Fetish, Recognition, Revolution

Fetish, Recognition, Revolution

James T. Siegel

PRINCETON UNIVERSITY PRESS

PRINCETON, NEW JERSEY

Siegel, James T., 1937–
Fetish, recognition, revolution / James T. Siegel
    p.   cm.
Includes bibliographic references.
ISBN 0–691–02653-X (cloth : alk. paper). — ISBN 0–691–02652–1
(pbk. : alk. paper)
    1. Nationalism—Indonesia—History.   2. Indonesia—Politics and
government—1789–1942.   3. Indonesia—Politics and
government—1942–1949.   4. Indonesia—Literatures—History and
criticism.   5. Indonesian language—History.   6. Indonesia—Social
conditions.   7. Language and culture—Indonesia.   8. Literature and
society—Indonesia.   9. Literature and revolutions.   I. Title.
DS643.S54   1997   959.8′022—dc20   96-32041

This book has been composed in Galliard

Printed in the United States of America by
Princeton Academic Press

10   9   8   7   6   5   4   3   2   1

10   9   8   7   6   5   4   3   2   1

(Pbk.)

TO THE MEMORY OF

David M. Siegel

Contents

PART III: *Revolution*

Acknowledgments

THE Social Science Research Council and the Cornell Southeast Asia Program supported this work financially. I thank them for their generosity. "Flunky + Maid" by Pramoedya Ananta Toer is published with the kind permission of William Morrow and Company, Inc. The translation and part of the commentary first appeared in *Indonesia* vol. 61 (1996).

I had hoped that this would be a work of collaboration with the historian Takashi Shiraishi. It seemed to me that the late colonial period of the Dutch East Indies was now, a half century after the Indonesian revolution, undergoing thorough revision and that Shiraishi and Rudolf Mrázek were the historians most active in that enterprise. Circumstances intervened. But the effects of the seminars we gave together at Cornell on the subject appear throughout the book. I fear that I have too often assimilated his thinking to the point where I can no longer distinguish it from my own and thus acknowledge it in the proper places.

I want to thank Rudolf Mrázek and Henk Maier for their commentaries on the text and for writing pieces of such strength that they stimulated my thinking beyond the ostensible subjects of their works. I also thank the anonymous reviewer of the Princeton University Press for the astuteness of his remarks. I am particularly indebted to Michael Meeker, who pointed out important gaps in my thinking and whose reading of the text revealed to me profundities I had missed.

It is odd to feel an obligation to someone who did not do something, but this is the case with me. In 1966 after the change of regime in Indonesia, the Suharto administration banned the leading scholars of my generation from entering the country, no doubt fearing what they would find. Even at the moment I write this, Ben Anderson, who is the primary interpreter of Southeast Asia today, has not been able to return to the country. Had he, Ruth McVey, and others been able to do so, the history of Indonesia today would look very different. I want this book to show that such censorship need not be effective and at the same time I want to say how aware I am that my shortcomings of vision, interpretation, and evidence are in part due to my inability to benefit from work that was prevented from being accomplished.

My fellow Indonesianists were banned as a result of the evidence they adduced that the Indonesian Communist Party was not responsible for the presumed coup that led to the change of regime, the massacre of hundreds of thousands of Indonesians, and the imprisonment without trial for seventeen years of tens of thousands of others. There is no model for thinking about this event. In place of a model, one has to think of violence and of what promotes liberation and its opposite. This book, which does not reach to those events, is nonetheless informed by them. There is another to follow which will take them up. But my comprehension of Indonesian history is made in the light of this occurrence. My understanding of the forces at play comes from reading Jacques Derrida, Jacques Lacan, and Martin Heidegger. I am particularly indebted to the work of Jacques Derrida; I do not mean to assimilate the three to each other. It seems to me that the path of thought he has opened, though it is becoming better known in the Anglophone world, has yet to be exploited by anthropologists and historians in the way it might be. It is in the first place because he shows the impossibility of our disciplines, precisely their lack of foundation. To continue after him means to accept this impossibility. But we must respond all the same, taking up in a context never imagined by him issues he has raised.

As for Anne Berger, her initials begin the alphabet. I owe those letters and the other twenty-four to her.

Fetish, Recognition, Revolution

> Afore I looked upon the Scripture as a history of things that passed in other countries, pertaining to other persons; but now I looked upon it as a mystery to be opened at this time, belonging also to us.
>
> —A. Evans, "An Eccho to the Voice of Heaven" (1653)

In 1975, Mrs. Suharto, the wife of the second president of Indonesia, opened a park she had created in Jakarta. A pond, more than eight hectares in extent, was filled with islands, each shaped like one in the Indonesian archipelago. To enable visitors to see this miniature of Indonesia from the proper perspective, the pond was crossed by a train suspended from a cable. Other sections of the park contained monuments and, one of its most important features, houses built in regional architectural styles. Each province was asked to contribute objects that symbolized it. A story about one particular exhibit circulated in Jakarta at the time and much after. The Province of Aceh, on the northern tip of Sumatra, had, during the revolution, collected enough money to buy an airplane that formed the greater part of the republic's air force at the time. They proudly donated it. The gift could not be refused, but as it was at odds with the authentic crafts of the regions, it was fenced off. Unfortunately for Mrs. Suharto, the elevated train by which one crosses this Disneyland made the plane again visible.

This permanent fair is called Taman Mini, "Miniature Garden," as it was conceived to be a miniature of the nation, a contemporary version of the colonial museum of ethnography. But it is not comprised entirely of miniatures. The houses, for instance, are full scale. Taman Mini is also a contemporary version of the colonial museum of ethnography in its insistence on a certain contemporary Indonesian notion of the authentic. It may be an even more forceful version of authenticity than the ethnographic museum. In his account of Taman Mini, John Pemberton quotes acquaintances who visit the park rather than making a trip back to their region of origin. " 'We go there regularly,' one Solonese couple asserted with peculiar sincerity, 'it's much less complicated than going back to Central Java.' "[1] Pemberton says that Taman Mini, by mixing monuments of the revolution and symbols of the regions, asserts continuity between them. It is his thesis that this continuity depends on an enhanced power of quotation; the Jakarta-built regional houses are authentic, for instance.

We do not yet have a word to characterize Taman Mini. It is a "theme park" à la Walt Disney. But it is more than that because it is also a museum, claiming to hold "authentic" features of the Indonesian past. Pemberton shows this new form to be the result of an enhanced power of quotation. One makes a monument that is similar to the national monument to the revolution and it holds the same sacred aura. Or it claims to do so. One makes a Javanese house and it is not a copy; it is original. One can go home to it.

I might add that the past reclaimed by this park-museum-monument is that of the nineteenth century, which is also the past of most ethnographic museums as well as that of the revolution. But to put dates on the exhibits themselves would be inappropriate. There is, in the thinking that guided the erection of the park, a timeless state, the "past" of Indonesians, which means not the events of the past but their "heritage" that somehow indicates who they have been, and the revolution that made them a nation and continues that heritage into the present.

The airplane upsets this construction in the first place by being anachronistic. It comes from the region, but it does not belong to the nineteenth century. It is part of the revolution, but it seems to bear a date. It is obsolete but not antiquated. But its size, tailored to human scale by comparison with today's planes, and the power of its engines, palpable even at rest, makes it possible to imagine flying it. If, for instance, there were a collection of traditional daggers and antiquated guns used during the revolution, would they create similar effects? As authentically Acehnese objects they would be put at a distance, in an Aceh which since the last quarter of the nineteenth century was famous for the resistance its people showed to the Dutch. The wielders of such weapons would be like the people of the Bible were to the Christian radical Arise Evans in the quotation I have appended above, when Evans "looked upon the Scripture as a history of things that passed in other countries, pertaining to other persons." Their story would be formally his as well, but it would remain a story of another place and another time. If these daggers were labeled as revolutionary weapons, they might be thought of like the sharpened bamboo poles Indonesians used at that time. These have become symbols of the determination to win independence and thus have lost all specificity. The airplane, by contrast, has a particular history. It came from a certain place at a certain time and never became part of the national myth of the revolution. The plane brings the past into the present; it sets off fresh stories. Perhaps because it is an airplane one can imagine reviving it for use today. It has a power of reference much less limited than the other objects of Taman Mini.

The plane reproduces the period of the revolution in a more powerful way than the icons of long-haired youth in lurid colors that cover billboards on the anniversary of the revolution. And it is, in my opinion, a more powerful sign than the various monuments of the revolution created, for the most part, in the mode of the gigantic and the style of socialist realism. For it is not a monument. A monument preserves a certain memory, replacing the possibly idiosyncratic associations that this airplane, so awkwardly placed, can awaken even in those who know little of the history of the Indonesian revolution. It stimulates stories about the president's wife. It is an object turned into a mystery, capable of awakening a gamut of thoughts requiring the sort of interpretations Arise Evans applied to the Bible once he had "awakened."

Taman Mini as a whole is filled with the effects of contemporary technology. It would be considerably different without the overhead train and it would be unimaginable without the example of Disneyland.[2] The overhead train furnishes the perspective of Taman Mini. It reverses the situation of the viewer of television who sits nearly immobile in front of moving images. Here, the viewer moves and the stationary objects, by virtue of the fact that they are to be seen rather than experienced, turn into images. One can also walk into the houses of Taman Mini, but this does not alter the point. One might see these houses as dwellings, but no one actually goes home there to live. The houses remain symbols, standing for all houses of the type, or perhaps images of the real house to be found elsewhere. That these objects are taken as authentic, that no difference is made between originals and copies, makes them close to the virtual reality produced electronically; but they are even more compelling.

Here one sees the technological put at the service of authority. It delivers only what it is meant to deliver and in doing so furnishes the "authentic" object of today. The couple who visit the park rather than going home visit a "home" purified of the usual complications. Visiting Taman Mini, they avoid, for instance, trouble with their in-laws and no doubt avoid also even remembering the difficulties they had the last time they went home. It is, as they said, "'much less complicated.'" It is a simplification inherently possible in the technologically produced image. On the other hand, that other symbol of twentieth-century technology, the fighter airplane, produces much less controllable effects. One must credit technology with delivering the effects of Taman Mini, but it would be a mistake to think that these effects are necessarily domesticating and completely controllable by authority.

I have used the story of the Taman Mini airplane as an example of the control of communication on the one hand and the breaking of that control on the other. The center of my interest is language and finding in language the equivalents of the Taman Mini airplane. Finding, that is, in language something that seems to provoke a flood of referents and sometimes breaks through the limitations put on identity by social hierarchy and sometimes is used to reinforce social identity. I start with the lingua franca, the language that mediated between groups in Indies society; groups who spoke different languages but used a language, belonging to none of them, when they dealt with one another. At a certain moment, the lingua franca took on new dimensions. It seemed to offer the possibility of hearing what had always been present but now seemed if not mysterious, at least intensely interesting. In particular, the communications that previously were contained within the groups of the Dutch East Indies who had, in a famous phrase of J. C. Furnivall, met only in the market, now seemed available to others. But the lingua franca brought not only messages from groups present in the Indies; it brought stories from most of the globe as well. This moment has been seen to be the beginning of Indonesian nationalism.[3] It is important to see that this nationalism began not in the nation and not with the colonial forces but with the reception of messages from Europe and Asia, from nearly all over the world. It is my purpose to trace the course of this international overhearing and its transformation into a bounded, national frame, which also produced the revolution.

I want to show that there is more than one history of Indonesian nationalism. There is one, for instance, that traces the ideas that conceptualized independence, ideas that were learned from the West. This is the history, in fact, of a conservative elite. There is another history of radical youth who pushed this elite to demand more but who never succeeded in achieving a social revolution.[4] My story supplements these. In it, independence will appear as the result of the history of hearing and overhearing that went on between groups of the Indies and between the Indies and the world. The prehistory of the Indonesian nation commences with the forces that dislodged the relation between Dutch and 'natives' precisely by making the world audible. It is a story of the decay of hierarchy. At the same time, it is the story of its reformation.

It is well known that, despite attempts in another direction, the Indonesian anticolonial revolution was not a social revolution. But the defeat of social revolutionaries by itself does not explain why Indonesian society was not transformed. One must understand that the lack of a social revolution did not mean the dominance of, say, court societies. It meant instead that another hierarchy was established, one similar to but not the same as the colonial version. What are the roots of this hierarchy? Is it a revival of regional, in particular, Javanese ideas? To some extent, indubitably. Is it an inheritance from the Dutch? It is clear that to some degree the forms of national authority in Indonesia today reproduce the colonial model. I believe that there is yet another source of this hierarchy and that it is to be found in the very processes of the formation of nationalism that led to the revolution.

Takashi Shiraishi has noted that it is usually possible to get access to important government authorities, at least eventually. One needs only to know someone who knows someone and finally one arrives. The indifference of the present Indonesian state to its people, the way it tolerates very little in the way of contrary voices, makes it similar to the colonial state. But by the fact of access to the center, it differs in Shiraishi's opinion from the colonial state. He has pictured Indonesian society today as a vast network of connections comparable to tribes. It is not merely that people in the regions reach out to officials in Jakarta out of need. It is also that they feel that the recognition the nation offers is essential to them, whether it be in the form of favors or simply of diplomas or other written forms of acknowledgment. Unlike African tribes, the Indonesian variety does not begin locally but at the center. Men and women have been known to weep when, after much hoping, they receive a long number identifying them as civil servants.[5] The capacity of the nation via the state to confer recognition surpasses the structure of patron-clients common to much of Southeast Asia. This is a personal matter not immediately reconcilable with a national identity. But the sense of being recognized of which I speak transcends persons. One may have received one's civil service number with the help of someone else to whom one is grateful and owes allegiance. This much alone would make it merely a matter of patrons and clients. But the number is not merely an administrative designation. It is taken as a form of national recognition. One may feel indebted to the person who helped one get it, but it seems to come, mystically enough, from the nation itself. The nation seems to have found one; with that, one belongs to Indonesia in a profound sense. One supposes oneself truly at home; more so than in one's house of origin.

I intend to trace the path by which recognition became centered in the Indonesian nation. At least I will trace this path up until the revolution. This history is indissociable from the history of "communication," in the sense I use that word, that began to connect the segments of the plural society toward the end of the nineteenth century. The plural society, in J. C. Furnivall's formulation, is one whose groups live their lives apart from one another, each with its own culture, meeting only in the market and administered by colonial authority. I use the word "communication" in the bare sense of "to connect" in the way that the airplane connects the present and the revolutionary past, quite apart from the content of the stories it then evokes. My claim is that the history of the nation is made not from autochthonous sources and not from foreign borrowings but from the effects of these connections.

Where can one find this history? The national language of Indonesia, called Indonesian, developed out of a lingua franca called "Melayu." I have tried to show the course of this development through writing, for the most part. I have analyzed 'native' and Sino-Malay productions.

However, it is always possible that one speaks only of a small group. H. M. J. Maier has stressed that in 1930 only 6.44 percent of the population classed as 'native' could read and write in Latin characters.[6] Clearly, one risks grossly overestimating the influence of these few if one considers only 'native' writings, even adding Sino-Malay. But the percentage of literate people is not significant here. We look at writing at the point where it first emerged in the course of developments toward a national language. We see the restrictions that it imposes on itself and the freedom it sometimes offers. We find in particular the source of the desire for recognition that the Indonesian nation has monopolized for itself today. The processes I describe begin within the play of languages that can best be seen in writing and that are coopted later by the state in the development of the national hierarchy. Precisely the autonomy that is refused to writing when it diverges from social norms is a topic I consider. What is at stake is the possibility of literature itself; its origin and its continuation, for not all cultures have literature.[7] By citing Arise Evans, I risk being thought ethnocentric. Am I not imposing a Western, even a religious notion of communication on an Indonesian phenomenon? I might reply that I rely on a notion of communication that has best been expounded by Jacques Derrida who is the most powerful thinker today in the line that continues the thinking of Claude Lévi-Strauss, Jacques Lacan, and Martin Heidegger to name only the most immediate of his predecessors. Even so, I might not avoid the accusation. Are not these theories, though they appear secular, a revision of religious ideas? The answer is yes and no. The ability to awaken references that were not intended, that seem to come from somewhere else, edges closely onto religious phenomena. That there could be these effects without Christianity, outside of Islam, and that they center on communication simply raises the immensely difficult question of what we mean by religion and how we can understand the nature of boundaries.

The effects I describe cannot be understood solely in terms of the culture of any part of the Indies or of Holland or of both taken together. On the other hand, there are specific features of the lingua franca that was used in the Indies to which I will refer and there is an important role played by communications technology. A lingua franca by definition operates between peoples of different languages and cultures without belonging to any of them. And technology, too, is available to anyone who can use it or, more importantly for us, who begins to fantasize about it. It, too, is a means, an in between point. It is precisely in this middle point that I begin my story. When Arise Evans spoke of scripture and history pertaining to the present where before it was confined to the past, he spoke of scripture as a means of transmission or communication as well as of a particular message. Whether religion is an example of language and technology or the converse cannot be settled.[8] It is clear to me, how-ever, that an understanding of the particularity of Indonesian history depends on understanding a middle point that produces cultural effects.

I have used the word "identity." I do not mean to imply, however, that identity is ever fully achieved. My view is contrary, therefore, to the stream of current thought that sees identity as achieved, negotiated, crafted, and in other ways the product of a self which, knowingly follow-ing its interests, invents itself. I think of it in the tradition of Hegel. There, to find a place of self-definition is to be thrown off balance unless one can be convincingly self-deceiving. Identity exists only at the price of enormous confusions and contradictions. I intend to make some of these confusions and contradictions clear because it is against these complicat-ing factors that identity becomes almost achieved.

The book ends with the Indonesian revolution. The usual under-standing of revolution pictures a surge of desire that overwhelms existing structures. The history of the Indonesian revolution is an exception. The freeing of desire occurs not with the relations of colonial peoples to their masters but with their relation to the world. Toward the end of the nine-teenth century, the Indies began to produce translations from, it seems, every part of the world. It is here that one can find the freeing of identity from social structures that precedes rebellion. Nationalism, as I picture it, domesticates desire, confining it within forms that produce recogni-tion. Before that, however, there is a demand for recognition that is not fully met. I do not try to explain why this demand should have arisen and why it should have taken the forms it did until I first trace the paths it took. When finally I arrive at my explanation, it concerns translation. Translation turns a foreign language into one's own. And yet translation in the Indies at the end of the nineteenth century took place in a lingua franca, a language that is by definition not anyone's. Thus, it produced something that was not completely foreign or completely domestic. The effects eventually were of liberation and later of belonging to certain groups.

I have shown how 'natives,' to use a translation of the Dutch term, felt themselves to be surprised by the recognition of the police who saw them, dressed in Western clothes, to be trying to pass for westerners, thus escaping the restrictions on movement imposed on them. In the accounts I rely on, 'natives' did not dress as westerners in order to de-ceive, however. They merely followed the fashions of the time, without thought of changing identity. They did so, one might say, in the mode of translation; that is, taking on forms thought to belong not to Dutch but to the world in general. They found themselves clothed in a fashion be-longing to no one in particular, just as translators brought the world to the Indies in a language that was no one's in particular. At the same time, they were wrapped in what to the eyes of the police was foreign fashion. 'Natives' were astonished to find that they might pass for someone from another social segment. I call this failed possibility the "fetish of appearance." It is a fetish in the Hegelian sense of an orientation to a power which cannot be appropriated but which, nonetheless, one feels one possesses. The lack of success in making this power one's own merely makes for persistence.[9] The history I trace is one of the progressive but by no means linear limitation of this power precisely as a certain national identity is achieved.

By the time of the revolution, one could be recognized as a nationalist. There were not only forms of dress and language and ideas to mark one, there were also inventions of a nationalist leaders who verified one's national credentials. This very success, however, contributed to a strange bifurcation in the period of the revolution. The Dutch, returning to reclaim the Indies for themselves after the defeat of Japan, were a menace not because they threatened punishment but because they promised pleasure, wealth, and position. Revolutionaries with whom Indonesians wanted to associate themselves were, on the contrary, menacing because they could detect one's true or false national identity. The fetish of appearance relied on an orientation to an other who could recognize, even if initially that recognition was conflicted, on the one hand, attributing to the person recognized the capacity to change identities and on the other condemning him for it. The replacement of national for colonial others was, in a certain way, too successful. Believing oneself to be a nationalist did not exhaust the overwhelming sense of power that was thought to stimulate recognition. Indonesian revolutionaries might find in one antirevolutionary desires one was unaware of oneself. In this situation, revolutionaries were strangely like the Dutch police of the turn of the century, detecting signs of inauthenticity unknowable to the person bearing them.

The achievement of national identity and national forms of recognition preceded the revolution. The Indonesian revolution was not, at least for those not part of the revolutionary youth, the unleashing of desire and the freeing of identity. Instead, it continued the domestication of both that was begun under the Dutch. "Awakening," which we can understand as hearing unexpected messages from the world at large, and the formation of national identity were thus different processes, the second establishing itself against the possibility of the first.

PART I

The Fetish of Appearance

CHAPTER ONE

The "I" of a Lingua Franca

MELAYU AS A LINGUA FRANCA

How does it happen that a language comes into existence? Where does one look for its precedents? One cannot say that at 10:00 A.M. Language A did not exist and that at 6:00 P.M. it came into being. No doubt one thinks that speakers of a certain language became isolated from one another and began to speak dialects that became incomprehensible to one another. New languages seem to mark a limit of communication; common sense demands a sociological explanation for their formation.

Perhaps. But although all known languages must have had their origins in previous ones, there are examples of another sort of development. In what is now called Indonesia and what was called the Dutch East Indies and on the Malay Peninsula, there was a language, Melayu, that was the language of certain courts and of villages, though not the language of the largest groups of the archipelago.[1] A language similar to this became a lingua franca, used first in trade. It developed apart from the traditions in which Malay was embedded and with different linguistic features. The lingua franca became the national language of Indonesia, called "Indonesian," and is spoken now throughout the archipelago alongside the approximately eight hundred local languages. Here it was not mutual incomprehension but the extension of communication across the boundaries of languages that brought a new language into being.[2]

As Pramoedya Ananta Toer points out, the translators used by traders tended to be Arabs or other foreigners to the archipelago. Such people were unattached to the literature and customs of traditional Malay and so the spread of the lingua franca did not bring with it the culture of the courts or the villages where the language may have originated.[3] Melayu, the lingua franca, was thus unsettled, lacking the contexts that stabilize usages. As the Dutch established their hegemony in Indonesia, they used Melayu as the language of administration. But as John Hoffman points out, they were continually worried that they could not make themselves understood in the language.[4] The problem was not Dutch grasp of Melayu but their subjects' use of what they termed a low form of the language, "low Malay," and their subjects' ignorance of what Dutch administrators considered the real language, court Malay. Dutch felt that the Melayu that came to be used in the major cities of the Indies was inadequate. They searched for the source of Melayu and claimed to have found it in the Riau Archipelago. In these islands, remote from the big cities, they felt they had the developed form of the language which, if only it could be taught to those later called "Indonesians," would make communication certain. They made increasing efforts to encourage "standard" or "high" Malay and to discourage "low Malay."[5]

Dutch needed Melayu because very few non-Dutch spoke their language. Partly this was because the colonial government did not make a great effort to teach Dutch to any but a few. But partly it was because there seemed to be an inability to learn the language even when the opportunity was present. In her outstanding study of Batavia, the historian Jean Taylor points out that the children of Dutch fathers and Indies women often could not speak their fathers' tongue unless they were sent to study in the Netherlands.[6] Indos, as the children of Europeans and 'natives' were called, could nevertheless be considered Dutch in the eyes of the law if their fathers either married their mothers or legally attested that they were the childrens' fathers. If these conditions were not fulfilled, such Indos were subjected to the laws of their mothers and missed the privileges the law accorded Europeans.[7] Separate legal codes were, indeed, a feature of what J. C. Furnivall calls "the plural society," a society in which Europeans, 'natives,' and 'foreign orientals' lived separately, without a common culture.[8]

Melayu was the language of the plural society, used between 'natives' speaking different local languages and between them and Indos and Dutch. It was the tongue that connected most of the 'native' world with Europeans and European culture as well as the rest of the world outside their local communities. It was the language of authority meaning not only governmental but also sometimes parental authority. In the major cities, Melayu became a creole, the first language of many speakers. But even as a creole it kept much of its character as a lingua franca. In the first place because, from the Dutch point of view, that was its function. Dutch used it to speak to those whose first language was or should be Javanese, Sundanese, or other local languages. Even as a creole, Melayu lacked some of the characteristics of first languages. In particular, it only weakly defined its speakers' identities. We have seen already that Indos who were creole speakers and nonspeakers of Dutch could be considered "Dutch," for instance. But these were only a small minority. Consider this ironic characterization by H. M. J. Maier, the leading contemporary Dutch scholar of Melayu literature:

> One thing was clear: the Malay that was used in Batavia and the other big cities . . . was gibberish, not at all in tune with the rules for use in administration and trade that scholars and administrators were tentatively formulating behind their

writing desks. Would it be possible for a foreign elite to actively engage in creating a standard Malay that was alien to almost everyone?[9]

The native speakers of Melayu were told by the colonial authorities and sometimes by their fathers, that their first language was not a language. It was, perhaps, almost one, or merely the degraded remnants of one spoken somewhere else, far away. In effect, they were told, they could not communicate with authority; neither in the language of authority, Dutch, nor in the one they had learned from their mothers if their mother spoke Melayu and not a local language. The Dutch message went further; the daily communications that speakers of the creole no doubt found satisfactory when speaking to each other were "gibberish." What they surely must have assumed made sense did not do so. They learned from the Dutch that they could not fully inhabit their "own" language. This is of course usually the case also for speakers of a lingua franca that is not the first language of either speaker and that does not have to be fully mastered to be used in trade. Speaking Melayu as a lingua franca meant that one could not rely on the same assurance about the language that one had in one's own language and one often did not need it.

But at the same time, the weightlessness of a language that is severed from culture makes it less intimidating. One can chance speaking it without the fear that it is the tongue of Racine, Shakespeare, Dostoyevsky, or the Gouverneur Generaal of the Dutch East Indies. It offers one the opportunity for a certain excursion if not into a new identity, at least away from an old one. In the case of Melayu as a creole, speakers did not form a cultural group in the same sure sense that, say, Balinese, Chinese, Javanese, or others did whose languages were at the source of some of the vocabulary of Melayu. There was a fantastic side to the culture of Batavia, as we will see, that can be attributed to its retention of some characteristics of the lingua franca.

The spread of Melayu as a lingua franca was rapid and strange. Pramoedya reports, for instance, that Dutch missionaries learned to preach in high Malay and did so to groups particularly in eastern Indonesian sometimes without realizing that their audiences did not understand them. Nonetheless, missionaries were important in introducing the lingua franca into certain parts of the archipelago. Or perhaps it is more accurate to say not "introduce" but "produce." Maier, in a remarkable sentence, lets us see how this could be:

> This language was the result of learning by reciprocal imitation of rudimentary language forms.

That is, one learned the lingua franca by imitating what the other said while the other was doing the same. One pictures the 'natives' who heard but did not understand sermons in high Malay, simulating what they heard, repeating it to their preachers who, not understanding, imitated them in return. The lingua franca took shape in the middle, between the speakers. Eventually they could comprehend each other. In the process, the language was stripped to "rudimentary language forms." It may be a historical fable, but one is necessary to imagine how communities separated from each other by different languages begin to communicate.

Maier describes a changing of places, each speaker taking the part of the other, as the normal course of the development of Melayu. It was a language that one learned by taking on the speech of the interlocutor while he did the same with one's own utterances. In such a situation, the speaker could have no assurance of his language, the second person being the superior judge of his words. This would be the normal course of learning any language were it not that the same was true for the second person when he came to speak. A community that begins with mutual imitation starts without the definitions that promote differentiation. And it begins without the usual generational transmission that establishes its authority. It is the opposite of the case we first sketched; it was not a question of the discovery of mutual incomprehension between communities, each concerned to defend their own linguist property and therefore to mark their mutual difference. It was a matter of each saying the same as the other, taking from the other what they found he had but which had no property rights attached to it. No important social distinctions can be generated at that stage of development. Instead, one feels the force of the medium in the way that one often does learning a foreign language before one starts to speak it.

Melayu was thus a language without the built-in authority the taking on of which gives one not only a sense of mastery but, as a speaker, the reassurance of having a place in the world. What Maier says about the first writers of the language must have been true of other speakers as well:

> In the shadow of Dutch authority, Malay-writing authors in the big cities of Java cannot have felt much self-confidence, not about the language they had to use, not about the topics and material they were supposed to use. Educated in a defective manner and thus moving between all sorts of cultural and linguistic communities, . . . it was impossible for them to accept blindly the Dutch concept of a knowable community: they did not know their place, they did not know the colonial community.

Their "defective education" consisted in not knowing what the Dutch knew about literature and history and about themselves. What they should write about and in what form were better known elsewhere. And not understanding the Dutch view of themselves, they did not know colonial society. Ordinarily, a language is a tool to make one's way through the world. Learning the language usually includes learning a map of the society of its speakers. Maier, however, pictures those who learned low Malay as never gaining the usual advantages of a language. When it connected them with authority, it was only to find out that someone else knew their language better than they did and that their grasp of the words in their minds meant only that there were matters they could not know. Turning to each other, they could only find themselves locked in ceaseless alternation. Such a community would be riven with anxiety. One could only know that being in the world meant being no where locatable. I subscribe to Maier's description. I would only qualify it by adding that their angst became apparent only at a certain moment, toward the end of the nineteenth century, and only in oblique ways. Maier goes on to say this:

> A new structure of feeling arose among the nonwhite population, inspired by an ambiguous desire to self-definition in reaction to Dutch claims of improvement which the natives themselves did not necessarily conceive of as an improvement. This search for a new identity manifested itself in a staggering polyphony and heterogeneity in printed materials, aimed at an inchoate readership.

The "desire to self-definition" here is "ambiguous" because it lacks the usual basis. One speaks of "self-definition" ordinarily when in a certain sense one feels one is someone already but lacks a form of expression. But Maier speaks of an "inchoate readership," for instance. He means that the readers of the works that began to be published in Melayu were not identifiable by ethnic group. Chinese, Javanese, Batavians, and Indos all read the same things. The identifications given by colonial society in terms of ethnicity were not shaken. But, despite these terms, uncertainty about language itself set in motion "a search for a new identity." It took the form not of defining relationships, as searches for identity usually do, but of a "staggering polyphony and heterogeneity in printed materials."

We will comment later on this "polyphony." But for now I only want to correct an impression of tone. One reason there could be such enormous diversity of material, without discernable direction, is because anxiety about language was concealed by the auxiliary character of Melayu. It was thought of, I believe, even by many of those for whom it was a mother tongue, as a second language. Its function as a lingua franca continued and gave the impression that, after all, there was (another) first language to fall back on, even if one did not know it oneself. This accounts for the fact that what was read in the language tended to lack weight, as both Pramoedya Ananta Toer and Maier have pointed out.[10]

By the end of the nineteenth century, a multitude of translations from world literatures began to appear in Melayu.[11] These appeared most often in newspapers as well as in book form. But it was not solely in print that these translations became available. They were also copied by hand and rented out in lending libraries. What is remarkable is that what was translated and what was written in Melayu was so diverse. It includes not only the literature produced at courts throughout the archipelago, Persian tales, and Chinese stories but also accounts of the Russo-Japanese war and of local events, including a bank robbery. There had always been translations into regional languages, but these were of a different order. In Aceh, a Muslim sultanate at the time, there were, for instance, translations into Acehnese of Arabic texts, particularly religious ones, and of historical or epic stories that connected the situation of Aceh with what it took as its relevant neighbors. The same is true of Javanese, mutatis mutandis. But Batavian newspapers published an epic about Napoleon, Chinese sagas, Persian tales, Sherlock Holmes, and various Dutch literature. It did not seem to matter who the readers were. It was not felt that readers would read in their own ethnic identities. And, indeed, there is evidence that the borrowers of traditional Malay works from lending libraries included, for instance, Chinese. Furthermore, such lenders cannot accurately be called readers. They were, often, listeners, the works being read aloud for small groups of people in the fashion of recitation of traditional literature.

One is dealing here with the formation of new audiences in the sense that the ethnic composition of audiences no longer seemed to matter.[12] The question of who listened to traditional literatures is more difficult than it might seem. For instance, wealthy Chinese commissioned the performance of Javanese shadow puppet plays and ordered the construction of Javanese orchestral instruments. This is rightly taken as an indication of their Javanization. But with Melayu literature and translations, it is not possible to say what effect on identity such broadening of reading and listening had. Readers of Melayu included people from many of the ethnic groups of Indonesia and prominently included among not only readers but also translators and writers "Indos," those of mixed European and Indies parentage.

This new audience did not always depend on a new mode of reception. One does not have isolated readers who silently picture to themselves what they read. The newspaper eventually had its own mode of reading, the one we know today. But at the time of its expansion in the Indies, at the end of the nineteenth century, modes of reading and listening were unsettled.[13] Before the displacement of chanting by silent reading was completed, the Melayu language world was invaded by the world at large. Melayu, the lingua franca, began to bring to the Indies the literatures and the events of the world and of one's neighbors. Manuscripts were recopied, borrowed from lending libraries in big cities, and recited in front of small groups. The contents of these manuscripts were often the same, and sometimes even borrowed, from what appeared in newspapers. There was an interchange between the newspaper and traditional rhymed forms. The newspapers printed traditional literatures while contemporary events sometimes based on newspaper accounts were retold in old forms on hand-copied documents. The impulse in both cases is not toward the enclosure that governs the formation of a new language when dialects become mutually incomprehensible. Rather, the possibility of speaking to a broad range of peoples in a lingua franca and the interest in hearing of a wider variety of events and listening to a broader range of narratives than was previously the case occurred together.[14] Somewhat abruptly, via the medium of the lingua franca, most places in the world began to be felt in the Indies. The messages of the world could speak to anyone and, for a while, it seemed that many did not shrug off what they heard around them with the thought that it was not intended for them. The feeling that there was something to be heard, and no one could know in advance just what it might be, loosened the constrictions imposed by identity. Even though anonymity of readership was not a feature of the lending library, nonetheless it seems inherent in it in the sense that one could not entirely predict what people would listen to by knowing their ethnic identification.

We have seen that translations existed in the courts but that they were chosen according to assumptions of identity. It is difficult to imagine, for instance, an Acehnese version of an epic about the Russo-Japanese war. But the listeners of the lending library or the readers of Melayu newspapers seem to have heard about nearly anything at all. If they still were interested in traditional Melayu texts, it seemed that they did not value them more than the story of the robbery of the Java Bank. One might see this as the vitality of the traditional form in which it was told, and it would not be entirely mistaken. But the same story would be told in prose in the newspapers. It is first of all the vitality of the language that seems to carry any information about anything, or the acuteness of listening perhaps, that is at work. In any case, for a moment, no hierarchy of literary form or literary works imposed itself.

It has never been satisfactorily explained just why Melayu literary activity became so energized at the turn of the century. But one can continue to follow Maier: "Educated in a defective manner and thus moving between all sorts of cultural and linguistic communities. . . ." Defective education, one that does not let one know one's place, prompts movement between communities. One sees here the lingua franca continuing its formation. The other, the person from a different community, exerts an attraction, one that, when it appeals from outside the Indies in particular, takes the form of translation. Translation is not imitation, but it is not entirely different from it either; one repeats what the other said, this time, however, using one's own code. This assumes a code already formed, but, as we have seen, in the case of Melayu, one is uncertain.

The effect in some cases was the same blurring of the difference between speaker and interlocutor that we have already seen in the formation of the language. The most striking example I know of occurs not in translation but in the disruption of the conventions that governed the copying of texts. The philologist Henri Chambert-Loir has studied one of the copyists of Melayu texts, Muhammad Bakir, a man who also had a lending library in Batavia. Chambert-Loir's study shows how this copyist introduced emendations into traditional texts. Of course, in traditional literatures it was perhaps even the norm for copyists and chanters to introduce changes in their texts. Those described by Chambert-Loir, however, are unusual in that they make the copyist a character in the text he copys. Even this is not entirely unprecedented. The chanters of Acehnese epics, in northern Sumatra, when they wished to take a break used to sing that they wanted coffee, interpolating the word "coffee" into the rhymes of the epic. Muhammad Bakir was more extreme:

> When, for instance, a princess relates that she is an orphan, her listeners sob and cry, and the story goes on: "Many tears were shed, and the writer started crying as well, because his father died when he was still young and his mother did her best to comfort him."[15]

The writer in this passage is not, or not merely, someone who knows what the text says and adds his own commentary. He shows himself within the narrative as someone who listens to a character in life, identifying with the character's suffering; her problems suggest his own experience. He presents himself as being in the story itself. But he also identifies himself as the copyist or "writer" of the text, moving between these persona without comment, as though he were there taking down what happened and as though he were also the copyist of a previously existing text.

Muhammad Bakir conflated historical time and the time of the text. Thus, in a copy of a manuscript dealing with mythical figures, "the King of Ngastina sends a letter to Darmawangsa, the King of Ngamerta, requesting the head of Arjuna, and the letter is dated Betawi, lst of May 1897."[16] The "lst of May 1897" is not necessarily the day of that date on the calendar; it is equally well the name of the day on which the King of Ngamerta sent a letter to Darmawangsa. One might think that mythical and historical time are conflated here, but it is not quite the case. Muhammad Bakir added a date to the events in the text he copied in the same way that dates were added to various other kinds of accounts at that moment, including obvious fictions that were not mythical in origin. During the same period, original texts dealing with contemporary events began to be written both in traditional rhymed form and, in the newspapers, in journalistic fashion. Here again there is an insistence on historical time with precise dates cited; places are also specified. Other stories about murder and about love specify the city and the neighborhood. "This is a true story," runs one of Muhammad Bakir's emendations. "It happened this very month, the 15th of November 1909. It took place on the side of the street." But the side of which street? The specification of date and place in this circumstance does not mean a certain "there." It means it happened in the world. When Muhammad Bakir wrote "15th of November 1909," and then adds, "this very month" he claimed that the language of the text speaks "now." But it is a "now" that extends from that time to the moment the reader reads "this very month." At that instant, the reader is in "15th of November 1909" along with Muhammad Bakir. To say then that he is in the text is no less true than to say that the text exists "now" in the world. It implies that through language, one finds oneself in the world and the text indistinguishably.

Hearing what the text says, or reading what the text says, the writer shows that he too is "there." What he reads as he copys seems to speak directly to him, as though, in the passage quoted above, the princess were in front of him. This assumption is carried further when the writer addresses the readers. "When having quoted a verse of the Qu'ran, he adds, 'Oh you, my fellows who are sitting, please say Amin.'" At that moment, the "readers" are not only those who might have heard the text when Muhammad Bakir finished his work, they are also characters within the story. The writer is not only present as a witness, he is also addressed directly by the characters. One of the mythical gods sends a messenger to other mythical characters and to the readers at the same time. Or, the characters address the writer and beg him to change the story.

> "O writer, enough, stop writing such things. I can't stand such pain. Change to another tale. Don't go on with this. O writer, who are you, and where do you stay, that you have the heart to make up such a story, so painful. You don't feel it, that's why you write whatever you like."

The writer, who should exist before the character can speak, is spoken to by the character in a time that is paradoxically before the time the writer writes and yet, as evidenced by the existence of the text, after it as well. One also notes the agonistic relation between the characters of the text, at least one of whom is named as the writer himself, as though he were struggling to make himself different from those he writes about.

These are all interpolations of the copyist. But whether the copyist distinguished himself from the narrator any more than he did from his characters is unclear. The same word, *pengarang*, is used for both "narrator" and "character." If these were merely conventional emendations, one could dismiss them. But they occur at a specific moment—a moment when in many parts of the Indies, languages began to be heard by those who had been deaf to them before. It is a moment when the copyist, looking at the text he copys, hears it speak. It speaks so strongly it surpasses the sense of the words he is transferring to another piece of paper. The copyist therefore adds more words. The words he hears in his mind seem unavoidable, hence addressed to him. The apostrophe is not from the writer to his muse or from the writer to his characters or his readers, but from inside the text, from the character to the writer. The character wants not only the story changed but wants to know who the person with the pen is and where he can be found and slurs him. The writer hears what he reads so acutely that he feels addressed by it directly. At that point, he is brought into the picture and asked for his identification. When he gives it, where is he? In the text? Outside of it?

"Muhammad Bakir" almost oscillates between the text and the world. But he nonetheless says, "this very month." When he adds dates he makes the text appear in the world even if at the same moment the world becomes an adjunct of the text. One can think that his "confusion" is really an insight into the interplay of language and event. That he adds dates is what makes him exemplary for us. He exemplifies a historical moment when the Indies social and political world became informed not merely by the currents of political and literary events from outside the archipelago but by a rich "confusion" of language and world. Even without literary texts, linguistic events similar to his penetrated the political world. "This very month" and "on the side of the street" mark an urgency that take linguistic processes out of literature and insist that they take place in one's ears and before one's eyes.

In a strange way, Muhammad Bakir was at home with his texts, even if we cannot say whether he was inside or outside them. This feeling of being "at home" in the literature was produced as well for others. In 1955, Nio Joe Lan described the way Indies Chinese, who were among the earliest to make translations, worked. He speaks of the period under discussion:

> After several generations, Chinese who settled here [in the Indies] could no longer speak Chinese. Only one or two Chinese families could still speak Chinese after having left their fatherland for a period of time. After awhile, . . . the Chinese language became foreign to them. As time went on, their everyday language became the local language (Melayu in Djakarta, Sunda in Sundaland, Javanese in Central Java and East Java).
>
> For this reason they no longer read Chinese stories in Chinese. But the pull of Chinese stories was powerful, either because they heard them told by storytellers which earlier still existed in Jakarta or because they saw displays of Chinese puppets or dolls (*potehi*). Eventually they made the decision to translate and publish these Chinese stories, which for the most part were folk stories.[17]

In this synopsis or perhaps tale, Nio Joe Lan, an Indonesian of Chinese descent and a loving critic of Sino-Malay literature, reports that first Chinese, after settling in the Indies forget their language but are reminded of its literature through storytelling and through the mute presence of dolls and puppets. They desire to hear what they feel they have forgotten. And they realize their desire in translations. They hear what is theirs but they know that they have forgotten it. What they hear is brought to them under the assumption that this, in particular, is what they can no longer remember. But even though Chinese took on local languages, one of which Nio Joe Lan names as "Melayu," the local language of Batavia, the vast bulk of translations were not into these languages, but into Melayu lingua franca. It was the lingua franca in which home was brought back to them. The lingua franca, after centuries of operation in the Indies, seemed to open recollection.

Nio Joe Lan felt that most of the original translators from Chinese did not themselves know the language but rather relied on newly arrived immigrants who were illiterate in Melayu. They were thus not so much translators as copyists or more precisely transcribers of tales translated orally and taken down at the same instant. "They ignored commas, periods, question marks and so on." They did so perhaps because, Nio Joe Lan says, these transcribers were themselves barely skilled in writing. One five-volume work used only a single period. It was written in one sentence beginning, of course, with the first line of volume one and ending with the last line of volume five. No doubt Nio Joe Lan is correct in pointing out the rudimentary skills of the transcriber or translator. But one sees in this five-volume sentence the pressure under which tales that demanded translation arrived in the Indies. The urge to hear and to continue the story through transcription and dissemination overrode linguistic self-consciousness. In their lack of attention to punctuation, Nio Joe Lan says of the transcribers that "they were not different from people telling tales orally." Thus in the rush to pass the story on, transcribers in effect became speakers. As copyists themselves become performers we recognize the gestures of Muhammad Bakir.[18]

Once reading or hearing of texts is so acute, the best defense would no doubt be to reply. This is more or less what happened, if not in the mode of Muhammad Bakir, more usually in the form of taking credit for what one had read. At the time Muhammad Bakir was living in Batavia, it was quite common to publish stories under one's own name that one had merely copied from someone else. The introduction of an author's name was recent. Just at the moment that the name of the author began to appear in published texts, in copied texts, the author, the narrator, and the characters are conflated, or at least, the "same" person is shown to move easily between them. It would be a mistake, I believe, to think of this as plagiarism induced by the market, although that would not always be entirely wrong either. Initially, however, the author appears when he is the copyist and is also sometimes addressed by the text he writes. In copying the text, Muhammad Bakir repeats the motions of learning and forming Melayu. He imitates the other who wrote the text before him and then, finding himself in the other's place, gives himself his own name in that place. He copies himself copying down the text, thereby introducing a series of duplicates of himself that begin with making a copy of someone else's words. It is out of this tangle of reflections that the Melayu author was born.

The copyist, the author, is someone who speaks the text or who writes it down. He is the one who, hearing what he copies, is moved to speak. And to speak not only the exact words, but sometimes other words beyond those that he reads or hears in the extended sense of the word "hear." This identification with language that exceeds the literal and that moves one to reiterate what one hears is at the origin of the Melayu convention of the author. A first person or a speaker appears who is both that of a person in the world and a character in a text and, as author, both. The first person is the "I" who speaks out of the text, whether the text is the one marked on the paper in front of the person with the pen or the "I" that is a word in Melayu—*saya*—as it is a word in English. To reverse the perspective, a speaking being inhabits the word "I" in the text to be copied, as we have seen in the example of Muhammad Bakir, and in the world outside that text. To say this word is, as Benveniste points out, to shift oneself into the text as the person who utters it.[19] We conventionally keep the identities of the different "I"s separate. But it takes a convention and the strength to maintain it to define these identities and to keep them apart. Before convention is settled, "I," the word, belongs to language, which is to say, language and speech are not distinguished.

The copyist is of course not a recent phenomenon. It is often the case that in Malay languages the copyist introduces himself, often asking forbearance for mistakes he might have made and presenting himself as someone particularly ignorant. When the copyist is also the owner of the manuscript that he rents out, however, he may add something more. E. U. Kratz notes that a writer in 1886, presumably a copyist but perhaps the first to write down the particular manuscripts of which Kratz speaks, was also the owner and the lender of the manuscripts.[20] He adds not only the usual apologies but he also pleads with his customers to take care of the text they have borrowed, not to hold it too close to an oil lamp, not to fold it, not to have children near by, not to eat *sirih* while reading as the red juice could fall on the paper, and to return the text on time. In effect, the copyist has identified himself with his text as a commodity. This has merely intensified his presentation of himself in the text as the copyist. He is even more concerned to reach his readers in order to effect the return of the manuscript on time in good condition, the rent paid. He appears in the text in more extended form to do this. This identification with the text as intermediary form occurs in Muhammad Bakir when he speaks out of the text to his readers and back to the characters. Muhammad Bakir was also both the copyist and the owner of the manuscript. No doubt we see in him, as in Kratz's examples, the intensifying effect of commodification.

Copyists presented themselves within the prosodic forms of the texts they wrote. But when they address their readers as consumers we see the tendency toward the use of prose. The boundaries between text and audience become blurred. Traditional prosodic forms no doubt had many functions, serving, as has been often noted, as aide to memorization, to delimit a certain space of performance in which the voice of the readers of the text and the voice of the characters are merged as in the theater. When the reference within the text is to the identities of buyer and seller outside of it, however, prosody loses its usefulness. The very success of identification with the characters, the identification of the copyist as a character himself, reaches a limit with the possibility of addressing the reader as a consumer. At that point, at the point of payment and return of the goods, it is the voices of everyday life that are called for. This does not mean that such voices have a given normalcy. Rather one sees the literary figure, the copyist/author/character about to inhabit ordinary prose. The result is visible in the convention of the subtitle of the prose works of the time: "A Story That Actually Happened in. . . ." The story told is likely to have been merely the gossip that circulated at the moment or the retelling of a fictional account. That "it actually happened" means not that language is distinguished from the events that it represents but that the author/copyist now speaks from the same linguistic milieu as his readers.

The borders between "traditional" and "modern" literature were never so firm as they have usually been made out to be. One sees them crossed at the point where the copyist begins to be confused with the translator and the owner of the manuscript. The intensified commodification of life in the Indies at the end of the last century accentuated possibilities within the lingua franca which, in any case, grew up alongside trade. But if one sees the beginning of modern prose at the moment when the owner-copyist-translator speaks to the renters of manuscripts, still one has to note another aspect. It is marked by the great variety of kinds of texts translated for the first time into a language of the Indies. The important aspect for us of this phenomenon is not the new varieties of narratives, it is the displaced origin of stories that allows these narratives to be heard in the Indies through an "author." When the author manifests himself in the Indies, he is not himself at the origin of what he writes. The convention of the subtitle is "An Event that Actually Happened. . . ." The author remains a scribe. What he transcribes, however, is not the result of his witnessing of the events. It depends, instead, as we shall see, on the events being already known in the community. The author writes down what everybody is saying, when he comes to write "original" narratives; or he writes what is heard via other languages in written form; what others have said. When "An Event that

Actually Happened in Batavia in 1886" refers to what people say about the event, and not what can be independently established about it, the origin of the story is in the speech of the community. Which is to say that the author transcribes language rather than describing events. The important move to modern prose did not happen all at once. The same events, bank robberies, for instance, were sometimes reported in the newspaper and described in rhymed forms. The authors of these stories continued to speak like the copyists of ancient texts; they spoke from within the narratives rather than as their originators. What marks the beginning of the author in this tradition is two things; the attempt of the author to reserve monetary rights to his production for himself and thus to reach readers in a new form and the extended sense of hearing that comes when the lingua franca is not felt to be a particular language, but somehow language itself, able to open a path to anything said anywhere. At that point the Indies author identified himself with language. He claimed to be the vehicle through which language arrives in the world, making it available to those willing to pay.

"If I Were a Dutchman"

From a social perspective, the lingua franca is ambiguous. As we have said, Dutch administrators promoted it as the language of colonial administration, at least between Dutch officials and most 'natives.' But at the same time, they feared that 'natives' did not understand the language. Melayu was a language tied to colonial structures, but it was tied loosely. It was intended by the Dutch to bind the Indies population into a colonial hierarchy, but the weakness of its social investments made it useful for political purposes colonial authority did not approve of. It is precisely the ambiguity of the lingua franca in its capacity to be the vehicle for political and social authority and on the contrary to be the instrument of communication that overrides social and political definition that is the starting point of our study.

When one speaks two languages, one of which is one's first language and the other not, one has two "I"s and one habitually shifts between them with the possibility always opened of developing different persona for each. At certain moments, the hearing of language becomes acute and the possibility of shifting between texts, between languages, locating oneself in different worlds alternately, without making one of them primary, or even merging these worlds is taken advantage of. It is this possibility that we have availed ourselves of to speak of the origins of what was to become "Indonesian" nationalism at the turn of the nineteenth century.

We turn to a famous episode in the history of Indonesian nationalism: the publication of an article in Dutch entitled "Als ik eens Nederlander was" by Soewardi Soerjaningrat. Later, when he was known as Ki Hadjar

Dewantara, he was an important figure in the development of education. In English, the title has been translated as "If I Were a Dutchman" but it could be "If I Once Were a Dutchman." The article was published in the newspaper *De Express* on 19 July 1913. It was republished as a small brochure with the title in Dutch and in Melayu, "Djika Saya Nederlander," on the same page. In his commentary on it, the historian Tsuchiya Kenji notes that Dutch government documents say almost nothing about the contents of the article although authorities were much upset.[21] Presumably what made the Dutch so sensitive was the idea that a Javanese could think of himself as a Dutchman. Legally this was a possibility. Various natives were "equated with" Dutch, that is, subject to the same code of laws. What seemed to upset the Dutch was not that Soewardi could be Dutch but that he and therefore anyone else could imagine himself doing so. Surely one has to consider this a major step forward in the movement toward independence; one does not have to think hard of the possibilities it offers for political mobilization.

But one should be sure that this indeed was its political significance at the time. If we look at what Soewardi actually said, something the Dutch did not much talk about, we see that Soewardi denied being serious about putting himself in their place. The article was written at the moment when the Netherlands was about to celebrate the one hundredth anniversary of the establishment of its monarchy. Soewardi rhapsodized about his joy; were he only a Dutchman, at this moment:

> My voice would become hoarse from singing the "Wilhelmus" and "Wien Neerland's bloed". . . . I would collect money from the Dutchmen in the Indies not only for the celebrations, but also in order to carry out . . . the plan to increase the army of our nation in order to protect the freedom of the Dutch. I would . . . I really I don't know any more what I would do if I were a Dutchman, because I feel I would be able to do everything. (Scherer, 298–299)

The point, however, is that, were he a Dutchman, he would not ask 'the natives' to join in the celebration:

> We will hurt their sensitive feelings because we are here celebrating our own independence in their native country which we colonize. . . . Does it not occur to us that these poor slaves are also longing for such a moment as this, when they like us will be able to celebrate their independence? Or do we perhaps feel that because of our soul-destroying policy we regard all human souls as dead? (299–300)

At this point, when he says, "does it not occur to us," he imagines the Dutch not aware of the Javanese. Not seeing the Javanese, but nonetheless in their presense. Soewardi imagines, were he a Dutchman, how he would notice the Javanese, whereas real Dutchmen do not. Were he a Dutchman, he would warn his fellow Dutchmen about the danger of holding independence celebrations:

> Their hopes are being encouraged, unconsciously we awaken their wishes and aspirations for future independence. Unintentionally we are shouting to them, . . . We love freedom. (300–301)

The Dutch do not know it, but they are sending unintended messages to those whom they do not notice. It is an embarrassment. It is this that explains that no notice was taken of Soewardi's article by Dutch authorities when it was published in Dutch. It was only when it was translated into Melayu that Dutch concern was aroused. In a way, it proves Soewardi's point. The Dutch ignore a message addressed to them from a Javanese, even one who announces the possibility of himself and thus any Javanese imagining himself Dutch. But a picture of themselves, or the mere sentence that proclaims, "If I were a Dutchman" in the lingua franca leads them to see what Soewardi says: They are observed by Javanese. They are observed at the point where a hitherto invisible Javanese has imagined himself in their place, where Javanese hear not only what Dutch say but what they are not aware of saying. There are two points here, analytically speaking. Dutch do not know that they are encouraging Javanese toward independence and Dutch do not know that Javanese overhear them.

Soewardi, as I have pointed out, said he did not mean it. The thrust of Indonesian nationalism in 1913 was not for independence; it was for a certain recognition. His warning, I believe, expressed Dutch anxieties, exaggerating the political fears of the times. By not recognizing Javanese, Dutch were raising expectations that would bring trouble. He takes it all back. "We must put aside all this sarcasm," he says. He does not seriously imagine himself taking the place of the Dutch. He knows he cannot do so. He says, early on, "I wish I could temporarily be a Dutchman, not a nominal Dutchman [that is, one given the rights of a Dutchman] but a pure unadulterated son of the Great Netherlands." But, he says later, "I am not a Dutchman, I am only a brown-colored person from the tropics, a native of the Dutch colony." Because he is not a Dutchman, he will not protest, he says sarcastically. And then, seriously, he says that he will join his group in sending a telegram of congratulations but also he will ask the Dutch government to establish a native parliament.

Soewardi swerves between imaginative and sociological identities. He mobilizes the "temporarily," the impermanent possibility of being someone other than who he is. One cannot be sure how much is play built on allowing himself, for the moment, to imagine himself in another guise and at what point the play becomes serious. He concludes as a Javanese imagining himself Dutch: "If I were a Dutchman I would never celebrate the independence of a country which is still colonized." Here is the final sentence: "I would first give the people whom we still colonize their independence, and then celebrate our independence." The "I" here—"I would first give the people . . . independence"—is Soewardi as Dutch; those about whom he speaks include Soewardi as Indonesian: "and then celebrate our independence." He freely imagines he is Dutch. But he is not Dutch and so his fantasy is "sarcasm"[22] and not to be taken seriously. But it was nonetheless forceful because it was noticed by Dutch authorities and found by them to be embarrassing. The possibility of moving back and forth between identities was not, therefore, dismissable simply because it was imaginary.

And what was the position of his Melayu readers? Consider again the fact of translation. In the original language, in Dutch, the title, the only thing the Dutch spoke about, did not matter. One might think that the capacity to pose as a colonizer in the language of the colonizer, appropriating for oneself his language, hence his ideas, would be threatening. Think of other colonial situations. Imagine an Algerian in 1913 or perhaps the 1930s or 1950s saying, "si j'étais un Français." The sentence, just as in Dutch, has a silent conclusion: "mais je suis Algerien," or perhaps, "je suis Arab," or "je suis Berber." When one says, "mais je suis Algerien," "but I am an Algerian," in French, the colonial dilemma is joined. One speaks to the colonizer in his language and turns his ideas against him. The colonizer listens, is threatened, and they contend with each other. But for the Dutch, a native who spoke Dutch to them still was not heard. For them to hear, there had to be a native who could speak Dutch somehow telling anyone who spoke Melayu and not Dutch, in Melayu, what the Dutch were thinking. This they found embarrassing. The lingua franca opened a route to the Dutch, whereas the Dutch language did not.

It was not, of course, that the Dutch did not understand their own language. It was rather that they did not credit non-Dutch with understanding it. They had a different problem with the lingua franca. As we have already seen, they thought 'natives' were insufficient masters of the language and tried, therefore, to standardize it, the better to make themselves understood.[23] They saw the lingua franca, that is, as a lingua franca and not as the language of the 'natives.' When a 'native' speaks to them in Dutch, they do not attend; when he says the same thing to others in Melayu, they listen. The language that is properly no one's language is effective. It is the change of language, and the change to the lingua franca, and not what is said that is critical. It proved, for one thing, in the case we are discussing that there were actually hearers, numbers of people besides Soewardi, who seemed to know what they, the Dutch, were up to. It is the communicative power of the language, the possibility simply of transferring a message from one point to another, that mattered at least as much as what was said. It was only the lingua franca that could "communicate" in this sense at that moment in the history of the Indies.

The doubts Dutch had about the lingua franca are useful in understanding the case of Soewardi. On the one hand, the lingua franca was the administrative language, the language tied to authority, and on the other, it did not communicate Dutch intentions. But it did transmit something, even if it was not what was intended. Precisely Dutch fears that they were not reaching 'natives' were also expressions of miscommunications, "gibberish." It is not far from "gibberish" to false understandings. To feeling that in fact "I" am heard falsely, which is to say, "I am heard." " 'They' do not understand, but 'they' hear." This, it seems to me, is what creates alarm for the Dutch when Soewardi's piece appears in translation. On the one hand, a language supposedly is bound to hierarchy; on the other, the same language allows an interchange of persons contrary to hierarchy. More is involved in this interchange of persons than psychological anxiety. It is also a question of language or of mediation.

Let us return to our comparison. One is an Algerian who speaks the language of the colonizer, who is potentially freed by it because he evokes a response from French authorities. But such a person is also imprisoned within the colonial language, unable to make the phrase appear with its maximum effectiveness in his first language. The dilemma is well known. But Indonesians seem to have evaded it. That is, the force of Soewardi's sentence depended on its ability to be translated into a second language, one that was not the language of the colonizer and was not the language of the colonized. In the Algerian case, the force rests on the real possibility of substitution. The "I" becomes "they" or one of "them."[24] But in the Indonesian case, its force rests on the "I" not taking the place of the other; but, rather, embarrassing or observing him. It rests on the possibility that when one says *saya*, "I" in Melayu, it can mean *Ik* or "I" in Dutch. It actualizes the possibility that the Dutch language can rest inside Melayu in a way that native speakers of Dutch cannot control. It is a problem with two moments. In the first, speakers of Dutch find that *ik* is also *saya*; that "I" has two forms. They find themselves doubled. Embarrassment is the effect and also the solution to this doubling. The presumably unitary subject now has two first person singulars. But the one labeled *saya* becomes the one who sees the one labeled *ik*. *Ik*, embarrassed, withdraws back into himself. The two forms are now differentiated. Or at least they are for the one who commences as *ik*.

The question is how this can take place and also how it can involve masses of people. It is not naturally given in Melayu lingua franca. The one who embarrasses is someone who sees what he should not see. He is present inappropriately. In the case we have examined, his presense is not noticed. He is invisible; he is present without being seen. That is, the "I" of the sentence, translated into Melayu, is one that suddenly appears to the Dutch, having been there all the time; a fact that one knows only in retrospect, only after the title of Soewardi's piece is produced and then translated. The ordinary colonial dilemma, the one we noticed in our hypothetical Algerian case, assumes the inadequacy of languages to each other. Translated from Arabic into French, the sentence produces effects because French is not Arabic. What one says in one language is not identical to its translation, even if the translation is said to be exact. To say in Arabic, "If I were French," is implicitly to deny the possibility of being so; to say the same sentence in French is to make it seem possible. In this case, the inadequacy of translation is borne mainly by the first person singular. "If I were a Frenchman," "si j'étais Français," is powerful to the extent that one can actually inhabit the first person singular in the form *je*. The "I" is then my "I," as it were; it is really me. But if French is not my first language, the degree to which *je* says "I" and the sentence grants my independence, imaginatively of course, is also the extent that "I" am no longer "x"; no longer, that is, fully Algerian. I am free of French political domination, but I am a prisoner of the French language.

In the Melayu/Dutch/Indonesian case, by contrast, the political force does not rest on taking the place of the other; it rests on being first invisible then on appearing suddenly. It depends on the "I," that is, not taking on its full sociological import; not defining the person in such a way that he is fully present to his interlocutors in Dutch. Soewardi was already *ik*, "I" in Dutch; however he went unnoticed. He was an unfelt presence, as a ghost is an unfelt presence until a certain moment. He was there, but was not recognized as being there until afterward; until his Dutch presence was noticed in Melayu, when *ik* became *saya*; when the "I" of Dutch appeared in the "I" of Melayu. That is the moment of embarrassment; a moment when Dutch appears in Melayu; a moment of the perfect adequacy of two languages to each other: something not thought possible.

One notices that this is close to the position of the "I" in a lingua franca. Neither party, neither the speaker nor the listener, has the lingua franca as his first language. And it is not a "real" language; that is, a language with a culture attached so that one can be both intimidated by its authority and try also to take that authority for oneself. The "I" of the lingua franca is not fully inhabited by its speaker. It is a language of substitutability; a language of commerce, where it is easy to replace one party by another. Where *saya*/ "I," announces the speaker as present, holding to what he says, in whatever deal is being concluded, but where the assurance that that is so depends on him being another "I," that of whatever language he normally speaks. The lingua franca as such thus does not create Soewardi's effects, though one can think that it prepares the way for them. The lingua franca becomes activated, we might say, when the presense of the "I" in one language becomes noticed in the second; when there is no reduction of the lingua franca to an original language. At that point, the sheer mediacy of language becomes apparent.

The lingua franca was exterior to all speakers in that no one thought it originated with them; it existed merely, as it were, between them. Of course, all languages mediate. But the lingua franca is always, by definition, a language in some way foreign to both the speaker and his interlocutor. It contains the possibility, therefore, of changing the "I" of the original language into a second "I," an "I" incipient in dual form in the other as well as myself. Once it becomes the medium that generally pertained between the groups of the plural society and once it was "activated" in the way that we have suggested, other languages, and even other forms of mediation, take on heightened powers of transmission as well. That Soewardi wrote his piece in Dutch does not matter in this case. Here, unlike the hypothetical Algerian case, we see at least the possibility of one language, perhaps Javanese, his mother tongue, or perhaps Melayu already inhabiting Dutch. It is equally possible that Soewardi imaginatively took the place of a Dutchman in the way of the Algerian example. There is no logical or linguistic necessity involved; it depends on the moment in time in which it took place, a moment of a certain excitement and perhaps panic.

Even though the actual political effects of Soewardi's statement depended on embarrassment, one can imagine that what we call, only for the sake of argument, "the Algerian possibility," the hypothetical taking of the position of the colonizer for oneself, remained open. Once one has imagined himself in the place of other, and Soewardi imagined himself as a Dutchman in the Dutch language, one could see this as initiating the course of Indonesian nationalism. This possibility remained for some, as we shall see. But the same heightened sense of communicative power that we see moving Soewardi also initiated another path, one that put the Dutch to one side and that made the rejection of Soewardi's position necessary. We locate the beginnings of this position in the original forms of Melayu literature, those forms that the writer Pramoedya Ananta Toer has called "pre-Indonesian."[25] Like Muhammad Bakir, Soewardi swings between different identities, without disguise. He is, for the moment, what *ik* says, what *saya* says he is. However, Soewardi, whose first language was Javanese, and who then mastered Dutch as well as Melayu, always returns to an original position: "but I'm not . . . I am only. . . ." Knowing both languages, Dutch are always present for him; he cannot maintain the freer stances of Muhammad Bakir, who was more deeply immersed in the lingua franca. Within the lingua franca there was, by definition, no permanent identity offered. Probably Muhammad Bakir actually used Malay as a creole, as his first language. But the fact that Melayu had a dual position in colonial society—a lingua franca for some and a creole for others—meant that it took on less cultural authority than other creoles that develop along a more singular path. Even as a creole, Melayu offered an easy possibility of being merely between identities, of offering only a weak reference to a "real" position, that is, a sociological and cultural as opposed to merely linguistic status, one where "I" is almost the same as "s/he."

The position of the lingua franca, however, remained ambiguous, not only for Dutch but also for 'natives.' If it was a language that to a certain degree freed its speakers from hierarchically given identities, it was also, to some, the possibility of closer communication with the apex of the colonial administration. For Javanese peasants, for instance, it could cut through the layers of Javanese hierarchy and tie them to Dutch officials. The relation to Dutch authority was of course not the same for those who knew Dutch as for the great masses of 'natives' who spoke only a regional language and perhaps had some capacity in the lingua franca.

Soewardi's article appeared in 1913. In December 1912, the first political rally was held in Indonesia. The Sarekat Islam, the first important nationalist mass organization run by and appealing to 'natives,' that is, not mestizos or Chinese (though not always excluding these), held huge rallies in 1913. The historian of this movement, Takashi Shiraishi, comments that the organizers and speakers of these rallies were journalists because "only journalists knew how to write in newspapers and talk at rallies to unknown numbers of unknown people."[26] One might ask what it means, or what it meant at that time in history, to speak to unknown numbers of unknown people. Are the nameless people in front of a speaker at a rally the same nameless people in the mind of the journalist when he writes? How did they become nameless? That is, how did they get the identity, "nameless"? Did they give it to themselves? Were they nameless? Did they not have identity cards, for instance; that is, membership cards, in which their personal names mattered less than the title, the name of the organization holding the rally?

Perhaps it is helpful, in answering the question, to ask what speakers expected of their audience. Tjokroaminoto, the most important leader of the Sarekat Islam at the time of the rallies, explained why his organization grew so rapidly. There were others, he said, but they could not establish themselves.

> But once the Sarekat Islam emerged, thousands of people became members, bound by the rope of the religion of Islam. That is why the Sarekat Islam has become an extraordinary association.

His statement is barely an explanation. The Sarekat Islam, he said, "is no ordinary association, but an extraordinary one, bound by the rope of the religion of Islam."[27] It seemed to him natural that his organization should succeed. It proved the power of Islam, he says, though there were other Islamic organizations as well. His explanation rests on his assumption of the rightness of the organization, its basis in Islam, its "lofty purposes." In other words, Tjokroaminoto expected no resistance to his words. If there was an assumption about writing for and speaking to an anonymous audience, this, perhaps is it. What "I," the speaker, say, will naturally be accepted by my hearers. There is no difficulty to be expected. One might think that this a purely religious expectation; the power of the word is sufficient. But this was a new form of preaching; to preach to those whom one does not know and for the greatest part never meets, indicates something more. The difference between the speaker and his interlocutors, his multiple interlocutors, is not problematized. If it were, it could mean, for instance, that the speaker would fear the dissolution of his identity into the multiplicity he faces; or he could fear that his message would reach no one; that, in front of hundreds, he was talking to himself. But nothing in the accounts I have read speaks of such failures. The assumption was one of perfect communication, though not because of the special power of the word; the speeches were, after all, highly secular. Tjokroaminoto's reiteration of the loftiness of the movement's aims suggests that the speakers were, in Javanese fashion, selfless. But this selflessness can confound itself with the replaceable "I" of the Melayu speaker, the "I" who speaks not out of his own interests, that is, not out of his history and experience, not out of his own identity.

But who, in the minds of the speakers, were the audience? We have seen that Soewardi, speaking of himself as a Nederlander, sees Javanese as, unbeknownst to him the Dutchman, understanding even what he, as a Dutchman, does not intend to say. Javanese natives, in his piece, are perfect listeners or perfect readers. Indeed, they are uncanny readers. This, of course, is the presumption of "If I were a Dutchman." That is, Soewardi the Javanese can imagine himself in their, the Dutch place; can imagine what Dutch think and what they say even if they do not intend to say it. He knows them better than they know themselves. This may be only "sarcasm" as the English translator has it, or *ironie* as it is in the Dutch, or *sindiran* in Melayu. "But . . . I am not a Dutchman." The "But" means exactly what follows: "I am not a Dutchman." It does not deny, however, what he has said while imagining himself as a Dutchman: that the celebration of the anniversary of the Netherlands will raise longing for freedom in Javanese. Indeed, the article has no point if that is not so. He speaks with irony, with a distinction between "himself" and his words. But the force of the irony, the force of his argument, is such that one believes him able to think in the terms of his opponent and to warn him, for his own good, of how he, the opponent, will be understood. Where is the irony there? It rests in him identifying himself as distinct from the position he has allowed himself to imagine. When he has to label his "own" position, he does not give it his name, "Soewardi," but "Javanese." "Javanese" are perfect listeners and "Javanese" have been present inside the Dutch mind all the while.

Now imagine him, or anyone like him; imagine, that is, anyone who believes he hears and who thinks that those with the capacity to hear are called "Javanese." Imagine him before a rally. Is he not faced with an audience capable of understanding what is said and what is even unintended? It, the audience, is mere replication of himself, understanding everything said. The assumption of these rallies, of an identity of speaker and audience, is not simply an identity of interests; that both want the same thing from the Dutch, at least potentially. Nor is it an assumption about common social identity: that both speaker and audience are Javanese in the sense of being subject to Javanese customs. Such an assumption would raise questions of Javanese hierarchy in terms of which the rally has no place.[28] Remember that the rally is without precedent; those who come bring assumptions that have no place there. If, nonetheless, the audience hears what is said, it is because not only the members of the audience but also the speaker are hearers despite traditional notions of Javanese identity. They are, precisely, "hearers," "auditors" who hear even what someone is not aware of saying. This is the effect, not of a definition of "Javanese", traditional or not, but of a linguistic situation that prevailed at that time in that place, in which those who spoke their "original" language no longer found themselves fully enclosed within that linguistic community. It was a situation where the lingua franca not only mediated between groups but seemed to imaginatively place members of one group within the ambience of another, that of the colonial authorities.

This assumption supposes that the message of the rallies arose not with the speaker but before him, with the Dutch. This, in fact, was the assumption on which the organization developed. Dutch authorities sought to control the movement by getting the cooperation of certain leaders. Once it became known that the Dutch Advisor for Native Affairs supported Tjokroaminoto, the most prominent orator of the first rallies, it was not a source of accusations but the contrary. Shiraishi writes:

> In the eyes of local SI leaders it was clear that Tjokroaminoto enjoyed the blessing of and direct access to the governor general, through [the Advisor for Native Affairs].[29]

When Tjokroaminoto spoke, one could hear the supreme colonial authority through him. "Direct access" to the Gouverneur Generaal, taken literally, has a charged meaning. It means not only being heard by his excellency, having one's case considered; it means knowing what his excellency has in mind.

This opening to the Dutch was, I believe, the cause of much of the excitement of the rallies. The audience heard what it had no right to hear. They heard what the Dutch thought to themselves. One adds that they were addressed in translation; not in Dutch, not in Javanese, but, at least for the most part, in Melayu. That is, what was transmitted came not in the language of the original speaker or his listeners, not in the language of the colonizers, but in the lingua franca, which is easily taken to mark the foreign origin of its message.[30] Anonymity was already a convention in newspapers. But for the illiterate masses at the rallies, this convention was not known. Anonymous hearing was reinvented at the rallies. It came with the passing-on of the hearing of those not intended to receive the message; thus, it came not with hearing but with overhearing. An overhearing, again, that was indicated by being in Melayu/Indonesian and not in Dutch.

The frequent complaints of rally speakers was that audiences were enthusiastic but no sooner did they leave the rally than they forgot what they heard. That is, they did not consolidate what they had listened to with their everyday identities, even though the speakers, voicing local complaints, tried to do that for them. The anonymity of the first rallies was not simply namelessness but also lack of identity. You will reflect that the person who hears outside of his own personality is already, in a certain way, overhearing. What he hears does not reach "him" in his constituted identity, but someone, if one can use the term, "not him." There is a peculiar structure to these rallies: on the one hand, overhearing or disseminating the hearing of something intended for someone else; on the other, hearing outside of social identity. One perhaps promotes the other; hearing what "I" should not hear, "I" leave my identity. In the fusion of these two lies the new identity of the audience of mass media, the group, the individuals, who become used to hearing what was not addressed in particular to them.

Overhearing meant hearing what the Gouverneur Generaal had in mind. For Soewardi, this meant hearing unintended consequences, words that stimulate independence. But for the peasant audience, access to the Gouvernor Generaal did not mean what it meant for Soewardi. Rather, it meant an improved place in a reformulated colonial hierarchy. From Soewardi to the audience of the rallies there was a reversal. One that concealed again what Soewardi had revealed took place in Dutch. To cover up the exposure of the Dutch was to make colonialism work again, even if it brought with it a step outside everyday peasant identities or perhaps precisely because it suggested such a move.

The routes taken toward nationalism and toward revolution do not start with a confrontation of colonial identities, between Dutch masters and colonial slaves. They begin rather with translations on a global scale. In such an age of translation, when "I" speak from within the text and embody the communicative power of language, there are political effects. The "I" of the lingua franca is important not because through it one imagines other identities and can, therefore, mentally replace colonial masters. It is, in our examples, in its power to compel a strange overhearing, its capacity to displace or fissure subjects that its political force resides. It remains to trace the metamorphoses of this "I." We will look at how "I" tries to secure communicative power and consolidate social identity at the same time. The reader should be warned: This is not a success story.

CHAPTER TWO

What Did Not Happen to Indonesians

THE LINGUA FRANCA SEEN THROUGH DUTCH

THE lingua franca figures in Dutch literature and in the writings of mestizos. It is shown to have the capacity to link people regardless of sex and nationality. But it is, nonetheless, still tied to Dutch authority in various ways. Eventually, Indonesians were able to identify themselves with this force, at least to some degree. But to see how this occurred, one must first look at the language as it figured in wishes and nightmares. First the wishes.

Toward the end of the nineteenth century, there was a strong reforming sense emanating principally but not exclusively from Holland. The motivation for reform has not yet been satisfactorily explained. It is conventionally said that it is due to the increasing numbers of Dutch women who arrived in the Indies with the opening of the Suez Canal and who found the state of European society there less than desirable, in particular the practice of concubinage. There were also reformers bent on stopping the opium trade. Stories of the latter sort tended to be anti-Chinese, the trade being largely in their hands, but it also pictured the corruption of Dutch officials involved. These stories accompanied the opening of the Javanese interior to the market, the monetizing of the countryside being accomplished through the sale of opium as has been well-described by James Rush.[1] Taking the two sorts of stories together, one gets a picture of authenticity disrupted. Genuine Javanese peasants, dependent on Dutch protection, are exposed to the evils of money and lust. And authentic Dutch women are exposed to the loose morés of white men in the tropics.

Both types of stories see the Indies from an imported view point, that of Holland. They are the result of the increased communications that came with the opening of the Suez Canal and with the clearing of the Javanese interior, the building of railroads and roads, and the penetration of the Dutch into parts of the Indies that were not yet under their control. They were generated under the pressure of the vastly augmented commercial economy toward the end of the nineteenth century. These stories picture a certain Dutch shame. They, the Dutch, are responsible for the condition of the Indies and it is not as it should be. There is something in its condition that they have not or cannot address. They invented figures to account for their failure: the lustful, greedy Chinese merchant; the corrupt Dutch official; the venal Arab; and the deceitful "housekeeper" or *njai*. Often, sexual, governmental, and financial corruption were pictured in the same story.[2]

We are familiar with these arguments about the corruption of the tropics and the projection of sexuality onto native women and men. What distinguishes the history of the Indies, among other points, is that, as Jean Taylor was the first to point out, *njai*, or concubines, were defended by certain Indo and Dutch women writing in Dutch. Generally, these were women who defended the ways of the Indies against those newly arrived from Holland who were both ignorant and insensitive.[3] In reading some of these stories, we see how the place of the lingua franca was accounted for from within Dutch and how it was seen to operate within the confines of colonial hierarchy.

I want to turn to Thérèse Hoven as one such example. In the series of vignettes from the Indies she published first in either 1893 or 1894, narrated by a newly arrived young Dutch wife, there is one which relates a theme common to many stories written by women at the time. It tells of a government official in a remote area of Java.[4] He hires a young Javanese girl as a servant but

> he was young and could not yet think about fidelity. She saw nothing wrong in it. He was far from a mother's watchful eyes and far even from the civilized world. The mountains, where he lived, lay miles away in the interior, he was the only European and she saw nothing wrong with it and he saw nothing wrong with it. (28)

The narrator, quite sympathetic to the 'native' woman, is also sympathetic to the Dutch man. It is a feature of these women's novels that they take an understanding view of male sexuality when it has no outlet in "the civilized world" and feel that Dutch women in the home country, by contrast, have no comprehension of the special quality of life in the Indies.

The couple have children. After a few years, he receives a promotion. He must move and leave his *njai*, his "housekeeper" behind. He plans to provide for her and for the children and he thinks, at his mother's instigation, of marrying his childhood sweetheart who is back in Holland. There is, however, the problem of the children. How can he marry his Dutch sweetheart unless he abandons them? For her part, his housekeeper is fiercely attached to the children. To leave the children with her, however, means leaving them in the village. "But, no, little Louise, with her fine, European face could not become a village child," he thinks. And the housekeeper refuses to give the children up. There are stories, he knows, of abandoned housekeepers who have poisoned their masters. In this case, the housekeeper tells him she would do him no harm: "My heart belongs to you, but you must not take away my children; absolutely not" (34). (It is a feature of these stories that the voices of housekeepers do not differ from those of

Dutch women.) Even though he is aware that if he were to marry Constance, his Dutch sweetheart, he would be happy, he refuses his mother's offer to arrange the marriage. After he has more children with his housekeeper, he marries her. His mother finds this out only by reading the announcements in the paper in Holland. "Oh God, that I should have to read such a thing of my boy" (35), she says, foreshadowing her attitude later when she will meet her granddaughter.

The marriage is not happy. The housekeeper is now a wife, but at heart she remains a village girl. The man sometimes forgets that he entered the marriage of his own free will. But in any case, the problem is not his wife but his children. His oldest son, Frans, has the worst of two worlds. "He was as insolent as a Dutch street urchin and along with it he had all the tricks of a ['native'] village child" (37). His mother has no authority over him and his father very little. His teachers find him intractable. His father decides that despite the cost, he must send his son to a boarding school in Europe and that his daughter also should be sent to her grandmother's in Holland. Otherwise, she will not have the skills she needs for marriage. He does so, and there is a touching scene of separation from the mother. The girl speaks much better Melayu than Dutch (her mother has tried but is not fluent in Dutch) and she knows that the grandmother speaks no Melayu. The mother will never see the daughter again and, being illiterate, will have to depend on her husband to read her daughter's letters. The daughter will never again be able to communicate directly with the mother. The mother recovers herself, in part because her husband is unusually sympathetic and tender; but she knows that the "tender chord of sympathy which existed between herself and her daughter now was broken" (39).

In Holland, the grandmother and her daughter await the ten-year-old Louise, understanding that they must receive her. They are reluctant both out of prejudice and because the family as a whole had wanted the father to marry his childhood sweetheart. When Louise arrives, they treat her coldly. Louise shows her unfamiliarity with European ways and, in answer to her aunts' and grandmothers' snappishness with her, becomes unresponsive. The story ends happily, however, when Constance, the father's childhood sweetheart, herself now married, arrives to see Frans's daughter. Constance is married, but not happily; being a woman, it is explained, she is able to love only one man. She has no children. Constance puts Louise to bed and kisses her good night tenderly. Until that point, Louise had been unresponsive. But when Constance embraces her, without knowing why, the tears, so long pent up, flow and Louise whispers, "Net Mama; Mama zoent ook zoo" (Just like Mama; mama kisses like that). Constance is shocked. The child found her "just like Mama," in Dutch even stronger; literally, "precisely Mama," and an idea forms of taking her to her own large empty house. Which is what happens. The father visits on his vacations. Louise becomes a

> genuine lady [*echte dame*], but nonetheless not ashamed of the village woman who had her in her heart. Constance saw to that. She, Constance, was "precisely Mama". . . . but the other remained her real mother and as such the girl [*nona*] honored and loved her.
>
> The End.

The child, when she arrives at her grandmother's, speaks broken Dutch. After she asks questions that reveal her ignorance of Dutch ways, and fights with her aunts because they insult her mother, she says nearly nothing until the end. This is said to be a characteristic of her background. Dutch children, faced with the bad temper of her aunt, "would have cried, but a *nonnie*, an Indische girl, seldom cried. To everything that was asked her, she answered, 'don't know'" (49). Her Dutch grandmother and aunts silence her. They are upset that their son and brother had children with a Javanese woman. To them, Louise is the sign of her father's less-than-perfect morals, little improved by marriage with the mother of his children. The child remains a reproach to their family. At the same time, the child is innocent. She shows no shame and she defends her mother. She is innocent of what she embodies in the eyes of Dutch society. Her innocence, however, counts for nothing in her relatives' eyes. In Dutch, Louise cannot be heard because her relatives are not willing to listen to her and because her Dutch is imperfect.

The role of the good Dutch woman, who is often times shown to be one who understands or who learns about the Indies, is to provide what the real mother cannot. She is a perfect substitute for the mother. But the Javanese mother is herself a substitute. She filled in for the lack of Dutch women. Constance understands; she recognizes that motherhood, rather than being unique, needs substitutes and, understanding this, is enabled herself to become the mother of her former sweetheart's child. It is a question of seeing that one term of the least replaceable human relation, mother-child, is in fact replaceable. It is so because the child is not simply the daughter of the mother, but of the father: "his child found her." And when the child finds Constance, Constance's relation to Frans, the father, is restored. This does not mean that the child forgets her Javanese mother, the wife of her father. It means that there is room for both, the Javanese woman and the Dutch woman; both, serving the father, can be mothers of the same child—mothers of his child.

This theme, as I have said, is repeated. In one of Thérèse Hoven's stories, "Reconciled" (Verzoend)[5] a Dutch woman, newly arrived in the Indies, has a fear of her servants, whom she calls "'brown monsters.'" She gives birth to a child but does not have sufficient milk for her. She refuses to have a brown wetnurse, even though her child's health is endangered. Finally, her husband, with long experience in the Indies, forces her to do so. The child recovers her health, the mother gratefully kisses the Javanese wetnurse, and in the final words of the story says that the woman who has a husband such as hers at such moments is "blessed." Again, the real mother is supplemented by a second and the problem, again resolved, is to overcome the prejudice of the motherland and make room for both, a possibility that exists through common relation to the father via the child. I could cite other examples.

As Jean Taylor points out, these stories are usually sympathetic to the *njai*, but it is not by the possibility of one being in the place of the other. The stories do not exactly repeat the "If I were . . ." of Soewardi. They picture one person in the place of the other only in order to say that there is room for two. And there is room for both because paternal authority, which is also colonial authority, makes a place. It is a question of acknowledging the ties that lead to the white father. The right of paternity in one story forces the inclusion of a Javanese mother and in the other leads to the recognition of his progeny in the eyes of Dutch society despite the color of the mother.

What interests us is how, in one case at least, acknowledgment is won. In our first story, it comes with the kiss Constance gives Louise. This kiss enables Louise once more to speak; she says, "precisely mother," *net moeder*, "just like mother." The kiss sets Louise talking; she speaks Dutch and she begets the strongest of reactions: "A shock went through Constance's heart; his child found her; "just Mama"; at once an idea came to her." (53). The idea was to bring Louise home with her. The child had the idea first: just mama. Constance's idea comes from her. The child speaks and thereby creates a second mother for herself.

But the assumption of the story is that Louise could not have the effect she has on Constance if she were not the daughter of her father and if her father were not her second mother's old sweetheart. "His child" was the embodiment of his disapproved sexuality, but she was also the sign of himself. Acknowledging the second makes the first acceptable. Louise, then, embodies more than she knows. She is her father's daughter; she does not know that that is shameful. She says, as it were, more than she is aware of and she makes it heard and accepted.

But it would not be accurate to say that Louise reveals a secret. The secret, her father's promiscuity with a Javanese woman (promiscuity in the eyes of his relatives who remain in Holland), was known. One of those to whom it was shameful is made to accept it. It is not revelation; it is, rather, that the known fact is now part of accepted social life. The Javanese and the Dutch woman are then linked. One can say that paternity has been made communicable and with it, color.

All this happens when Louise begins to speak again and says "just mother," *net moeder*. She speaks broken Dutch, confirmation of her mother's fear that she was at home in Melayu but not in Dutch. Her laconic phrase no longer indicates her reluctance to speak but her unfamiliarity with Dutch; she still thinks in Melayu. When she wins acknowledgment for herself, her mother, and her father, Melayu is seen transformed into Dutch. Louise conveys her past—"just mother"—through translation from the language in which that past occurred. A Dutch woman, hearing it, is struck. But if a path is opened from Melayu to Dutch it only conveys the effects of the father. Melayu heard in Dutch leads back to the activities of a Dutchman. Through the child and the woman, the reluctance of "the Dutch" to understand that someone else can speak their language and must be listened to is overcome. The resistance is the resistance of the Dutch language to penetration by Melayu. But certain people, those who understand the Indies, understand this possibility and write stories that communicate their knowledge. The discovery of the possibility of translation from Melayu to Dutch, however, is predicated on the origin of what is translated in the activities of the father. When the girl conveys what she experienced with her monolingual mother in Dutch, she is heard, but only because the real reference of her words is the Dutch father. Melayu in translation here turns out to have been Dutch all the time.

One cannot say that the path goes in two directions. Constance sees to it that the fear of the Javanese mother, that her child would forget her, does not happen. But the author does not think to tell us of the reactions of the Javanese mother when, for instance, she hears that her husband's sweetheart is now the mother of her daughter. The Dutch language remains a barrier for some. And, for that matter, one can see the play of jealousy between Dutch women in Holland and those established in the Indies. The former are excluded in favor of the *njai* in the writings of Sloot, Hoven, and others.

Soewardi wrote in Dutch and nothing happened. In translation, when Dutch was made to be heard in Melayu by 'natives,' there were political consequences. These women's novels close off the availability of translation to both sides and thus alter political consequences. The novels obscure the effects of male sexuality; male sexuality which is inextricably connected with Dutch political authority. These effects are not only the exercise of that sexuality with 'native' women. Louise's father has given up his Dutch sweetheart, Constance, in order to keep his children. He has not only taken a 'native' woman, he has neglected or forgotten Constance. Constance is connected with him again, at a great distance and yet in another manner closely connected. This is the working of translation, hence communication, in favor of one side only. It denies that certain Dutch women are excluded when Dutch men exercise their power in the Indies.

It denies that they are ever out of the minds of men, even when these men are not aware of all they have communicated. The native mother, at that point, is relevant as an indication of the Dutch man's force.

Again, it is not when Soewardi put himself in the place of a Dutchman, but when he conveyed that fantasy in Melayu that his effort mattered. What he conveyed had a double message: If he were Dutch, he would see that Dutch do not say certain things about themselves. He would see that they keep some things to themselves and do not allow Melayu speakers to hear them. He points to the consequences of Melayu listening: desire for freedom will be awakened. He imagines himself a Javanese hearing what the Dutch might, later, say. And he imagines Dutch men suffering the consequences of being heard to say what they did not intend to convey. He envisions himself on both ends of the lines of communication. He is not so much a speaker or a writer, but someone who overhears, in no stable identity, what one side did not mean to say and what the other would suffer from hearing. He is not the first person or the second, but an impossible third; one who hears inappropriately. He offers the Dutch advice: Do not say what you do not want to be overheard. He offers himself as someone who will close off what goes on in Dutch mens' minds—their celebration of freedom—from Javanese hearing of it. In these Dutch women's novels, the Dutch language, in the end, fills the role Soewardi proposed for himself. There is no need for the native woman to be jealous; she, scarcely knowing Dutch, illiterate, dependent on her husband for communications in Dutch, is not likely to be fully aware that she shares her place as mother with a Dutch woman, a former lover of her husband.

As for Constance, in Hoven's novel, when she hears "just like mother," she does not think, "If I were a Javanese. . . ." The role of languages here is not to stimulate identification; it is merely to establish a fantasy of connection. Identification, perhaps, occurs only when communication is thought to work in both directions. Soewardi alternately finds himself with the Dutch and with the Javanese, traveling somehow between the two sides. His political effectiveness was not to be one or the other nor one taking the place of the other, but to make communicable what was thought not to be so. With Thérèse Hoven, what comes from Melayu is really Dutch. Or, put another way, in the Dutch hierarchy which is widened to include natives, what is translated into Dutch already is known, approved, and originates with the Dutch. The figure who knows more than she knows she knows, thereby creating embarrassment, is neutralized. Hierarchy encapsulates communication; nothing escapes. The sign of male pleasure is given a place of honor. Soewardi, overhearing, shows that there is more in Dutch than its speakers thought; an increment that is revealed in translation and that threatens to end hierarchy altogether. Soewardi, one might say, put himself in the place of Melayu, not on either side, but in motion in the middle, opening Melayu to Dutch and Dutch to Melayu.

The circulation of language without authoritative control was a nightmare written down by a Dutchman in 1887. Hangings were a feature of nineteenth Century political life in the Indies. In 1887, Isaac Groneman (1832–1912) described one he had witnessed.[6] The public display, Groneman thought, had a deleterious effect; it transformed criminals into martyrs. He says that those hanged are "admired and honored." And yet when he gives his impressions of the hangings, another impression emerges:

> I have seen them die, one by one, most apparently indifferent; a few presumptuous, unashamed, proud, as warranting a well-deserved homage of the whole people, against the contemptible troops of the hated Dutch [*landas*]; another half dead of fear of dying, with grim pale brown countenance and hopeless twisted steps, powerlessly sunk into the arms of the executioner's assistants.
>
> I have read on the faces of the native spectators—and there amongst them were certainly again some whose turn should come—no compassion, no horror, no fear or awe and scarcely any interest.
>
> Only a few female faces were a little less indifferently creased than usual.(169)

Groneman's point is that executions create martyrs by stimulating defiance. But only "a few" are of this type. Of the others, one is contorted by fear of death. But most show no reaction: "Most apparently indifferent," he says. And this includes the spectators, including "some whose turn should come." He catalogs the emotions they do not show: "no compassion, no horror, no fear or awe." These people whose turn on the scaffold can be foreseen, do not seem to put themselves in the place of the one whose death is imminent or, perhaps, just arrived. Or, if they do see themselves to be like those on the scaffold, it is only like the condemned who are "most apparently indifferent."

Faced with death, most of the 'natives' Groneman watched showed no reaction. He looks at their faces and "only a few female faces were a little less indifferently creased than usual." The others do not move. The face is the part of the anatomy that most intensely displays feelings and it does not function. The owners of these faces seem not to think that the death that is approaching is their death, although it is. Or, if they are aware of it, it does not matter to them. They are "indifferent" to death, Groneman feels. This indifference makes them already almost dead, their faces no longer animated. These immovable visages, severed from their source of animation, could be called masks, but then one would have to posit a wearer of the mask different from it. Groneman's difficulty is accounting for what if anything is behind these immobile faces.

Groneman believes executions create martyrs. He knows this by reading the faces of a few who are "presumptuous, unashamed, proud, as warranting a well-deserved homage." These are the faces that stimulate rebellion. They are a threat to authority. But the indifference of the spectators is no less threatening, though the threat is less apparent. If these 'natives' are afraid of death and if death, in the form of the execution, is controlled by Dutch authority, their faces would show it. They could not disguise such a powerful emotion. Appearances here are set in a certain hierarchy; or they should be. They should acknowledge the power of death and the power of political authorities at the same time. If Groneman speaks of the rebellion of certain figures and yet describes most as indifferent, it is perhaps because he finds both reactions to be menacing. A society consisting of inanimate appearances acknowledges no authority, not out of rebelliousness but simply because it responds to something other than authority. Groneman saw Javanese criminality as an effect of gambling and he saw gambling as an obsession. Those who gambled believed in chance. They responded to a mythical call and in so doing, they were impervious to the social and the political and to a certain civil or colonial religion.

All that was available to Groneman, the spectator of those already condemned to death and those soon to be, was mere appearances, entities inhabiting a world other than his own, yet occupying the same territory and nominally belonging to the same state. Political authority uses its most powerful weapon, legalized killing, but the sight of it scarcely causes a single muscle to contract. For Groneman, mobile faces would indicate the integration of colonial society. Even rebelliousness would show a relation to authority, which, though regrettable, is preferable to complete divorce from the colonial world. In Groneman's nightmare, mere appearance, irreducible to anything reachable by him or those like him, governs 'native' society. For him, the face is where the fear of death is transmuted into signs. When he believes this does not happen, he fears that colonial society is broken apart, unable to transmit indications between its segments.

This does not mean, however, that nothing at all is transmitted. Groneman feared addiction to gambling which made those on the gallows, in his view, respond to some other source of animation; one not controllable by the Dutch. But those on the gallows lack animation altogether. He complains that he sees in the spectators not merely no fear and no compassion, but "scarcely any interest." And yet, even without interest, there is mutual regard. The spectators look at the victims and the victims look at the spectators. What can a lack of interest that nonetheless sustains mutual viewing mean? It means that there is no attempt to see beyond the face, to penetrate to the feelings of one whose death is imminent. The expressions of the victims are taken, we dare to say, at face value. They mean only what they appear to mean and nothing more than that. There is nothing of additional interest. The extinction of human life, in Groneman's view, was not an occasion for 'native' spectators to wonder at death, to try and glimpse in the face of one who was to die in the next minute an indication of something that cannot be experienced and told about.

What does it mean to take something at face value? There were spectators, people whose presence at the execution in some way meant that they vicariously experienced the fate of the victims, if only, perhaps, contrary to what Groneman supposed, to distinguish themselves from them, to say, "but I'm not. . . ." Groneman, however, insists that many of them were obliged to say, "If I were . . ." because they, too, were criminals. They put themselves in the place of victims without attempting to learn more, without trying to discern an invisible force or an impulse that came from somewhere else that would mean that they too will vanish. Perhaps they were entirely without expectation, having already accepted their deaths. That would account for their indifference, but not for their presence at the scene. Their presence as spectators indicates that they had an identification of some sort with those about to die or already dead, an interest in seeing themselves through an other. And yet death, administered by the Dutch, did not affect them.

If we extend Groneman's thoughts about spectators, we can say that spectators imagined themselves on the gallows as though the disappearance of the ones they saw did not leave a gap, an empty sign. For them, from the start, the sign of the person, the appearance of himself, was all there was. It is the assumption of Muhammad Bakir who, moving between persons within his texts, does so of course in the form of signs, not of physical persons, and never leaves himself behind. Muhammad Bakir never says, "but I'm not . . . I am only" as though to imagine himself someone else would also be to imagine the disappearance of his original self. He identifies himself only as whatever "I" he takes on. He could and in a certain way did, say, "I am dead"; it was no different for him than saying "I am so and so."

Those hanged and those watching were not necessarily speakers of Melayu. Groneman's scene, in any case, took place without any particular linguistic code, being a matter of appearances. And yet, Groneman reflects the situation of the lingua franca; the situation of a certain noncommunication between languages that makes the lingua franca necessary. Groneman hears and sees that he does not hear. He knows that there is something that excludes him. Sometimes he thinks it is nothing at all; sometimes it is something he disapproves of; and sometimes it is something he knows he cannot imagine. He puts himself in the audience if only to say that he is not like "them." He, the implication is, would certainly, in their place, imagine himself about to be hanged. In saying this, he shows us how one comes to feel addressed. They should understand the message of the gallows; he,

Groneman, certainly does. It is how he knows it is not meant for him. He has put himself in their place, felt the message addressed to him, only in order to deny that he is in their place. At the point where the message is not meant for "him," Groneman the European, Groneman the colonial figure, he feels himself addressed and denies it. He is, then, not so different from Muhammad Bakir who felt himself addressed, quite inappropriately from the point of view of sociological and cultural conventions and definitions, but who, instead of denying, responded.

This is Groneman's nightmare of colonial society. People respond not to what is intentionally addressed to them, but to another message, hidden in the first; the message that there is a message. The spectators at the hanging have displaced the center not only of colonial but of linguistic authority. They refuse to respond to what is said to them but they do respond, through their indifference plus their viewing, to something else. They respond to what they should not respond to. They thus find themselves within a circuit of communication outside the circuit defined sociologically. The result, Groneman recognized, is unreadable. But it is realized for such 'natives' as Muhammad Bakir within Melayu. No doubt there were others unlike Muhammad Bakir but similar to Groneman. Such people would have said that what they hear does not apply to them. They would have then found themselves, like Groneman, back where they were originally. It is my contention, however, that denial came much later. And that before it arrived, there were still other responses to messages not intended for oneself. Response to these put one inside the text, outside "normal" social discourse.

A Society of Appearances

"Above all avoid display" was the foremost rule that must serve for life in the Indies. One could be as one wished, do and permit what one wished; if one did come in conflict with good morals or conventional forms but . . . [kept it] inside the house, one could stay respected and honorable in the Indische world. Then it never came up that one was a usurer, a lecher, a deceiver.

The quotation is from a novel by J. A. Uilkens, a Dutch writer who lived in the Indies and whose novel was published in 1877.[7] It comes from the mouth of one his characters who is learning the ways of Indies society.

So long as the appearance [*schijn*] was avoided. If you made yourself seem energetic you could be lazy in the Indies; seem honest and you could be the opposite; seem temperate and you could in quiet be immoderate in your person; seem virtuous and you could be without morals; seem honorable and you could injure those closest to you to your heart's content; seem to understand and you could be stupid as an ass; seem rich and you could be tons of gold in debt. The one who in the Indies did not avoid appearance but shows himself as he is, stands in the way of his own career [*staat zich zelven in zijne loopbaan in den weg*]. Sincerity is not in demand and the showing of the bad side of character is the greatest mistake that one can make. Seem to be an angel and then without difficulty you can be a devil. So thought Mevrouw Villany. (261–262)

"One who in the Indies did not avoid appearance but shows himself as he is, stands in the way of his own career," Mevrouw Villany, a person in one of his novels, went on. The result is a society built by social exigency. Truth appears only when imagery is put aside. "Sincerity is not in demand and the showing of the bad side of character is the greatest mistake that one can make." For Uilkens, appearances favor social acceptance. They thus make it possible to act in any way one wishes. "Seem to be an angel and then without difficulty you can be a devil. So thought Mevrouw Villany" (261–262).[8]

The contrary of "appearance" here is "real moral character" not, of course, ethnic identity as in the cases we shall see in a moment. These oppositions are not in doubt; one genuinely is a rich lecher, called Priaap, for instance, in another novel of Uilkens, avid for money and women at the same time, pursing the wives of one's employees, blackmailing them and so on.[9] But one appears respectable and is taken for such. Most of the unfavorable characteristics Uilkens names have to do with sex or money. The two are confounded and they form an underlying reality always betrayed by appearances.

But the bottom line or underlying reality is only one feature of money. Uilkens equates money with greed and lechery; through their operations, appearances and reality diverge. One would think Uilkens had read Marx on the power of money:

> Money's properties are my properties and essential powers. . . . What I *am* and *am capable* of is by no means determined by my individuality. I *am* ugly, but I can buy for myself the most *beautiful* of women. Therefore I am not *ugly*. . . . I am bad, dishonest, unscrupulous, stupid; but money is honored and hence its possessor is good. Money, besides, saves me the trouble of being dishonest; I am therefore presumed honest.[10]

In Marx, money's power to effect substitution generates the false appearances of the rich. One item is exchanged for another unlike the first and is equatable to a generalized form. When people respond to the power of money, they respond to a source of circulation at odds with normal social values. Uilkens's capitalists are thus similar to Groneman's Javanese. They are a node or source from which false impressions emanate, resulting in the formation of an undesirable society set within normal forms but responding to an entirely different imperative. Again, as with the women's novels, there is the problem of male sexuality, though of course Uilkens is less tolerant than Hoven. Hoven accommodates Dutch male sexuality through the workings of the lingua franca and links 'native' and Dutch circles. Uilkens instead generates villains, makes no accommodation and sees only social disintegration.

In the novels of P. A. Daum (1849–1898), a Dutch newspaper editor and writer of the Indies, there are subtler treatments of money and sex having to do with the *njai*, or concubine. In the story *Nummer Elf*,[11] for instance, George Vermeij keeps a *njai*, the daughter of a Dutch soldier and a 'native' woman of whom he is quite fond. However, he is greatly in debt and feels that it is time to marry. He arranges a marriage with a Dutch woman, Lena Bruce, principally in order to pay his debts. He is, however, still attached to his *njai*, called Ada in the Melayu translation and Yps in the original Dutch.[12] Ada does not want to give him up. Eventually, out of jealousy, Ada poisons Lena Bruce, or so it is rumored.

The *njai*, as an institution, was founded on the market. However, here George Vermeij's affections are with the *njai*; it is the Dutch woman with whom he arranges a bond based at first on money. In this context, the questions of the status of the *njai* are raised: Is she commodity? Is she the object of sincere affection? George asks himself, "How can I chase her away like a servant or like a dog?" (46; II/6, 31 July 1904). He is genuinely fond of her. But money and love are confounded as Vermeij comes also to have an affectionate relation to his wife. The question becomes how to rid himself of his *njai*, who refuses to simply disappear (46; 13 July 1904, Bintang Betwai).

When the break between Ada and George is definitive, Ada's mother tells her she is stupid because she only wants to take money from one man.

> Just think for a minute; is the money of that *tuan* different than the money of other men? If you want money, you can't refuse the European or Chinese men who come here with full pockets.
>
> Njai Ada thought her mother was right. From that night on she accepted the men who came to her house for their pleasure and got money enough to soothe her hurt. (XXI/50, 23 September 1904)

The status of the *njai* has in one sense been clarified. The role of money has determined respectability and sincerity. All money from European and Chinese men is alike; therefore, why be faithful to only one man? Njai Ada is not necessarily less fond of her former *tuan*. But in the passage quoted she sees the "reality" of her situation. At the same time, the question of money comes up in the family of George Vermeij and Lena Bruce. There is another man who chastely loves Lena and who is wealthy. He gives them f5000 to name their child after him. Even though George has married for money, the couple come to be attached to each other. They first agree to accept the offer but in the end reject it (164, 166, 189). But they consider it, and the result is that the name is for sale although the sale is never consummated. Fathers can be replaced, bought and sold, just as *njai* can. The idiom of money is used to show a "reality" that may be ambiguous, in distinction to Uilkens's Indies, but that underlies appearances and renders them deceptive. The result is that the world of Daum is, finally, similar to that of Uilkens. People look respectable, but the operations of money hollow out appearances.

In the Indo *Story of Njai Dasima* by G. Francis, which we will turn to shortly, money is important as it is turned into the gift. Njai Dasima is grateful to her *tuan* because he is generous with her. She is not shown as earning a living by being his housekeeper; what she gets is a sign of his tenderness for her. In the relations of the *tuan* and the *njai*, there is no difference between the stories of the Dutchman Daum and the Indo Francis or, for that matter, with the later Indonesian versions of Njai Dasima. Or at least that is true up until the point in Daum's story where Ada, who has been pictured as genuinely attached to her *tuan*, realizes that the money of all men is the same. Then, money comes to play a different role; it becomes an indication of desire. The speech of Ada's mother redefines the role of the *njai*. Being a *njai* is merely a commercial venture. At that point, money exchange indicates the sexual desire of the man and the desire for money of the woman. The institution of the *njai* could be questioned just as marriage itself might be when the name of the child can be bought and sold.

A scene in *Nummer Elf* illustrates how the role of language changes when money indicates a difference between appearance and underlying reality and male sexuality comes into view. Early in the story, George is tormented about Ada. He is desperate for money to pay his debts. He watches Ada adorn herself and he thinks, "The dear. She does that only to please me" (19). He decides that "Njai Ada is no different from a European girl so it would not be right to chase her out as though she were a servant" (31 July 1903). He approaches her, but as he does so, she hands him a letter. He trembles as he takes it. It is from a lawyer, demanding payment of his debts. He remembers again he must marry Lena for her money.

He hands her back the letter. Although "she was not really capable of reading or writing, and though she did not understand much Dutch, nonetheless she knew that it was a letter dunning him for debts and that he could not pay" (31 July 1903). When she asks about the letter and he explains, she is suspicious. Her suspicion is elaborated in the next episode.

"All right," thought Ada, "George wants to send me back to the village, that's just fine. It's better in the village than here in this big house. In the village I can talk with the people, and that's very nice. I stay with a Dutchman for the money. If it were not for that, of course I would ask for my leave right away. Now he is starting to hate me; later I can take my revenge on him." (1 August 1903)

She thinks George wants to be free of her and has had a friend write the letter so that he can make an excuse. This is not the case. Daum pictures the *njai* as self-absorbed, interested in her own appearance. Her nature will remain ambiguous throughout the story. On the one hand, she is interested only in herself and in him for what he can give her. But sometimes she is affectionately attached to him. Ada's narcissism is protected by a linguistic barrier. She knows only rudimentary Dutch and she is barely literate. She is thus part of a world that, from a Dutch point of view, is self-enclosed. But despite her rudimentary literacy, Njai Ada reads the letter correctly, not by knowing what it actually says or how it was generated, but by seeing what George had in mind before the letter arrived. She has guessed his secret thought with a certainty greater than his own and for no reason whatsoever. We are given a picture of an Indo able to read the mind of Europeans; an Indo who emerges from an entirely Indies background. And yet, George's thought is hers.

Ada knows; and George knows that she knows, though he does not say how. That night they sleep in separate rooms. Two days later he tells her. By this time he has no choice. He has told his friends and she has had her suspicion confirmed:

All of George's friends have *njai*s. They told their *njai*s that George wanted to let Njai Ada go because he wanted to marry. The *njai*s of George's friends told this back to Ada and her mother. The two were angry but they did not make a scene. (31 July 1903)

Here gossip makes reasonable a fear; but only after the fact. Daum offers no explanation for why Ada suspects the truth in the first place on the basis of no evidence. She thinks the letter is a forgery, the pretext for George to make an excuse. It is not. But she is right all the same; George wants to get rid of her. Precisely for reasons the letter, which she can read, only barely, but still sufficiently, explains. She rejects these reasons. She is right for the wrong reason. How she comes to have a suspicion is not made clear. True, it is a convention of the lives of *njai*s; they are overthrown at the convenience of the *tuan*. But this convention is invoked precisely at the point where a letter comes in George's language; a language she barely has access to. When her suspicion is triggered by Dutch, she seems to have access not only to the letter but to the whole of what goes on, in Dutch, in the mind of George. The *njai*, the dweller in native villages, controls thoughts that originate in Dutch. Here we have the danger of translation. Precisely the *njai*'s ability to read Dutch is conflated with her access to his thoughts.

When Dutch male sexuality is put in the idiom of money, the intimate relations of 'native' women and European men, each ideally a unique matter of sentiment, become contentious. What the man has, money, can be coveted by the woman. More generally, native poverty is no longer a mere consequence of native ways of life; it is a deprivation caused by the satisfaction of European desire. In the idiom of money, 'native' desire also can be aroused. In Dutch language accounts, when money makes itself felt, dangerous communications make themselves felt. The secret thoughts of Dutchmen become public knowledge. Passage between languages becomes the means to see that what colonial masters enjoy—freedom—is available to natives.

The lingua franca could operate as with Soewardi, at least in one understanding of Soewardi, revealing the secret thoughts of Dutchmen. Dutch literature, in any case, including Daum's novels, was already available in Melayu translation. If one places global translation at the origin of nationalism and one sees the Dutch fears of it that Soewardi himself expressed on their behalf, it is reasonable to think that the development of nationalism followed this path by which 'natives' could imagine themselves in the place of Dutch.

It is my contention that this was not the case. In part, it is a question of understanding Soewardi when he wrote "If I Were a Dutchman." One can see him as imagining what the Dutch think, as imagining himself as a Dutchman, and through that, opening the way for others to do the same. Or keeping in mind that his work was only effective once it was translated, one can see him demonstrating the power of translation, the power of language freed from social moorings. In the first case, "Soewardi" has a secure identity he never gives up as he thinks what Dutch are thinking. In the second, "Soewardi" is a figure similar to "Muhammad Bakir" who simply does not think about consolidating whatever fictional persona he might temporarily inhabit. As the figure who travels between, who has the power to do so, "Soewardi," like "Muhammad Bakir" would be indistinguishable from this power but unable to appropriate it for himself. "He" would remain in motion.

CHAPTER THREE

Fetishizing Appearance, or Is "I" a Criminal?

THE NJAI AND THE WHITE FATHER SEEN BY AN INDO: G. FRANCIS

Men born of European fathers and indigenous mothers often never learned Dutch, but their identity depended on whether their fathers legally recognized them as their children. Their legal status, what law code they were subject to, as well as their life chances depended on this recognition. But recognized or not, they had a place alongside the Dutch in a culture that fused European and Indonesian elements. When the Indies were opened up to increasing European influence, the position of Indos became questioned along with the whole of the culture of Europeans and their offspring as it had adapted itself to the Indies. This is the point at which the first stories dealing with events said to have "really happened" in a certain place at a certain time, told in prose and printed, began to appear. A new sort of literature, that is, began to appear when for some, the lingua franca not only was but was realized to be all they had to connect them to the legitimating power of colonial society. Precisely this awareness of language generated fear in many Dutch (language) writers as we have seen; a fear that is behind the increasing separation of groups in the Indies in the early part of the twentieth century.[1] Yet this anxiety could work as well to wish-fully rebond European fathers and their descendants. That was the case with certain literature written in Melayu by Indos.

I propose to look at an Indo story, one which, more than others, gained lasting popularity among Indos, 'natives,' and Chinese.[2] It is called, "The Story of Njai Dasima." *Njai*, as I have said, is a term used to mean "house-keeper" or "kept woman." It refers to the women who kept house for Dutch or other European and sometimes Chinese men and who often bore children by them. Dasima is the proper name of a woman kept by a European, Tuan W. Njai Dasima bears Tuan W. a daughter and Tuan W. loved Njai Dasima, we are told, "as though she were his wife. He gave her his wealth to take care of." Her wealth was the talk of the neighboring native community. Several men tried unsuccessfully to win her. Finally one, the Muslim Samioen, does so with the assistance of an old woman who entered Tuan W.'s house as a servant. The woman threatens Njai Dasima with punishment in the Muslim afterlife if she does not leave Tuan W. Dasima comes to believe this only when the woman uses magic, thus compelling her to believe she fears God and loves Samioen. She deserts her child and leaves Tuan W. desolated. It is soon clear that Samioen wanted only her wealth. He, and especially his first wife, treat her like a servant. Dasima comes to regret leaving; in the end, Samioen, to avoid having to give her back her riches, hires a thug who murders her. Samioen and his accomplice are easily captured by the police and admit their guilt.

When Njai Dasima tells Tuan W. she is going to leave, he begs her not to, but she is deaf to him, having been made so by magical means. He is overcome by sadness. The point is that she is not merely a mistress; she is the mother of his child and he loves her. In certain Dutch and Melayu literature, the family composed of a European man and a native woman was thought to be the equal or perhaps more of the Dutch family.[3] In the absence of European women, native women took their place, as we have already seen. To the degree that these women learned Dutch ways, they were, in these literatures, appreciated:

> This *tuan* was still young and had a certain *njai*, an Islamic woman from Kampoeng Koeripan named Dasima. This *tuan* had this *njai* from the time she was an adolescent. She was well formed, light skinned with long hair and she was willing to learn all the work of women, that is, cooking, sewing, cutting out clothes. She learned all this from Njonja Bonnet with whom she lived in Tjoeroek at the time. Because this *njai* was diligent and good at her work, Tuan W. loved her as though she were his wife. He let her take care of all his wealth. What's more, Tuan W. got a beautiful daughter from her called Nancy whom he loved dearly. So Tuan W. in no way felt it a loss to buy and give his *njai* all sorts of things for her to keep, such as a . . . diamond hairpin. . . . all of it with a value of more than f3000. Moreover, every month he gave her f100 for expenses. . . . All of which *njai* kept herself without the *tuan* ever paying attention. (3–4)[4]

Njai Dasima's qualities make her arrangement with Tuan W. into a perfect family. Her domestic abilities enhance her good looks, extending, as it were, her womanly qualities ("she was willing to learn all the work of women") but in the direction of domesticity. She is reliable; Tuan W. can trust her with his money;, she does what is necessary in the house; and she is the mother of a child he loves.

An old village woman gains entry to their household and later gives her view of the closeness of their relation to each other:

> "They love each other very much and the Tuan trusts her with all his wealth and the entire household. They live together even beyond the ways of those married, because the *njai* takes good care of the *tuan*'s money and saves it and isn't at all extravagant; she never buys anything she doesn't need." (10)

It is better than marriage: she is beautiful and a good housekeeper; he gives her money and she saves it for him. In these passages, there is an assumption of money exchange as the basis of their relationship. Furnivall says that in the plural society, communities meet only in the market. The relation of *njai* to *tuan* does not seem to contradict him; it is the extension of the market into the family. And yet it would not be correct to leave this statement unamended. The isolation of elements in the plural society rested on the ability of money to create restricted relationships. One's laborers might be merely that, with obligations limited to the exchange of labor for money. If they were more, they did not necessarily have much in common culturally. Here, in the description of the better-than-marriage relation of *njai* and *tuan*, however, there is a process of cultural conversion that is at the heart of the story. Dasima was trained in the household of Mevrouw Bonnet, a European. In the Dutch language version, published in 1926 by A. Th. Manusama, probably an Indo, it is made clear that Dasima first worked for Mevrouw Bonnet where she learned European household skills "to the great satisfaction of her mistress." It is there that Tuan W. met her. Dasima "was so exactly what he liked because of her beauty and her qualities [that is, her domestic skills] that he took her as a housekeeper."[5] Their relation begins as economic and it continues as one of exchange—he gives her money, jewels, and goods and she takes care of them and of the household and has his child. For her part, Dasima at one point tells the woman who wants to convince her to leave the *tuan*, she has "been with the *tuan* for eight years, ever since I was an adolescent, and everything was fine and I had a daughter" (18). "And everything was fine" presumably meaning that everything went well and that she received all that she might wish for. But the monetary aspect becomes obscure as the *tuan* comes to be fond of his *njai* and to trust her. He "pays no attention" to what she does with what he gives her. If exchange is at the heart of their relation, it seems to be the exchange of bourgeois marriage; interests rule and interests are general. But the point of the story is that no substitution is possible. Tuan W. is desolate when he loses Dasima and Dasima only leaves him because she is coerced. Dasima, we are told, "loved the *tuan* and she loved her daughter" (19). She tells the old woman, "I am fortunate [a phrase that can also mean, "I profit"]; God has allowed me to live with the *tuan*. He is generous and he loves me; I have enough to eat and enough to wear"(18).

The condition for this arrangement is that Dasima learn Dutch ways. It is because of what she learned from Mevrouw Bonnet that she is able to act like a wife. She has Dutch skills and these enable her to make a household that is the equivalent or more of a Dutch household. This, indeed, was the defense of the *njai*, found in both Indo and Dutch literature. Given the paucity of European women, European men were left only with the possibility of 'native' women. The picture of these women varies, but in certain writers they become valued not as sexual but as domestic substitutes. This substitution begins as buying and selling of labor but it becomes, it was sometimes said, better than the original. When something is better than the original, it is itself unsubstitutable. It is this idea that is reproduced in "The Story of Njai Dasima." But for this to happen in this story, by an Indo, the *njai*-mother-substitute-wife must take on Dutch characteristics.

It is precisely the incompleteness of this process that allows for the abduction of the *njai*. Various Muslim men try to coax Njai Dasima from Tuan W. in order to get her wealth. Samioen succeeds through the efforts of an intermediary, an old woman, who drugs or enchants her but who also offers her various arguments in favor of leaving. The old woman asks Njai Dasima, "What does one want in the world?" and answers her own question: "Respect, wealth, and security"(19). She menaces Dasima with Dasima's lack of security:

"You are taken care of by Tuan, but you are not his wife and not a slave. It is impossible that you would want to stay here like that. At this moment you are not Dutch, not Chinese; you are a Muslim and you must do your duty so that you are secure in this world and the next. Don't let things go so far that you have nothing on this side and nothing on the other." (13)

She argues another time that:

"if the *tuan* really loved you he would marry you. He is a white man and if he gets one of his own kind of course he will throw you out and, just like that, go back to his homeland taking the child. You will be stuck all alone without relatives and without acquaintances here. You live in adultery, without marrying as the Prophet Mohammed commanded. You have to follow religion so that you do not regret it later." (19–20)

Although Dasima may have Dutch skills, she lacks the security a Dutch woman would have, not having the legal status of wife; as a Muslim, she puts in jeopardy her future in the afterlife. She may be like a Dutch wife, but she is not one. Her lack in this regard is not actually threatening, we are led to believe in the story. It is not that her *tuan* would actually abandon her. It is that she believes the common view put into the mouth of the old woman and therefore comes to doubt the security of her relation to the European man. Her fear of being abandoned, that is, stems from suddenly realizing that she is not Dutch and therefore is not safe. Her insecurity stems from her comprehending the very identity that had offered her security and that until then she had never thought about.

Dasima is, the old woman points out, safe on neither side. Without knowing it, she has found herself in the middle, between Europeans and Muslims and without the protection of either. Were she to leave Tuan W., she would win what she lacks, namely respect. "You stay inside the house, you don't get the respect you would since you do not mix with people of rank"(19). As a *njai*, she was unlikely to mix with Europeans other than her *tuan*; the sentence refers primarily to the acknowledgment Dasima would get were she to live in the Islamic neighborhood. Questions of respect and of Islam are mixed with one another. As a Muslim and the wife of a Muslim, she would gain the honor due to her. As a *njai*, she is deprived precisely of social life outside the house and left only with a precarious domestic status.

The old woman's arguments are shown to be specious. But they succeed in translating her out of the house.

> Njai Dasima thought about what Ma' Boedjoeng [the old woman who was the accomplice of Samioen] said to her and what Saleha [Samioen's mother] said, that she would be respected in Samioen's house; her heart reversed itself and she no longer liked the *tuan*. (22)

When she moves to Samioen's house at first "she got the respect of many Muslim guests [in Samioen's house] but after a month" Samioen asked her to hand over her wealth and made her do the work of a servant.

"The Story of Njai Dasima" is a story with a moral; with several morals in fact. The subtitle ("It will be a lesson to all women who give in to the seduction of men") warns women about men and we have seen how the story itself warns against the teachings of Islam. The subtitle blames Njai Dasima for giving in to the temptations of life with Samioen. In the story, she has little choice, given the power of magic, other than to listen to what the old woman tells her about Islam, respect, fear of desertion, and promises of the afterlife. Her vulnerability, however, is first of all the fault of Tuan W. After telling us how he loved Dasima and trusted her and after the first admonitions of the old woman this passage appears:

> Njai Dasima listened to what was said and remained silent, unable to reply because she had never had true instruction in religion which would have enabled her to resist the lies of Ma' Boedjoeng. It's true that she was skilled in women's work but she was ignorant of religion, . . . because her man, Tuan W., never taught her and never had her taught religion. For that reason, the words of Ma' Boedjoeng were an arrow that entered her heart, startling and frightening her. (8)

Dasima is a domesticated woman; she learns domestic ways, and these fit her to recreate a European household in the tropics. It is the fault of Tuan W. that she is not completely domesticated. Had he married her, she would have the security that Ma' Boedjoeng tells her she lacks. But, the story asserts, at least implicitly, she need not marry Tuan W. He loves her, but he might have strengthened her against Ma' Boedjoeng's arguments and so preserved an arrangement superior to marriage. It is due to him that she did not get the instruction that would have enabled her to repel the invaders of his household. If she does not belong where she is, in the words of the old woman, because of who she is, Tuan W. should have seen that she was more thoroughly transformed. He should have seen that she belonged less to the world of unscrupulous men and women who use religion to get what they want, who are shown to be hypocritical and greedy, without the restraints in themselves that would also strengthen them against the unworthy advances of others. As it is in the story, Dasima, left defenseless, comes to want something, respect, she had never before missed. The story says, in effect, that there is a woman who is a mother and who belongs to a particular man, the father of her child, in whom a desire is raised that leads not to the social establishment of herself that she comes to want, but into humiliation. It is a case of a passion for the domestic; a passion that was already satisfied before and whose arousal a second time could have been prevented if the *tuan* had done what it was incumbent on him to do.

Dasima is coaxed into leaving Tuan W., but because of the use of magical drugs, one can also argue that she is abducted or stolen by another man. Samioen wants Dasima not for her herself but for her property; the property that the Tuan gave her. He deceives Dasima by promising her a domesticity that she already has and raising her desire for something he never plans to give her. His desire for her property is conflated with a desire for her "beauty." He wants someone who is a mother and who is the sexual property of the father. And who is the thief? It is not the son, but the dealer. Samioen, we are told

> looked young but ugly, his face was dark and he mixed with all sorts of opium addicts and thieves. He was a dealer in stolen goods and stolen water buffalo and as a result had a lot of money, several fruit gardens and a big house. (9–10)

He is a dealer in stolen goods, of which Dasima is merely the last example. It is a suggestion that his winning of Dasima was in fact a theft and way of emphasizing as well the impossibility of her finding a place in Islamic society. Even were she to leave Tuan W. of her own free will, as, in form at least, she does, she remains, by association with Samioen, stolen goods, without legitimacy in her new home. She is given respect at first, but this soon changes.

One could imagine a happy ending: Dasima arrives to find what she lacks in the house of Tuan W. But this is prevented in the story by Samioen's mother. Samioen is already married to the daughter of someone with rank and his mother much values this. Whenever there is the slightest difference of opinion between Samioen's first wife and Dasima, the mother intervenes to say that "Njai Dasima is of no more worth than Si Koentoem [a servant], which wounds Njai Dasima" (28). Thus, Dasima belongs in neither place. She does not belong in the house of the white man for the reasons that the old woman gives, reasons which were the conventions of the time, so far as they concerned the uncertainty of tenure of unmarried housekeepers and also because Tuan W. did not sufficiently form her in the ways of Europeans. Nor does she belong in the Islamic neighborhoods where, rather than receiving respect, she is said to be unworthy of it. In her new setting, one can make the comparison not with the prostitute but with another figure of commerce, the slave: "she had been waited on by servants; now she had become the slave of others" (28). She crosses the lines between the communities of the plural society but she can settle nowhere, remaining an object of exchange, unable to satisfactorily return to her original sector.[6]

"Njai Dasima" is a symbol of wealth; simply as *njai* she is herself a sort of possession. The term *njai* makes her the *njai* of someone in a relation that begins as a commercial transaction. In this transaction, she is not merely the receiver of certain benefits and, as housekeeper, the bestower of others in exchange, but is herself, in her beauty, one of the benefits. She seems capable of being owned, apart from anything that she brings with her such as her wealth or her services, which would form part of a normal commercial exchange. However, she has an indefinite status. She is neither a prostitute, a woman openly available on the market, nor in the fullest sense a slave. And yet, as *njai*, she is possessed nonetheless. It is precisely her status as "possession" that is raised by the implication that she is not won but stolen. Even when she joins Samioen in his household, she is still called "Njai Dasima"; she never attains the full rights of a wife. "Dasima," as "Njai Dasima," remains a possession never fully possessed.

Before Dasima is abducted, she is the subject of gossip. But to hear of "Dasima" is always to hear of "Njai Dasima," of her relation to Tuan W., hence of the wealth she controls as well as of her beauty. To hear about her is to hear about the objects that attract Europeans and to learn about what goes on inside a European household. "Njai Dasima" is not quite a type in the way that "Samioen" is a type. "Samioen" stands for every village man, and especially every village man who is poised to overhear what goes on inside the European household. "Njai Dasima" is initially idealized as part of the idealization of the Indies household. Then she becomes the subject of gossip. First, news of her travels to the Islamic neighborhood, and then she herself is translated there. She thus comes to embody gossip. Being at once possession and at the same time out of place makes it possible for us to see in Dasima a materialization of gossip. In a larger sense, she is the materialization of the lingua franca: the language that does not belong in any one community, which no one truly possesses, in which one sees what one wants and bargains for it, and which, of course, passes between communities. It is, as well, the language in which whoever says "I" has more than the usual trouble finding herself enclosed in her own or any other community.

Francis is concerned that "The Story of Njai Dasima" remain concluded. "Francis" is one, perhaps "the one," who speaks on behalf of the other victim of the story, the *tuan*. Tuan W. did not know what was happening inside his own house. He did not know the turn events were taking inside the mind of the native woman just next to him. He could not hear the servants, Njai Dasima nor Ma' Boedjoeng. One thinks again of the Dutch who could not hear Soewardi even in their own language and who were not aware that they were overheard by him. Tuan W. needs someone to overhear the villagers and to tell him what is going on right next to him. Francis does that for any future versions of Tuan W. Of course, in doing it, he makes himself into a figure like Samioen. He hears the story others have told and he acts on it. The difference is that he wants the story to end. There are, in the story, two stories that are overheard. The first is the one passed on by gossip: Dasima is rich and beautiful. The second is the continuation of that story after it is heard by village men and in particular Samioen. Francis tells both stories in order that all those who figure importantly—Samioen, Dasima, and Tuan W.—never repeat, in the form of contemporary persons, what he, Francis, describes.

The story was both written and published (the verb for both activities is *mengeluarkan*) by G. Francis . The verb *mengeluarkan* has the root *luar*, meaning "out," set in a form that indicates action or production. *Mengeluarkan* can be translated into English as "to put out." As such, it does not necessarily claim the originality that an author claims for his fiction. It is rather that G. Francis has put the story into circulation, or back into circulation. And, as the publisher/author/copyist, claims perhaps no more than to repeat the story but to do so with a set of warnings and with all of the steps necessary to print and distribute the book. Tineke Hellwig believes that because Francis was English by descent, and that the story has an English *tuan*, and that it takes place during the British interregnum, that Francis fabricated the story rather than merely retelling it. This remains a disputed opinion.[7] Whatever the case, however, the fiction depends on Francis, the author, presenting the narration as something from seventy-five years earlier and taking place in familiar settings in Batavia. The subtitle reads "AN EXCELLENT STORY WHICH OCCURRED NOT SO LONG AGO." It is a story that, even if he made it up entirely, came to him from somewhere and in that sense was not merely circulated but recirculated.

In his powerful commentary on "The Story of Njai Dasima," Tsuchiya Kenji says of the tonality of the narration that it is "cold, stoic" and that there is "fact after fact in long reportive, periodless compound sentences." He sees it as a "non-fictional, almost reportive writing style" and a "very objective way of telling the story." He distinguishes this style of the body of the work from the tone of the title. The title is "moralizing"; the work itself is "objective."[8] The "cold" and "objective" style he notes is characteristic of Melayu works. It is also a feature of translations made into Melayu. Often, the person designated as "author" is really the translator; in addition, the translator translates without giving any indication of his social identity. Here, works designed for one group—Chinese, 'native,' European, Arab—were read by all. This is the style of intercepted language. The style in which something is retold to be passed on rather than reinflected in the retelling. The author is in effect the mouthpiece of the story. At this point, Melayu functioned more like a code than a language. More, that is, as though the translator merely found neutral equivalents for what might have been said with idiosyncracy in the original. Here, what Kenji Tsuchiya called coldness of tone can indicate a belief in the perfect adequacy of Melayu to any language, an adequacy that finds its expression not in the equivalence of voices between languages but in the absence of a need for voice, as though ink itself spoke.

The title, however, is different. Here the author takes a position on his characters and his voice shows through. It is in this light that we can ask who it is who gives the admonitions of the subtitle. The complete title and subtitle are as follows:

The Story of Njai Dasima

A Victim of Seduction

AN EXCELLENT STORY WHICH OCCURRED
NOT SO LONG AGO

It will be a lesson for all women who
give in to the seduction of men

ADVICE FOR THE YOUNG

DECORATED WITH A PICTURE OF
NJAI DASIMA

It is someone who distinguishes himself from Dasima and anyone who would be like her: "a lesson to all women who give in to the seduction of men." The second warning in the subtitle, "ADVICE FOR THE YOUNG," is directed to Samioen and anyone else who might do what Samioen did. It is a warning to anyone who might hear of a beautiful *njai* with money and try and hook her away from her *tuan*. In the body of the work, the story is heard as though it tells itself. In the subtitle, one is given a reaction to it. In the body, one is given what circulates; in the subtitle, the author announces himself as someone who has heard the story and speaks. He is a reteller in the second degree.

The admonitions of the subtitles suggest that the Batavia of Francis's day was full of characters similar to those in the story; readers were considered capable of reenacting the events. These warnings, of course, are directed against certain parties. Those tempted are those "like," sociologically speaking, the characters of the story. In issuing his warnings, "Francis," the author of the subtitle, says, "I am not Dasima" and "I am not Samioen." He is not the object of desire in the story and he is not the one who wants this object so badly he steals it. But in telling the story, he necessarily puts himself imaginatively in the place of his characters; he takes their places in his mind. He thus says, with Soewardi, "If I were . . . but I'm not."

When he denies that he is Samioen, however, complications arise. "Samioen," we have said, stands for one who overhears what he should not hear and who wants and takes what he hears about. Francis, the publisher and author, has, in one sense or another, overheard a story and he has taken it for his own—writing it down, printing it, and selling it. There is, however, a difference between the two. "Samioen" hears what has been repeated and acts on it. It is through him that the story of Dasima adds chapters; he continues the story he first hears about. The story is presumably over when Samioen is captured and confesses. But the warnings set by Francis indicate that he thought that might not be the case. The story might be reenacted were others to do what Dasima and Samioen did. Francis repeats the story in order that it will not be repeated except in the form of literature.[9]

Francis sells what he has overheard; he sells what he did not buy. If he then denies that he is Samioen, the dealer in stolen goods, it is not surprising. Doing it, he guarantees the validity of his goods. By adding the subtitles, Francis claims to stand against the thief and the dealer and at the same time to stand on the side of legitimate authority. It is a way of saying that, as the author and publisher, as one who puts something into circulation, he is neither Dasima, the person who comes to embody what passes between, nor Samioen the thief. His goods are authentic, not stolen. But "Francis," the author, is implicitly a character in his story. His name on the title page, his voice as it speaks in the subtitles, enters him into the text. Just at the same moment that he distinguishes himself from his characters, he adds himself to the text as did Muhammad Bakir.

"Francis," retelling a story he claimed "really happened" starts as a witness or as someone who has heard what a witness said (no matter at how many removes). He begins by selling goods he never bought. If he did not steal them, if they just came to him, it is much like the excuse of many found red-handed with the goods and accused of theft: "someone gave them to me." What he sells did not originate with him. And yet he claims a right to sell "his" goods. He is Samioen and he claims he is not. When he claims, "but I'm not . . . ," he could still be another character inside his text, à la Muhammad Bakir. When, however, he speaks from the subtitles, he claims to stand outside the text, therefore not to be Samioen or anyone else named in the story. His radical attempt to disengage is his claim to separate himself from all of them by calling himself "author." Even if his production is not from scratch it does not matter. He assembled the story; he "put it out." The sale of his story confirms that it circulates not freely, as gossip circulates, but within the limitations of the market, as purchasable. It is his announcement of himself in the subtitles, thus outside the text, if only ambiguously, that says "but I'm not . . . I am only."

However, as Jacques Derrida has shown, the frame of the story given by the title is itself part of the text.[10] The author of the subtitles writes himself into the text; he is an effect of his writing. But he is so ambiguously. The success of his claim is the degree to which one attributes to him a fixed position within the course of circulation of the story. When the story emanates from him and is therefore only a story, even if it is a true story, it forces a separation between imagination or the product of the author and action. It thus approaches a notion of fiction since fiction is at once something made or produced and something separate from the world of nonfiction. With stories of the type we have been considering, an institution of fiction begins. From its inception, this story is directed at the inhibition of action and also at the limitation of imagination. The story should not go further. There should be no new chapters, in life or in fiction. Such inhibition depends on respecting the rights of the author that are both economic and moral.

For the admonitions of the subtitles to be effective, they need to show the possibility that readers could find themselves in the text and the possibility as well that there is an outside of the text to which they can return when they say, "but I'm not . . . I am only." The first step requires showing that there are possibilities that readers may not have imagined. The text suggests that they have in them the possibility to be those they read about. But the institution of the author, depending as it does on the author not being a character, thus on drawing a line between text and outside-the-text, assures that they can break the identification and remain who they were originally. Otherwise, they risk having the adventures of "Muhammad Bakir." These two possibilities involve contradictory ideas of the power of language. The lingua franca has to open the possibility of being someone other than who one is initially; it is, we have seen, its special possibility during the period to be able to do so. To then add "but I'm not . . ." also requires enhanced linguistic power.[11]

The admonitions are not addressed to the Dutch. And yet readers who are potential actors include Dutch fathers as well as native thieves. The inhibition of action and the limitation of imagination applies to the second. The reverse is true for the first. The difficulty is that Tuan W. does not hear. As Soewardi said later, the Dutch are not listening. One reading of

Francis's story says in effect, "If only you would listen, you would under-stand that you must listen. The 'truth' is that events repeat themselves. They do so because hearing, overhearing, and imagination provoke action. You, the Dutch, must act; but to act, you must first know; and to know, you must listen." By contrast, those addressed in the subtitles are already guilty of a listening that is too acute. They hear, they overhear, they act, and there is catastrophe. Such persons should limit their listening which is, in any case, already begun. The Dutch, however, have not even begun to hear. For them, Francis's story is an attempt at generating a message so highly charged that someone who is not listening will start to listen. It is a contradiction that can only be explained by a belief in the communicative power of language that surpasses its contents. It reaches those whose first inclination is to set it aside and others whom it is feared will take it too seriously. "The Story of Njai Dasima" is at once an attempt to limit linguis-tic force and an indication of its enhancement.

It sometimes seems that at the turn of the century everyone who wrote about the topic agreed that something was wrong with Indies colonial authority. The reform movement was clear that the problem was the laxity of authority and the inappropriate closeness of Europeans and 'natives.' When a woman such as Thérèse Hoven answers these charges, she, none-theless, does not disagree that something is lacking. She is as phallocentric as her Dutch opponents, perhaps more so, wanting a place within the sphere defined by male desire. Francis, writing so that Dutch men will hear, is similar. It is a question in both cases of tracing the way back to European men and making a claim of connection. These arguments say that authority is heedless and weak. Others, whose work is better known and whom we have not dealt with, argue that authorities have too much power, and that they use it improperly to keep native women, to make themselves rich, and, here for once all are in agreement, neglecting the welfare of 'natives.' Authority is corrupted by tropical forces; it does not keep itself within the law.

In different ways, Hoven and Francis concern themselves with the power of the lingua franca to force its way across cultural and linguistic boundaries and with the limitation of that power. We have already seen how this was made use of later with Soewardi and in the rallies. Hoven and Francis show also how one could locate and be connected with a center of authority. Here, again, we have the example of the rallies, whose audiences wanted to be connected with the center of governmental authority. It was, we have seen, more than an administrative center. For the rally audience, it was a source of messages; for Francis, it was an address, reachable by the same route of communications. The 'native' audiences of the rallies must have conflated colonial and indigenous authority, the latter of which is also very much a center.[12] But our examples show that it is nothing Javanese that prompts the locating of a center of languages in the center of administration. When it is claimed that "Europeans do not hear," the claim itself indicates that they could hear. It would only be necessary to speak forcefully enough. The opening of this route is important because it locates a linguistic center and thus makes this available later for revision.

There is also another topic whose significance we will see later. It is the question of legality. Indeed, the question of the law is central. For instance, Tineke Hellwig astutely points out that the murder of Dasima depended on the fact that at the point of separation, Tuan W. had registered Dasima's possessions, the things he had bought her, with a notary, thus certifying them as hers. The law, via this legal document, allowed her to make a claim that Samioen could not refute. This, of course, offered her no protection; on the contrary, it led to the taking of her life. The law, rather than guaranteeing order, leads to murder.[13] Thus, reformers argued that the law was not sufficiently enforced, whereas Francis seems to say that the law itself was a cause of disorder.

This difference of opinion about the law simply highlights the problem of identity in the Indies. The legal status of Indos, we have said, depended on whether European fathers recognized the children of *njai*s as their own. If they did not, genealogy and legal descent diverged. In the Indies, this was more than a problem of inheritance of goods because one would be subject to another code of law, that applying to natives, were one illegitimate. But for Francis there is the suggestion not that he wants legal recognition, a question not raised in his story, but merely the father's recognition of his son's allegiance and indeed of his presence. The law merely disrupts.

For Thérèse Hoven, the question of origins and of connection to authority is somewhat different. The legal status of the child is not at stake, but the question of who is the "real mother" and the place of the other mother implies a legal dimension. The connection in question is that of the Dutch woman to her former sweetheart. She keeps a claim on him; she is the mother of his child via long distance. Her claim, of course, is entirely outside the law. The connection is made only via language. "Just like mama": the lingua franca makes itself heard. In Francis, unlike Hoven, the complications of a language at once too powerful and not powerful enough are made evident. But if only European men will hear, they can keep their *njai*s, attend to their children, and a connection will be maintained even if it is not recognized in law. It is at once a question of a force outside the law and a question of the effectiveness of the lingua franca.

Take, for instance, the child of Hoven's story. We are never told that Constance adopts Louise. And the "real mother," as Hoven has it, remains the mother in the Indies. Is Constance a thief? Clearly not. Has Constance not taken advantage of a child's confusion to have what she, Constance, also wanted, namely a child and in particular the child of the man she loves? Constance does all she can for the girl, saving her from an undesirable situation. The mother, who already released her child to live in Europe surely would appreciate that. Today, raising Louise as a "genuine lady" might be thought akin to theft; it deprives the child of her original identity. But this, too, Constance safeguards by being sure that Louis recognizes her real (biological) and legal mother as such.

But suppose that Louise had not taken to Constance; had not said to her, "Just like mother." Without the words of Louise, what right would Constance have to the child? Given Louise's reluctance, Constance would merely reproduce the deplorable conditions pertaining between Louise and her grandmother and aunts. And Constance would not have the right of possession that comes from a relation of kinship to the child. She would be like a thief. When Louise begins to speak without reluctance, it is all different. There is a bond between her and Constance that starts with Louise's regaining of language. Her first words at this stage, "Just like mama," reproduce her experience in the Indies. It is Louise who establishes the similarity between Constance and her real mother, a similarity that no one could possibly have guessed at without her words. What justifies Constance in her motherhood is the speech of the child. This speech has the force to create an alegal if not illegal structure of kinship, one outside the law if not clearly to the point of being against the law.

Said to any other woman, these words would not have the same force. Constance, for instance, does not inquire into the characteristics of the girl's mother that cause the girl to see a resemblance. The kiss is enough; mother kisses just like that. The kiss of the mother and the kiss of Constance are identical. Judged, of course, by the child. Constance is shocked. Constance substitutes for the mother when she recognizes the truth of the child's statement. The legitimacy or illegitimacy of this substitution depends on how deeply one reads the significance of the kiss. How much can the words of the child, which I have claimed are a translation from Melayu into Dutch, convey? The stronger they are, the less legitimate the connection between Louise and Constance because it awakens the imagination of an extralegal relation with the father; or just because it awakens imagination. On the other hand, the girl's statement, conveying her experience in the Indies and finding it reproduced in Holland, carries the father into the picture, perhaps standing by the bedside as the girl is kissed goodnight. Here, he is the benevolent presence who sees that things are as they should be. His presence seems to confer a right to the girl; but the stronger his presence, the more illegitimate the connection to Constance.

The lingua franca cannot make anything legitimate. Rather, it forges a connection to authority and demonstrates its own force. It also does the opposite perhaps whenever it causes one to imagine. Francis's prose does not convey the same reassurance as Hoven's because it evokes not merely the absence of the legitimating figure but his deafness. Were he to listen, he would be expected to confirm the author in his denial. To say "But I am not Samioen, I am not a thief, I am only the author" is insufficient. "I" the author may not be Samioen but unless "I" can separate myself from my production, he could be a criminal for all the reasons we have already pointed out. The establishment of the author in the subtitles is a step toward this denial, but we have seen that it is ambiguous. The person who could give an aura of legitimacy—who could confirm that the author is not a criminal, that he is entitled to sell what he has produced, that he stands on the side of the law—is evoked, but he remains unavailable. Francis lacks the law's blessing. We are at the beginning of the institution of authorship where rights remain vague and where there is precisely a conflation between European fathers and colonial authorities. The author appeals to a legitimating figure in both registers. Francis wants to wake him up in order to receive his recognition. The difficulty in doing so stimulates more demand for recognition. And it opens a difference between legitimate authority and another force, which is associated with language.

EVADING FICTION

It was common practice to put stories such as that of Njai Dasima on the stage. Njai Dasima, one commentator noted, was staged "countless times." One company alone put the play on 127 times. The anti-Muslim tone was generally suppressed. Wiping out its religious coloration, however, still left it a racist story, picturing 'natives' derogatorily, showing them to be greedy for wealth, users of black magic, murderers, and, in general, criminal upsetters of domestic harmony and social order. The story was nonetheless popular with 'native' audiences. Why would a group of people go to see something that showed them to be criminals?

In 1929, Njai Dasima was made into a film by the Indies Chinese firm, Tan's Film Company; the anti-Muslim aspect was left out.[14] An article in the Sino-Malay magazine *Panorama*, written in Melayu, sees the making of the film as a critical moment for Tan's Film Company and, in fact, for the Indies film industry in general.[15] Many companies had gone out of business, unable to compete with foreign films with their famous stars. They were unable to appeal to the "educated classes" while the "cheap class," to use the language of the article, preferred foreign clowns and foreign battles, especially American ones. What was left was to make a film for the 'native' [*bumi putra*] cheap class, which would be "what the people of that class wanted." Tan's Film Company was apparently saved by the film. The author says that "so many Indonesiers came to see it that some had to be turned away. Almost no Europeans were visible but the number of Chinese viewers was also large. If the film gets viewers in other places as in Batavia, Tan's Film Company will do well." Indeed, according to Salim Said, Tan's Film Company went on to make two sequels to *The Story of Njai Dasima.*[16] But, again, why would an audience go repeatedly to see a movie that presented them in an ill light?

The writer, Kwee Tek Hoay, or KTH as he signed himself, limits his praise for the movie mainly to what we would call the special effects and the general technical excellence. He says in a scene where Tuan W. (he refers to him as Edward) dreams of a snake that wraps itself around Dasima's neck, that viewers "feel repelled . . . even though the snake that mounts to the bed is visibly false." After Dasima leaves, Edward looks at the servant and, for an instant, her face is that of Dasima. "This is something really true to life and is often experienced by men whose lovers have just left them." He has very little good to say about the actors; he criticizes their dress in particular. In any case, the various faults of the film do not matter too much considering the audience:

> We could write several more columns if we had to recite all the faults visible in this film, but it is not necessary because most viewers from the cheap class are not aware of them and so think highly of what is actually far from perfect.

If the author is correct about the naivete of the audience, it only means that they accept the story with all its faults of presentation. Of course, that still leaves us ignorant as to why they wanted to see the movie at all.

What impresses the author of the piece, Kwee Tek Hoay, is almost only technical progress. In this, he is not different from the critics of present-day Jakarta who praise films for the lower classes for their technical effects. For KTH, these effects make the film more "realistic" (he uses the English term). The film is "so real and clear [*njata dan terang*] that it is almost no different from European films." By "real and clear" he refers not to the story, but to a purely visual characteristic. He tells his readers that it is not necessary, for instance, that an actress wear a real silk blouse because

> its quality and beautiful colors will not be apparent. It is most necessary that sarongs or blouses be worn which have white backgrounds with dark or black flowers so that in the film they will be clearly outlined.

He is unconcerned with the story, and from his comments about the poor characterizations, he feels that their faults will not be noticed by the naive audience. What will attract them nonetheless is the "realism" or verisimilitude of the film to which he attributes its success.

KTH is prejudiced against what he calls 'natives' and sees them as naive and therefore easily deceived. I reject this supposition; it makes it all the more difficult to explain why the movie was popular with audiences it insulted. Suppose, however, that KTH were correct in the latter part of his explanation; suppose it was the realism and clarity of the film that attracted 'native' audiences. What would this mean? To KTH it is evidently an aspect of the modern, judging from the number of times he compares this technical excellence with that of European companies. Such clarity is the work of an instrument that performs as well in the hands of technicians in one part of the world as the next. It has the power to attract no matter what it shows, no matter what narrative it finds itself recording. It gives the story what he says the actors deprive it of: "realism." The camera makes the viewer believe he sees real silk when he gets only the "map" or "outline" (*terpeta*) of clothes (and clothes are what KTH comes back to in judging the story). It is not that the camera sees what the eye sees. In seeing, it transforms ordinary cloth into silk and in so doing, it makes this ordinary cloth seem more like silk on the screen than silk itself might seem. Somehow, this makes up for the imperfect rendering of the story.

KTH, as we have said, sees the imperfections in the telling of the story, the anachronisms, the faulty acting, as unnoticed by the 'native' audience. It is worth looking at his criticisms. He complains that the *tuan* is played by someone "who in no way looks like a real European" and that he is too young, the result being that his *njai* is "much older." He complains that Samioen is also too young, younger than Dasima; "and his face is not right, he looks more like a servant than like a youth who could turn the head of a beautiful *njai*, driving her mad." Samioen

> should be someone who, even though he has no money, looks chic [*tjakep*], with menacing or cruel eyes and older than Dasima. But Samioen in this film appears hickish and his clothes do not show the fashionableness they ought to have. . . . Samioen ought to be tall and slim, his skin not too dark, with a waxed mustache, glasses and a suit coat and tie, with pants or a long sarong.

KTH complains about many of the other characters as well. The old woman who lures Dasima out of the house ought to be "clever and sly." Instead, she seems to him like an "idiot" of the type known on the streets. The comical characters are not funny. Samioen's first wife wears clothes almost identical to those of his mother-in-law. He also points out anachronisms: the appearance of a type of police that were created only recently, whereas the story is set earlier, and a picture of a recent Sultan of Turkey.

KTH himself, however, points out that the book was well known. Indeed, the story itself, even for the illiterate, surely was well known, given the long history of theatrical presentations before the movie was made. The audience knew the story. The question is whether they saw it in the same way as KTH did. It is possible that they were interested precisely in the deviations from the plot. KTH accuses the audience of interesting itself in what is "realistic and clear" (*njata dan terang*). He uses the phrase in two senses, both of which it has in Melayu. *Njata* means "clear" as a synonym for "evident" and it means also "real" or "actual." But it also means "clear" in the visual sense, as does *terang*. But in another place, he speaks of *njata* as a technical question. He says that he thought the atmosphere in Java would prevent making a clear (*terang*) picture. But the photographer was, he says, very skillful. Here, *njata dan terang* is a technical question. In another place, he uses the English word "realistic" as a substitute for the phrase in question. He thinks the audience responds to the technical side and was simply too dull-witted to attend to the deviations from the story and the anachronisms.

The first editions of "The Story of Njai Dasima" bear, as part of the subtitle, just after the warnings, the phrase "DECORATED WITH A PICTURE," the picture being a photograph of Njai Dasima. The year after Francis published his version of Njai Dasima, O. S. Tjiang published a version in verse, noting on the title page that it was taken from the book (though not mentioning Francis's name); it was also furnished with a photograph. As Tineke Hellwig points out, the women pictured are different. She takes this as evidence of the fictional character of the story since the woman is not "Dasima."[17] But who is she? That is to say, why, in an edition that proclaims itself to be based on the book, did the author not take care to see that there was at least a closer resemblance to the presumably original woman in the first photograph? It indicates that the purpose of the photo is not to say "this is Dasima, the historical personage."

Again: Who is in the picture? It is not Njai Dasima, the historical person, if there was such a person. But it is certainly "Njai Dasima," the character. There is her picture; therefore the story in the book is "true," meaning that it has a reference. The story, the title insists, but in a conventional way, "actually happened." The existence of Njai Dasima, independent of the book, is affirmed. But the photographs are not of anyone who lived in 1813 and it is evident that no care was taken to prevent anyone who made a comparison from exposing the photographs as a fraud. In any case, although the period saw many accusations of defamation based on stories and reports, I know of no case where anyone claimed that a story called true was false to the point of involving entirely fictitious characters.

The picture is an illustration if that means an image of something already established in words. The photo does not establish historical authenticity. It is, rather, evidence that there is something outside the book. The photograph has to have an original and this original has to exist before the book, unlike the story, which might have been entirely made up and have come into existence with the book itself. The photograph, with its separation, as it were, of an image from an original, shows that there is a path from outside the book to what is told inside it. One cannot be sure that the original of the photograph was the subject of the story as it actually took place. But one knows that there is a gap between the original of the photo and the photograph. One sees evidence of a certain transmission. The interest in the photograph is an interest in this transmission. To see this image is to feel that something comes from a distance, "1813," and yet is close, "here in Batavia." The picture of "Njai Dasima" is a picture of "The Story of Njai Dasima."

When the story circulates, a clear image emerges. KTH conflates the technical clarity of the film with its verisimilitude. Complaining of anachronisms, he insists that a knowledgeable viewer compare the adequacy of images to historical provenance just as he wants the actors to be true to the book that existed before the film was made. But his interest in the film is not that of the viewers. They might start from the technological. Such an interest would lie in seeing how cotton, in the process of being photographed, turns to silk. Which is to say, an interest in the difference between the two as evidence of something transmitted and clarified in that process.

> A woman servant comes bringing coffee. When she gets close, in the eyes of [Tuan W.] she changes, becoming Dasima, but a moment later she is the servant again.

KTH explains that such scenes, utilizing the technology of the movies, attract an audience that will ignore the faults of presentation and, one might add, the deviations from the story. It would not be dull-wittedness that would allow such an interest. It is rather an example of the scene Groneman witnessed at the hanging. It is an interest in appearances without the attempt to read their motivations.

The photographs, like the film, through their unconcern with adequacy, display the manufacturing of appearances. One thinks of the scene in the film where, says KTH, the *tuan* dreams there is a snake wrapped around Dasima's neck. This "makes many spectators shiver it is so big and powerful, even though the snake that rises onto the bed is obviously a false snake." The falsity of the snake is evident, but it moves, it acts like a snake, and it is an illusion allowed by the camera. It is the visible deviation from the original that points to the power of the camera to produce "clear images."

The film shows the fabrication of signs in the process of transmitting them. But this occurs in the story as well:

> After about two years, Njai Dasima was well known [*tersohor*] in the Islamic villages. [They knew that] she was nice looking [*bagus*], rich with lots of money, gold and jewels, so many Muslim men badly wanted to hook her in order to get her wealth. Many Muslim men sent women to her to coax her away, but Njai Dasima did not care to go along with their plans and angrily told them to go home.

It is made evident that Dasima does not know Samioen before her servant introduces them. She is known to the village in the way that newcomers are known to their neighbors and to the people on the street well before they themselves come to be acquainted with these people. It is not hard to find the path of such knowledge. Servants tell servants, and they tell the peddlars who call at the house each day. It would not be possible to cite the names of those who own the eyes who see these newcomers after the first few. In a short time, identities are in circulation through a process of anonymous seeing and public diffusion. Is this not already a primary characteristic of the movies? Is not the anonymous seeing of the camera—which produces an impressive "clarity" rather than a story, which is an instrument through which what is seen is disseminated—comparable to the mechanism we call gossip? It is comparable precisely because gossip is what we invoke when we want to explain how something became known and want to attribute it to a nameless reception and a nameless dissemination. It does not matter who sees; or it matters as much as knowing the name of the cameraman or the make of the camera.

"At that time in Pedjambon Village," we are told,

> there was a young Islamic man called Samioen. Like many, he too had heard of the good looks and wealth of Njai Dasima. He knew that many had tried to coax her away without success. So he worked up a plan with a woman named Ma' Boedjoeng who lived near his house.

Samioen is one of the young men of the Muslim villages who hears about Njai Dasima. In fact, "Samioen," I am told, means, "to hear" or "the one who hears" in Arabic. Samioen, like the others, hears of Njai Dasima and then he acts. It is the hearing of "Njai Dasima" that, in the story, provokes actions that become the narrative.

The "Story of Njai Dasima" is itself a story of the manufacturing of signs. "Njai Dasima" in the photo did not designate a long-dead woman but rather a figure whose reference was what was said and was being said about her. The photograph of "Njai Dasima" in this case is not exactly an illustration. It is called, in the subtitle, *hiasan*, which one easily translates as "ornament." But "to ornament," is a word that in Indonesian has the synonym *berdandan*, which means "to dress up" and to "complete." It means, one can say, to bring out a quality that is somehow inherent in whatever is completed. "Njai Dasima," the photograph, is the completion of the story of Njai Dasima in the sense that it makes her story evident. It is the process that KTH describes where cotton turns to silk when it is filmed. One sees something somehow inherent in the original that the original itself does not (and cannot) display. Only after the supplement is added, the nature of the original is known. By this logic, the photograph of Njai Dasima is a photograph of the words of the story.[18]

If we accept KTH's account, the audience was not interested in the veracity of the story or even its coherence. They were attracted by the effects of the camera, which for them were the story in its fully developed form. Such an interest, which does not interrogate motivations, leaves the audience looking at the screen in view, as it were, of actors who look back without generating a response. It makes the Indies movie theaters, often not theaters but open-air arenas, the equivalent of public hangings. There, too, spectators saw versions of themselves displayed in an unfavorable light. But there, too, they looked. If they put themselves in the place of criminals, it was not to think that "I too" will find "myself" on the gallows later. Absence, death, the "but I'm not . . ." of Soewardi are all lacking in such scenes. Instead, the visualized lingua franca sweeps up viewers, enabling them to think "I" in the form of another and another and another. It is a question of saying, with Soewardi, "If I were . . ." but, unlike Soewardi, not being able to finish the phrase.

Indonesian lower-class audiences watch movies today in the way I have described, as anonymous viewers, without commentary afterwards on what they have seen.[19] They watch nearly any sort of movies: Indonesian movies, Indian movies, kung fu movies, and, particularly, those with special effects. They watch, that is, without editorial comment, as those who do not identify with their own names, as anonymous not only in the view of those on the screen, if they could see, but to themselves.

Njai Dasima was retold several times and it was filmed at least twice by Indonesians.[20] And while the story was modified, Samioen remained a villain. The transvaluation of values one might expect if the story were to be retold by nationalists never takes place; the thief remains a thief and not someone who, it might have been seen in revision, merely took back what was his originally. The confrontation within the terms set by colonialism never occurred. At the level of the plot, the story remains weighted in favor of the colonial father.

If, nonetheless, the story was favored by the proto-nationalist masses, it is because they looked at it in a way that was already prepared by the lingua franca. That is, as those for whom the lingua franca is not theirs any more than it is anyone elses. As those for whom what is transmitted through that language means not simply what it says, but that it says. Again, like the spectators before the scaffold, they respond to a message inside the message; to the message that there is a message. They are responsible viewers not when they defend their social identities but when they watch silently, without denial.

At that point, they inhabit and are inhabited by the characters, one surmises, as Soewardi inhabits the Dutch or as the Dutch "I," the *ik*, inhabits the Indonesian "I," the *saya*. Such viewers are fascinated. That is, they have no means at their disposal to exit from their impermanent dwellings except to move to another, equally not that of their "original" selves. If their presence in the characters were felt, one would call them ghosts. They do not take the place of those they occupy; they rather find themselves inside them as a ghost is "inside" as well as "besides" the person it haunts. In this way, they escape the interpretation of Njai Dasima that we have attributed to its author. Rather than the lingua franca designating characters who are to be heeded according to who one is outside the performance, all characters are potentially equatable with any member of the audience. The subtitles, so important in the book, have no place in the movie.

The admonitions of the author do not touch the movie audience. In place of the warnings, the poster for the movie boasted that the movie was "clear and perfect." The poster reads in part:

> See the Great and Absolute Difference between the Melayu Stage and the Film in this most popular story and enjoy the Sadness, the Comedy. It's Packed and Holds Attention. Cruel and Extraordinary Action which cannot be forgotten. Real and Perfect.[21]

The "Melayu Stage" only imperfectly expresses "this most popular story." It is the camera makes it "real and perfect." The appeal of the movie is that more than any form before it, it brings out the text through photography. The movie claims to be a photograph of what one already has heard ("this most popular story"). In a certain way, the camera usurps the place of the author. But the lack of admonitions means it is not exactly like the author. Its claim is not the moral value of the story but that the perfection and clarity of the film hold attention. Thus, the identifications we have described are allowed to take place.

The audiences of the movie seem to have moved behind the intentions of the story to be gripped instead by the processes of production. The movie audiences of *The Story of Njai Dasima* stood outside the institution of fiction that we see beginning with the author of this novel (and of course others of its day). But it does not mean they were outside the grip of language. Just the opposite. If the movie audiences avoided the convention of fiction, it was for a powerful reason. They had something not necessarily better but at least stronger. They had the entire text to inhabit and to be inhabited by.

THE GHOST OF THE LINGUA FRANCA

Dasima keeps reappearing. Even as late as 1970,[22] the "Story of Njai Dasima" was retold in Jakarta as a movie. "She" is a figure that keeps on arriving. This is a characteristic of ghosts. Ghosts, we know, in Java at least, appear on the site of disappearances. Thus, in Surakarta in 1980, a train collided with a bus. The numerous passengers killed reappeared as ghosts for long afterwards. A ghost is often a reappearance, as is Dasima in the repetitions of her story and in the repeated appearances she made particularly to 'natives.' Ghosts, we know, are seldom welcome. They sometimes remind us of what we would like to forget. Often enough, however, we never knew them or about them in the first place. But the other characteristic of ghosts, important to us here, and less noticed, is that they are local. At least in Java, they belong to particular places. The ghosts of the dead passengers appear on the site of their deaths. As messages, as reminders, even of what we would like to put out of mind, they arrive in our minds and make us want to dispose of them. But ghosts are indisposable, that is, both unfit for the world and invulnerable to being displaced. They cannot be moved from their own sites, at least without special knowledge of the occult. They are, in that sense, messages that stay in place and that, instead of moving on, reappear. This is the case of "Dasima," whom we have presented as a figure of communication. But she communicates only in the sense that ghosts communicate: through repetition and the refusal to be disposed of. Her constant appearances attest to her less-than-full arrival.

Java, it is my impression, is more densely populated with ghosts than other places. By comparison, the world mediated in Indonesian has many fewer ghosts. Dasima, for that matter, is not generally considered a ghost. However, she appeared as a specter on a certain bridge in the neighborhood of her murder.[23] This, however, is different. A ghost that appears as a ghost can be dealt with. In Java, one avoids haunted spots and, if one is affected by ghosts, one calls in people skilled in evicting them. A ghost that does not appear as a ghost is a different matter. A phantom that simply appears and reappears, a disturbance that cannot be avoided and comes back to mind, lacks a cure. One has to ask, for instance, about the provenance of such a specter. We know the place-names of the story of Njai Dasima. Among them are the place of appearance of her ghost. It is not just any place, however; it is a bridge. That is, even as a recognizable ghost, Dasima haunted a place of communication. As an unrecognizable ghost, she appeared in the theater, in films, and in books; to my knowledge, her story has been rewritten at least five times. Her places of reappearance, her localities, are precisely the places where language appears. Not, however, language as such but "Melayu" before it is certain of being "Indonesian." She is the ghost of "pre-Indonesian" as Pramoedya Ananta Toer called the lingua franca, and she continues to haunt the language that never fully replaced it, the national language, Indonesian. She illuminates the nonarrival of language, which is to say its continuous failed attempts to convey something.

When does a ghost communicate? We say that ghosts remind us of what we cannot forget. But why do they have such an intention? The ghosts of the railway accident simply refused to be forgotten. They continued to insist on their existence. They communicated not a message but simply themselves in the paradox of their nonexistence. They spoke when they had nothing to say other than that they had disappeared and yet still appeared. They had no message at all. In that sense, they could not be said to speak but only to make their appearance, and, equally, their nonappearance, felt. Ghosts, in this sense, are simply messages that refuse to move on, that stay in place, that is to say, out of place. They ought to be forgotten or they ought simply not to come to mind. They should have said what they had to say and then passed out of mind. Njai Dasima, likewise, simply appears and refuses to disappear forever. Her locale, however, is less specific than the usual dwelling places of ghosts.

In the "Story of Njai Dasima," hearing of Dasima, we have pointed out, means hearing of European authority and hearing as well of its weakness and its unawareness of what it disseminates. To hear of women, in these narratives, is to learn of European males, of their sexuality, the limitations they surpass, and the authority they cannot fully exercise. With the clear images of the movie and of the printed story, the native viewers arrive not at white authority but at the production of the imagery. Cotton turns to silk. "Dasima" in her photograph indicates that something appears. If behind the silk there is cotton or if "Dasima" is not the woman who lived seventy-five years earlier, before the camera was in use in the Indies, it merely shows that there is something to hear, to be turned into imagery, and that it comes from somewhere. "I," in no capacity at all, have intercepted it or been intercepted by it. Stripping away the structures of hierarchy, one finds the elemental communication on which hierarchy is constructed.

The ghost of the lingua franca appears with the perceived weakness of hierarchical communication. But it also appears in the weak establishment of that other source of the control of words, the author. When appearances and words seem to have no provenance they seem to simply reappear, the double of themselves rather than the reflection or the representation of events or creators. Thus, the story of Njai Dasima is said to be well known before the book appears or the movie refers to "the well known story." What is brought into evidence is the circulation of information that is without particular location. It indicates, by comparison with traditional ghosts, how unlocalized the hearing of the lingua franca was. This is what we might expect of a symptom that hearing occurred between cultures from across the world. Njai Dasima arrived to 'natives' before and after they were "Indonesians." The place of her haunting is no longer the bridge where part of the story took place but the movies and the writing themselves. Dasima reappears now as the refusal of language to fully deliver what it transmits, which thus stays in place, flickering in and out of sight.

Appearances Again

The thief in Njai Dasima never reads the mind of the master. Instead, he has a spell put on Tuan W. so that he never has to worry about what Tuan W. is thinking. Only the thief is shown as having desire. The man with money already, the *tuan*, is oblivious to what goes on around him, which means he never defends himself, and so his desire is never pictured. He does not have "desire" as the word is used in the market to mean a generalized form of energy as such expendable on one object as well as another. He has affection for Njai Dasima, "his *njai*" in all the ambiguity of that phrase. What he owns is not shown to be the effect of his wishes or an indication of them. His relation to Njai Dasima remains merely a fact, an instance of the way things are ordered sentimentally, domestically, culturally, and politically.

Hence the poverty of 'natives' is not seen as deprivation caused by the satisfaction of European desire. The thief, given that context, is merely a criminal, not someone who takes what is, in a sense, already his and therefore a possible model for incipient nationalists. Even in later Indonesian versions of Njai Dasima, this remains the case. In the Dutch literature we have glanced at, however, it is quite otherwise. Money is the middle term between parties who exchange. It offers a means to trace desire and to show that appearance is no indication of reality. When money comes into view, the result is conflict.

The nationalism that we are beginning to trace does not begin with the feeling of deprivation that could have been provided by the story of Njai Dasima if only it had been told a little differently. If the motives of the European had been exposed by, for instance, showing him alert to what was going on around him, he would be seen to be involved in a jealous contest for ownership in which his right to the *njai* could be questioned. It is primarily in the Dutch literature that the motivations of the European are questioned.

Despite the difference that remained about the place of money and desire, 'native' accounts share the Dutch view of society as a set of appearances. These accounts begin early, as we shall see, and continue to a point where, in 1938, R. S. Soerohadipoerno, a police officer from Pemalang, published a booklet entitled *Book of Frauds*.[24] His aim was to alert the public. Various frauds are being practiced which people are not aware of, sometimes even after they have been their victims. The frauds are not merely described, they are narrated, each with a title. "The Story of the Swindler of Counterfeit Money," for instance, tells of a "rich man" (*orang kaya*) who "one day" was "approached by a swindler." The swindler offers to sell him counterfeit f5 notes for f2.50 each. They arrange a rendezvous on a certain intersection. But as they are about to exchange suitcases, a police agent arrives. The rich man flees, leaving both suitcases behind. At home, he is relieved to have escaped arrest. "This rich man, at home, thought he was safe, but he was swindled out of f500. Sometime later, the rich man realized he had been swindled" (1–3). One notes, although it is not commented upon, that the police agent himself was a fraud.

In this story, the swindler is identified only by his actions; in others, the victim is sometimes "a Chinese" (*Tionghwa*), but the swindler is simply identified as "swindler." It is not a question of nationality. He is "a swindler" and this is enough. His looks are unimportant; it is sufficient that whatever or whoever he looked like, he stimulated credulity. The swindlers in this book have no origins. We do not hear where they come from or how it is that they make themselves known. There is no attempt to indict certain classes for their behavior. People and, we will see, ghosts simply appear and their appearance is taken as normal even if undesirable. The victim, for his part, accepts this normality often for sometime after he has been swindled. The subtitle of the book stresses this aspect of the swindle: "Stories of swindlers who work subtly and neatly to the point where the persons swindled are completely unaware of it."

. The word for "subtle," *halus*, is used often to refer to ghosts. *The Book of Fraud* includes many ghost stories. They are not singled out as such. For instance, in one story, common enough in Java, a man engages in conversation with someone he meets on the road. Later he learns that the man has been dead for fifty years. In another story, a man sleeps with a woman who then turns into a snake. Between swindlers and specters there seems to be no boundary. Whoever simply appears can defraud one. Sometimes the fraud is monetary, but sometimes it is simply an encounter with someone or something in disguise. One speaks to a pure appearance and that alone can constitute the "fraud" (*tipoean*) of the title.

The point of the book is to make the public aware that they are, in fact, in the presence of the disguised all the time. It is not important what their real identities are nor, in every case, even to know their motives. What matters is that one is, without knowing it, within the ambience of mere appearance, the result of which is sometimes but not always loss. For that reason, money cannot play the role it takes in the Dutch stories we have looked at. There, money makes all respectable appearance suspect. In *The Book of Fraud*, all appearances become suspect simply because appearance has no necessary attachment to reality, much less to social identity. The function of money to summon up a sense of the bottom line, the reality that counts, versus what otherwise is dismissible, is not available. Appearances can be ghostly and one can never be sure, perhaps not even in retrospect, whether one has been dealing with a ghost. The point of *The Book of Fraud* is to alert readers to this. But very little of it can be remedied. One lives among ghosts indistinguishable as such.

The problem in these stories is language. Usually one speaks and one's language reaches only people who are present. In *The Book of Fraud*, one speaks and later learns one has had intercourse with a ghost. Language carries too well. One responds to a voice that matches an appearance, but the appearance is not what it seems and may have no physical existence at all. One speaks and one reaches what one assumes is beyond reach. It is this linguistic power that creates a society of appearances.

Some of these same ghost stories can be heard today in Java. Ghosts penetrate Javanese society, but they always reveal themselves as ghosts, at least at some point. Here, ghosts and swindlers are conflated. Swindlers are not supernatural; they cannot be said to come from outside conventional social life. If they cause material loss, that is a way to know that they are not who they seem to be. Nevertheless, one cannot be sure that the swindler will be eventually known as such. It is, in a way, a more serious situation than living in a society penetrated by ghosts because it is more difficult to account for the gap caused by the credulity that arises when one merely speaks. The deception of appearances is generalized and permanent.

Exposure of an underlying reality was not the route to the nationalist consciousness we are tracing.[25] There was never an Indonesian explanation of the role of language equivalent to the Dutch exposure of the place of money. The Indies, in the early part of the twentieth century, was indeed a society built on appearances for both Europeans and 'natives.' But the 'native' reaction to this condition was quite different from that of Europeans. Here is an example from Tirtho Adhisoeryo (1830?–1918), the first 'native' editor of an Indies newspaper and the person Pramoedya Ananta Toer said was at the origin of Indonesian nationalism.[26]

A woman sent a piece to one of his papers about wearing hats. Dutch women, she pointed out, both wear hats and carry parasols. They do not wear hats because they need to do so, therefore. The author, Raden Ayoe Dwioso Wijoto, noted that Dutch women wear hats "only to ornament themselves and not in the least in order to keep out the heat or the rain and because of this Dutch ladies' hats are beautiful" (*Poetri Hindia*, n.d. [July 1910], 114). Tirtho took the time to comment. He repeated the Raden Ayoe's distinction between practicality and ornament and added that wearing hats "long has been a general wish [*keingingan oemoem*], especially for intercourse with other races." He continues:

> "Kleeren maken den man niet," a Dutch proverb says, which means clothes do not make the man;[27] indeed but in the Indies clothing is a topic that preeminently gets attention.
>
> Imagine that we see a native [*anak negri*] who has his diploma from the school for officials dressed in European clothes with his wife, the daughter of a regent. She simply wears the usual clothes of a native. How astonished we would be

when one of our friends going along with us whispers, "look at that Indo's *njai*; very pretty!" Now this is progress gone astray, because that native in European clothes is really Tuan Djoanis, while his Raden Ajoe [his wife] is not different from the *njai*s brought along by the *tuan*s! Think if the Raden Ajoe wore the dress of a Turkish woman. Even though her husband had on European clothes it would not matter. In the eyes of natives or other races he would not be faulted. (115)

In addition to practicality (health) and ornament, the hat, of all items, serves to identify the wearer. It is a sign of nationality. But everyone wants to wear a European-style hat, and this led Tirtho to a discussion of clothes and ethnic identity on a broader scale. It is a serious matter. To confuse identities can lead to gossip, even to slander, as a respectable woman is confused with a *njai*. One must get the sign right and if one does not, the result is the notice of others. The other who notices here is someone from one's own nationality. The police agent, we will see, might arrest the man in the hat because he thinks the man is a Javanese posing as an Indo. In fact, he is a Javanese who, no doubt because he has graduated from a school for officials, has been given the right to so dress. The danger here is from the person of the man's own group. He thinks the man really is an Indo and this leads him to think the man's wife, dressed, appropriately enough as a Javanese, is his *njai*. The question for Tirtho is not exactly how to straighten out the misunderstanding, but how to neutralize its consequences.

There are several steps to Tirtho's fantasy: first the Javanese on the street thinks a Javanese he sees is an Indo. Then he thinks that the man's wife is a *njai*. At this point, the man on the street is dismissed and Tirtho invites his readers to imagine the woman dressed as a Turk. Readers thus take the place of the anonymous viewer on the street. There seems to be no limit to the amount of substitution Tirtho can imagine. What triggers it all is thinking of European hats as signs misidentified when worn by Javanese. But Javanese cannot be stopped from dressing like Europeans; it is part of life at the time. Tirtho does not want to drag the European-dressed Javanese back into unmistakable Javanese dress. Dressed as a European, the Javanese man is unknown to his fellow Javanese. He passes perfectly and there is nothing wrong with doing so in Tirtho's view. Tirtho would extend the right to dress differently to the man's wife as well. Were she only to exchange her 'native' dress and put on a Turkish costume, there would be no trouble. The man on the street would no longer think of her as a Javanese and therefore would not believe she is a *njai*. The couple's respectability would be saved. Saved precisely because false conclusions built on partially correct recognition would be precluded. Dress, instead of guarding identity, would hide it in both cases, not, of course, to make the couple deceptive but rather to keep their marital propriety untarnished. The best society is one built on sheer appearances.

As Tirtho pictures them, the couple had no intention of deceiving anyone and certainly not of creating the impression he attributes to the man on the street. But dressed as they were, and they were, we would say in English, "dressed up," the sight of them in public stimulated interpretation. It is a question of being seen and thought about when one did not have it in mind to be so. Tirtho protests not against the lack of prudence of the imaginary couple, but against the intention to interpret of "everyone," the anonymous person on the street who turns into his reader. This interpreter is the accidental interceptor of an unintended message. Tirtho does not present a means to stifle the curiosity of this person. Nor does he advocate sending unequivocal signs as might be suggested by someone who thought along the lines of the Dutch writers Uilkens or Daum. For Tirtho, the interpreter of the street will always be there, but the effects of his work can be avoided by making it impossible to equate dress and identity. Tirtho wishes the Javanese woman wore a Turkish costume. He advocates further dressing up in order to make recognition impossible. Misinterpretation would be avoided by the assumption of innumerable kinds of appearances.

The flaneur, wanting to know who someone was, would be left in a position similar to Groneman's at the hanging. He would suppose that something was going on between the couple he saw, but he would not know what their appearances meant. Is it a European with a Javanese? A Javanese with a Turk? And so forth. The code of dress would lack a key. One would only know that a man or a woman wore the dress of a certain nationality. The flaneur would be left permanently baffled, knowing at most that he could not understand. Uilkens thought that underneath appearances, money was at work. Daum thought sexual desire, affection, and the workings of money were confused but could be seen under what passed for social reality. A society of appearances without money at work leaves a society of images without originals. It is a society entirely infested with ghosts. The man or woman on the street might be aware of being seen but would be securely insulated from the opinion of the viewer, a little like a character in a movie, removed from the interventions of the audience. The ghosts would be happy.

Dutch and 'natives' often agreed that the Indies of the turn of the century was a society of appearances. The Dutch solution was to reestablish "real" identity. This is the beginning, for instance, of the intensification of government surveillance. But the 'native' response, at least the one that we trace here, was to ignore the identity of the other. It is particularly important that it was Tirtho Adhisoeryo who formulated this odd solution, since Tirtho has been placed by Pramoedya Ananta Toer at the beginning of the nationalist movement.[28] A nationalist movement developed not, in its popular forms, by reading the mind and the desires of the other, the result of which could well have been conflict, but by keeping the other out of mind.

With no notion of an underlying reality and no fear of the look of the other, anyone is secure in taking on the appearance of anyone else. If the spectator is in the position of Groneman, the person on view is positioned like Muhammad Bakir, ready to be any character and to change from one to the other. The text here is the street itself, full as it is with dress of various nationalities and with the irrepressible desire to dress as one sees others dress; the working of fashion before there was much material for it. We have seen this desire to clothe oneself in various forms already with Muhammad Bakir. We can identify the effects of the lingua franca, capable not only of summoning the other through language that has gained in force but also exercising its power to put oneself in the place of the other across lines of nationality. The question that Tirtho's fantasy leaves us with is how one might exit from this paradise.

In Tirtho's scenario, the hurt is suffered by the couple misrecognized; it is the flaneur who is wrong. Those who follow the ways of the time and put on the clothes of others have no intention of passing for him or her. They do not demand recognition of their desire; rather the opposite. They are not swindlers or deceivers. They are not criminals; they intend no harm or deception to anyone else. And they violate nothing in themselves when they imagine themselves in the place of the other. The couple are innocent even if what they wear is misleading about who they are. The innocence of the couple is protected by preventing recognition, but this protection extends to the person who does the recognizing. He is prevented from imagining, for instance, a shameful relation. He is left with an expanded view of the world without his own fantasies being exposed as such. Tirtho's schema is paradisiacal. One can imagine at length, put on any form of dress, and one is never ashamed and never subject to the disapprobation of others. One can interpret at length and one remains innocent.

The flaneur cannot recognize, which means that the possibility of recognition has been raised. The flaneur has been ruled out, for the time being, as the important source of recognition. But that only means that somewhere else there exists the possibility of a recognizing agency. One is seen, at this point, in the eyes of whom? It is exactly this question that is raised when Tirtho says that the person who sees cannot understand. There is, nonetheless, the possibility and even perhaps the desirability, however much denied and hidden, of being recognized. Tirtho refuses to locate this possibility in the anonymous public. At some point, recognition became important, which means that it was locatable somewhere. We will return to this later.

Dress and identity are separated in Tirtho's fantasy, but in a society of ghosts, one is hard put to say in what social identity would consist. When someone recognizes, however, the question arises. There are two possibilities. One is the crime of deception; the denial of identity given by birth, which lies under appearances of whatever sort. And there is the crime of imagination, one that stems precisely from innocence of the first. The couple who dressed up did not intend to deceive. They did not have it in mind to impress anyone else with their fantasies of themselves. But, recognized, noticed, and taken for what they appear to be, they are then guilty precisely of secret imaginings—of having dressed up only for themselves. They have used a social form to enact a private reality, a little as though they were caught talking to themselves. We shall see that neither of these was entirely the case.

THE CAMERA AND THE LAW

In 1903, Tirtho Adhisoeryo ran a series of short articles on photography in his paper. It concerned technical explications of the camera. But these technical considerations evidently answered to a larger notion of photography. The camera figures also in Tirtho's political articles. Tirtho had exposed the corruption of certain officials and been sued in return. He accused a Dutch resident, Donner, of engaging false witnesses. Had only the camera (the movie camera) been present, his case would have been proved:

> If a photographer had been able to make a film, it would have shown the entire world how during the Donner period in Madiun, false witnesses were brought forth. . . . Let the world know how between them the Resident [and] the Prosecuting Attorney carried out robberies, hold-ups and caused tumult.[29]

"If a photographer had made a film . . . the entire world" would have known the facts of the case. What the camera sees, it shows accurately; apparently not like the camera that filmed Njai Dasima. Once filmed, what is filmed is known and known by all the world. Between the camera and the making known of what it records, there is no gap. What his opponents hid, Tirtho's cameraman would have made evident. The camera here is an instrument of revelation.

Apparently what the camera shows lacks the distortions that Kwee Tek Hoay saw as interesting 'natives.' But it is not only its accuracy that was important to Tirtho. The Resident and the Prosecuting Attorney were Dutch and important officials of the colonial government. Against their warping of the truth, the camera not merely records but, in Tirtho's plea, somehow makes known what they would conceal. It is an instrument of dissemination. Its ability to counter the officers of the law, to impose on them a truth that they denied, depends on making the facts known. Tirtho adduces another court other than the Indies, one where the case would be properly judged. It is a court composed of "the entire world," that is, of anyone who would see the film. Against colonial justice, there is another justice, one administered by someone who has no nationality in particular. Tirtho, of course, has no camera. He wishes one into existence. "Camera" stands for the capacity to break through whatever barriers prevent making disgraceful events known to everyone. It is the instrument he wishes were there in order to record and to transmit the scandal to everyone, thus across any borders, whether ethnic or political. Tirtho's camera is a version of the lingua franca.

If Tirtho's camera seemed to ensure that images transmitted would be correctly received, at certain times he thought the contrary. Consider this:

> We got [the newspaper] *Bintang Hindia* and cut out the pictures of our re-spected Royal Highnesses the Most Noble Soesoehoenan of Solo and the Most Noble Sultan of Jogja and the most highly esteemed Kandjeng Raden Adipati Sosrodiningrat, Rijksbestuurder of Solo, among others of our nobles. We framed the noble rulers of Solo and Jogja because we could not bear to see the pictures of these nobles sitting next to several pictures of store employees, *seran Borneo,* sidewalk soup sellers and so on.[30]

This passage appears in a piece on advertising. *Soenda Berita*, his paper at the time, accepts ads at low rates he says, "because we want to help" and "especially so that 'natives' [*priboemi*] without education can have the benefit of seeing the pictures" the advertisements contain. Here, the photograph accurately conveys the image of the original. But just that causes difficulties. Tirtho forbids the mixing of photographic images of nobles and shop attendants in the same newspaper. In fact, he frames the pictures he has cut out, in order to isolate them from their new surround-ings and to restore to them a setting appropriate to the respect he feels they deserve.

There is no distortion in the photograph; there is, if anything, too much reality, a function, perhaps, of his assumption that the camera reveals what otherwise would be out of sight, in this case if for no other reason than because of distance. Via the workings of commerce, the pages of the news-paper become the context in which those in the photographs find them-selves. Without their consent, the rulers of Java sit next to sellers of soup. The camera has the capacity to recontextualize; the most improbable, even delusionary, settings are conjured up when photographs are set next to each other in the newspaper. It is as though royal presences are actually mingling with the popular classes; but their social identities no longer have any force. There are the images of rulers, but images that, no longer gov-erned by their originals, mix with any other figures on the same page. The newspaper becomes a movie theater, its commercial images responding to scenarios found nowhere in the actual world.

Tirtho differs from KTH as, we will see, he differs from the Dutch. He does not fear that the generation of an appearance, an image, brings with it distortion. Rather, he sees that context can actually be changed by the camera and the newspaper. He sees that in the course of transmission, clear images emerge that are not merely images. The camera, for him, in its operation does not leave behind the object it records; it somehow brings the original with it. But this is absurd because Tirtho knew the difference between image and original. The difficulty is that the image is too powerful. It is not merely a visual imprint; it seems to contain all that nobility meant for Javanese. It is, like the photograph of Njai Dasima, not only an image of a specific person but a condensation of what is known and said about these persons. The photograph of the soup seller is not different. When they are contiguous, the photographs set off suggestions of social intercourse that Tirtho finds unacceptable. The soup seller would offer the sultan a bowl of his soup; the sultan would refuse. The photographs, in Tirtho's fantasy, seem able to speak. When they do, registers of language, culture, and society are unacceptably mixed. In Tirtho's scenario, the soup seller and the sultan cannot remain apart. Set on the page of the newspaper, they speak across its columns and across the borders of advertisements. He assumes that it cannot be different; otherwise, he would not cut out and frame the pictures of nobles. He refuses the Dutch solution, which would be to say that these are merely images, the originals of which are somewhere else, immune to the improper mixing he imagines. Tirtho seems to be unable to restrain himself from imagining that each recognizes the other and compels the other to respond to him. It is the source of his objection.

This power of the image to compel recognition and response is also, of course, what makes his imaginary camera an instrument of justice. Tirtho wrote before movies had sound. Yet, the viewers of the scandal he revealed would understand what they saw without words. It is because the photographic image for him, as for Francis, was not only a representation of the physical but of the linguistic. Tirtho's photographic image is condensed language.

Here is another story of appearances. In an issue of *Soenda Berita*, Tirtho discussed the "law of disguise" (*wet samaran*). He cited the law:

> Whoever appears in public [*dihadapan orang banjak*] wearing clothes that are not those of his own nationality [*bangsa*] or if a man wears women's clothes or if a woman wears man's clothes in order to disguise themselves, or if a person goes out wearing a mask or other sorts of clothing (3 April 1904)

will be fined f16 to f20. Tirtho cites a Dutch legal expert who explains that it is necessary to intend to deceive (*bikin bodo*) or delude (*berdaja*). "'Thus if a person simply wears something not ordinarily worn by his nationality, for instance a Javanese wears a necktie or a Chinese jacket, that cannot be called disguise.'"

As the law is stated, it is not a question of deception but of how one appears in public. At issue is being in public and how one looks. Then, Tirtho cites a Dutch expert who explains that what is at stake is crossing lines of nationality. It is not merely a question of dressing as someone else but also of deceiving "the public," that is, those whom one does not know. Sexual cross-dressing is not discussed. As Tirtho develops the question, however, he insists not on the intent to deceive but on the fate of a person who simply dresses up and goes out in public. He takes the instance of a Chinese who has cut off his queue and goes out in European clothes, wearing "a European hat, a necktie, European pants, and shoes." Some think he is violating the law. Others disagree because the queue is a sign of loyalty to the Chinese emperor and it is already customary for Chinese to wear European clothes. So "if he is sentenced by the [justice of the peace] the justice of the peace will be embarrassed" because the sentence would be overturned if there is an appeal. It would be different if, "while he was out roaming around he was asked his name and denied it, giving a non-Chinese name." Or, if he was stopped in an area where he needed a pass and did not have one. Then he could be convicted on two counts; one for not having a pass and the other for intending to disguise himself as a European not needing a pass.

The question of disguise is, viewed legally, a question, in the instances of the Chinese, of deception. The Chinese could look just like a European and there might not be a case against him if his dress was not an attempt to conceal his identity. In Tirtho's examples, the Chinese are simply in public, on the street one supposes, when the police stop them. They might be in disguise. It is the job of the police to see that their European appearance, already a commonplace for them, is not severed from their identity. So long as appearance and identity can be put together, there is no delict.

Again in *Soenda Berita*, Tirtho gives a similar example of 'natives' who might be vulnerable to the law:

> For instance take the case of one of our race, a native [*anak negri*] and follow the analogy. A *hadji*, for instance, wearing a tie, pants, hat, *stamboel* hat, taking his pleasure, wandering through the city with no special intention, only because he is dressed up and he likes to do so; if he is arrested. . . .

The person has nothing in mind, only pleasure in wandering through the city, in wearing certain clothes. Then the police appear. The wanderer has not intended a crime of any sort. Yet the police stop him. In the example, he is let off. But anyone dressed like a European can be uneasy. Even if he is not convicted, he could be subject to a control. The man can evade this easily enough.

> But if he puts a turban around his hat, even if it is only one strip to indicate that he is a *hadji*, there will be no difficulty these days because the desire of natives to mimic all Dutch ways is already commonplace today. Just so long as he indicates he is a native.

The *hadji* has no other interest than wandering through the city. He does not intend to deceive anyone. He only wants to dress up and go out. He does not intend to be anyone other than who he is, but he intends to look the way people looked at that time when they wanted to be fashionable. He thus comes to look like someone of another nationality. The Dutchman appears, one might say, on the form of the 'native.' There is no fusion of the Javanese and the Dutchman and no substitution or attempted substitution of one for the other. The two appearances are simply superimposed. One cannot, at this point, use the word identity. That would come into play only if the *hadji* wanted to deceive someone into thinking he was really a European. But he only wants the pleasure of appearing in public. He does not propose to be identified at all, only to be on display.

Identity becomes a question only at the moment when the police agent suspects that the man he sees on the street looks like someone he might not be. The police stop him and in effect say, "You are not a Dutchman." It is the law that insists that identity always be maintained. It appears, in Tirtho's accounts, by surprise. It thus contrasts with the law in "The Story of Njai Dasima" or in another story of the time, "Si Tjonat" by F. D. J. Pangemanann.[31] There, officers of the law show up at the end to arrest the murderers. Their appearance is the natural culmination of the story. They ensure that it ends as it should; because of the police and the courts, those who want what they should not have and try and get it are punished. Here, the policeman seems to intrude where he is not called for because there has been no desire to appropriate anything; merely to look a certain way. It is a desire that never thinks of ownership. But when the law appears, "his" identity is raised and established.

The Chinese who dresses like a European to avoid the pass laws is one thing; the *hadji*, simply out for pleasure, is another. The concern of Tirtho is not the concern of the law; he is not made anxious about the possibility of being deceived. He rather wants to warn people that when they dress up they could be accused of being deceptive. Someone who is simply following the trend of the day might fall into legal difficulty. His assumption is that this could happen because appearance is no longer necessarily a clue to identity. This is because, in the course of things, appearances have come to have a certain autonomy. Images have been made available and made attractive; 'natives' want to look like what they see in advertisements. Tirtho claims that it happens "because the desire of natives to mimic all Dutch ways is already commonplace today." The mime here does not think he is impersonating; he is doing the commonplace. That is, it is not just the Dutch who are mimicked, it is "everyone." Were it just the Dutch, there would be a question of motivation and of appropriation of the object. But to do what everyone is doing, as we well know from our experience in mass society, is not to assume a change of identity.

Appearance was a cultural question, a matter of the camera and the market. Identity was a legal matter. Like other newspaper editors of the time, including Francis, Tirtho translated law compendiums from Dutch into Melayu. His effort to allow the Melayu-speaking world to stay within the law, however, met a certain limitation. Tirtho sent his book to the Melayu language paper, *Selompret Melayoe*, where the editor thanked him in its columns and, after noting the usefulness of the book, stated also its limitation:

> But readers of the book must be careful. Do not think you can be your own attorney because legal regulations [*hoekoem-hoekoem oendang*] indeed cannot be clearly translated into Melayoe. It is only hoped that the reader of this book gains some clarity into the laws that are valid for trade. (13 June 1911)

A person without knowledge of Dutch cannot be his own attorney, not because one needs to have the specialized education of the lawyer but because of the impossibility of translation from Dutch into Melayu. Here, again, we meet the assumption that Soewardi was to break down. The invulnerability of Dutch to Melayu indeed would have no place in the translation of a law book. There, if one cannot be precise, there is no point in approximation. If nonetheless the editor of *Selompret Melayoe* thought there was a value to the book, it is perhaps to indicate the difficulty that this notion of translation brought with it. The law, instead of being something one can know and thus obey, becomes an instrument of chance. At best one learns that, without knowledge of Dutch, one is necessarily ignorant of the law and one can be prepared to be surprised. There is no way to prevent the law becoming chance if it is not translatable. One in all innocence does what people do at the time and one is hailed by the police. The effect of Tirtho's description of the law of disguise is thus ambiguous: It lets people know that under certain circumstances, they might break the law and that under other circumstances, they might not. Because one cannot be sure of the circumstances, readers can only know for certain that they are in the presence of a force whose actions they cannot predict, which therefore they cannot guard against and which can reveal them to themselves as appearing as someone else when they had no intention of doing so.

The ability to take on the "I" of any language, we have said, involves an assumption of perfect translatability. Therefore, it seems contradictory to see on the one hand a naive dressing in the mode of the other and at the same time, an assertion that the law is not translatable. It has to be kept in mind, however, that dressing in European fashion is not exactly the same as standing in the place of the other, à la Soewardi and the Dutch. It does not bring with it the idea that one has penetrated behind the image of the Dutchman, that one knows what he is thinking. Rather, it is that one dresses as "everyone" does, the "everyone" who appears in photographs and advertisements. It is not identification with the other, but identification with the commodity, with the commodity pictured in the press. With, in other words, the points of transmission or communication between Dutch and others. It is before, as it were, the point where translation would reveal the peculiarities of Dutch language and Dutch thinking. The difference between Dutch and Melayu does not prevent communication between two worlds speaking different languages.

The editor of *Selompret Melayoe* did not say why he thought the law was untranslatable into Melayu. Presumably, he passed on the fears of the Dutch about the inadequacy of Melayu as well, possibly, as an assumption about the interpretation of the law and its relation to language. However, asserted without justification, the statement that the law is untranslatable made to a reader of the lingua franca could mean that he did not have to bother thinking what the Dutch had in mind. The assertion would be a reassurance that he need not try and imagine "If I were a Dutchman . . ." at the moment when he might be taken for one. It could equally well mean that there is an asymmetry in communication. Initially, "I" hear, see, feel something that arrives from a world whose language "I" do not speak. But "I" take on its attributes, "translating" them as it were not into "my" or even "our" language, but assimilating them as best as I can to my body; ornamenting myself with them, letting "myself" appear through them.

If, then, "I" am surprised by the police, it is because the police says that "I" am really not a Dutchman, "whereas I" thought "I" was simply amplifying my original appearance, not disguising it. "I" am surprised because "I" believe that, contrary to my intentions, "I" might really have been taken for a Dutchman. If the policeman had not almost thought so, he would not have stopped me. In any case, a limit has been reached. One has heard about and read and seen pictures of what is chic, *perlente*, in the word used at the time. But this has brought one to a point beyond which one can see or hear. One cannot know, without a knowledge of Dutch, what one's own appearance means. With a knowledge of Dutch, out of a knowledge of Dutch, it might be possible. That is, the power of the law is a power contained in Dutch. One has followed certain trains of information contained in gossip, newspapers, and books and one has been left surprised. One has been taken for someone other than oneself. The law says or might say, "you have deceived." But one's reply to the police is not only to say, "I am innocent; I had no intention to deceive. I am really *hadji* Mohammed Ahmad." It is also possible to think, "He thinks I could pass for a Dutchman." That is, "I could be what my appearance indicates."

Such a statement raises the possibility of thinking that a native becomes Dutch in the way that, via the camera, cotton turns into silk or turns nearly any woman into Njai Dasima; merely through a certain appearance or appearing. The original is no longer in question. It is only the police who think of it. A change of appearance can somehow leave the original behind. If one is no longer interested in reclaiming the original identity by saying "but I am not Njai Dasima, I am really . . ." it is because the gap between appearance and origin appears as a kind of magic or a newly discovered power. Simply dressing up, having no other intention, one is taken for someone else, just as the Sultan of Jogjakarta, having his picture taken, finds himself somewhere else, next to a shopkeeper. No one in these scenarios notices that it is not true, that one's "real" self has been left behind. No one but the policeman. And the policeman, when he notices that, notices that you have the ability to pass for a Dutchman. The policeman is not interested in your total lack of intention, thought, or desire to do so. He would not stop you for trying to deceive unless he thought that your appearance made it possible to do so. The policeman knows something more about yourself than you do. He understands the possibility of cotton turning into silk.

Such is the magic that one has oneself, even without a camera, and that one did not know one had. It is the creation of a fetish, a magical instrument that claims a false relation to an origin. "False" not by an absolute standard of truth, but false after the fact, by the claim of the very authority who shows that an ordinary practice is in fact magical when he demonstrates its falsity. It is the police who establish that one could be a Dutchman, and thereby leaves one to think that assumption of appearances shows more to others than one had ever dreamed of.

The policeman sees me dressed as a Dutchman. He arrests me. I have not said a word; I have only made an appearance. It is possible I cannot speak Dutch. But for him, "I" have already spoken. The policeman hears me dressed up the way that Tirtho hears photographs. For them, the image speaks. "I" when "I" dressed up did not make the same assumption. "I" never thought that if "I" put on "a tie, pants, hat" "I" would come out *ik* instead of *saya* when "I" opened my mouth to speak. It would be absurd even if "I" shared Tirtho's notion of the photographic image. The policeman, however, when he applied this idea to "me" made "me" think it was nearly possible. The next step, as it were, would be to speak Dutch.[32]

The magic of the fetish of appearances is not the ability to look like anyone at all. It is the welding of appearance to language in such a way that, through authoritative recognition, "I" seem to have taken linguistic power for myself. In the texts of Muhammad Bakir and in some of Tirtho's scenarios, the textual "I" speaks and compels the recognition of other characters. Now, with the invocation of the law, appearances on the street do the same. The delirium of an "I" that moves between social identities of any sort has been displaced from newspapers and manuscripts onto a person in everyday life. Such a person is no less a textual entity than his predessor. That, as we have said, is his magical power. If there had been no law against cross-dressing, one would not have the amazement that Tirtho shows that it is really possible to appear as another.

What is needed for this to be more than an ordinary historical fact but to result, as I believe it did, in a fetishizing of appearance, is a third party. This third party is reached without intention. It is through the reaction of the unintended addressee that one learns one has signified something or that one is the bearer of signs. When, additionally, the third person is the police, it means for Tirtho that one must attend to what the police say. Whoever is recognized by the law has to take this recognition seriously. In Tirtho's account, the policeman is not what he was for Francis. We have seen that for Francis the police ensure a proper ending, but in the meantime, the law distorts social order. In place of the law, the power of authoritative recognition is held by the father. The same was true for Thérèse Hoven. But in Tirtho, even when the law does not work, there is still the court consisting of all the people who see his film and there is still the flaneur and the newspaper reader. The indefiniteness of these groups and their anonymity and even lack of identity indicate that the recognition that is demanded through the imagined intermediary of communications technology is only uneasily given by socially defined figures.[33]

There are two points to make about this. First is the freeing of the capacity to authoritatively recognize from any place in particular. This we have already seen. Next is the relocation of this capacity. Tirtho has no recourse to paternal figures to replace political sources of recognition. On the contrary, he seems to welcome the policeman and he never complains about the law as such. But this is because the law, being unforeseeable, incomprehensible, and descending without warning approximates the third person. The third person is the one not present; the one not addressed but who is thought of anyway because even if one cannot predict who will get a message when its delivery is deferred, "someone" will. Tirtho's cheerfulness about the police when they accost the innocent comes no doubt from a relief that would be strange if we did not set it in the terms we have already used. The person accosted is guilty of impersonation; that is a crime. But he is innocent because he had no intention of deception. He only dressed up to satisfy a whim. But then he should be not guilty but instead ashamed of being interrupted in the midst of a private fantasy. It is precisely the turning of the moment of recognition into the thought of having a magic power, capable of impressing policemen, that allows Tirtho not to resent the police or the law. Through the magic of the fetish of appearances, "I" am not a criminal and am not ashamed.

With Tirtho's formulation, emphasis is placed on recognition. The law appears without, it seems, anyone summoning it. And yet the law appears in response to "I." This law is unintelligible to "I." And yet, in retrospect, it is evident that it was "I" who made it appear. The position of legal authority has then shifted from most of the Dutch texts. Legal authority is no longer the source and limitation of messages as it ideally was for Groneman. And the force of communications is no longer identified with paternal authority even outside the law. Rather, anyone stopped for breaking the law of disguise could reflect that he did indeed have a force he never suspected himself of possessing. In retrospect, he is, or perhaps almost is, a criminal. It is simply because after the fact he sees he has a force of communication that is outside the law and that unwittingly reaches it. The police enforced the law of disguise in the Netherlands East Indies. But for the law to have consequences for identity, for it to be serious, it had to be embedded in myths of self-consciousness such as Tirtho's.

"I"s awareness of its power would not be achieved if he did not summon the law. If the notice "I" collected was benign and not open to interpretation, "I" would exist within Groneman's society of those who take everything at face value. Such people are not threatened by death and are immune to the law.

This power of communication that had always been thought of as being the property of colonial authority or, if not, of Dutch paternal authority, now falls onto 'natives.' The consolidation of this ability, or rather its attempted consolidation, I call the "fetish of appearance" or "the fetish of modernity." I use the last term because modernity is associated with the ability to achieve an identity as opposed to being always defined by identity given by birth and because modernity and Indonesian nationalism were almost indistinguishable for most of the first half of the twentieth century.

It is clear up to this point that the formulation of a national identity does not start with the claim of roots. 'Native' is not the basis for "Indonesian." To be "Indonesian," one had first to feel the currents of world communications.[34] And, there needed to be further considerations of the power of communication.

PART II

Recognition

CHAPTER FOUR

Student Hidjau and *The Feeling of Freedom*

MAS MARCO KARTODIKROMO (c. 1890–1932) belongs to the generation
of Tirtho Adhisoeryo from whom he learned journalism. He was also
influenced by Soewardi Soerjaningrat. He was a leftist of the time, a founder of the most important Islamic political organization of the day; and he
was well known as a journalist and a master of political sarcasm. His political career has been well told in Takashi Shiraishi's *An Age in Motion*; Henri
Chambert-Loir has defined his place in Indonesian literature. According to
the latter, Mas Marco's "novels and stories reflect the Javanese nationalist
conceptions of the twenties; they are also among the best specimens of the
serials which had a very important role before the creation, in 1917, of a
government publications house." Mas Marco apparently taught himself
Dutch, though rather badly, and spent five months in the Hague, his only
trip outside the Indies except for two months in Singapore.[1]

Student Hidjau, which Chambert-Loir says is "worthy of being studied
in the framework of Indonesian literature" and was published in 1918–19,
tells of a Javanese youth, Student Hidjau, who is sent to study in Holland.
Whether or not he should go is, in fact, the issue that opens the story. Here
is the first paragraph:

> "Kanda! Kanda! [a term of address] your son sent to Holland! No!" Thus Raden
> Nganten Portnojo wept in front of her husband when he he let it be known that
> their son would be shipped to Holland to attend a school for engineers. (5)

Her husband tries to pacify her, but the Raden Nganten is alarmed to the
point of panic. It is during the First World War and she is afraid his ship will
be sunk before he arrives. When her husband tells her not to worry, that
life and death are in the hands of God, she is not soothed. They have only
one child; if he is in Holland, what will she do? "If I don't see him for a
single day I feel sad"(6). Another fear comes into her mind: "If your child
marries a Dutch miss, would you allow it?" (6) Her husband is "offended"
and tries again to reassure her. But she persists. Even if Hidjau promises
not to do such a thing, "Women in Holland aren't like they are here" (7)
and if he goes to Holland, when he comes back, he may no longer want to
marry a Javanese woman. Were that to happen, the Raden Nganten says
she would "die" because she dearly loves her son and his Javanese fiancée.

We never see the mother reassured. And while this may have been meant to be amusing, we can speak here of panic or of fear disproportionate to its cause. This panic begins with apostrophe: "Kakanda! Kakanda!" *Kakanda* means older sibling and is used by Student Hidjau's mother to address her husband, as is the convention. She makes an appeal and she begins with the naming of the second person, duplicating it both as an indication of her emotion and to ensure that she really has a listener. The first sentence of the story is a reply, or an attempt at a reply. It does not work, both in the sense that Hidjau's mother does not succeed in canceling the plan to send Hidjau abroad or in the establishment of a conversation. Each time her husband speaks and tells her that death is in the hands of God, or what the advantages are of a Dutch education, she merely finds another argument. She rejects all of his replies. One might say that her initial apostrophe is a failure, as is the case with panic.

The source of her fears are in Holland; "Holland," to her, means separation from her son and his moral corruption by Dutch women, not to mention war and death. Her husband cannot speak to these fears. Instead, he talks of the advantage of sending their son abroad. "Don't be discouraged" he tells her:

> "I am merely a merchant. You know yourself, these days people like me are still looked down on by people who have become government functionaries. Sometimes we have a child of our own who works for the government and he doesn't want to mix with us because he thinks he is superior to us merchants or farmers. My intention in sending Hidjau to Holland is simply to make those people who ridicule us understand that humans are all alike and the sign of it is that our child too can study like the children of regents and princes." (6)

For Hidjau's father, something is wrong with Javanese society. He and his class—merchants and farmers—do not have the position of respect he feels they deserve. The way to right this situation is to show that he has access to Dutch education for his child, just as they do. The implication is that if *prijaji*, or officials, feel superior, it is because they, the regents and others like them, can send their children to Holland. If he could do the same, he would be their equal. The superiority of *prijaji* to merchants is not intrinsic to Javanese society; it is a result of privileged connections with the Dutch. The answer is to establish these connections himself. His position, in other words, is that of the audience at the rallies. But in this instance it will be shown to be inadequate.

Hidjau's mother does not accept this argument. She tells her husband that their son has already had sufficient education to become a *prijaji* and he is better educated than the children of that class. And in any case, there is the important question of women; here, she raises her fear of Dutch women. She is not worried that Hidjau will be rejected by Dutch society.

She is, rather, afraid that what her husband wishes for their son, acceptance by the Dutch, will occur with all together too much success. What for Hidjau's father is a solution is a problem for his mother.

The argument could be reformulated. Hidjau's father sees Holland as part of the hierarchy of Java. If "all humans are equal" or should be so, it is because they all have, or at least should have, equal access to Holland. For Hidjau's mother, "Holland" means not the top of Javanese society, but war, death, separation, and menacing women. He, the father, sees Holland as the source of the structuring of Java; she, the mother, pictures Holland as the unstructured outside of Java. The place of Mas Marco is shown, of course, by the story: the mother's view prevails. What is at stake in this argument are two views of Indonesian society. I want to show how the conflict of views is underlined by an unstated assumption about language and languages.

The mother's panic, in this view, is justified. "The Netherlands" becomes the outside of society, but as we shall see, an outside of a special type. The first words of the story are an attempt to reply to the words of the father. We never hear the precise words he spoke that incite the mother's reply. Those sentences are uttered before the story begins. They come from outside the text. Following the same logic, the words of the father are informed by a sentiment that comes from outside what Mas Marco considered cultural if not national boundaries. If Hidjau's mother cannot engage a voice, it is because the words of the father are only passed on by him, they do not originate with him. His words rely on an authority found not in himself and ultimately not even in Java, but in the Netherlands. They encompass what has been said in Dutch.

Student Hidjau's mother feels panic because she hears the undoing of kinship that comes as a second language speaks from within a first and from a place somewhere far behind the speaker. The father, the speaker, is unaware of this. He is, in a sense, already in Holland, in that, whether he knows it or not, the sentiments he utters originate there. The mother's inability to engage him shows that he is someone who only seems to be present. From that point of view, her panic is justified. This not only because her view will prevail in the novel, but because she knows that she cannot communicate beyond certain boundaries and that some relationships in Indonesia, those through which Dutch passes in the guise of Melayu or Javanese, have already been hollowed out. The course of the novel will show that it is not she, in her panic, who is beyond rationality; it is the father who only mouths what someone else, some place else has already said.

It should be evident that what is at stake is the status of the lingua franca. As the medium of the story and the language into which others are eminently transferable, it furnishes the assumption around which the story turns. It is not, however, named as such. Everything in the story still occurs as though the lingua franca is transparent. One can say that the lingua franca occurs through its effects rather than through being conceptualized.

When he arrives in Holland, Hidjau enrolls in a school in Delft. He finds lodgings with a Dutch family. Hidjau is a diligent student. In Solo, when he finished school, he continued reading, even when he was with his fiancée. He continues his habit in Delft. Or at least he does so until he is invited to the theater. There he hears the opera Faust "Which is very much liked by most Dutch" (69).

> Faust is a story of a man who likes to study very much, to the point where he has no time to feel the pleasures of the world. Faust was a wealthy man, but he was not happy taking care of a woman in the way most people are and he did not like other pleasures. So Faust was able to live happily with several hundred books which he enjoyed. From the time he was young till he grew grey, he never wasted an hour; he always studied. Of course as time went on he grew wealthier. Faust always thought about death which had to come. . . . According to the story, Faust was assured that in the end he would have a place in paradise. But . . . Faust fell in love with a married woman. Because of this intense love Faust no longer cared for his wealth which was in the millions and he was not afraid of going to hell. . . . Faust no longer bothered with the excellent learning which filled his head.
>
> With the help of satan, Faust became a handsome young man and finally the woman he loved came to love Faust and. . . . . of course because of Faust's improper behavior, all that he owned—paradise, wealth, learning and so on—vanished. (70; ellipses in original)

One might expect that Student Hidjau would find a lesson for himself in Faust. In fact he does, but it is not one his mother would approve of. He is much affected by the performance, not least because of the girls who sit next to him, one of whom says, "Tuan Hidjau . . . in the end you will be like Faust. Because now you like to study but . . . finally. . . . . ." (70; ellipses in original). When he gets home he cannot put the story out of mind. He thinks to himself:

> "If when I am old I act like Faust its better to do it now. Because if now I follow the ways of young people who like pleasure, that's not awful because its generally thought all right. But later, when my hair turns grey, if I act like Faust, bah!" (71)

Faust as interpreted by Student Hidjau proves an irresistible model; in the next chapter, he is seduced. One can ask why Hidjau draws such a conclusion and one can point to the suggestion of the girl who sits next to him. But this is the wrong question. One must say that Mas Marco asserts that in the Netherlands Student Hidjau cannot resist suggestion. One might also ask what is wrong with being seduced; in *Mata Gelap*, Mas Marco's earlier novel, it happens frequently and pleasantly enough.[2] In Holland, however, it is different. There, seduction threatens to lead to what his mother fears. Hidjau begins an affair with the daughter of his landlord but he becomes troubled: "In the midst of this pleasure, Hidjau felt very upset; he kept remembering letters [which he had just received] from Woengoe and Biroe" (81). Biroe is the name of the Javanese woman whom he and his mother expect him to marry. Woengoe is the name of the Javanese woman he marries in the end. It is not just these women that bother him however. "If I keep doing this I'll upset my own parents and. . . . . and. . . . finally. . . . ." (81; ellipses in original).

Hidjau, at this point, cannot name all the troubles he might find for himself beyond those with his parents and his Javanese women friends. He goes off to meditate at a vegetarian hotel in Amsterdam. Through this effort, Hidjau is able to think clearly; his love for his parents, for Woengoe, Biroe, and Wardojo, his Javanese friends, increase. The conclusion he reaches is that he must leave Holland:

> "I have to return to Java," so said Hidjau to himself as he sat under a tree and looked at the expansive sea.[!] "Because if I continue to study here in the Netherlands, maybe it won't be long before I become a Dutchman, because it is certain I will marry a Dutch girl. If I do that it's the same as if I were to leave my relatives and my nationality. Bah!. . . . . . *Europesche beschaving*. . . . ." (83; ellipses in original)

To marry a Dutch girl is the same as leaving behind his women friends, his fiancée, his male friends, and his parents in Java. To marry a Dutch girl is to "leave my . . . nationality" and become Dutch. The conclusion of his meditation is that there is no possibility of combination; of marrying a Dutch woman and remaining Javanese. His mother was correct; her nightmare could come true. If he went to Holland he might find a Dutch girl, and if that happened he would be lost both to his mother and to himself.

The problem is love (*cinta*). If he loves Betje, the landlord's daughter, he will end up being Dutch. And loving her is the inevitable concomitant of studying in Holland. Learning means progress; it is the learning of the West. But progress, *kemadjoean*, leaves him vulnerable to *cinta*, love. One day after he has been to the theater to see Faust, he hears a knock on the door as he sits in his room.

> "Mag ik U storen [Could I disturb you] meneer Hidjau," said Betje after Hidjau opened the door.
>
> "Zeker! Zeker! [Certainly, certainly]" Hidjau answered happily, but he went on reading his book.
>
> "Close your book, tuan, I want to talk with you for a moment." (72)

Books cannot protect him from women. As Hidjau says, "If I continue to study here in the Netherlands, maybe it won't be long before I become a Dutchman, because it is certain I will marry a Dutch girl." The danger is not that he will study, however, but that Betje will take away his book. There is no equation here of knowledge with power and sexuality as part of that power.

> "What do you want to talk about?" said Hidjau, standing before the chair; but he kept on reading the book. "Close the book first," said Betje showing her impatience. (72)

They could have become Paola and Francesca, ending in Hell but celebrated by Dante and Tchaikovsky. Instead, Hidjau leaves Holland and returns to Java and they are never heard from again. Mas Marco's book is remembered far more in Europe and America than in Indonesia, where it is today almost entirely unknown. Hidjau is saved from the destructuring power of Holland which, in another context, would have been the possibility of memorialization. Here, it is the commencement of forgetting.

Student Hidjau does not fear exile; he does not fear being a Javanese in Holland. And he does not imagine the formation of a new, egalitarian society, one forced open by the possibility of sexual enjoyment open to all humans. Rather, he fears assimilation. If he stays longer, the danger is that "it won't be long before I become a Dutchman." As in Tirtho's discussion of the law of disguise, the problem is not the ability to disguise oneself but the possibility that inadvertently one might take on the identity of one's dress simply by doing as one pleases.

It might have been different. Sexuality might have been the force that opens society to everyone. But in this story, sexuality does not mean that Hidjau gains what Dutchmen already have; instead, it threatens Hidjau's loss of himself as he knew himself to be. Hidjau goes to Holland and finds himself in the place of the Dutch not simply geographically but as one who enjoys what Dutchmen enjoy. Mas Marco, showing us the thoughts of his character about seduction and assimilation, says that if one follows the strongest fantasies of desire in Holland, one ends up Dutch. Mas Marco says, in effect, "If I were a Dutchman. . . ." His next phrase is not, "but I'm not" but, "I would always remain so." He says in effect, "I could be Dutchman and if I were, I would be lost to Java." Hidjau's solution is to leave Holland, which means also to put it out of mind and with it the possibility of rethinking Soewardi's formula. To put Holland out of mind while the Indies were still Dutch, however, could not be easy.

Hidjau's seduction begins in the theater. When Betje succeeds in getting Hidjau to give up his book long enough for them to talk, she invites him to the Princesse Schouwburg to see Lili Green. Hidjau watches the women on stage dance "naked" except that they have on thin silk dresses.

Hidjau in his entire life had never seen anything like it; his heart pounded as his eyes detected [*mengetahoei*] these naked girls.

They leave at the intermission and his seduction is accomplished.

This critical moment is mediated. "Very fine," said Betje who sat on Hidjau's right after she had watched these girls with opera glasses. "Have a look with these glasses" (75). Hidjau sees more than he could see with his own eyes as the opera glasses seem to bring the girls closer to him. The glasses bring only the images of the girls closer to Hidjau, of course, but these mere images are crucial to his seduction and thus to his fear of becoming a Dutchman. If Hidjau simply saw the dancing girls with his own eyes, there might have been a different scenario, one in which the girls would have stayed on the stage. One remembers Tirtho Adhisoeryo shocked to find the Sultan of Jogjakarta next to the seller of soup. Images are replaced in a context that is inappropriate to their originals.

Let us return to the fetish of appearance for a moment. That, we have said, depends on a colonial context, one in which the law recognizes "me" and finds more in my appearance than "I" knew myself. This is an ambiguous situation because, on the one hand, the law that sees that there is more to me than my origins would indicate, forbids me from becoming what I appear to be. In Holland, however, Student Hidjau experiences no check on what he can have, on what he desires, nor on what he can become. In Holland, a woman awakens his desire or perhaps recognizes it where he did not know it existed. He did not know that he wanted what he had never seen before but, finding out, he is threatened with becoming someone he never suspected he could become. The barrier between communities and cultures that the law maintained in the Indies does not operate in Holland.

The possibility of this breakdown depends on the dancing girls being delivered to Student Hidjau through the opera glasses. "Hidjau in his entire life had never seen anything like it." An imaginary scene occurs that is improper by standards his mother implicitly sets at the beginning of the story. It is not merely sexual, it is a scene of easy communication across a cultural and political frontier. And it is a scene that suggests an expansion of imagination not so much by its content (women, or even Dutch women) as by the fact of easy conveyance through a technological device. The glasses are like the camera in that merely through the possibility of conveyance one sees what one never expected to see even if one sees the "same" thing one has seen before—the sultan, for example, or the woman whom one has seen on the stage a moment earlier.

This opening of imagination does not dissolve the boundaries of colonial society. They remain intact, but one imagines what one sees delivered across these frontiers. But traffic goes in both directions. Student Hidjau decides he has no place in Holland. It has become a foreign land, one to which Java does not belong, just as his mother said. Usually one is aware of being a foreigner because one cannot imagine having a place. Here it is the opposite. Having a place in Holland would be perfectly possible for Hidjau, but he would become Dutch. Hidjau finds he has arrived in a foreign scene once he has what he did not before know he wanted.

Student Hidjau marks the point where one could imagine anything, and thus the beginning of literature and the surpassing of the fetish. But it ties desire and imagination to identity, and it thus tries to close down what it has opened. It poses an argument about whether or not Java is part of colonial hierarchy. Factually, in terms of existing political conditions, it was, but linguistically it was not. And culturally it was not, the novel claims. This was not because of the differences of culture and morality between Java and Holland, nor because of the difference between a traditional and a modern society. Instead, it was because it was so easy to find oneself there. It is a result of the fetish once again operating across the ethnic borders interior to colonial society. Someone Dutch sees me; sees that "I" could be Dutch and "I" realize that it is a possibility of myself "I" had never been aware of.

In Holland, Hidjau is wary of going to the theater with just Betje. When she invites him, he replies " 'Fine, but who will we see it with?' " Betje tells him that he will see it with her. " 'Yes, but are we going by ourselves, not with anyone else, your father or [illegible]?' " She wants to go alone. He protests, " 'But I would be happier to see it with lots of friends from here.' " They go by themselves. In Java, there is no need to go with others because they are always in the midst of those who know them. At one point Hidjau takes his girlfriend Biroe to Sriwedari, the pleasure garden that contains a theater. They find chairs in front of the restaurant in a place "which is a bit dark and people cannot see them clearly" (15). This choice of place prompts Biroe to say, " 'Djo, why do we have to sit here? . . . people who look will have a bad opinion' " (15). But Hidjau reassures her by saying, " 'Ach, not at all. Of course everyone already knows that you are my fiancée' " (15). Later, they go to see the Javanese theatrical form called *wayang orang*. On stage a man, Djanoko, in paradise, is seen by nymphs. As they watch, Biroe turns her attention to Hidjau; she looks at Hidjau's face "as though tracing it" (17).

In Solo, darkness does not protect the couple from being seen. But being seen is actually reassuring. Hidjau says that everyone who sees them will know who they are. When he goes to the theater with Betje, he goes with no one they know and they are anonymous. In Solo, as the nymphs watch Djonoko, so Biroe watches Hidjau. But this doubled display of admiration and desire does not have unwished-for consequences; the result no doubt of feeling themselves in the presence of those who recognize them. What is at stake is not social control. It is not that, in the presense of those who know them, they restrain themselves. It is rather that pleasure, desire, does not deliver either of them into another scene, one where they find themselves unfamiliar to themselves. They remain in the same context, seen by the same eyes, unlike, for instance, the Sultan of Jogjakarta who, looking out from the newspaper, would find a stranger looking back.

The distinction between Javanese or Indonesian and European women is made not in order to distinguish the moral and the immoral, as is often done in Indonesia today, but to ensure that pleasure in women is quite possible without leading to the uncanny. Indonesian women are, from early in the nationalist movement, placed firmly in the position of the domestic and the domesticating. They are one of the early replacements for colonial law in the attempt to reconstruct the fetish. The woman I desire is not foreign; therefore my desire does not lead me to a foreign context. But in Student Hidjau, there is not only Biroe, Hidjau's girlfriend, there are also those who see them and there is also the stage. Those who see are, like Biroe herself, familiar. And Biroe, though she repeats what is happening on the stage, suggesting a process similar to viewing the stage through glasses in Holland, neither has glasses nor watches something foreign. What she sees is one of the classic scenes of Javanese mythology. All of this reinforces the familiarity of scenes of desire.

One might think that there is nothing left of the fetish here because there is no suggestion of change of identity. But Hidjau and Biroe are not traditional Javanese youth in this novel. They are nationalists and, in one scene, they go to a nationalist meeting in an automobile. They are the modernist youth of that day. Their flirtation itself is something modern. Biroe and Woengoe as Hidjau's sweethearts are figures who see in Hidjau something new, something with little precedent in Java. At the same time, by their contrast with Dutch women, they show that in the new there is only the familiar.

Student Hidjau gives another reason to turn one's back on the Dutch, this time in the Indies. Often times Europeans who leave Europe for the Indies are not who they claim to be. Instead of coming from the highest realms of Dutch society, they come from the bottom. A long portion of the novel relates an anecdote in which one such person is exposed.

> People who understand the Indies are not surprised by these stories. But for us there is a highly important meaning. Dutch themselves admit that in the Indies there are many former coolies and low people who here go mad, inflate themselves, insult us as though we were their slaves and even worse, animals. Those who have never been to Holland seriously think that this conceited being has high origins. (114)

Dutch themselves admit that many of their friends when they arrive in the Indies, "become mad about status and no longer want to mix with their friends from the Netherlands." This allows the writer of the pamphlet to draw a distinction. Those Dutch who are of "middle and high" origins are fine; they are willing to help and are satisfying to be with. But some, though not all, those of lowly origins become of bad character when they arrive in the Indies and particularly become *gila hormat*, or "mad for deference."

There are various reasons for this. These Dutch are ignorant of the Indies. They know only servants who cheat them. But it is also a condition that arises because Javanese are afraid and most do not know Dutch. Most Dutch use Melayu or low Javanese. They do not pay attention to the difference between low and high Javanese, which indicates differences in status; they respond to the deference they get in Javanese with low language or with coarse Dutch. They invite one to speak Dutch. That is fine. But readers should not speak in high language if they are not answered in kind.

Although the text is missing the page that concludes this argument, the point is clear. Dutch in the Indies are often false. They demand deference in Javanese and they do not repay it. They make a claim to high status when by birth they are lowly. They forget their origins and succumb to a certain obsession. In the most ordinary situations, even amongst themselves, Europeans in the Indies are revealed to be other than who they pose as being.

Javanese in Holland can wind up as Dutchmen without being aware of what is happening to them. And Dutch in the Indies pose as being other than who they are born. But this is not a simple parallelism. In both cases, the victims are Javanese. Sometimes without knowing it, Javanese pay respect to those who are not entitled to it and, moreover, to people who are incapable of paying the proper respect to Javanese. It is a linguistic matter. There is no ability to establish an adequate exchange. Instead, one side, Javanese, are compelled to speak in a way that elicits an inadequate response. No matter what they say, the Dutch with whom they speak return something that falls well short of what should be said. There is, properly speaking, no exchange. When, consistently, there is no exchange, Javanese cannot remain who they are in their relations with Europeans. It is not merely that they are maltreated but that they are unrecognized. It is the Europeans who are said to be obsessed, "mad about deference," but it is Javanese who feel themselves in a situation of madness; obliged to respond with words that have nothing to do with themselves, thus merely repeating formulas, becoming creatures whom they can only try and disown.

There is a picture of *gila hormat* (obsession about deference) in another novel by Mas Marco, one he published under the name Soemantri.[3] This novel, *Rasa Merdeka* (The Feeling of Freedom) was written in prison and was published in book form in 1924. It is the story of a man whose father is an official (*prijaji*) about to retire. His father and mother want their son to become a *prijaji* as well by first serving an apprenticeship. He, however, is reluctant. He resents the obsequiousness one must show to others, Javanese and Dutch, higher in rank. In particular, he resents a sort of duck walk (*djongkok*) as well as the respectful raising of the hands to the head (*sembah*) that often had to be repeated:

> "Be an apprentice? What, have to waddle like a frog, cringe and put on an agreeable face? It's true what they say [*kata orang*]; these days such customs aren't right. Even so I always see my father duck walk and *sembah* on and on whenever the boss asks [him something] or if he wants to ask the boss something. Can it be pleasant when someone is treated as. . . . . ." (6; ellipses in original)

Soedjanmo's father speaks to Controlleur Vlammenhart in the most respectful Javanese which is put into Melayu in the novel with a particularly comical effect: "Keroenia Kangdjeng Tuan atas hamba empoenja diri, soenggoeh aken berharga besar bagi hambamoe" (The blessings of your honorable lord on your slave are truely of the greatest value for your slave) (16). Or possibly Soedjanmo's father says this in Melayu; the language of the author, as in the other texts we have read, is treated as though it were transparent. In any case, the Javanese feel that the language that emerges out of their mouths is vacuous. And it is, moreover, precisely the words that, in another epoch, would do most to establish the identity of the speaker. Again, it is not merely that the speaker is obliged to give a false representation of himself. It is also the Dutch who do not understand that these words are merely formulas, inapplicable in the situation and therefore senseless. The Dutch official in this novel demands these respectful forms thinking they redound to his credit. But the character in the novel feels otherwise. They show not merely the official's cruelty and insensitivity, but his self-deception. There is merely an alternation of words; there is no exchange. It is Javanese who feel it to be so, not Dutch. The controlleur in this novel does not know what is happening around him. It is a version of the deafness of the Dutch, of their inability to hear what Javanese are really saying.

But this time, Dutch deafness to Javanese is part of the constitution of colonial hierarchy, an unjust constitution, to be sure, rather than itself a threat to hierarchy. The initial assumption is that there is a single framework or ranking that comprehends both Java and Holland. But certain Dutch are dishonest. They assert they are from high social levels when they are not. In particular, such people demand respectful forms of address when they are not entitled to it. It is not a question of whether one uses respectful forms but whether they are used properly. In Javanese, the giving of deference establishes a place for the speaker which, although it may indicate his inferiority in rank, shows that he is a person who knows how to speak properly and is therefore of value. Speech and political hierarchy are bound together so that the proper operation of the first ensures the second. It is this principle that is upset when respectful forms are required when they are improper. Improper speech does not undo hierarchy, but it makes speakers want to flee.

Soedjanmo, the protagonist of *Rasa Merdeka*, tries to do as his father wishes. He consents to taking a position with Controlleur Vlammenhart. Soon, he speaks and acts in the same way as his father. Hearing that he is accepted as an apprentice, he feels that "From that time he will be bound by regulations and customs that make his freedom as a human disappear" (19). Nevertheless, he accepts the position and because of his intelligence he is soon the most skilled of all the apprentices. He is unhappy. He is confronted with Tuan Vlammenhart, whose approval and disapproval depends on whether his employees cringe before him.

> Tuan Vlammenhart himself loved to see his employees creep in front of him, even if they were only bringing a letter or just doing their job. . . . Whenever Tuan Vlammenhart asked his apprentices anything at all they had to squat and come, offering *sembah* and if they did not, of course they got a sour face. (20)

In time, Soedjanmo can no longer tolerate this. "Now its been six months that I've tortured my thoughts following the wishes of my father" he says to himself. He grows thin because, finding no way out, "his brain is disturbed [*menggangoe otaknja*]." He is sorry for his father but he wants to flee. He thinks he might not be able to provide for himself if he leaves. But at that point he thinks what "nobility" (*moelia*) means. It is nothing else than "freedom to desire and freedom to do" (*meredeka boeat berkehendak dan merdeka bagi berboeat*) (22).

At this point, exiting from hierarchical position, Soedjanmo discovers "freedom," which is political freedom (*merdeka*) and is at the same time freedom of desire and freedom of action. Freedom in its various dimensions is then a release. He is now free to want what he might never have imagined wanting. His action is not understandable to his father, who tells him he thinks like an infant. He is himself unclear about what he wants:

> Apparently Soedjanmo had the seeds of the opinions that are carried by the stream of the era of progress, but he himself did not understand why he had these opinions, because the "foundation of freedom" [*dasar merdeka*] that blossomed in his heart had not yet opened or been cultivated by him. It was only that he was not happy to see the old ways that were still used in an era that had changed [era of progress], and he could not bear to see the human poverty that he looked at everyday though he himself did not understand the sources and reasons for that poverty and the general suffering at that time. (5)

Soedjanmo knows he is unhappy and he knows why: We have seen the reasons in the description of his father and Tuan Vlammenhart. He knows "the old ways" will not do. But he does not yet know what else there might be. The "foundation of freedom" was there, but only the foundation. In the mixed metaphor of Mas Marco, the foundation had not yet "blossomed," thus the objects, programs, and thinking that accompany freedom remained unknown. What he was sure of was that deference was wrong and that he wanted something, something which in this passage he sees is lacking in the lives of the poor; thus, he wants something for others, but also something for himself. First, he wants release from an unbearable situation and beyond that, the discovery of what it is that he wants. Soedjanmo feels freedom before he knows its contents. What he wants could be anything.

The possibility of wanting anything, thus the discovery of desire, and the political possibility of freedom are tied in the first place to an interethnic situation, to the communication that pertains between groups and that, as we have seen, distorts true hierarchy. But this interethnic communication passes as well through the family. In both the novels of Mas Marco's that we have discussed, the father is the conduit of Dutch influence. Even speaking his "own" language or languages, he betrays something foreign in his speech. It is after the father's authority is shown to be foreign that "the feeling of freedom" arises in *Rasa Merdeka*. In *Student Hidjau*, desire and freedom are not equated. But there remains the linkage between foreign-inflected speech and the opening of desire. In *Student Hidjau*, Hidjau gets what he did not know he wanted as a result of following his father's wishes. But the father's sentiments and the very basis of his authority, in so far as it depends on connection to the Dutch, is wrong. The lack of effect of authority in turn is connected to its foreignness and is followed by the opening of desire.

In one way or another, Mas Marco ties together the discovery of desire itself, that is, the possibility of wanting anything, with the misworking of authority because it is inflected with foreignness. But the foreignness of authority is discovered not through the strangeness of what it commands but through the languages it uses. It is hearing one language inside the other, Dutch in Malay or Dutch in Javanese in one case and the making foreign of Malay and/or Javanese by Dutch command in the other that reveals authority to be alien.

Against the alien quality of the language that governs hierarchy, there is, in *Rasa Merdeka*, a communication that seems to come directly to the new nationalist. Soedjanmo sees the faults of his father easily enough. For instance: "someone old-fashioned [*kolot*] like that never thought beyond what he could see, to the point where of course it would not be easy to change his thinking to follow the new thought that was occurring from day to day" (7). His parents are excused because they are old and brought up in different times. But he, Soedjanmo, feels that new ideas are arising around him. These new ideas are never specified; they are simply in the air. "Apparently Soedjanmo had the seeds of the opinions that are carried by the stream of the era of progress, but he himself did not understand why he had these opinions, because the 'foundation of freedom' . . . had not yet opened." His new ideas are not attributed to an particular agency beyond the "era of progress," or to the "new ideas arising everyday," or to 'what people say."

The narrator finds it unproblematic that one living at that time would pick up such ideas and it is never considered that anyone young might reject them. Soedjanmo ponders his situation and he resolves it as the result of an act of hearing:

> "It felt as though someone said to him, 'fear is evil' [*ketakoetan, itoe kedjahatan*]." He was shocked because the voice came from his own heart and with it, the difficulties of thinking he had just experienced were over." (22)

The voice of nationalism speaks so directly that it speaks in his own voice. At the same time, what it says is what is being said. It announces that Soedjanmo desires but, the narrator tells us, he does not yet know what he wants. He hears something that sets him on his way. But he leaves and joins the nationalist movement precisely to find out what he wants. Somebody knows him better than he knows himself. It is no one Dutch and it is not his father.

In *Rasa Merdeka*, there is a picture of a public meeting or *vergadering*. It occurs after the character Soedjanmo has decided not to follow his father in a career as an official. He goes to the city and there is taken to a political rally. The speaker, Soedarmo, talks about charges that "internationalism" means "selling the fatherland into the hands of other races" (77). This, he explains, is not the case. The problem is international capital. It has forced its way into villages, making it impossible for many peasants any longer to own their lands. They are "free" (*merdeka*) meaning that they own nothing. They come to the city to be laborors. Even the great wall of China could not keep out the capitalists. Today there are only two groups—those with capital and laborers. As Soedarmo speaks

> The people listening almost did not move or make a sound so that Soedarmo's clear voice resonated in their ears [*terdenger dengen djeli-djeli sekali*]. Only when Soedarmo was finished speaking did people move and clap vociferously, showing they really agreed with the explanation of internationalism that had just been given. (81)

The audience remains nearly motionless until the end. Soedjanmo also is fascinated:

Soedjanmo too all this while listened so intently he did not blink an eye. He did not forget to use his pencil to make notes of Soedarmo's very important presentation in a notebook.

And so too several newspaper correspondents who were present while Soedarmo made his presentation. They wiggled their pencils so fast it seemed as though fire would sprout from the ends of their pencils.

After the speech, various people raise objections. Mohamad Abdulgani says that

> "If there are those who become poor and those who become rich its because of what they do themselves. They are poor because they are spendthrifts, while those who become rich do so because they are capable of gathering wealth." (The *vergadering* stirs.) (83)

The audience is unanimous and all in favor of Soedarmo. When Soedarmo answers Mohamad Abdulgani, he returns to his seat with an untroubled expression on his face. Abdulgani, however, "could not move because he could not answer."

The audience here, played off against the unfortunate Mohamad Abdulgani, is treated as an undivided entity. It has only one reaction and its reaction is the measure not only of the effectiveness of the speech but of its truth.[4] Their judgment is conveyed first by their attentiveness to what is said and then by their enthusiasm afterwards. They "clap vociferously." But their stronger reactions are reserved for the debate that follows the speech. The audience is

> loud with cheers because Abdulgani could not reply. The noise of yelling was so loud it seemed it would make the walls of the building collapse. (89)

Identification with the speaker is unanimous with the result that the arousal of the audience only confirms the truth of the nationalist speech. What we have here is the *vergadering* seen from the point of view of the speaker, the author himself being a nationalist publicist. The stimulation of the audience at this point brings no danger of division. At the same time, it is a public audience, an anonymous one, rather than the Javanese public that frequents the theater and knows everyone else in the audience. We are at the moment of transformation of the audience at the time this novel was written.

If there is no danger of creating division, there is, however, another effect created. Someone else besides Mohamad Abdulgani speaks after Soedarmo. It is the peasant Sariman:

> He wore a torn shirt with a sarong hitched way up and oversized short pants. His turban was merely wrapped [perhaps rather than tied in the fashion of a Javanese

belangkon] a sign that he was a villager without much understanding due to lack of education.

He spoke in an amusing Javanese dialect, to the point where every word made people break out in laughter.

"*Blegandering*!" [rather than *vergadering*] Sariman said first, fixing his turban, which had come undone. "I am from the village and not good at speaking. But because I am so happy and agree hearing the talk of this here tuan, I got the itch to talk too." (84 f.)

Sariman, saying, "because I am so happy and agree hearing the talk of this here tuan, I got the itch to talk too," examplifies the arousal of the audience. But in him the effect goes beyond approving cheers and applause. He not only agrees with the speaker, the stimulation of the speech makes him also want to speak. This amateurism is pictured also in a novel we will speak of later, *Tan Malaka di Medan*. Seeing or hearing something agreeable, one wants to reproduce the action that caused it. In the frenzy of his identification with the speaker, Sariman's turban comes undone. He continues:

"In short because I cannot talk much I. . . . . . .I. . . . . agreee. . . . . . . with that there talk. Enough, because I myself many times saw, its clear, about that there people leaving my village; and many even signed up to go to Deli."

"In short, I agree with this here blegandring."

When he finished with this words, which came out with such difficulty, Sariman descended from the podium with a comical walk. The noise in the *vergadering* was overwhelming as people clapped and cheered and roared with laughter, they were so tickled. (85; ellipses in original)

Suppose we take his first sentence seriously: because he cannot talk much he agrees with the speaker. Having no means of expression of his own, he takes the speaker's words as his own. As he says, that is "enough." Meaning he need not say more; the speaker has already said it. But he wants to add something. He saw what the speaker was talking about. Having taken the speaker's words as his own, it is left for him to agree with their contents; to find something in himself that matches what the speaker said. Then he tries to say himself what the speaker said and what he also wants to say.

The speaker has roused in him the desire to speak. He lacks the speaker's words. They are foreign to him. But nonetheless they make him feel that he has already seen what the words convey. Certain words have reached him, which are alien but which arouse a feeling of déjà vu. Sariman, we are told, speaks "an amusing Javanese dialect." When he tries to put what he has heard into his own words, in the dialect of his village, it is more than he can manage. Not only the speaker's words are foreign to him; his own words are as well. Of course, in the village he can speak. In front of the speaker, trying to say what he means, he cannot. He is estranged from not only the speaker's words but from his own.

Sariman is not entirely different from Soedjanmo, who also knows that he wants something but does not know what it is. Soedjanmo, too, finds what he did not previously know he wanted to say in the *vergadering* where he furiously notes down the speaker's words. Soedjanmo has left home, too. If, unlike Hidjau, he is still in the Indies, he is nonetheless addressed in an alien tongue; not the language of his parents but the language, new to him, of nationalism. As with Sariman, he is pleased and excited by what he hears. There is a sense that these two characters, members of the audience of the *vergadering*, find themselves someplace new and someplace alien. The alien for them is not what it was for Hidjau. It cannot be identified in ethnic terms. Its foreignness rests in the language of the *vergadering*. It is this foreignness that seems paradoxically to stimulate in them a feeling of already knowing what is being said, of having already experienced it. But this experience merely locates the alien within them. It is part of them, but it is strange. At this moment, the alien becomes no longer a matter of different ethnicities, different nations, different linguistic codes. It is inherent in nationalism itself. At this point, one has the bizarre condition that the nationalism common to Indonesians rests in the recognition that they encompass something foreign in common. Therefore, they find themselves in a foreign scene, even if it is Java and they are Javanese. It is no longer necessary to leave their native place to be in a foreign country.

These members of the *vergadering* audience have become nationalists through a process of recognition. They recognize the accuracy of what the speaker says, and they see that they knew it already without being able to say it. They recognize the foreign in them. This foreignness is first of all the language of the speaker. This language, considered as a code, is one that Soedjanmo shares with the speaker. Soedjanmo is not limited by being able only to speak a village dialect. But it is still foreign to him in the sense that he never before heard such words. If they correspond to what he "feels," as in "the feeling of freedom," it is still the case that he had no language for his feelings before; he needed to learn a foreign tongue. Soedjanmo and Sariman here do the recognizing. But it is also true that the speaker recognizes them. His words reach them. When they do, these members of the audience speak and write. They make the speaker's words their own. But these words are meant for others. Sariman speaks to the meeting and particularly to the speaker when he says that he is in agreement. Soedjanmo's notes are meant to be read by him later in order that he can more fully understand them. They remain the speaker's words. Soedjanmo will take them in in the deferred presense of their originator. When Soedjanmo understands, it will be at the point where he feels these words fully present to himself. Here we can see that the speaker recognizes him, even if at a distance.

Soedjanmo will not encapsulate his knowledge. He will be a nationalist capable of speaking like a nationalist. Like Hidjau, he will find himself in a new scene; and like Hidjau, he will discover that he can belong there. But he will not flee back home, feeling that he has left himself behind. Hidjau might not either had he not looked at Lili Green through opera glasses. Through the opera glasses he saw what he had already seen magnified and close up. The déjà vu had a reality stronger than the initial experience. Events in Holland confirmed that he himself was part of that second scene. Precisely what he feared was being at home in the uncanny.

When it is nationalized, the fetish retains the foreign. But somehow the uncanny was concealed and thus neutralized, one dares say "naturalized," in the process of recognition. The political possibilities are obvious, since the person who finds a surprising element in himself needs the political leader to assure him that he really belongs to the nation; that what he feels to be foreign is knowable and sayable. He need not flee back home. This is the beginning of the nationalist hierarchy, a hierarchy that starts to replace the Dutch version even before the later has been dismantled.[5]

CHAPTER FIVE

Scandal, Women, Authors, and Sino-Malay Nationalism

CHINESE WRITERS of Melayu should have much of the credit for the establishment of popular writing. Fiction in the Indies written by Indos, and often serialized in newspapers, did not have anything like the circulation of Chinese-written stories. Achmad Adam estimates that vernacular papers, before Chinese established their own, only had circulations in the hundreds.[1] This increased into the thousands. The popularity of Melayu stories, before this, was owed more to their performance on the stage than to reading.

As is well known, Chinese fiction developed alongside Chinese nationalism. For this reason, we must relate some of the history of this movement. Chinese nationalism developed radidly after the turn of the century. One might say that before that time there was no need for it if nationalism here means a reflection on group identity and self-consciousness about one's "own" institutions. There were Chinese in the archipelago before there were Dutch. But the institutions of colonialism were, as usual, the ones that gave rise to nationalism. Before the turn of the century, the most important Chinese political and economic institutions rested on their relations with the Dutch. In particular, a system of revenue farming gave an important place to certain Chinese. Chinese bought the rights to monopolize certain goods, especially opium, in particular areas from the Dutch. These concessions made some Chinese wealthy. They also brought with it freedom from the pass laws that governed transit through the Indies for non-Europeans. They, or Chinese connected with them, could sell other goods as well in the hinterlands. Those who held revenue concessions were usually chosen by the Dutch to be the head of the Chinese community, that is, to be responsible for the maintenance of order in their communities.[2]

With the economic crises of the middle 1880s and with Dutch reformism, certain monopolies were no longer allowed the Chinese. At the same time, the special access to Dutch power and other privileges allowed Chinese officers were curtailed. Lea Williams points out that the system of access to power was never representative and this did not matter.[3] But when access to colonial authority was blocked and when these same officers were no longer holders of concessions, a demand for representative institutions began that resulted primarily in the foundation of schools.

One senses that there was an unproblematic "Chinese" identity before the end of the nineteenth century. There was no need to question who one was in relation to the economy and to authority, and there was no serious attempt to do so. But the beginnings of "Chinese" nationalism left open only certain possibilities for development. Chinese nationalism in the Indies predated the Chinese revolution of 1911, but neither before nor after is there a Chinese Zionism. Certain Chinese returned to China, of course, but the path of Indies Chinese nationalism was not to see in "China" a place where, uniquely, Chinese identity could be developed. At the same time, Chinese in the Indies naturally enough had adapted themselves in important ways to life, particularly Javanese life, without becoming "Javanese" but rather "Indies Chinese." In addition, they tended to adopt Western ways available to them through the market. Further, the multiplicity of Chinese languages and the process of local adaptation, the place early taken by Chinese in Melayu publishing, all made Melayu the major language of Chinese nationalism.[4]

Chinese, many of whom were brought to the Indies as laborers, had established themselves in the market early on. But the market has various functions. The wealth that some Chinese were fortunate enough to gain through the concessions they bought from the colonial government was transformed into social position by the same government when it appointed them captain or lieutenant of local Chinese. These offices structured the Chinese community. The Dutch appointed the wealthiest people as head of their communities, thinking, says Williams, that "they would be the most respected." But it seems not simply that wealth was respected but that the Dutch did much to make it respectable. The end of concessions was important because it brought with it the weakening of the framework of the Chinese communities. The community officers, Lea Williams points out, served the interests of the Dutch by passing on colonial orders and being sources of information for the government. It is not surprising that with the beginning of nationalist feelings, this structure was felt to be unrepresentative. Officers lost their prestige if they were not also nationalists.

Williams points out that the institution of Chinese officers lasted, unquestioned, for centuries and that suddenly it was found "unrepresentative." Instead of having a privileged relation to colonial authority, officers became mere subordinates of the Dutch. Chinese were, in a sense, pushed out of their place within the colonial framework. Nationalists wanted this place back. In particular, they demanded that the privileges that had been allowed officers of the community be made available to all Chinese. In the event, they had to restructure their community, making it less dependent on ties to colonial authority. In their situation, they could not demand independence, but they needed to redefine their relation to themselves and to their neighbors. The market remained the most important arena for

Chinese economic activity. And Melayu, the lingua franca, was the language available to them for "assimilation." Had Chinese abandoned Melayu for Chinese or for Dutch or Javanese, everything after would have been different for them. It would have meant becoming wealthy and becoming Dutch, or attempting to do so, at the same time. Instead, they became "modern" and "Chinese" just at the moment when "Chinese" was a difficult category. The market itself, somehow, had to provide not only wealth but also a means for its validation. This left them with the difficulty of developing a "national" identity in a place that was not "Chinese" culturally, politically, or geographically, within an institution—the market—whose characteristic it is to mediate between different peoples, and with a language—the lingua franca—that did the same.

In the early writings of Chinese, the market, taken in the largest sense, instead of being a place where one could establish oneself, is a source of trouble. For instance, *The Flirtatious Girl, or The Influence of Money* by Venus,[5] was written, according to the subtitle, as a warning to those obsessed with money (*mata doewitan*). The parents of a girl marry their first daughter to a man because he is rich. They do not care that he is a womanizer. Their second daughter shares her parents' greed for money. She, the "Flirtatious Girl" of the title, uses her seductive talents to gain a rich man. She finds one, but with the same descent name (*she*) as hers. Her father changes his name so that she can have a rich husband. But he is disgraced in the end. He is "ashamed to meet people." He has lost his name and gained nothing that matters. At the same time, the husband of his first daughter leaves her, as could have been expected. Even though she is attractive, men will have nothing to do with her because they know that her parents are avaricious (*mata doewitan*). What Venus imagines is how it is that following economic interests one forgets everything else and ends in ruin. The family's imaginings, their ambition, has led to failure and they are exposed to public view. When economic interests take hold, one sees not rationality but blindness.[6] Unable to see how they should behave, unheeding of other's perceptions of them, people behave incorrectly. When economic and psychological interests are merged, the second encompassing the first, when one wants too much money, there is financial and moral disaster.

There are three elements in the stories of this period that are inventively combined and recombined: correct familial sentiment, love, and desire for wealth. The last is posed against the first two, but the first two are sometimes posed against each other. "Love" is an ambiguous category; when it disrupts the family it is not *cinta* (love) but simple desire. When money is the issue between lovers, one of them has *cinta* and the other is false. But there is always a close relation between the two and the result is threatening to the family. In the typical story, familial sentiments that should govern the welfare of the family are replaced by insatiable desire for gain. The very basis of social order, the sentiments of kinship and loyalty that assure continuity between generations, are threatened. "Chinese" identity, centered as it is on familial piety, is menaced.

But just why this should be so is not immediately apparent. The curious feature of stories such as *The Flirtatious Girl, or The Influence of Money* is not that there is an exchange of women for money but that the story, from the title onwards, is conceived that way. A father who sought a rich husband for his daughter in another time might have been thought to be looking out for her welfare. When this literature comes into existence, it is with stories that show such exchange is suspicious. The father, instead of providing for his daughter, is full of inappropriate desire.

Furthermore, in the stories of these authors, women are presented differently. The *njai*, who in Indo stories and in some Dutch accounts, is a domestic figure, begins to look like a prostitute. And the prostitute herself becomes a center of attention. The most famous prostitute of the day, Fientje de Feniks, became so after her murder. Neither she nor the man who killed her was Chinese. However, the story, which remained well known for decades, was told most strongly by a Chinese writer, Tan Boen Kim.[7] I use it here to show how an interest shared by various groups of the plural society was considered by him. In the view of Tan Boen Kim, the attraction of Fientje de Feniks was her ability to appear as a member of any of the prominent nationalities of the Indies:

> From the way she tied up her hair, this young *nona* looked like someone of Dutch descent, but when she wore [certain hair ornaments and kinds of dress], this girl looked like a native of Batavia rather than a European. (1)

Later, she is mistaken for a Chinese. Whomever a man wants, she is it. As Ann Stoler points out, women cross the boundaries of the plural society.[8] But one has to add that they do so in exchange for money. The equivalence between women and money is as strong as it could be in Tan Boen Kim's description. "Fientje de Feniks" is a figure not merely of a desirable woman, but of a woman who fills all (male) desires. She is not someone in particular, but the possibility of the satisfaction of desire in general. She is an analogue to money in its generalized capacity to buy anything, and thus to satisfy any want. Money has no use in itself; it is a means to obtain what one can consume. In its generalized form, it can stand for anything one can imagine wanting. It is a substitute for what one wants when one thinks one knows what in particular one wants. Before that point, as a substitute, it is a focus of desire in general. The father of the flirtatious girl, when he looks for a wealthy husband, is guilty of wanting. Instead of being the father who provides for his daughter, he is a father who sees in her a means to satisfy himself. He acts according to desire when he should act out of obligation. Again, much of what he does might have been thought correct in another time. Phantasms of the father's desire invade scenarios that previously were unthreatening.

Under the pressure of this anxiety, perhaps out of repugnance of *mata doewitan* (avarice), one could turn against wealth itself. This was not a real possibility for those deeply engaged in the market. The problem in any case was not involvement in the market as such; that had been true for a long while. The difficulty was that, when wealth seemed to have no social purpose, it seemed put to bad purposes. It lost its specific raison d'être, to support the community as a whole, by assuring connections to power.[9] Now, wealth, having no use, was thought to stimulate transgressive impulses. It caused people to imagine too many possibilities.

It was too late to assert that people should not imagine and be as they used to be. This left the possibility of reappropriating wealth to put it in a social context. Precisely the equation between sexual desire and desire for money seemed to make this possible. One could have all one wanted in the form of a woman. And this would be a domesticating trend, provided that somehow the woman was both everything one wanted and yet still herself domestic. She had to be at once not a prostitute but a wife and also the object of desire. This means that the woman had to be modernized, she had to be the object of desire in a context in which who one was was defined by one's relation to desire. And yet desire had to be tamed. The contradiction did not matter so long as one was blind to it.

In a much later novel, *My Dream House* by Liem Liang Hoo,[10] a man called Hok Kie imagines marriage. His enthusiasm for his wife is inseparable from the charms of the market. He will return home from work, greeted by his wife who has prepared fresh clothes and a bath for him. The house will have a *Gramafoon* in the corner so that they can listen to music. He will dress his wife in European clothes so that she will look "like a picture painted by an excellent painter" (27). He finds a woman he thinks will satisfy his dreams. On their honeymoon, they stay at the Hotel Hollywood whose floors are made

> from glistening marble tiles so shiny that anyone who passes by stops to look at them, they are so glossy, like mirrors.

The windows have "Parisian embroidery."

> It is evident that this is the best hotel, the most modern in the Dutch East Indies. To the point that guests who stay there feel like they are in a royal palace. (61)

In this ambience, his wife's beauty is enhanced by recent technology:

> The rays of the Electric lamp were enough to give her beauty even greater radiance.

At the hotel, Hok Kie is more than ever attracted to his wife. Her fine pale skin, her silk blouse, her movements, all make Hok Kie's heart beat:

> Looking like that made her face seem more noble, like a statue made out of marble. (64)

This is perhaps the apex of his attraction for her. Her face is like a statue's. Not a particular statue, but not just any statue either: one made out of marble. At the height of her attractiveness, something blank appears, the material of the statue, the marble (*marmer*), itself. The word is Dutch and it recalls the other time it is used, namely for the tiles of the Hotel Hollywood.

Mary, dressed in European clothes, slim, and petite, is "even more achieved [*tertjipta*]." Mary is more what she is, more herself, dressed in European clothes than she is dressed like a Chinese. She is not less Chinese for that. It is simply that the fulfillment of herself comes when she is adorned by what the market has to offer. She is "even more achieved, like a picture painted by a good painter" (27). Again, it is not a particular painting he compares her to but merely "a painting," any painting, so long as it is by "a good painter," that is, the best that one could afford.

Mary is associated with the market and with technology, electric light, and the movies. It is of course the same in the opening passages when, before Mary, his wife, has been mentioned, he dreams of having a wife. There will be, we have already seen, a *Gramafoon* in the corner.

> It won't be quiet like now, when I dream of having a wife. Every afternoon without stopping I will play records, His Master's Voice, Miss Riboet and Odeon while my wife sits in the corner sewing or reading the paper. (24–25)

They will listen to music. It will not be quiet, but Mary in this scene never speaks. What replaces her voice, what fills the void in his life, is His Master's Voice, Miss Riboet and Odeon, in a mixture of trademarks and singers' names. "Mary" is someone who, when he invokes her, makes him think of the transmissions of words and things from different languages and different places, which somehow she makes available to him. Through his wife, the modern world of communications technology speaks.

When Mary speaks in her own voice, she does not tell him what he wants to hear. She tells him she loves someone else. His dream is just a dream it would seem. But this is merely the chance for him to be a "gentleman" (in English), to fill a role out of modernity. Mary tells him that she loves another, that she has not married out of love but out of obligation to her parents, and that love (*cinta*) "is more powerful than anything in the world" (67). Weeping, she says, "I . . . I . . . do not love you." This forces him to consider:

The blood of a gentleman which still flowed through his body led him to noble feelings. He could not make a firm decision quickly. He could not chase out this woman who did not love him. He did not have the courage to do that because he knew that if he did so it caused people to lose faith in themselves as men. He could kill her, but even though this woman had spoiled his good fortune, he did not have the heart to murder her. It was because he did not want people to say that he was a murderer of a woman he was tired of [*satoe pemboenoe dari satoe prampoean jang lama*]. What was left? Divorce? Mhh, this would be difficult. . . . [*sic*] even though the wife was worthless and even though she had destroyed his hopes he did not have the courage to divorce her because he could not stand the shame.

And so what was left? There was no other way better than not using force and (not) violating someone's wishes. (69–70)

It is again shame, what people will think, that makes him refuse to be violent. The only thing left is to follow her wishes. This is *sifat gentleman* (the character of a gentleman).

Sifat gentleman is what appeals to Mary in the end. She goes to her lover. He, however, explains to her the nobility of her husband's character:

"Your husband has to be praised; he is wise and has noble thoughts. Remember Mary, if you had gotten a man who was cruel and bigoted (*cupat*) it is certain you would have been destroyed or at least sent to another world. Are you willing to ruin a man's good fortune?" (85)

If he were otherwise, not *sifat gentleman*, she would be dead. She is still alive; therefore she owes her life to him. His noblility of character consists in renouncing his urge to murder (and loading her with guilt). His murderous urge comes from having his desire raised and then thwarted. *Sifat gentleman* means giving up violence. Giving it up but in return being recognized by the woman for what he has renounced.

Mary sees what Hok Kie could be but is not. In her eyes, he is not only innocent he is someone capable of being guilty. He could be guilty of two things: He could be a murderer when it seemed he could no longer have what he wanted; but he could also be a traditionalist, insisting on having what he wanted by right of customary marriage arrangements. These are both ways of mastering Mary, of having her when she seems unavailable. What would make him a criminal is taking by force what the market lures him into wanting. But what makes him innocent is playing the "gentleman," that is, playing the role that is appropriate to guests of the Hotel Hollywood. Mary is not responsible for Hok Kie wanting to be a gentleman; rather, Hok Kie wants Mary in order to be a part of that world. She gives him the chance to be not by recognizing in him that he inherently belongs there but that he could very well not be the sort of guest the Hotel Hollywood would like to have.

Mary returns to Hok Kie, recognizing his value as a husband, because she sees he has a possibility in himself that he gives up. This is, of course, quite different from being taken for what one appears to be in the mirrors of the Hotel. This reversal is necessary once it seems possible to simply buy one's way into the modern world. The possibility of having everything that one wants leads to scenes of depravity such as we find in *The Flirtatious Girl, or The Influence of Money*. When the girl is no longer flirtatious (but is still seductive but loves her husband because he could murder her), it seems that the difficulty of having desire and limiting it at the same time is solved, at least in a certain manner.[11]

Indonesian-Chinese writers, or at least some such as Liem Liang Hoo, put money to use, building a middle-class ideal of life in the market and life at home. In building this version of the modern woman, they depend on showing jealousies and their mastery. And this in turn depends, as always, on the complications of triangles. The triangles are often expanded to include not merely three lovers but an amorphous "everyone," or public, who knew what was going on: "It was because he did not want people to say that he was a murderer. . . ." thinks Hok Kie when he is wants to kill his wife. Shame and an amorphous everyone play a role in jealousy early in Sino-Malay writings. For instance, Fientje de Feniks is the prostitute who appeared in whatever ethnic identity men found most appealing.[12] Fientje is murdered by an ex-lover, the notorious Brinkman. Brinkman wins her away from a previous lover, but then he loses interest in her:

> In fact Brinkman loved Fientje only at the beginning, and as time went on got bored with her. This is because Brinkman only loved Fientje for her prettiness while Fientje, for her part, liked him only for his capacity to spend. (17)

Here we have a picture of the market at work: She loves him for his money and he loves her for her looks. They get along well, and then interest fades. In the normal course of affairs, perhaps there would have been no more to the story. But Brinkman and Fientje are the subject of much gossip in the bordellos and outside them as well. The result is that their problem is magnified. "That's the way it is with idle people; they usually like to talk about others. Small problems are made large" (20). A friend of Brinkman's, an Englishman called "Rymond" [*sic*] reports to him that he has seen Fientje de Feniks out with another man. This infuriates Brinkman and leads to her murder.

The cause of the murder is that Brinkman becomes jealous, but it needs gossip to make him act. Tan Boen Kim is precise about this, and he insists that Brinkman found out about Fintje's other interests through an intermediary. The connection between sexuality and an exactly pictured circuit of gossip is made in other ways. The madame of the bordello, herself a former prostitute, is said to be a police informer, for instance. This connection between jealousy and gossip is repeated in works by other authors.

The role of gossip in producing jealousy and murder is reversed from the story of Hok Kie and Mary. There, it is precisely remembering what everyone will say that prevents Hok Kie from killing his wife. It is not enough, it seems, simply to consider the changes in conceptions of women; one must also see how the place of "everyone" altered over a few decades. There is novel that lets us see this change in process. In 1918, a pseudonymous author who called himself "Chabanneau" published a book called *Secrets of Bandung, or a Love which Transgressed Chinese Custom: A Story that Actually Occurred in the City of Bandung, ending in the Year 1917*.[13] The first chapter is entitled "Everywhere People Are Whispering" and the first sentence, part of an epigraph, is "Secrets cannot be kept." The chapter pictures the spread of gossip on the street. People are talking about a scandal that forms the substance of the story.

What people are said to be whispering about is this: Hilda, daughter of Tan Djia Goan, has fallen in love with Tan Tjin Hiauw, who is unsuitable because he is a member of the same *she*, the same descent group. Hilda's father, being someone who "likes progress," sent Hilda to a missionary school where she took the name Hilda.

> Hilda had a European-style education and her father gave her a lot of leeway to mix with European girls and to read all sorts of Western books and stories. Hilda fell into the abyss of love (*cinta*) and the one she loved was, in fact, Tan Tjin Hiauw who was from the same *she*. (43)

It seems as though this is the story of an educated girl whose European books and friends lead her to un-Chinese ways. It is more complicated, however. Tan Tjin Hiauw, whom she marries in the end, wants her not out of love but for her money. For most of the time he courts her, he keeps a prostitute on the side. Hilda, after much effort, escapes her father, who has kept her under watch, to run off with Tan Tjin Hiauw. Tan Tjin Hiauw gets Hilda, but he does not get her money, as her father, furious with his daughter, settles that on a relative outside the immediate family.

The setting of the story is "everyone is talking." The talk of everyone gives way to various descriptions of the language and languages that circulate between Hilda, her suitors, their intermediaries, and those who look on. In this novel, language is shown to be at the very core of the relation of the lovers as well. One can say that what makes Hilda desirable to Tan Tjin Hiauw is her money. But what makes her available to him in the story is her education. Reading and speaking in foreign languages, we are told, is what makes her susceptible to an illicit relation. This is the point at which the questions of money and of the widening of desire slide over into a question of language—or, rather, of languages—and at the same time, of gossip and the fear of gossip. For instance, Tan Tjin Hiauw meets Hilda after school and they take walks in the park. When she does not show up, he writes her love letters. These letters, we are told, are in the hands of the author. They were written in Dutch:

> These letters, though they were not too long, softened Hilda's heart; these letters, now in my hands, were written in Dutch and went something like this: (70)

The letters, before reaching "Chabanneau," fall into the hands of Hilda's father, who is furious and beats her and, by mistake, even beats her mother when she gets in the way.

Love letters, are, of course, no surprise in novels. But these letters are perhaps a bit unusual for two reasons. First, they are translations, being written in Dutch and appearing in the novel in Melayu. Second, when a question of translation arises in the story, there is also a case of transgression. I will give examples. Tan Tjin Hiauw, Hilda's lover, has a friend, Tan Bo Hok, who is also his business associate. The two, with Thio Hoek San, are partners in the Vertaal Bureau Trio (The Trio Translation Bureau). It is here that Tan Tjin Hiauw often brings his prostitute and mistress, Nji Enon (60). Hilda and Tan Tjin Hiauw become lovers via an exchange of books. Hilda was at school and told her friend Margaretha that she, Hilda, regretted that Tan Tjin Hiauw was the same *she* as she, Hilda. Hilda says to her friend, "'If he weren't from the Tan *she* I really would marry him'"(92). When Margaretha Thio heard this she "did not stay silent" (97), but told Thio Tjom Swe, who told a friend who was a friend of Tan Tjin Hiauw, who told Tan. The emphasized figure in this chain is Thio Tjom Swe, who is identified at length. Unlike other Chinese figures with Western education, he has not only taken a Western first name but also a Western family name. "Thio Tjom Swe was a Chinese who was recognized [in law] as Dutch and was now known as Theodicus de Bopro"(93). The reason, we are told, that Tan Tjom Swe got the legal standing of a Dutchman was so that he could enter a school that was closed to Chinese (93).

Once Tan Tjin Tiauw heard of Hilda's interest, the two began to exchange books. This is described in a conversation between students reported by the author:

> "First they started to exchange schoolbooks but after awhile it was any sort of books, no matter what kind. . . . This borrowing and lending of books went way past what anyone might have expected. Once, about March, 1914, Tan Tjin Hiauw got a book from Hilda with the title *Nana* written by Émile Zola, a famous French author. This book wasn't a schoolbook, as he thought it was. It was a dirty book (*boekoe tjaboel*), just as dirty as most of the books Émile Zola wrote."

"On the front page of this book, in Hilda's own writing, there was a line in Latin script in German which went this way, 'Zur andeken van deiner lieben Freundin,' meaning in Melayu something like, 'A souvenir from your sweet woman friend.' Not only was there that line in German, but there was a red ribbon in the book (red means love for Westerners) for a bookmark and on it is said, *ANDEKEN*, which in German means 'souvenir.'"

"Not only did they loan books to each other, but Hilda often wrote him secret letters." (93)

Hilda sends the book to Tan, where one might expect the converse. However, the point is that it is an exchange—of letters, books, of foreign languages—that culminates in either a French book in Melayu translation, or in Dutch translation, or in French, with a German inscription and a "Western" sign. It culminates, that is, in the words of the author, with the sending of a "dirty" book. The two of them exchange foreign languages at an accelerating pace, through the help of a person, Thio Tjom Swe/Theodicus de Bopro who has, in the interest of non-Chinese, non-Melayu learning, already become non-Chinese—and this ends in transgression.

Hilda and Tan Tjin Hiauw must keep their relation a secret. Their exchanges take place through intermediaries. This is even more the case once Hilda's father has discovered their connection and has isolated Hilda in a remote house where she is kept under surveillance. There is, in these scenes, an exchange of languages in which what is perhaps most important is the address: Will they reach their destination? Initially they do so only through one intermediary, who in himself represents a number of languages and with them a double identity, and a second, a Chinese who is a student at the "Hollandsch Chineesche School."

There is another exchange of letters that presents a different problem. A second man falls in love with Hilda. Lie Tok Sim also has a bad character:

Lie Tok Sim could be called a clever, shrewd fellow, bold and resolute.

He was more capable of wounding than of praising, better at insulting than at paying compliments. . . . Lie Tok Sim was well known for his spending and was never without pocket money. . . . When he was young, Lie Tok Sim studied at the Tiong Hoa Hwe Koan [nationalist Chinese organization] school but those sorts of studies did not suit him so he took private lessons in English.

. . . He made good progress in these two European languages [the other being Dutch] because he did not lack the courage, no matter who was involved, to speak Dutch or English, so in a short time he could be said to be competent. His skill in reading and speaking Chinese was quite superficial but in English he made good progress while in Dutch he wasn't bad. (107–108).

This view of Lie, giving his education only in terms of the languages he learned, is common to the description of the other characters as well. Their culture is not the substance of their studies, but rather the languages to which they have gained access. And their immersion in foreign languages is intricated in their love affairs. For instance, Hilda says of Tan Tjin Hiauw, that there can, in Bandoeng, be no one more talented since he only went to "elementary school [*sekolah Melayoe*]," but by sheer determination

> he became fluent in Dutch and got a diploma in bookkeeping (double entry), but he also understood English, French and German which he still studies today with a private teacher. (72)

She sees in him talent, which she equates with learning four foreign languages outside school and, a language of another sort, bookkeeping. If he sees money in her, she sees languages in him.

Lie Tok Sim, Hilda's second lover, writes to Hilda in English, which is paraphrased by the author who says that "if it were put into Melayu, it would sound more or less like this" and then translates a proverb, presumably "love is eternal" (*katjintaan ada saroepa barang jang tida bisa dibikin roesak*) (137). Hilda answers him in Melayu, saying she understands his letter, but that as she "is not skillful in writing or speaking English [she] will write what [she] wants to say in this language," the language being left unspecified (139). Hilda refuses Lie Tok Sim's advances and asks that her letter be burned (139–140). By the time he writes a third letter, Lie Tok Sim has reverted to Melayu, but he nonetheless continues to quote proverbs in English:

> "THINK BEFORE YOU ACT which means something like, BERPIKIR LEBI DOELOE SABLONNJA KAOE BERBOEAT!'" (143)

When she answers this letter, Hilda says she does not know Melayu very well because she usually speaks Dutch (145). Hilda remains the figure who either writes the letters or receives them, although eventually they end up in the possession of Chabanneau. Writing only passes through her, as it were; she does not retain it.

Hilda quotes Dutch to Lie Tok Sim, although he does not have much grasp of that language. Nonetheless, he reinterprets the proverb she quotes—*unbekend maakt onbemind*—by paraphrasing another proverb and by quoting yet another English proverb—"other men, other minds"— which he says he is sure she understands (148) and by quoting a verse of Longfellow. The verse, he writes, is "more or less like this":

> Not enjoyment and not sorrow,
> is our destined end or way;
> But to act, that each to-morrow
> Find us farther than to day. (149)

After telling her again he is sure she understands it, he says, "When I read your letters, I am struck by a *pantun*," a *pantun* being a Malay verse form

in which the first two lines contain words vaguely alluding, either by their
sense or their sounds, to the last two lines. Only the last two lines need to
have a determined syntax. Lines one and three rhyme as do lines two and
four:

> "Satoe, doea, tiga, ampat,
> Ampat, lima, anem toedjoe,
> Saja mentjari dikoeliling tempat,
> Nona sendiri jang saja penoedjoe (150)

> One, two, three, four,
> four, five, six, seven,
> I looked everywhere,
> It is you yourself I like.

Traditionally, *pantun* are recited in contests, usually at weddings by the
parties of the bride and groom. Each tries to answer the other in a more
devastating way until no response is possible. In this modernized version of
a *pantun* contest, what is at stake is the ability to control the meanings of
the other person. When he sends one of his final letters, Lie Tok Sim says
that he

> "prays to God the Almighty that by means of this letter I can awaken [your] heart
> *and silence all the sense and the sound of [your] letters that I have already re-
> ceived.*" (157; emphasis added)

He adds that he hopes Hilda will answer saying that he has "succeeded"
(157).

The stakes here are more radical than in the usual *pantun* contest. The
exchange of proverbs is designed to change the mind of the other party
and beyond that to negate, to make sure that the meanings and the sounds
of the second party's words are no longer valid. The aim is nothing less
than to eliminate the possibility not only of the other making sense except,
we will see, for the sense that Lie Tok Sim wants them to have. At that
point, Hilda would belong to Lie Tok Sim. He could replace whatever she
directed toward him with pleasant thoughts of his own. She would only be
able to say what it was that Lie Tok Sim wanted to hear. He would control
her language and her heart. Here is a version of the woman as a figure who
can satisfy any desire at all. But this story does not issue in her reversal into
someone who recognizes the restraint of the man.

Hilda does not give in to Lie Tok Sim, but the contest is not over. Hilda
requests that Lie Tok Sim burn her letters. Lie replies that he will not

> "because these letters soothe my heart which is now troubled. I feel very happy
> when I see [your] writing which is so valuable and so fine. All the more so if in
> the letters it is made clear that [you] will accept my love the Himalayas them-
> selves would not be as big as my heart." (157)

It would be better if Hilda would say what he, Lie, wants to hear. But if she will not, still, her handwriting reminds him of her and he likes that, even if the content is not agreeable. This amounts to saying that he will keep her letters with their disagreeable content and, looking at them, one no longer speaks of reading them, he will have the pleasure of thinking about her as he would like to think about her. Hilda, so long as he has her handwriting, will say what Lie wants her to say.

Hilda, meanwhile, insists that he return her letters. She is not afraid that either Tan Tjin Hiauw or her father will read the letters—the contents do not incriminate her. What is at stake for her is that her name will be carried places outside of her control. Thus, at the end of the book, well after she has gotten rid of Lie and after she has married Tan and had a child, Hilda still tries to get the letters back. She sends an intermediary to Singapore where Lie now works.

Hilda has sent Lie eight letters, most of the latter principally devoted to getting back the earlier letters. Lie tells Hilda's emissary he has gotten rid of them on the ship between Batavia and Singapore. In any case, Hilda need not worry, " 'except of course if Tan Tjin Hiauw loves you only for your money.' " Here would be a fitting end to a melodrama. Tan did not love Hilda; he loved only her money and, albeit in a somewhat obscure manner, their marriage ends for lack of his love. We would be back to a story moved between the poles of Chinese ways and love, complicated by questions of money. But this is not what happens.

Hilda is not worried about the reaction of her husband. Lie has said that someone has approached him to purchase the letters. But, of course, he refused. He will not say who it was.

> Hilda was not frightened of her husband but she was afraid now that the book, *Secrets of Bandoeng*, would be published. (This was on December 26, 1917, when only the first volume of *Secrets of Bandoeng* had been published.)
>   Lie Tok Sim told Hilda that all the letters had been thrown overboard from a ship and that she need not worry. (239)

Lie is shown by the author to lie. He did not destroy the letters; he sold them to the author. Chabanneau himself has them. Of course, Chabanneau has said this earlier when quoting them: "I copied all of the letters without changing a word, without changing a single letter except for the names of the people"(138).

Hilda's wish, that her traces be eliminated, and Tan's, that he possess them to remind him of her no matter what they say, are denied. Hilda is mastered not by herself, not by Tan, not by Lie, and not by her father. She is not even mastered by fate. She is not shown, for instance, to suffer from the consequences of breaking Chinese custom; nor does she suffer from having her love for someone be returned by an interest not in her but in her money. These themes simply are left to dangle. It is true that she is blamed for her desire. Several times we are told that a young girl's desire cannot be controlled. But she wins for herself what she wants. Even this is not celebrated as step in emancipation. Rather, Hilda is mastered by the author when he publishes her letters. We have the assertion of the author against that of his chief character. His assertion is that he and not Hilda controls Hilda's words.

Chabanneau's story seems to be based on historical events. But how hallucinatory the notion of the control of the gossip that surrounded that event was we can see from this: The book is decorated by many photographs, principally of sites in Bandoeng, which are captioned as places where events in the story took place. But there are also two other reproductions. One is of Hilda's name card, with her writing on it. The other claims to be a reproduction of one of Hilda's letters to Lie. Chabanneau made a special point of saying that he was telling the truth, except that he changed the names. Either he lied and did not change the names, or the photographs are of forged objects. Either way, in his eagerness to show his control, Chabanneau finds himself in a contradiction. It is, however, one that only magnifies the menace of the author against his character.

No one controlled Hilda. As we shall see, this finally this was true even of "Chabanneau." But Chabanneau has a threat that is different than any of the characters of the book, and this has both political and literary importance. Hilda's father, for instance, is a strong supporter of Chinese national causes, as are Tan and Lie. All of the lives in this story are lived within that ambience, but they come to rely on various forms of colonial authority. Hilda's father locks her up, but she escapes after she finds a way to exchange letters with Tan. The father, unable to keep Hilda where he wants her, tries to control Tan. He uses the weapon of nationalists; he organizes a boycott of Tan's firm, to be put into effect unless Tan is fired. Tan is fired, but he ends up with an excellent position in Batavia. The father appeals to the Gouverneur Generaal. But the Gouverneur Generaal refuses to intervene. Hilda's father appeals to the church, but they refuse to help. Neither paternal law nor colonial nor religious nor economic authority can be applied against her with any effectiveness.

"Chabanneau," however, believed he had a weapon greater than theirs. He actually wrote three books on the same topic, only one of which, apparently the second, is available to me. After hearing the account I have just given of Chabanneau's book at a conference we both attended, Mrs. Myra Siddharta, with great generosity, sent me a typescript by Hilda's nephew, thus the grandchild of Hilda's father. This man says "the picture of my grandfather [in *Secrets of Bandoeng*] as an uncompromising autocrat and the rendering of the small-minded society were rather accurate." He grants this despite the fact that his mother told him the author wrote *Secrets of*

Bandoeng in order to blackmail his grandfather:

> "My mother told me, that the author had indeed approached my grandfather and threatened to publish the books if he did not receive a certain amount of money. My grandfather, furious, refused to see the man and therefore the book found its way to the public."

The author here speaks with a special voice. He reports, as the grandson of the protagonist says, gossip. The books would not have been published presumably if Hilda's grandfather had paid. It seems that when the grandfather did not pay, Chabanneau tried to get Hilda to do so.

Why should he have thought she would pay? The "secrets" were already known. "Chabanneau" himself says so in the first chapter. There are three books, apparently because each time no one paid, "Chabanneau" put out another one, obviously thinking that there was something about a book that was more potent than opinion in the form of gossip. Furthermore, "Chabanneau" does not claim to add anything to the story. What changes is that who might come to know the secret becomes indefinite. Hilda, when she asks for her letters back, says that there is nothing in them that is reproachful. She merely wants to keep them to herself, out of the regard of others. These "others" or "everyone" become a threat not because of the secret they might learn but because the publication of the event, its general availability, reveals them, the readers, to the person blackmailed. For the author/blackmailer and for his victim, readers themselves become characters. These readers, the blackmailer's menace, are figured in the story as those who gossip; they are of course the "everyone." But they are nonetheless different from anyone who may actually have gossiped before the blackmailer/author went to work.

One can imagine another course of events. The blackmailer might threaten to tell Hilda's father that she is in love with someone of the same *she*. Or, a blackmailer in another story altogether might threaten to tell the police about a crime. In both instances, there is someone named as the recipient of scandalous knowledge. It is their possible reactions, of course, that are the threat. But in our case, the reactions that could be predicted have already taken place. If Hilda is still vulnerable, it would be because the story was reopened in another context. Hilda feels endangered when she sees herself spoken about indefinitely by indefinite others. And this is the case when "Chabanneau" relaunches the story in print. Chabanneau's menace is to drag Hilda into the story and embarrass her. It is a threat that depends on intensifying the fear of a public which already existed but which becomes infinitely larger and whose responses become uncontrollable and even unpredictable when that public consists of readers. "Any one" could say anything about Hilda. Hilda, like Soewardi's Dutch, would suddenly find out that someone has been privy to her private thoughts.

There are thus two moments: the revelation of anonymous readers to the one blackmailed and the blackmailed person finding herself imaginatively in a scene she never anticipated entering. Why should Chabanneau think she might be vulnerable to his threat? It depends on his possession of the letters. He makes the letters capable of revealing an enormous amount beyond what Hilda wrote. We have seen, for instance, how Lie Tok Sim insists on keeping them so that seeing them, he can make them say what he wants them to say. This is a threat so absurd it could surely be disregarded were it not for its context. The bulk of the story of Hilda does not consist of showing what people say when they learn the scandal. It consists of the amazing feats of language when, for instance, via translation or the borrowing of books, one ends up with a "dirty book." The story Chabanneau printed developed precisely out of the exchange of languages in the form of books and letters. Time and again, Chabanneau focuses his attention on matters such the Vertaal Bureau Trio as the site of seduction. Chabanneau's threat is to associate Hilda with an extraordinary flow of languages that delivers her into the hands of any one now able to imagine anything at all about her. Hilda is menaced when her letters mean only what a reader imagines they mean. She is in danger when language has lost its authority.

Chinese did not develop their nationalist ideas in Chinese, Javanese, or Dutch but in Melayu, the same language as their neighbors spoke. Claudine Salmon long ago pointed out that what is called "Sino-Malay," the Melayu inflected with, among other languages, Chinese, was shared by other Melayu-speaking groups.[14] It was only after the "purification" of Melayu under the pressure of the Dutch that Chinese were left, after the fact, with the blame for "low Malay." It is an example of how, at a certain moment in the early twentieth century, there was contention for control if not ownership of the lingua franca. The Dutch wanted to secure it for the purpose of clear understanding as well as to blame Chinese for what they, Dutch linguists and administrators, called the corruption of the language. It was just at this moment that Chinese were guarding the language from what they saw as the dead formality they felt Dutch reform would impose.[15] In the complicated linguistic politics of the time, the language of the Chinese was in fact the language as it was generally spoken and printed in the popular press and shared by other groups. Instead of pushing hard for their own language, Sino-Malay nationalists wanted a language that guaranteed them a place within the colonial structure but was autonomous with regard to Dutch control.

Sino-Malay writers were reluctant to accept the reform of the language the Dutch tried to institute. Balai Pustaka, the Dutch-sponsored publications office, sponsored writing in what they hoped would be standard Malay. As an editorial in Kwee Tek Hoay's monthly paper pointed out, however, one need not be too concerned with criticism of Melayu that emanated from that source because "they are not free of the difficulties which make high Malay unpopular to the point where it is low Malay that has spread throughout Indonesia."[16] Kwee Tek Hoay, defending Melayu against colonial reform, seemed to have opened the possibility of claiming the popular language for Chinese themselves. This, however, was difficult in part because Melayu was the language of many others besides Chinese. But, it was most difficult because, at least in the opinion of Kwee Tek Hoay, Chinese themselves seldom mastered the language. They preferred to speak Dutch or they spoke incorrectly. He shared the view that the language lacked standardization and regretted that manuals of the language were not widely available. In the absence of an authoritative version of the language that was also popular, the result was that "Chinese-Melayu writers mix languages to the point where they can seldom write an article for long without mixing in Dutch words."

As if to prove his point, he uses the Dutch word *zonder* instead of the Indonesian term *tanpa* to say "without." In front of his readers, he has committed the very fault he deplored. Were he to reread his piece, he would no doubt have been embarrassed. However, the lingua franca had always used foreign words, as Kwee Tek Hoay was aware. But in the period between the two wars, this mixture appeared as a foreign presence not merely to Dutch administrators but to those from whose mouths and pens the language issued every day. One said what one was not aware of saying and it became evident to everyone. One sensed that one could not appropriate one's language, that as a result one said what one did not intend and it could be held against one, particularly when it was broadcast in the press. Who knows what people might think of one after that? Instead of the respectable newspaper editor, the authority on language, one might be taken for a charlatan or a fool.[17]

Kwee Tek Hoay complained in other articles about the scandal of Melayu publishing. Authors without authority wrote books of instruction, stories that made no sense, or they damaged morality by preaching the value of magic. There is less of that now, that is, in 1936, than before because publishers are losing money. But eighteen years after Chabanneau, Kwee Tek Hoay, pointing to the uncontrollability of languages and to the market, made explicit the climate of language and authority that allowed Chabanneau to combine blackmail and authorship.

The blackmailer takes advantage of the situation, but his effects are not always menacing. His claim is that, in the absence of the control of language, he will take charge. If only Hilda will pay, he will see that her letters are not published. But that is only a start. In doing so, he offers the possibility that when he does publish something else, it will be proper. Kwee Tek Hoay, seeing to it that Melayu is properly spelled and that books are not published that deceive people about magical powers, will offer instead books that will neither deceive nor harm. Chabanneau addresses Hilda in the form of a character in a book and a person outside the book at the same time. He is not entirely different from Muhammad Bakir or even from Soewardi. But the claim of the author, though it starts in scandal, ends in propriety. Language dislodged from social origins is vulnerable to having new origins attributed to it. Colonial officials may not control Melayu, but authors will. Between the fear of the figural and the absence of origins for language there is, as Neil Hertz has pointed out, a connection waiting to be made.[18]

"Everyone" will turn from those who imagine anything at all to those who understand what they should understand. It is at this point that we put the idea of "everyone" between literature and sociology. The demand for recognition, as also in the writings of Mas Marco, takes a path leading to the discovery of the foreignness and hence uncontrollability of one's language. The response is to locate the recognizing figure in women, in "everyone" in such a way that it is reassuring. Along the way, the institutions of writing take shape and always with the same goal of showing that language is controllable and that one need not fear recognition. The specificity of Indonesia comes not with the establishment of these institutions or even with their domesticating tendencies but with their success in transferring authority from authors, thus from writing, to the social. If literature has dissociated itself from blackmail, that is the reason. The locus of control of language has passed from writing to social institutions without leaving behind much space for fiction. The social has monopolized the power of recognition at the cost of literature. I see no necessity in this process. Instead, there is the fear that arises the moment after translating activities become intense. These activities are accompanied by attempts to find recognition in places where one will not be found a criminal, much less a poet.

CHAPTER SIX

Love Sick, or the Failures of the Fetish and of Translation

RECOGNITION

We have already mentioned the government publishing company, Balai Pustaka, which was responsible for large quantities of Malay language publications.[1] It was charged with providing "good and cheap reading material for the slowly growing number of literate Indonesians." Of course, a colonially supported publishing company could not very well print antigovernment material. Nor did it publish books advocating strong religious positions. "Good," the word used by A. Teeuw, a Dutch professor of Malay literature, in the phrase just quoted, seems to have meant morally and also linguistically correct. The Balai Pustaka novels, as they are usually referred to, were often stories of, as Teeuw puts it, "the clash of cultures." The clash is between the culture of the regions on one side, but it is not simple to name the other. At the time, one would have been tempted to use the Dutch term, *ontwinkkeld* (developed or educated) for the opposing cultures. The term "educated" would not refer to "educated in regional traditions"; instead, it would mean possessed of a certain "modernity" that reflected Dutch influence but was at the same time often thought of as "nationalist." To be a Balai Pustaka publication, a novel had to represent a nationalism that was not at odds with colonial authority.

Balai Pustaka had as one of its aims to replace the "filth" of Sino-Malay literature with more edifying materials.[2] The latter included the productions of many who considered themselves modernists and nationalists. These writers found no conflict between a nationalism that relied not merely on Dutch subsidies but, in the novels, pictured Dutch authority uncritically. That they were able to do so indicates the strength of Indonesian interest in hierarchy. I do not mean to read the Indies Chinese out of the nationalist movement when saying this. There is, however, a difference in nationalisms. The Sino-Malay writers found a place in the market with less reference to the Dutch, while the "Indonesian" nationalists of the 1920s and later often included the Dutch in a modern but still colonial system. Other writers, for example, Mas Marco, did not and these were also meant to be displaced by the writers of Balai Pustaka.

One Balai Pustaka publication is called *Djeumpa Atjeh*, or *Flower of Atjeh*. Written by H. M. Zainuddin, who latter wrote accounts of regional history and tradition, it was published first in 1928.[3] It is a typical representation of Teeuw's "clash of cultures." Such stories usually concerned arranged marriages; *Flower of Atjeh* is not an exception. On one side, are the parents of the girl who insist on the prerogatives given them by tradition, and on the other is the enlightened view that says that people should not be married without their consent. The traditional view is explicit and is restated in the novel. The rules governing marriage are set out in the *adat*, the word used to name the traditions and norms associated with regional cultures. The story is set in Aceh,[4] on the northern tip of Sumatra. Today a province of Indonesia, in precolonial days Aceh was an important sultanate and center of Islam. It has its own language, Acehnese. According to Acehnese *adat*, youths are the responsibility of their parents until they are married. Parents, taking into account the welfare of their children and given their experience, know better than children what would make a good marriage. In our novel, the notion of *adat* is set against *cinta*, or "love." Although it is not so stated in the novel, an Acehnese marriage traditionally was an economic arrangement made by the families concerned; it involved the exchange of rather costly amounts, and it was negotiated by the two families involved without the interference of the children to be married.[5] "Modernity" enters in the form of sentiment, which suggests that love is the basis for modern marriages.

In these novels, "love" (*cinta*) is above all moral. When it leads to conflict with traditional authority, it issues only in disaster. Were the couple to marry against the wishes of the parents, it is not only the parents who would be offended it is also the figures who represent "modernity." This is because "love" would then mean simply the expression of desire whereas modern marriage in this novel and many others of this type is selfless; it unites partners who struggle for the enlightenment of their nation or of their region and yet who desire each other. To offend against *adat* would be to betray ideals. Modernism in these novels asked not for the replacement of *adat* but merely for the reform of that part of it that governed marriage. How desire becomes selfless is a topic to which we will return.

It would be oversimple to state this as a conflict between love and authority. The problem is not *adat* or traditional authority as such. The rules of exchange between families, for instance, are described in the novel and are not questioned. In the preface to the edition republished in 1957, the author states his satisfaction that *adat* has changed and that, as a result, the fate of many women has improved. He says that "good" *adat* should be retained. What he describes in the novel does not challenge tradition as such. The responsibility of parents for their children, for instance, is not questioned. The problem is the unenlightened exercise of authority. It is not the rules, the content of authority, but the authorities themselves, parents, who do not live up to their own injunctions. The result is conflict between parents and child. The "clash of cultures" if there is one, occurs not merely because the daughter "loves" (*cinta*) someone and is no longer willing, as a traditional daughter would be, to give up her desire to follow her parents injunctions. It happens because the mother herself wants something and does not understand her daughter. The "traditional" world is pictured as "out of date," no longer adapted to the "modern" world.

The story takes place in Kutaradja, the name of the capital of the province of Aceh until after national independence. Aceh was defeated by the Dutch only after the longest colonial war in the Indies. It was considered "pacified" by 1914, after forty-one years of war. A conflict of that duration and intensity left a reputation for "fanaticism," a word often used to describe Aceh and Acehnese not only by the Dutch but also by Indonesians. The oppositionist side of Acehnese life, however, does not appear in our story. The novel pictures the "enlightened" section of Acehnese society, the youth who were receiving a Western-style education. Against them is not "Islam," in whose name most of the resistance to the Dutch was led, but *adat* (tradition).[6] A youth named Nja' Ahmat works for the Dutch government in an unspecified capacity. He is also active in the NIP, the National Indische Partay, as it is spelled in the novel.[7] Resistance to the Dutch, at this point, was associated with the "backwardness" of regional culture. There is no mention of resistance of colonial rule in the novel except that Nja' Ahmat, as a militant nationalist, writes articles about Aceh for the press in Medan, the major port of Sumatra and a center, at the time, of nationalist activities.[8]

Nja' Ahmat is described as "fluent in High Malay [the language of Balai Pustaka]. . . . Sometimes he mixed it with Atjehnese and Dutch just to make his speech more agreeable" (9). When he arrives in Kutaradja, he stays initially with some youths from the Acehnese nobility who are part of what was called at that time the "young generation" (*kaum muda*). This is the place where enlightened Acehnese meet; there is a sign in front, "Vereeniging [*sic*] Atjeh." Circumstances force him to move from there to the house of teachers. The woman of this enlightened couple, who are not Acehnese, includes among her students Sitti Saniah, who is studying contemporary ways to run a household. Sitti Saniah and Nja' Ahmat meet accidentally. They fall in love simply seeing each other on the train going to the capital. (Were the train going to the provinces, it would seem less likely.) They tell no one, not even each other. But the teachers, recognizing how well matched the couple are, arrange the marriage.

Sitti Saniah's parents agree to the match after the schoolteachers present it to them, having first consulted the couple. All would have been well had Sitti Saniah not gone to the movies. There, at the intermission, in the glow of the electric light, she is seen by T. B. Raman. T. B. Raman is the son of a regional noble. The "T. B." in his name probably was meant to signify a title, "Teuku Beuntara," that announces his noble status. He is young and a lecher. He has already been married eight times. He has been ordered to the capital as a punishment by Dutch administrators for creating trouble in his native area. He does not suffer much in Kutaradja, spending his time in pleasure rather than in learning. T. B. Raman goes to the cinema where by chance Sitti Saniah has gone with the schoolteachers.

> When there was break [pauze] and the lamps were bright, a youth could be seen looking in every direction. By chance not far from him a young girl was sitting between a man and a woman. (68)

It is, again, the girl revealed in electric light that stimulates a man. No longer able to see the movie images, T. B. Raman's attention is attracted to Sitti Saniah. His reaction is instantaneous:

> "Astaga!" the youth said when he saw the face of the girl, "how pretty she is. . . . Who is that? Hm, I'm going after her." (68; ellipses in original)

He sees her; he wants her immediately. His only thought about her aside from knowing that he wants her is to wonder who she is. By contrast, Sitti Saniah and Nja' Ahmat, meet, talk, separate, think about each other, and do nothing. Nothing further happens until the schoolteachers intervene. Their trajectory is first seeing, then wanting, then waiting, and then recognition of themselves and of each other by a third party.

Sitti Saniah's parents are said to be "proud" (*tinggi hati*) and because of that to have refused their consent to previous suitors of their daughter. It is not exactly their pride, however, that is the cause of the trouble in this instance. T. B. Raman insinuates himself into the esteem of Sitti's father. Having done so, he sends a matchmaker, an old woman, to convince the parents to marry their daughter to him and not to Nja' Ahmat. It creates a dilemma. The father finds T. B. Raman acceptable, but they have already accepted the engagement gift sent by Nja' Ahmat. If they return it, they may leave themselves open to a court case, either on the basis of *adat* (customary) or Islamic law. But all authorities agree that though a case might be brought, Nja' Ahmat would not succeed, particularly if they return the engagement gift with its value doubled.[9] They do so, taking the advice of T. B. Raman's intermediary to double its value in compensation for the "shame" they have caused. Nja' Ahmat refuses the gift, saying that he gave it not to them but to Sitti Saniah, thus revising its significance. It takes the effort of a judge to get him to renounce his claims on her and still not take back his gift. Nja' Ahmat has insisted that the gift was a gift, and therefore without the possibility of being valued in money. Sitti Saniah's side, however, has done just that, estimating the cost of the items Nja' Ahmat sent.

The case for the *adat* is made by a group of people that Sitti Saniah's parents call to advise them. They are unanimous in telling the parents not to break the engagement. Sitti Saniah's father is also persuaded. He tells his wife that Nja' Ahmat is from the same social and economic level as themselves. He quotes a proverb that says that that is the way marriages should be made. They should not have excessive ambitions for their daughter, who, they believe, will later be the wife of a local ruler, an *uléëbe-lang* (83), if she marries T. B. Raman. But his wife will not listen. The assembly thus turns its attention to how to return the gift. One of them explains that in *adat* the engagement gift is required so that a promise of engagement will not be made lightly. It can, nevertheless, be returned, but only with a penalty. One should establish the value of the gift and then add that amount in money. There is a reason for it.

> If it were not done this way, clearly people could renege on their promises when-ever they liked. In the end there would be major disputes. (85)

They thus bring out the gift: "It was put in the center of the gathering and evaluated by each person. According to their calculations it was worth f75."

At the same time, a more general case is made for the *adat* or custom. It is a question of order itself.

> "That is the way the *adat* has it. . . . As I said earlier, 'The *adat* is the local regulation. If there were no *adat*, of course there would be no order in the territory, like a ship without a captain or a farmed plot with no one to look after it.'"

The *adat* is thus essential and the novel does not dispute it. It is only a question of one of its aspects, that concerning marriage. When the assembly has agreed on the value of the gift, they still urge the parents not to return it right away but to take a few days to reflect. One person suggests asking the opinion of Sitti Saniah herself.

> "Don't bother," said the oldest person. "A girl may not interfere in this case. She rather must follow the orders of her parents." (86)

When Nja' Ahmat insists on his gift as a gift and not as a payment, he has thus cast doubt on the *adat* itself. It is essential to social order and yet it makes the most authentic signs of solidarity between persons into tokens of monetary exchange. The religious law, it is added, has no jurisdiction at this point because it is a question of engagement rather than marriage and therefore not of concern to it. There is something fundamentally wrong with law itself and yet it prevails. The engagement is broken against the will of the couple.

The *adat* authorities, we have seen, try and convince Sitti Saniah's mother not to break the engagement. The fault is thus hers. She will not do so because she wants too much, as Sitti Saniah's father has pointed out. T. B. Raman's intermediary points out his virtues:

"T. B. Raman is the son of a rich noble [*ulèëbelang*] with a salary greater than Nja' Ahmat's. He has a big house, extensive rice fields and much livestock. When he becomes an *ulèëbelang* perhaps he will buy her a car. . . . And [you] have to think of the times ahead as well. If [you] have trouble, of course he can help us. And if it turns out right for Sitti Saniah and she has sons, of course her son will later be made *ulèëbelang*. Wouldn't you want to see your grandchild a ruler?" (78)

Sitti Saniah's mother consents to all this; it is what attracted her to T. B. Raman in the first place. What is wrong with her action in the eyes of her husband is that she wants more than she should want according to *adat*. Moreover, T. B. Raman has been ruled out from the succession to the rulership because of his bad behavior. The mother will not believe this even when she is later told. She accuses the person who tells her, Sitti Saniah's grandmother, presumably her own mother, of being the dupe of Sitti Saniah and Sitti Saniah, in turn, of being magically enchanted by Nja' Ahmat. She thus will not hear the truth, not only about this but about many things concerned with the marriage. She turns facts around. Sitti Saniah falls ill and, in the end, dies as a result of the frustration of her love. At certain moments, however, she recovers a bit. The mother attributes her recovery to the magic medicine she has employed. "In fact, the medicine that freshened her up was nothing other than the visit of her girl friends" (128). Sitti Saniah's grandmother is her ally and comforter. But when the grandmother visits and Sitti falls ill again, the mother blames the grandmother, telling the grandmother she encourages Sitti Saniah in her disobedience.

When Sitti Saniah's mother compares the advantages of the two candidates, she takes into account, for instance, the fact that Nja' Ahmat has a government salary whereas T. B. Raman will live, she believes, off the proceeds of the region he will govern. Her calculations, in the light of Nja' Ahmat's insistence on the gift, make her seem as though she is avaricious and overly ambitious for both her daughter and herself. And yet what she is pictured as doing, calculating the future advantages for her daughter, is precisely what the *adat* prescribes. She and her husband are putting their daughter in the hands of someone else and it is up to them to see that she will be taken care of. That is, what she does is entirely normal; yet it is the strength of the novel to show the normal as mere calculation and to show Sitti Saniah's mother, in her deafness to others as she makes her calculations, to be, if not mad, certainly outside both the socially desirable and even the normal. Normality itself, in the form of the administration of the law, is at stake.

The *adat* is shown to be out of date, not in keeping with present conditions. The present has its own normality, which means that the desire of the girl to be married should be acknowledged. Sitti Saniah's mother believes her daughter falls ill because she has been magically enchanted. But "the girl was not effected by someone's magic, she fell ill of the sickness of love plain and simple and. . . . she despaired" (145; ellipses in original). Her illness is the sign that a certain normality, one that comes from nature, has been transgressed. It is even acknowledged by a European doctor to whom she has been taken by her father and who, after examining her, tells her father that he must give in to the girl's wishes. Sitti Saniah's illness and eventual death indicate the normality of "love" (*cinta*) and the abnormalities that attend its frustration.[10]

Love demands recognition. Of course, this means a certain love. Not that of T. B. Raman, for instance, which is mere desire. He, it is said, has "a cartfull of children" in various villages, from wives whom he has divorced. His inconstancy, his unreliability, is not part of the normal. But it makes one ask how it is possible to tell one sort of love from another. At the end of the book, desperate, Sitti Saniah runs off to meet Nja' Ahmat and wants to run away. He gently refuses. They could do so, but, he tells her:

> "Would our life be happy and secure? Would we set a good example for our nation [*bangsa*] which wants progress and proper behavior [*kesopanan*]?" (136)

Not only would this not be the case, but their example would be used by the forces of reaction. He goes on:

> "In fact, if we were to make this mistake, it would provoke [*menjadai provokasi*] reactionary forces to restrict the progress of youth gathered in the Atjeh Vereeniging and the NIP." (136)

He asks her if she does not love her parents; does she want to stain their good name?

> "Think first so that we do not disgrace the family and our grandchildren later on. And if we just did what we want to do, what will become of the efforts we have already made? We have tried our utmost to advance the cause of women in Atjeh, we set up Industrie-cursus so that girls can deepen their knowledge of running a home and can unite in girls' organizations. . . . Now parents have confidence in our organization [*pergerakan*] and allow their girls to go to school." (137)

If they run off, people will no longer believe in youth. The love that should be recognized is, thus, inseparable from the struggle for progress and especially from the partial emancipation of girls from the authority of their parents. Their love, moreover, is in the interest of creating proper genealogies. It is this that distinguishes love, *cinta*, from the sheer desire of someone like T. B. Raman.

Such love is not merely justified by its link to progress in the novel, it is recognized by the figures of progress without even the intention of the

couple. Before they have declared their love to each other or told it to
anyone else, one of the pair of schoolteachers, the woman, who gives home
economics courses to Sitti Saniah among others, thinks to herself:

> "Those two youths are well suited to each other already, like the moon and the
> sun, like rings on the ring finger. How wonderful it would be if the two adoles-
> cents became husband and wife! Looks, skills, politeness—really, those two are
> perfectly matched. I don't regret teaching that girl. . . . Oh, Saniah, you have to
> become Nja' Ahmat's wife; Nja' Ahmat a youth who is so well mannered, so
> committed to the progress of the nation. You have to become his wife to support
> him and help him in his pure and noble goals for nation and fatherland. You too
> have to be a model, a torch for your nation." (39)

The schoolteacher recognizes in them not their attraction to each other,
but their commonality of demeanor and ideals. She and her husband, who
agrees with her observations, make the match. Before this, the couple had
met on the train and been instantly attracted to each other though they
scarcely spoke to one another. Even at that point, each hoped the other
was someone progressive. But their attraction could not be true "love"
unless it was linked to progressive ideals through the recognition of an
authority. It is this authority who sees in them what each hopes the other
would be and who, acting on it, makes them potentially a couple.

Sitti Saniah and Nja' Ahmat show themselves not to each other but,
unintentionally, to a third party. This third party is endowed with the capacity to see that their intentions are good and on that basis brings them
together. She is thus similar to the figure of the law in the piece of Tirtho.
But there, desire leads to appearing as someone one is not. It is only intentions that are innocent. Here, what the couple want from each other is the
good of the nation and the good reputation of their families. They need
never say, "but I'm not," which in their case would mean not, "I am not
a Dutchman, I am only an Acehnese" but "I am not a nationalist, I am
someone with desire for a person of the other sex."

It is otherwise with the rival suitor, T. B. Raman, who at one point is
made to say he is in favor of parents asking the permission of their children
before marrying them off. The anonymous narrator comments:

> It's as though he really wanted to do away with the old-style marriage *adat* and
> replace it with new *adat*, which fits present times. But was that really his aim? Is
> it not rather that noble, valuable speech was used simply as a weapon so he could
> satisfy his desire [*hawa nafsu*]. (72)

But with Sitti Saniah, it is not the case. She is frustrated in her desire and
frustrated in her noble goals at the same time. This does not lead her to see
herself cynically, as someone who really merely wants. Rather, it is what
leads to her death. She is the victim of her parents and of old-style marriage
adat. Her parents' frustration of her love is also a frustration of the forces

of recognition. It is at once a check to progressive elements and, even more deeply than that, the constriction of a fundamental social power; the power to elicit recognition, to be sure that love, now seen as both an aspect of the modern and an aspect of human nature, results in social cohesion. It is a question of those in love emitting certain signs; of these signs being recognized by those qualified to understand them with a new family formed as a result.

Sitti falls ill. She becomes ill in the first place by overhearing her parents speaking about breaking the engagement. What she overhears connects her with authority as it did for the Javanese audiences of the rallies in the earlier part of the century. Here, this overhearing ties her to her parents; the result is that she pictures her own death. At the meeting called by her parents to discuss the change of bridegrooms, Sitti Saniah was in the next room, looking through the gaps in the wall. She does not understand at first:

> At first she thought they were speaking of the wedding fixtures, when they would be sent on. But then she heard the words of her mother: "Send back Nja' Ahmat's gifts," srrr. . . . . [ellipses in original] was the noise in her breast because she finally understood. . . . Her blood rose, her heart thumped, her breath came hard and her throat closed up. She was furious to the point where she rose wanting to leap into the meeting and refute them. But out of shame and fear, she restrained herself. (86)

Sitti Saniah cannot sleep. She thinks of her fate, she weeps.

> She thought, "If I cannot marry my beloved, it would be better to die and hold up the earth [i.e., be buried under the earth]. What is the good of living if I have only a corpse in front of me [*djika akan bertjermin bangkai*]?"

It is, of course, a way of saying that she must have her love, that her love and her ideals are one, that thinking of her future without the ability to realize her love, she sees herself not as she has presented herself but as "dead." The phrase I have translated as "if I have only a corpse in front of me" uses the Indonesian word for "reflection" and so could also be rendered "if only a corpse reflects me." She sees herself as though looking in a mirror but the mirror reflects her back to herself as a corpse.

Sitti, seeing herself in an imaginary mirror, pictures her inability to elicit a response, from herself first of all but from others as well. She is her image, the nationalist-sweetheart, or she is "nothing," a "nothing" that precludes herself being someone who merely desires, whose desires are not wrapped in idealism, and for whom any other presentation of herself is unthinkable. She is absolutely what she appears to be, someone with *cinta*, thus a nationalist, fully identified with herself. Or, ahead of her, she sees reflected back to herself only herself as wholly without radiance, appearance, life.

"But I'm not . . . ," said in the face of parental authority, leaves her dead in the midst of life. It is the result of absolute identification with the image.

This raises the questions about who or what she is vis-à-vis her mother. She is her mother's daughter and she remains subject to *adat*. Why does she never repudiate her mother in the manner of revolutionary youths in other times and places? Sitti Saniah never says, "but I'm not . . ." in face of her mother. She never says, "I am in love, I am a nationalist, and therefore I am not your daughter." She does not question her relation to her mother. She sees herself only in the eyes of the movement. But she is her mother's daughter by birth, and she does not deny her descent. The consequence is that she is subject to the legal authority that governs descent without ever thinking that such authority could be repudiated. Her mother makes difficulties, but in doing so she merely activates the law that governs marriage. Sitti Saniah in relation to this law is its victim. She is unwilling to be so, but neither she nor anyone else in the novel think they have a choice. Nationalism in this and many novels like it, is legal, particularly when it concerns genealogical questions.

Sitti Saniah does not say, "but I'm not a nationalist, I am only a daughter." The alternatives posed by Soewardi are reworked once modernism furnishes identity via the image. There is, in particular, no contrast between the image and its origin. She looks like a nationalist, she is recognized as one, she is one. She was nothing before that. She has reached modernity without seeming to leave from any place that can hold her except for reasons and powers that are out-of-date and that should simply be reformed away. Between original and image the difference is only that the image brings out something already inherent in the original. When an objection is made from the side of parents, it is shown to be without foundation; it is faulty because it is out of date and certain to melt away in the course of time. It is the victory of the fetish of appearance.

Or rather, it will be the victory of the fetish. In the meantime, Sitti Saniah dies because she is not allowed to love. The fetish is the solution but the problem of its actualization is still there. What exactly is the difficulty? What is it that prevents Sitti from accomplishing her love? Why is it that her parents do not allow her to make her choice? The novel is vague, suggesting on the one hand that there is something in the character of the mother, an ambition too large, that is the cause. And yet, from the point of view of *adat*, the mother is justified. One can say that what she did she did for her daughter, just as a mother should. Nor is it suggested that the *adat* as such is at fault; only the right to arrange marriages without consent. But this statement obscures the problem. The difficulty is not precisely the power of parents; it is their blindness in exercising that power. Nowhere is it suggested that parental authority as such should be curtailed;

instead, parental power is inappropriate when it is exercised without the consent of daughters in choosing a husband. The question becomes: What causes their blindness?

Sitti Saniah's parents are much concerned about her illness. Her father brings her to the European doctor who, after examining her, learns of her love. He then speaks to her father:

> It happened that the doctor did not understand Indonesian [or did not understand Indonesian well]. He said to Sitti Saniah's father: "We have examined your daughter's body and her blood and there is nothing wrong. We feel she has another illness. Has your daughter already been promised in marriage?"
>
> "Twice already, *tuan*, but she is not yet married. I refused the first fiancé because I did not like him."
>
> "Yes, perhaps that's the reason she is sick; we can't help. But you yourself can do something. Just give her what she wants, what makes her happy. You must follow her wishes." (124–125)

The difficulty of Indonesian here is the fault of the doctor. But it is not a matter of blame but of the nature of the misunderstanding:

> The doctor's words were not clear to Sitti Saniah's father. He did not understand the words "she has another illness" and "just give her what she wants, what makes her happy." He thought "another illness," *sakit lain*, was the illness *teukeunong*, "struck by black magic," "enchanted by someone," so that the doctor could not help, only a curer could. And the words "just give her what she wants, what makes her happy" he thought meant "whatever she likes to eat or to wear, give it to her so she will be content." (125)

Whatever the doctor actually said, the difficulty is that the father did not understand properly. He made the mistakes described. He heard what the doctor said, as when he heard "give her what she wants," but misinterpreted the sense of the words. The paragraph offers the possibility that the difficulty was the doctor's inability to use Indonesian that caused Sitti Saniah's father's misunderstanding of what should have been clear. Whichever the case, the problem arises between speakers of different languages. It is a failure of translation, but not an ordinary one. The Acehnese word, *teukeunong* (struck by magic) bears no resemblance to the Indonesian phrase, *sakit lain* (another illness). The first meaning of *teukeunong* is simply "affected by"; it could be followed by whatever word designated the agent at work. Without another word, it can mean "affected by magic." *Sakit lain* means "another illness." Instead of hearing what is said and taking it for what it means, Sitti Saniah's father reads into the phrase another meaning.

Indeed, whenever magic is involved, there is mistaken interpretation. We have already seen examples. The only explanation Sitti Saniah's parents have for her illness is black magic. This, indeed, is what she reproaches them for in a letter she leaves for them just before she dies:

> "My illness, father and mother, was not magic-illness [*penjakit teukeunong*] as you supposed; you, father, mother and the entire neighborhood. It was rather an evil and dangerous illness . . . love [*cinta*] sick it is called." (149–150)

It is not of course that *cinta* is an illness but that love when blocked turns into illness. It is the parents' fault for not recognizing *cinta* (love) for what it is. They can only see black magic. Thus, they miss the potency of love which consists, in the first place, of its seriousness. When they hear of youths who have committed suicide, they can only think it is black magic. But it is in fact that love has been misrecognized. Parents are unwittingly responsible for the deaths of their children. They misrecognize, they therefore use force. It is the power of parents, of the parental law, that kills children. Precisely the force that should compel recognition by authority, *cinta*, does not do so.

But in another way, this merely proves the power of love. It is the most intense expression of modernity. The "sickness of love" is the sign of the abnormality of what is taken as normal; the reign of an outmoded law. Love is itself powerful in its capacity to force another sort of recognition on the generation of parents. This is the reason for leaving behind a letter, which Sitti Saniah "hopes will be valuable to you, mother and father, and to my nation later on." In the end, after the novel, modernity will win; parents themselves will recognize not merely the value but the necessity of acknowledging the force of *cinta* just as schoolteachers do already.

This proper recognition is linked to the proper reception of signals. The doctor reappears on the last pages of the novel to tell the father about his now seriously ill daughter, "We told you before you had to go along with her wishes because she loves [*cinta*] someone" (145). But it is too late; too much damage has been done to Sitti Saniah's brain and the doctor fears she may commit suicide. The father misunderstood. He should have known that "another illness" does not mean "black magic." He should not have thought that she was in the power of someone else. He should not have seen either in the actions of his daughter or in the words of the doctor another presence behind the words. In fact, "the illness of love" is an illness like others, treatable by doctors; it is not one to be left to practitioners of magic. Although the doctor has no medicine for it, it is curable by following his advice. In fact, if he had medicine, he would not give it to Sitti Saniah but to her father and mother, for "the sickness of love" is curable only by curing them. Her father, had he properly understood the doctor, would have followed the doctor's advice. His lack of understanding is a defect or a symptom of cross-cultural transmission; it is a defect of translation. "Affected by another illness" (*penjakit lain*) he takes only as

"affected by" or *teukeunong* in Acehnese. But *teukeunong* is itself an abbre-
viation for affected by magic." *Teukeunong* simply means "affected by";
neither this word nor the phrases in which it is set indicate affected by what
or by whom. But misunderstanding, parents see too much and attribute
dark and evil powers to something that is actually clear. They are thus
themselves infected by the "illness of love." It is the result of a phrase that
has concealed itself through its transformation into a word of another
language.

The parents are the carriers of this transformation, which is also the
germ of the illness. It is what causes their blindness to their daughter and
her subsequent illness and death. It is precisely "an effect"; not "an effect
of magic" but "an effect of transmission between languages." It is the
"other sickness" (*penjakit lain*); the sickness of the other; the other language that still works its effects within the regional or domestic language.

What would the cure for love sickness be if not proper recognition, that
is, recognizing *cinta* for what it is: the power to compel recognition. More
precisely, it is the power to compel recognition of desire transformed into
idealism. That idealism is directed toward the advancement of the Indonesian people. At that time, this meant not independence and not equality.
It meant rather the possibility of having a certain identity. One which
marked one as progressive. A progressive person was in touch with the
modern world outside the Indies. The particular matters with which he or
she was concerned was secondary. It varied from the modern ways to manage a home to a range of political ideas. But in the Balai Pustaka novels, as
in Mas Marco, one does not get men interested in politics who go for long
unjoined by *cinta* to women interested in the domestic. In one way or
another, nationalist women in the novels we have discussed ensure that
desire does not lead one to unwanted destinations. *Cinta* is possible only
with proper women and is subject to recognition by the proper authorities.
And with it, the connection to the modern world never leads men outside
of the world of the Indies or of the Indonesian. And for the same reason,
cinta is never truly incompatible with familial origins.

Cinta as a force is absolute in its demands. Either the world acknowledges this force or the one in love dies. It is a situation regularly repeated
in the novels published by Balai Pustaka. But where does the authority and
the force to recognize reside? In this story, as in many others, it rests in the
union of nationalist and colonial enlightened figures who are connected
with the currents of thought that flow through the world at large. These
currents stimulate nationalism and love, but they must be rightly understood. The promotion of literacy and the reform of writing, spelling, and
linguistic usage work together for progress.

There is little substance to the idea of modernity in these novels. One
does not find expressions of equality between races, cultures, speakers of

different languages, or the two sexes; and there is no notion of independence. There is no insistence on equality just as there is no insistence on liberty. "Progress" exists as a question of belief and recognition. If it is a matter of identity, it is not because certain people, modernists and nationalists, were engaged in a political struggle. In this novel, as in many others from the period, nationalists and Dutch were allies. One joined their ranks not by sharing their ideas but by falling into *cinta*. *Cinta* opened a path to recognition and propriety. It marks the development both of a restructuring of hierarchy that could include Indonesian as well as Dutch figures at the top and the path that reading and writing took in the Indies. That path conjoined fetishism and literature, reducing the latter to the former. Literature would have made a place for the "foreign as foreign" and thus for the sense of possibilities, unrealizable or not, which the unincorporated foreign stimulates. In what took the place of literature, in novels such as the one we are presently considering, the foreign is reduced to difficulties of translation amenable to correction with further education.

The result is the reintegration of colonial society with an enlarged place made for 'natives.' Chinese publishers such as Kwee Tek Hoay tried to establish their own ideas of correctness in the face of Balai Pustaka. They, too, wanted an enlarged place for themselves within the Dutch East Indies, but with more autonomy in literary matters. There was more at stake than correct linguistic usage, we see now. There was a question of who was to be included in developed colonial society. *Flower of Atjeh* implicitly reads out not only Chinese but also "socialists" such as Mas Marco. The achievements of Balai Pustaka are not to be underrated. They did, in fact, do much to enlarge the number of literate people and to furnish them with material to read they found interesting. The lure they had was not different from the appeal of the rallies earlier in the time of Tjokroaminoto. That is, it was not only the substance of their promise, a place within the modern and the colonial; it was also the magical tool one used to get to that place. *Flower of Atjeh* is writing in the service of the fetish, putting it to use to draw youth into the ambience of the modern and the colonial.

The fuzziness by which "modernity," "colonial authority," and "nationalist authority" are scarcely distinguished might seem to undermine nationalist authority. There are indeed, instances, where Balai Pustaka novels celebrated persons later considered traitors to the nationalist cause and were condemned for it. But the strength of nationalists was on the whole uncompromised by its association with colonial authority. It is not merely that "the modern" encompassed both. Their advantage was to be able to recognize what parents could not, an advantage that came to them through their position on the edges of the international and the regional. Their superiority is in the first place linguistic. They, unlike parents, know what *cinta* means. They know it is a foreign word even if it was commonly to be found with a different sense in regional literatures, a sense that comes from outside the Indies. They show that translation can work properly. They, therefore, can recognize in nationalist youth what parents cannot see.

But if nationalist leaders remained uncompromised by their association with the Dutch, it is because their authority had another source. Nationalist authority borrowed from parental authority. It is not for nothing that it is nationalist schoolteacher couple who are the matchmakers. They did precisely what parents did traditionally; they found appropriate matches for their charges, acting for their own good. The schoolteachers' advantage is highlighted because it makes up for parental disadvantage. They are parental not simply by their matchmaking, but in particular by their supervision, one could say, even, super vision. Not only do they see but they supervise the activities of their charges in the manner of parents.

It is in particular the mother whom the novel faults for her blindness. The father is merely linguistically incompetent in a manner similar to the fathers of Mas Marco. The difference is that it is the father in these novels who furnishes a connection to the Dutch. The mother is not involved, in the present instance, in translating the doctor's speech. Showing the incompetence of the father breaks the connection with Dutch authority. Women's authority, or a mother's authority is, however, nameless. It is her position as "mother" rather than the *adat* itself that is put at stake in the novel. But that position is put at risk only to be recuperated by the schoolteacher and in particular the woman schoolteacher; her husband plays practically no role. She does what the mother should have done.

Her supervision (or, super vision) is the result not merely of her modern education but also of her capacity to act as a mother. Through her, "mother" is inscribed among the nationalist authorities, dragging along with it, "father." It is, in any case, this ability to do better as parents than parents themselves that bolsters nationalism. In particular, the ability of parents, substitute parents, and especially mothers to know their children better than they know themselves gives fetishism its orientation.

These substitute parents are the guarantee of innocence practiced against the view from within kinship. Later, parents tend to fall out of the picture entirely. It is the Dutch who frustrate the fetish of recognition. The difficulty they come to offer is that they once again satisfy desire, as in *Student Hidjau*. This is only to be expected. Modernism begins with the raising of desire and the promise of the possibility of appropriating it for oneself. Nationalism makes desire proper; first against the claim of parents, then against the possibility of satisfaction that remains associated with "Dutch." This opposition of authorities, one good because it confers propriety and the other to be opposed because it recognizes desire in order to satisfy it improperly, became important later during the revolution, as we will see. For it to develop, however, nationalism had first to align itself with political authority in the manner of this novel and to set itself against outmoded but undiscardable parental authority. Once nationalists could do well what parents were charged with doing badly, the way was open to reevaluating the place of the Dutch in the path of modernism and nationalism.

PHOTOGRAPHS

In the preface to the second edition of *Djeumpa Atjeh*, published in Aceh in 1958, the author announces that he has changed several words to bring them up to date and that he has "adorned" it "with several illustrations." The first of these is one of the author himself, face on, in the manner of an identity photo. The last is also of the author with his family. Those in the picture are various relatives, come to celebrate his sixty-fourth birthday. The other twenty photographs are of Acehnese places and objects. Each picture has a caption. Some have two, for instance, a photograph of a steam engine pushing two wooden cars across a bridge:

> The Extra Train Carrying Members of the V.A. [Vereeniging Atjeh] Congress.

This appears above the photograph. Below it is another:

> *Kruëng peuët ploh peuët.*
> One of the railroad bridges in the forest of Seulawaih between
> Seuleumeum [Atjeh Besar] and Padang Tidji [Pidië] called
> "Kruëng Peuët Ploh Peuët." There is only one river but it twists
> so much that it needs 44 bridges and because of that Atjehnese
> call it "Kruëng peuët ploh peuët," which means river 44. (11)

These photographs all have to do with Aceh, but only some of them, such as the one above, allude to the story. There is no picture of Nja' Ahmat, for instance, comparable to the picture of Njai Dasima. The references are, rather, outside the story, as though they might in some way continue it simply by adding further thoughts rather than by developing the plot. For instance, there is a picture of the council of the Vereeniging Atjeh for 1916–1919. The caption identifies its members in one case like this: "1.Abubaker schoolopziner, secretaris kedua*" The asterisk refers to a note:

> *now the head of the Division of Education and Culture for the Province of Atjeh.

Another note identifies a second person as "presently a merchant in Penang [Malaya]" (20).

The pictures "adorn" the text, but they do not direct one's attention to what one reads. Rather, they join the text to the landscape and to certain historical persons, not mentioned in the story, and to the situation as of the time the novel was published for the third time in 1958, thirty years after its first publication. But they unite the text with the place in a specific way. For example, the picture of the Governor's Palace notes that it stands on the site of the former palace of the Sultan of Aceh. This is also where a great battle was fought in 1874 between Dutch and Acehnese for control of the sultanate, as it then was. It was one of the first major battles in the long struggle that resulted in Dutch domination of Aceh, but only after forty years of resistance. It is odd that a book that supports nationalism would not find this picture a bit embarrassing even if, as was the case, the nationalism of the author's group at that time was one that wanted a place within Dutch political control. Precisely for that reason, the remembrance of the battle is odd.

Another example is a picture with the title: "*DARABARO*, the Acehnese word for 'bride.'" The picture shows a woman dressed in traditional Acehnese bride's costume, surrounded by flowers. Under the picture, the caption reads:

> The Clothes of the *Dara Baro*
> (The Bride)
> Made of silk and worked gold ornaments and covered with jewels.
> The silk referred to was cut to pieces by Sitti Saniah. (142)

This is the single mention in the captions to the text. It refers to an episode in which, after Sitti Saniah's bridal outfit has been put together, she cuts it up. Of course, if one is to read the caption literally, one is looking at the silk outfit that was cut up in the text. I do not believe in this case, at this point in time, the reader is meant to believe that he is seeing whole what has been cut up in the text; rather, it is probably intended to illustrate an example rather than the image of the original. In any case, there is a second picture with a title that reads: "*Teupeuen* = Weaving Cloth" (47). It shows a woman sitting at a loom and others spinning. Beneath the picture is this legend:

> Women in Kampong Lamgugob weaving silk for the clothes of "*dara-baro*" [brides] and Lintobaro [grooms]. [capitalization as in original]

The wedding silk has its own story in the photograph. One learns of its production, one sees the product in such a way that the destruction mentioned in the caption now has its own context; it is not the story of the unfortunate Sitti but of the unfortunate silk, woven in one picture, displayed in another, and cut to pieces in the caption. Perhaps it is not so unfortunate since in the picture the silk remains whole.

The caption of the picture of the Governor's Palace says "Previously this was the site of the remains of the Palace of the Sultan of Atjeh, erected in the year 1880." What was erected in 1880 was the Governor's Palace, of course, not the ruins. The ruins resulted from the destruction of the palace by Dutch troops. The destruction of the palace was pictured in the popular Dutch press of the time. It is an image that remained for a long while in popular imagination. The text we are discussing here, whose third edition was published in Aceh, alludes to the ruins of the Sultan's Palace, but it makes no mention of Dutch and Acehnese antagonism. Instead, there is an image of wholeness and propriety, comparable to the image of the properly dressed bride with its reference to the sliced silk. In the photographs, the destruction caused by conflict is undone. The photographs, that is, seem to have been selected not merely by association with the story, but, in a certain way, in opposition to it. In the story, there is conflict. In the picture captions, conflict and destruction is referred to only to show that "now," in the picture and at the time of publication, everything has been repaired. They also show that there is a wholly different story, at least another one than one reads on the pages next to the pictures.

There is conflict and destruction in the story, but none is visible in the photographs. One can see the motions by which one moves from story to picture within the book itself. At one point, T. B. Raman is described going out for pleasure, something he does regularly.

> Every afternoon he went around the city wearing beautiful clothes, sometimes as far as Peunajong and Vredespark (now called Taman Sari on Radja Umong Road) in front of the Julianaclub [*sic*], because there many European men and women played sports and there was frequently music to be heard.
>
> As it happens, Malays call it "Kebun Radja" [King's Garden] and Acehnese call it "Radja Umong," meaning "king"s rice fields." The reason Acehnese call it "Radja Umong" is because in ancient times in the era of the Acehnese kingdom of Sri Sulthan Iskandar Muda, when it was time to have the people of the kingdom begin work in the rice fields, that rice field was the first to be worked. (63)

We are given the visit of T. B. Raman to a certain place. But instead of telling us what he did there or what he saw, the place itself is explained. The name of the place stimulates the author to give its etymology. This happens several times. Here is another example:

> Then T. B. Raman went on to Neusu; there there are pleasant views, especially toward Kroeëng Daroj where the water is particularly clear and where on the bank of the river there is a small mountain made of stone [*gunungan*], from earlier times. This hill was built by the Atjehnese Sultan Iskandar Muda as a place for princesses to bathe. In the hill there are several small chambers and a place for

shampooing and for relaxing for the princesses also made of stone. Outside of it there is a large stone mortar; it is said that this mortar was used to crush sinful people in ancient times when the kingdom of Atjeh was still strong. Not far from the hill there is a gate also made of stone called "Pintu Khob." People say that is the gate used by the princesses when they went to the rice fields. Nearby there are rice fields called Putroë Umong, that is, when the seeds and seedlings were set in the fields women began at that field led by princesses or royal consorts. Now this land has become an electric station. (65)

On the next page, there is a picture of the "Gunungan"; the building is described, again explaining that it was a bathing place for princesses. In this instance, the text gives us a picture of a place visited by a character; it is not just any character but the villain. He is following his desires, "satisfying" them, we are told. "T. B. Raman liked to tour around and satisfy his desires (*hawa nafsu*)" (67). But the description of his satisfaction leads away from pleasure and toward etymology; toward what it is people say about particular places, their legends, as it were, their embodiment in tradition and linguistic usage, and finally to photographs.

We emerge out of the text onto a scene in which pleasure has been left behind in favor of the citation of linguistic usage. Or at least, we might. T. B. Raman's tour ends at the site of pictures themselves, the cinema. It is there that he sees Sitti Saniah for the first time. It is there that her disaster begins. But there is another exit from the text via the photographs, an exit that seems to want to ensure not that the events will not be repeated but that they will not be remembered.

The diversions of the text, from the story of T. B. Raman to the legends of place, end logically enough in the photographs. The photographs are inherent in the text, as the description of T. B. Raman's pleasure tour makes evident. If there were no photographs, as was the case in the first edition, the descriptions of places would be close enough. The photographs "adorn" the text, but they do so as outgrowths of it, as the place where the diversions culminate. They consolidate the moment when one can forget in whose eyes these scenes were seen or the sting of the particular references to the story that might occur were one to read back from them to the points from which the diversions began.

The photographs of the text, showing only what should be seen and distancing themselves from the text, are not different from postcards. Printed separately with the text placed on the reverse, they could be sent through the mail, no doubt along with the usual messages one puts on postcards. Here, "technology" is transmission, but only of the superficial, almost only of appearances. The conflicts of the past are mentioned not to evoke them but to emphasize the long distance between them and the photographs, separated as they are by the diversions we have mentioned. Appearances, we have already learned, should be taken as such. Without the need to think about what informs them, there is no problem of interpretation. The transmission between points does not close a gap between different kinds of understanding. The sender and the receiver will have the same impressions.

One photo caption notes that a member of the Vereeniging Atjeh of 1919 is "now" the head of a government department. Here "now" refers to the moment in which the fact was recorded. Perhaps the reader is supposed to calculate the time between his reading and the recording of the date, and then to guess where the man is "now." The use of the word "now" suggests the presence of someone, (the author of the caption), which is similar of course to authors' presentation of themselves in the subtitles of earlier books. The time between the photograph and the writing of the caption, like the time between the moments of writing and reading, can easily be estimated by looking at the date of publication. But one wonders at the significance of the gap in time. Eventually, a reader will assume that the persons pictured are necessarily gone from the world. One might feel the pathos and, with Roland Barthes,[11] think that the persons photographed died twice, once in life, and again, in the time of the photograph after the picture was taken. In other words, photographs can evoke both presence and absence. But one of the pictures suggests another reading. It shows the author in the midst of other persons:

A picture of the author and his family: children, mother-in-law, grandchildren and nephews and nieces who has just celebrated his 64th birthday on 15 Muharram 1376—22 June 1956.

It is not odd for an author to put his photograph in his book. But what makes this picture strange is that author presents himself not as author at all. There is nothing about his pose, for instance, that suggests that he thinks, he writes, he sees. There is nothing in his face to see except for the fact that he is clearly posing for the photographer. But he is posing as the central member of an extended family. Around him, men and women hold babies; children, presumably grandchildren, sit at his feet, while next to him sits his aged mother-in-law. The picture is labeled in the list of photographs, "The Author's Family." The author, that is, appears precisely in the context which, in his novel, is the source of trouble. This is not the author who controls circulation; it is not the person who from out of the subtitles announces his presence by warning his readers what they will be vulnerable to if they do not read his book. It is the author as one more sight, and one more site, of the Acehnese capital. It is the author on an occasion which he marks just as he marked the fall of the Sultan's Palace. That is, the author does not have any obvious relation to his story; his relation is no more direct than the photograph of the Governor's Palace. He simply is pictured in a setting which, like the Governor's Palace, indicates another story.

H. M. Zainnudin here points to himself as one of the outgrowths of his story. He is part of one of the other stories that someone familiar with Aceh might know and that others can guess at as they wonder, for instance, why his wife is not in the picture or, if she is, why she is not named in the caption. With enough distance and enough time, the picture becomes a mere snapshot in which one is given the image of the author to recognize and which evokes little interest at all.

When the photograph is merely a snapshot, the author has been reduced to the mere image of himself. But it is as such an image that he is most readily transmissible. When he is seen by future readers, he will be taken up in a circuit of transmission that, as of 1994 when this is written, has already extended outside Aceh and outside Indonesia. H. M. Zainnudin, were he able to do so, would find himself recognized in places and in ways that he never anticipated. But, by the very factor of distance, he would be reduced merely to his name, "H. M. Zainnudin," and to his image. He inserts himself, then, into the structure of the fetish with the assurance that only that part of himself that is proper and that he wants recognized is so. He would not have to fear the recognition of something of himself that he would prefer not to have revealed. Or at least, he would not if the structure of distancing works as the captions suggest it should.

It is a structure that differs from that which binds texts to readers in that it does not ask for comprehension. That is, it does not demand that one think of *Flower of Atjeh* in its various possibilities of interpretation and credit H. M. Zainuddin with them. Rather the opposite. The attachment of the author to his text here is merely tangential. If H. M. Zainuddin is extracted from the setting of his family in order to be restored as the author of the book in which he appears, it is because his family is as little relevant to him as the battle for the Sultan's Palace is to the Governor's Palace or the shredded silk of the story is to the silk of the photographed dress. What is at stake is binding a speaker, a writer, to a set of signs. In this case, it is accomplished by finding another circuit, here the transmission between reader or viewer of photographs and what is seen. That circuit escapes complications in the interest of transmission and recognition.

The photographs with their captions repair the damage that occurs in the story. The wedding dress is whole again; the effects of the misunderstanding between modernity and tradition disappear. The wedding dress, the landmarks of the old sultanate, and traditional ornaments are now to be found in a sort of modern museum, the photograph album. Modernity has encompassed the past while erasing its conflicts. Precisely what caused all the difficulty in the story, the failure to transmit properly and with correct understanding, is corrected. One can understand, then, why the wedding dress might be shown. And one can understand why, in the search for diversion, various Acehnese monuments are pictured. But it is more difficult to say why the Dutch are brought into the picture, particularly at the point where the bloody transition between Acehnese and Dutch rule is marked. That there is an assumption of colonial rule is one thing; that the clash between powers is alluded to is another.

The modernism that the principal characters of *Flower of Atjeh* are devoted to is one that brings them close to the Dutch. Nja' Ahmat is a member of the important nationalist organizations of the time and he works for the Dutch administration. There is no contradiction; rather the contrary. Modernism comes to them through the Dutch, and the connection to the West is assumed. That the novel makes no distinction between the culture of the West and the politics of colonialism is not surprising in the context of the time. Moreover, as we have noted, the aim of the state publisher, Balai Pustaka, was to further just such modernism as a way of both enlightening Indonesians and drawing closer bonds between colonists and colonized.

In *Flower of Atjeh*, the Dutch are shifted to the side of the story. There is no Dutch person in the story who speaks except for the doctor. But the coincidence of Dutch and Indonesian authority is assumed. Nja' Ahmat is both a member of the colonial administration and a member of nationalist organizations. The Dutch are pulled into the story as the context in which modernism can take hold. It is necessary to get something from them or through them that can, for instance, solve the "Atjeh probleem" about which Nja' Ahmat writes newspaper articles. The "Atjeh probleem" concerned the obstacles to progress formed by elements who remained from the period of resistance to the Dutch and who, in the 1920s in Aceh, still occasionally killed Europeans. From the point of view of modernists, such people were seen not as elements of political resistance but as traditionalists who did not understand how the Indies could become a modern country. From this point of view, "Dutch" signaled an opportunity. If the Dutch were foreign to Aceh, their foreignness meant precisely that they brought something rather than that they took what belonged to the inhabitants of the Indies. In particular, "Dutch" represented the possibility of Western learning. The picture was ambiguous politically since modernization could bring with it a political claim. But the assumption of authors of novels such as this one was that for there to be modernity there had to be a connection to the Dutch. It is exactly this that the photographs provide all the while they idealize.

The caption to the photograph of the Governor's Palace notes that it stands on the site of the Sultan's Palace, the latter destroyed in a famous battle of the war between Dutch and Acehnese. Yet, somehow the palace can be mentioned without its implications being evoked. It is the nature of the photograph as it is used in this book that it makes whole what was cut to pieces either in the text or historically. It is a version of the logic used in speaking of the movies: cotton turns to silk. The logic of the photograph makes the Governor's Palace appear as the restoration of the Acehnese Palace. Were the Governor's Palace to mark the ruins of the Sultan's Palace, there would be a wholly different interpretation. These ruins, of course, would be the residue of conflict; restoration is a form of continuity. With the latter, there is a simple sequence, but one in which what was destroyed is made whole, in the way that the silk dress, once cut up, appears in its original state. Somehow, the movement from one moment in history to the next is no longer set in time with its irreversibilities and its residues. Instead, is a question of transmission via the photograph that not merely records what is in the picture but brings forward the past while at the same time making what had been in shreds and cinders regain their original states.

The photograph and caption thus create a continuity between the sultan and the governor when in fact the sultan was the enemy of the Dutch. The succession from one to the other was achieved only through a bloody war. In the book, the only other residue of this war is the mention of the "Atjeh probleem," the subject of Nja' Ahmat's articles in the press. Nowhere in the story is the damage of the war attributed to the invasion of foreigners or, the reverse, to elements who did not recognize the advantages of colonial domination. It is not a question of interpretation of events but of seeing a transition without interpretation, consonant with the use of photographs we have already discussed. But, again, why bring up the issue at all; why are the picture and caption used?

In KTH's description of the attraction of films, the image counts for more than the original and the process of reaching the image fascinates. In the pictures of the Governor's Palace and the bridal dress, one sees what photography adds qua photography. There is a motivation to show certain pictures that stems precisely from their rectification of unwanted conflict. In that sense, they come from the story itself, even if by a process of erasure and reversal. But the bulk of the pictures are mere diversions from the story; they are surely expressions of the wish to go beyond the conflicts of the narration and to end in imagery. One can see this process in a wider setting by comparing the story with Mas Marco's *Hikajat Soedjanmo*. There, the father is shown speaking either antiquated Javanese or antiquated Melayu to the Dutch controlleur. The father's language is out of place; the controlleur does not merit the respect the language is supposed to express. The effect is thus both comical and irritating, the sentences being void of significance for the speaker. But the speaker is compelled by the Dutch official; he has no choice but to speak words alien to him. The Dutch official feels otherwise. He speaks from the position of Dutch authority; the lack of significant exchange demonstrates the impossibility of translation. The implication is the need for separation; a separation which would be at once political, cultural, and linguistic. By contrast, *Flower of Atjeh* advocates relations with the Dutch and thus encourages exchanges between languages. The failure of translation between the doctor and Sitti Saniah's father is finally the effect of the backwardness of the father; it is not inherent in the relationship between different languages. True exchange brings proper understanding and enlightenment, though perhaps one should not say "exchange" since it is a one-way street; enlightenment passes from Dutch to Indonesian exclusively.

The burden is thus on Indonesian and on this novel to take in as much as possible, to show that it can contain not merely the story as a narrative but everything associated with it, including the setting and the objects that might disrupt the wish for perfect communication. Rather than avoiding the mention of moments of historical difficulty, the novel goes out of its way to point to them. It thereby demonstrates that it is a vehicle for perfectly smooth transference, for communication that does not stimulate complications. Indonesian here is like photographic film, able to take in whatever image sensitizes it. But this is too passive a simile. For the language to be seen to work as it should, for modernity as it is understood in the story to work, the language has to encounter difficulties and smooth them over. It has to show that, precisely, it can take in Dutch and it can take in the traditional and that in doing so, boundaries are crossed without complications. It is, in other words, not by chance that there is a picture of the Governor's Palace and of the bridal dress. They indicate the reach of the language and the fascination with the possibility of reception.

But whatever assures the recognition of "everything" could also recognize in "me" something I would not care to have recognized; something that did not fit the "modern." It is my supposition that the Dutch component of the setting of the story is specified precisely for that reason. "Dutch" at that time meant modernity. The setting of the story, its context as given by the photographs, is more than its physical or geographical context. It is the ambience of the story, the associations that not only come out of the story but give the story its tonality, which is precisely a mixture of the modern and the traditional. It is within the ambience of the remains of the sultanate that the story takes places. One example of those remains is the bathing place, which is not only shown in the photographs but, in the story, reported as seen from a car window. There is also the Governor's Palace, the Dutch government building on the site of the Sultan's Palace where Nja' Ahmat presumably works, and, from the side of tradition, the wedding dress that Sitti Saniah was compelled to accept. If there is a demand that they be inserted into the book, some in words, some in photographs, it is because they represent the threat on which the story is built.

It is the threat that the past continues to assert itself and therefore the photographic museum is necessary to embalm it.

More and more is taken in. But in to where? The location of the domestic, the nonforeign, is no longer the traditional. The traditional, with its insistence on magic, is foreign in the way that "Dutch" could be also foreign. "Could be" if one thought that by becoming modern one became Dutch, a bit like Student Hidjau. One could accept becoming modern and being like the Dutch through a belief in equality of peoples, for instance. But the Indonesian nationalism that was associated with Dutch as the path to modernity did not find a home in ideology. Although there was a nationalist ideology at the time, it was not the ideas of independence or equality, of freedom from racism, and so on that inform the novel, even implicitly.

"Modernity" as it is understood in many Balai Pustaka novels, is associated with a domestication of the foreign where the domestic is neither the assertions of traditions of regions nor of a national culture nor of an international culture. It is the process of transmission itself whereby origins of whatever sort no longer make themselves felt. "Dutch" may equal the modern, but only because it no longer means "the implantation of Dutch in the Indies" or "living like a Dutchman in Holland." It means that one "sees" the Dutch, their effects in photographs, as one hears them in translation. In the perfection of translation, the perfect adequacy of languages, illustrated through the perfect transmission of imagery, one finds a new home. It is the place one belongs; within the photograph; within the national language. This is the place the characters of this novel inhabit; it is a place where the monuments of the sultan and the palace of the Dutch are both there and are equally "ours."

What is taken in, either from the past or from Europe, creates the ambience of the novel. There is an interest in taking in more and more, on challenging what might resist the translation to modernity. It is closely related to the fetish of modernity we have discussed. This fetish compels recognition. It insists on recognition of "myself" that extends beyond what I know myself to be. Once recognition is linked to propriety and authority, it insists that "I" am discovered to be part of the modern world, subject to the same processes of making oneself at home that govern the transformation of the Indies into Indonesia.

In this notion of modernity, which equates it with transmission, the foreign is located on both sides—in the traditional and in the European. The narratives of "modernity" show that one is bound to family by an identity that is no longer functional and that is not repudiated. Sitti Saniah is the daughter of her parents. Everyone in the novel insists on it, not least Sitti Saniah herself. That her parents are mistaken about her and that their mistake is lethal only shows that her identity as their daughter is undeniable. She bears something in herself that is foreign to her identity as a nationalist. It is not the foreignness that comes from Europe; it is the foreignness that comes from Aceh. If she, like the other fetishists of the modern, within and outside novels, lives her life in the hope of recognition of something about her she does not know, it is because it is assumed that there is a foreignness to oneself that one is born with. It is odd to think that one has a natural foreignness. But this is the result of the supplementary notion of recognition by which I discover something in myself always there and that makes me what I have become. It is not evident until the point of recognition. Afterwards, an origin clearly not transformed reasserts itself. This, now, is the foreign, itself a product of fetishistic recognition.

The foreign does not arrive from abroad in the form of foreign languages. Rather, the perfect translatability of languages fails and creates misunderstandings that makes parents blind to the natures of their children. In the view of the novel, parental failures at translation mask the adequacy of languages. *Cinta*, the novel asserts, is both understandable in Indonesian and universal by its nature, so that it should be equally comprehensible to the Dutch doctor and the Acehnese father. *Cinta* is a word taken from literary Malay, where it means "devoting much thought to. Of care, longing, regret, love, mourning and solicitude generally."[12] Suppose instead of *cinta* the author said "love." Then his characters would be in danger of finding themselves European when they fall in love without having to leave for Holland. The fetish in the context of nationalism reassures that one belongs where one started, thus to the region, as well as to the new, the modern, and to the nation. It is a question of seeing that one is born with the possibility of having *cinta*; it is natural and not a translation of a European object. When translation does not work, *cinta* is "love" and misunderstood locally as "black magic." When translation works, the foreign element appears as always having belonged to the local scene. The contradictory phrase, the "domestic foreign" is a question of translation.

It is precisely here that one can locate the borrowing of the authority of the mother for nationalism. The nationalist schoolteacher who acts as a mother, arranging the marriage of her students, does not replace the original mother; she rectifies her errors, or at least tries to do so. Mothers will be restored to their true functioning at some later point, when, for instance, the female students studying home economics themselves become mothers. At that point, regional traditions, nationalism, and modernity will be wholly compatible. It is not the repudiation of the mother but the wish to retain one's tie to her, indeed, to render unthinkable breaking that tie, that informs the picture of the schoolteacher. She, within the lingua franca that is now also the national language, makes the foreign that originates in Aceh forgettable. Between her and Sitti Saniah's mother there is hoped to be, in the next generation at least, the same seamless transition as between the Sultan of Aceh whose palace was burned to the ground and the Governor of Aceh whose palace occupies the same site. In the idiom of kinship, to return to the case of Sitti Saniah and the schoolteacher, a vast denial is constructed which is also the appropriation of the authority of the family for nationalism.

The change of registers from linguistic text to photographs and captions reinforces the denial of the inadequacy of languages. The pressure to do so indicates how a fiction that works against fiction worries about itself. This worry about what cannot be taken in without producing an alien form of oneself not only shifts the scene of fiction to photographs, it creates different stories there. If these in turn are denials, they show how the attempt to find the modern in the process of transmission and to make this an instrument of incorporation into the colonial hierarchy is not successful. More stories are required, equally devoted to the elimination of fictions that seem so without purpose as to be distractions.[13]

Borrowing the authority of mother for nationalism established a source of nationalist power apart from the Dutch, a power of recognition that the novel asserts cannot be denied. But the very establishment of nationalist authority, its ability to recognize love and idealism, its reorientation of the fetish from colonial police to nationalist schoolteachers, one might say blinded it. For the power to recognize the genuine nationalist and the purity of love is also the power to see its opposite. Or rather, the very establishment of an authority that recognizes innocence raises the fear of guilt. That fear is located not in those who have acted wrongly but in those who believe that nationalist idealism means innocence. Anyone who knows more about me than I do myself might well find guilty residues. This is the topic of the following chapter.

CHAPTER SEVEN

The Wish for Hierarchy

Just before World War II, in the port city of Medan on the island of Sumatra, there were several series of popular novels which, because they sold for a very low price (about 18 *sen*) came to be known as "dime novels" (*roman picisan*). Tamar Djaja, one of the authors of these books, says that "ten penny novel" or *roman picisan* was a pejorative term used by someone who thought the novels were merely extended short stories hurriedly written and confused in their aims and execution. Tamar Djaja names as the author of the term a leftist who may have had ideological reasons for his criticism of the novels. In any case, another objection was made against them on the grounds of their language, that is, it was not the proper language supported by the Dutch. Tamar Djaja, however, points out that the novels were both popular and they created effects. The Muslim political organization PERTI demanded that the books be burned and that the three people they considered responsible for them be cursed at Friday prayers for a month. One of those to be cursed, Hamka, was, to be sure, a rival Muslim figure important for his religious writings but who also wrote novels, including *roman picisan*. Attacked from the right, the left, and by the Dutch, these dime novels merit our attention.

According to Tamar Djaja, *roman picisan* leaned toward "fantasy and agitation"; the favorites were detective novels and stories of ghosts and similar uncanny manifestations. They appealed to boys and to men. I have never met a woman who has read one, but of course there may have been some. The authors were youths who were obviously deeply immersed in the urgencies of their day. This urgency expressed itself in the speed of writing. Tamar Djaja says that one author wrote five eighty-page novels in a month while another wrote one overnight, having it ready for the printer the next day. Professor A. Teeuw, one-time professor of Malay Literature in Leiden, deplored the language of these books, but Tamar Djaja points out that it was the language used by readers and for that reason the books were popular. It is clear that, linguistically at least, these authors escaped the constraints that the Dutch imposed on Melayu. It indicates that to a certain degree they stood outside the official culture in which, for instance, *Flower of Atjeh* was written.

Contrary to Professor Teeuw, Tamar Djaja praises the Indonesian used by comparison to the language of the Sino-Malay authors. He regrets the state of Indonesian written after independence, claiming that it fails to attract readers because, he claims, they do not understand it, implying that the present national language is the heritage of Dutch-reforming efforts. The language of the *roman picisan*, by contrast, was close to speech. For Tamar Djaja, at least, these novels escaped the standardization of the language and therefore retained a certain closeness between authors and readers.[1] We shall see that some of these books had strong political connotations.[2] But the urgency reflected in the language seems to have stemmed not from political involvement so much as from a desire to be immersed in the popular culture of the time. For instance, there are interesting novels about sports, frequent references to the movies, and much comment about dress.

Noriaki Oshikawa has shown that several dime novels by various authors had the revolutionary Tan Malaka as their chief protagonist, albeit not always so named. In some novels, he is pictured under the pseudonym "Patjar Merah," or The Scarlet Pimpernel.[3] One such novel, not mentioned by Oshikawa but fitting his description, and by an author of a Tan Malaka novel, is Matu Mona's *Detective Rindu*.[4] The detective, more or less inexplicably, solves a crime. The point of the novel is not how the detective uncovered the identity of the guilty, it is, rather, that those suspected are innocent. The detective, who is not described as detecting, is more of a judge; his role is to relieve the innocent from suspicion. Indeed, relieving the innocent from suspicion is the function of the fictional version of "Tan Malaka" even when he is not a detective.

The historical Tan Malaka, born in West Sumatra in 1897, called himself a Trotskyite. As Rudolf Mrázek has shown, he adapted a Minangkabau dialectic to world history thinking all the while he was in the socialist tradition.[5] He was popular in the Indies before World War II as a political figure who, through his travels across Asia and Europe, showed how Indonesians could appear on the world stage. Tan Malaka was apparently put to death in 1949. In fiction, Tan Malaka was celebrated for his capacity to disguise himself and to speak the languages of the countries through which he traveled. He was pictured as a chameleon, taking on whatever ethnic and linguistic characteristics would allow him to blend with his environment.

Moechtar Nasoetion's novel, *Tan Malaka di Medan* (*Tan Malaka in Medan*), is the story of a youth who is a member of a secret nationalist organization.[6] Marwan, as he is called, belongs to a group of which Tan Malaka is the "Pedoman Agung," or "Supreme Guide." The members of the organization are not known to each other, being referred to only by numbers and attending their meetings masked and disguised. At one of these meetings, it is announced that the Supreme Guide is about to arrive in Medan. Just then, several people reveal themselves to be police agents.

The others escape by a secret exit. Later, Marwan receives notice that the organization has sentenced him to death for betraying them. The remainder of the novel consists in the youth clearing his name.

The police arrest a Chinese, thinking he is Tan Malaka. While he is held in jail, however, letters signed by Tan Malaka are sent to the newspapers and to the police. These are actually the work of Marwan, who succeeds in getting the police to release the Chinese, whom Marwan then follows, thinking he is Tan Malaka. He is not, but for a reason that is not made clear, Tan Malaka is nearby and has understood what Marwan has done on his behalf. Tan Malaka takes Marwan to the leadership and they agree to give him a week to clear himself. The evidence against him, however, is strong: a letter with a signature matching Marwan's informing the police of the organization's meeting. Eventually, Marwan is arrested because the police think he is Tan Malaka. Marwan's sweetheart forces Tan Malaka to turn himself in in order to clear Marwan. Marwan is humiliated to learn what his girlfriend has done. He forces his way to the radio studio and broadcasts a message: Radio Moscow has reported that Tan Malaka is ill in the hospital in Moscow and his passport has been stolen. The police believe it, though Tan Malaka insists that he is really himself. Not believing him, the police release him.

The youth's broadcast convinces Tan Malaka of Marwan's fidelity and innocence. The three, Marwan, Tan Malaka, and Marwan's fiancée, leave for abroad to continue the struggle. At the end, it is said in passing that Marwan's uncle has betrayed the organization and Marwan to the police for money and vengeance; but vengeance for what is not said. The sweetheart knew this, but she is relieved not to have to reveal it. After they leave, rebellion breaks out "all over Indonesia," apparently a reference to the 1926–1927 Communist uprising. The rebellion is the result of misunderstanding the Supreme Guide, who wanted not "force but nobility and humanity."

In this novel, Tan Malaka is uncapturable because of his disguises. He is capable of all appearances. The police, knowing his talent for costume, arrest a Chinese; Tan Malaka, however, has taken on the appearance of a Bengali. In other novels, he appears as various other nationalities as well as as a woman, a beggar, and so forth. When he appears as himself before the police, showing them his papers, the police believe his passport is genuine, but they do not believe that the bearer is really the person the passport identifies. And when they arrest the Chinese, thinking he is Tan Malaka, the police refuse to believe the innocent Chinese, again being confused by Tan Malaka's reputation for disguise. A police agent speaks:

> "Och, och, och, you are extremely skillful, Mr. Tan Malaka, in theater. . . . your disguise is excellent. Charles Laughton has met his match." (22)

One notices the reference to the movies, whose influence on these books is clear.

"Tan Malaka" in these novels is a polyglot; in one novel, he speaks Thai and French among other languages. In another of the Tan Malaka novels, one by Matu Mona, Tan Malaka is described this way:

> He can speak the languages of the people of the country, starting from Siam, India, China and the Philippines. He knew two or three Western languages too such as English, French and German not to mention Dutch.[7]

We have seen, in speaking of Soewardi, how, in the conception of the Melayu lingua franca, the first person singular of any language could appear in Melayu. The Tan Malaka novels modify this formula. In these novels, Tan Malaka, the figure of Indonesian nationalism, takes on the appearance of any nationality, any individual type. If the assumption before was that an "I" of any origin can appear in Melayu, here the "I" of Indonesian, spoken by the nationalist leader, can appear at will as the "I" of any nationality and either gender. But the reverse movement, from other languages into Indonesian, does not take place. In particular, the Dutch *ik* does not become the Indonesian *saya* or "I."(When the Dutch interrogate Indonesians, the language they use is unspecified.)

Unlike Soewardi's piece, the purpose of this movement between languages is not to expose but to conceal. These novels do not show Indonesians contending with Dutch; they show Indonesians evading them. The fight against the Dutch meant staying out of their sight. Tan Malaka is famous; he is well known in these novels both to the Dutch and to Indonesian nationalists. His great feat is to be both famous and uncapturable because he is unidentifiable by his pursuers.

The political stance of Tan Malaka is perhaps shown by this puzzling passage from *Detective Rindu*.[8] The detective, as I have mentioned, is thought to be modeled on Tan Malaka:

> He did not work for any particular country, but as a private detective. Wherever there was something difficult that happened that terrified a country and that bewildered the Crimineel Recherche of a country, Rindu was called to straighten it out. He took part in exposing the rebels of Indo-China, of Burma and was a Siamese counterespionage agent in 1936 when there was a movement that wanted to overturn the old fashioned despotism of the kingdom. The voice of the people [*soeara rakjat*] overthrew the nobility who wanted to be praised and flattered like holy gods. (66)

Detective Rindu works for the authorities of any country, meaning colonial authorities. He puts down rebellions; he is a counterespionage agent. This might seen hard to reconcile with the fact, surely accurate, established by Oshikawa that both the (Indonesian) Scarlet Pimpernel and Detective

Rindu are modeled after the revolutionary, Tan Malaka. And yet the very name for him, "The Scarlet Pimpernel," refers to the counterrevolutionary in the novel of Baroness Orczy, who saved French nobles from revolutionaries' guillotines. The Scarlet Pimpernel was known in Indonesia from the movie made after the book. The resemblance to the figure of Tan Malaka is clearly not to his revolutionary politics but to his secret international operations. He appears in disguise across national borders. The idolizing occurs when national boundaries, diverse languages and, one can add, disguise, are invoked. What makes him an extraordinary man is not the content of his politics but the international celebrity claimed for him combined with his unrecognizability to the Dutch.

In Matu Mona's novel about Tan Malaka, one character tells another:

> Understand that he is not just anyone, not just an ordinary man. In Europe people say his name along with Mussolini, Stalin, Kemal, MacDonald and others. Isn't it true that on this ship there is a reward of 50,000 *ticals* offered by a foreign government to whomever can catch him alive? But none of his friends would betray him. (33)

He is not ordinary. Neither are Stalin or Mussolini, who are equated in this sentence with each other and with the Scarlet Pimpernel because "in Europe" people say his name in the same way they say their names. A Trotskyite equated with Stalin and with Mussolini, he is wanted by "a foreign government," the same one for whom he worked, in another novel, as an antirevolutionary. It does not matter what he does. What matters is coming to the attention of authorities and evading them. No matter how well known he is, and he is world famous, he is unrecognizable by authorities when they search for him. On the other hand, as in the passage cited, he is not merely acknowledged by world authorities, he is equated with them. He embodies an adolescent's notion of invisibility, but at the same time one associated with the glamour of the market, particularly of the screen heros we have already seen. He is a celebrity, someone well known, appearing in different roles in different movies, different novels, but reduced to a "real person" outside his roles by his readers. "Tan Malaka" is another effect of the technology of the camera.

In these novels, others have the chance to prove their identification with him. In *Tan Malaka di Medan*, for instance, it is not important to expose the actual betrayer. It is more important that the false accusation of betrayal offers Marwan the chance to prove his fidelity to the Supreme Guide. In doing so, Marwan, too, shows his capacity for invisibility. But he evades not the colonial authorities but the nationalists who have sentenced him to death. Dutch who look for Tan Malaka are replaced by nationalists who look for Marwan. Marwan demonstrates his political sympathies not by action against the colonialists but by proving that even at the risk of his life, he remains a loyal nationalist. Tan Malaka's role here is to be conflated with all government and at the same time to be a nationalist opposed to colonial government.

The idea of the "national" and the "international" as it is expressed here depends on colonial imagery; that is, it depends on figures that appear in Dutch from the end of the nineteenth century onwards, rather than the figures that appear in "traditional" Sumatran or Javanese literature. For instance, in the latter case, there are nuanced differences between various Javanese, but few distinctions are made between those outside the group. The imagery inherited from the colonial world passes through Melayu, the lingua franca, and latter Indonesian, the national language. The Tan Malaka novels show an "international" world, with not simply Dutch and Indonesians, but Chinese, Indians, Thai, and, in some Tan Malaka novels, French, Filipinos, Russians, and others. These images express presumably fundamental identities in each case, but ones which are at the same time transferable from one into the other through the medium of Indonesian and through the figure of Tan Malaka-Scarlet Pimpernel-Detective Rindu. Indonesian thus keeps its character as a lingua franca in the sense that, through it, international differences appear but at the same time they are reduced to an Indonesian fundament.

As we have seen in the last quotations, "Indonesians" now make their own appearances on a world scene. But when they do so through Tan Malaka it is not as Indonesians who take a part vis-à-vis their international counterparts. It is in the guise of the other, the way that an Indonesian actor might play the role of a Filipino. "Tan Malaka" conflates the power of Indonesian to be converted into other languages with the taking of their part. But there is now an underlying reality, if that is a term one can use in something so thoroughly imaginative: the actor is Indonesian. But he is a screen actor, an effect of the camera, as is evident from the influence of the film of the Scarlet Pimpernel but particularly from the celebrity we have noted. He is a celebrity in the way that Edgar Morin, for instance, thinks of celebrities.[9] Morin's contention is that "stars" are those whose private lives and screen roles are conflated by their fans. But of course the private person is known only through publicity and is as much an effect of the movies as the screen role. There is no point, that is, where it is easy to find the difference between "Tan Malaka" in the forms he takes in this novel and the historical figure. As a result, the new set of international differences that appears in these novels remains imagistic.

One can see the image constructed within the novel itself through its motif of disguise. In *Tan Malaka di Medan* Tan Malaka's disguise is always effective. But Marwan's disguise involves him in complications. He, like the members of his organization, goes about in robes, calls and is called by numbers rather than names, and uses passwords. Disguise, one notes in passing, not only keeps members' identities hidden from the police, but from each other. Nonetheless, their meetings are discovered by the police, and someone inside the organization knows Marwan is a member and falsely accuses him. One can say that Marwan's disguise is not adequate; someone has found out his identity. But it would also be possible to say that Marwan in disguise has attracted the attention of someone. His disguise brings him to notice. In another instance, while in hiding, Marwan visits his fiancée to explain to her what has happened. He comes to the door dressed as an old beggar. She thinks, " 'It's someone asking for alms I suppose.' " But the disguise is too effective because when Marwan calls out her name, "Hajati almost screamed to hear her name said by this man whom she did not know" (56). Marwan explains that "I am in disguise" and refuses to enter the house "so that people won't be suspicious because my clothes are unusual"(57). The assumptions in this case are that, in disguise, he is noticed and that the disguise is effective. But Marwan's disguise deceives those whom he wants to know his identity and brings him to the attention of someone from whom he should have been concealed.

The novel begins with a description of dressing up which has unintended consequences. Here are the first three sentences:

> The youth Marwan finished dressing: a grey gabardine suit, a glistening pair of black Barrath [Bata?] shoes, a blue bow tie with white polka dots adorned his neck; on his head he wore neatly perched (*terlekap rapi*) a *petji*, the Seremban model. He was chic, fashionable, 28 years old and handsome. Seen in passing he would certainly be placed among those called "snazzily dressed youths," many of whom "adorned" this Paris of Sumatra; that is, the group of youth who did things and went out for pleasure night and day. (3)

Marwan is about to go to the *vergadering*, the meeting of his nationalist organization. He is carrying papers he wishes to conceal. As he finishes dressing, his fiancée comes in. She does not believe he is going to a meeting; she thinks he has a date with someone else. Marwan dresses up here as a disguise. Anyone might think that he is merely out for pleasure, just like other youth. And he is successful to the extent that he fools a person he does not want to deceive. But equally, he is a modern youth of the day; he is interested in romance; his disguise is the dress which is appropriate to him. Hajati, his sweetheart, is not surprised he has such clothes; only that he wears them without her. He is taken for what he wants to appear to be, but that creates difficulty for him.

Marwan, like the others of his group, dresses up again at the nationalist meeting, the vergadering. The meeting is held in what appears to be an abandoned building. Near the building "two or three black shadows like ghosts approached the building and then disappeared." It is dark; black shadows keep on appearing and disappearing. These ghosts are not ghosts at all. They are members of the organization:

> black robes covering their entire faces and heads. Only two eyes and a nose appeared from out of holes. (7)

Despite this disguise, someone knows that Marwan is one of these wearers of robes and hoods. Marwan has dressed up with good intentions and yet he has been taken for someone with bad intentions. He is understood as such not by the antinationalist authorities but by nationalists. His disguise reflects his authentic political beliefs. But it is misread by those with whom he wants to be identified.

Tan Malaka's successful passing between identities depends on his devotion to ideals that come before any relation that threatens permanence. Marwan tries to do the same. But Marwan's sweetheart becomes involved in his nationalist activities all the same. At one point, she goes to Tan Malaka to ask for help in clearing Marwan. Tan Malaka agrees, but he tells her that there is a love that is greater and more noble than romantic love. She accuses him of not knowing love. He replies:

> "Perhaps." When she looked at him, his eyes were staring into the distance, but only for a moment. Then he laughed and laughed. "Love, oh love, what enormous influence you have." (72)

The idealism of Tan Malaka and of Marwan is connected with a renunciation of desire, which means for Marwan conflict between his sweetheart and his loyalty to Tan Malaka, at least till the end of the novel when Hajati, the sweetheart, joins him and Tan Malaka in the struggle. Hajati, for her part, is jealous of Marwan's political involvements:

> "I love just you, but you, besides me, you have another sweetheart—your movement and the Great Guide." (77)

Love is related to disguise because the woman loves not only the person in disguise, who is also the political person, but the everyday figure. The course of the story shows Marwan in his disguises noticed by Hajati who does not understand. This, of course, makes Marwan's efforts more noble, a sacrifice similar to Tan Malaka's. Ideally, he should be able to combine the two, at least in the sense that Hajati appreciates Marwan's sacrifice and loves him more. He would then be noticed in his absence and able to combine two identities. But his disguises work too well. He fools Hajati who, when he dresses as a smart youth to hide his nationalist papers, thinks he has a date with someone else and who nearly calls out when, dressed as a beggar, he pronounces her name. The difficulty, that is, is that he is overtaken by his disguise, which is more effective than he figured it to be.

He is taken to be what he is dressed as even when he does not want to be. Dressing up, as a nationalist, he again merely activates a potential in himself that was always there. The difficulty is that in doing so he surpasses himself, as it were. The fetish is out of control as he becomes recognized for what he looks like, for who he is beneath his robes. He makes trouble for "himself" just as often as the reverse. It at once confirms the power he has to stimulate recognition and the need for an authority of some sort to stabilize and confirm identity. This, of course, is the role of Tan Malaka.

VENGEANCE

> What was special was that the courageous youth was thought to be incapable of committing the treachery of which he had been accused. In this situation, Hajati secretly felt relieved because it was no longer necessary to expose the secret of Marwan's uncle, the merchant Sjahrir, whom she had seen . . . receive 5 bills of 100 *roepiah* from the officer of the PID. . . . Without Marwan's knowledge, his uncle apparently was also a member of the leadership of the organization and from one or another motive wanted to take revenge on his nephew on his wife's side, to the point where he had behaved shamefully in trying to plunge Marwan into the fatal abyss. Further, he knew Marwan was commissioned to deliver the organization's communications. (80)

It is Marwan's uncle who has caused Marwan to be suspect and for motives of revenge. Had someone betrayed Marwan only for money, it would imply that he was a bad type. His desire for money, his lack of political faith, might be only a question of a flawed personality. But it is not anybody at all who casts suspicion on Marwan. The uncle's motives are never given, but one thinks of the tension between nephews and maternal uncles in some Sumatran societies. It is their family connection that has given rise to an unmentioned situation that makes the uncle want vengeance. Marwan's difficulty comes, that is, because he continues to be associated with his uncle.

In the logic of vengeance, there is no end. If nothing intervenes, if peace cannot be made, there is more vengeance and one has the feud. Vengeance is a form of reciprocity in which each deed begets another. Each act of vengeance is a response to a previous wrong. It is exactly as a "response" that Indonesian phrases the definition of revenge (*dendam*): "the strong desire to reply to a wrong"). To "take" revenge is to give back to the other what they gave to oneself; in taking, it gives back to the other their own, something rightly theirs and not one's own. Vengeance is a logic of the foreign, possession of which begets response. "I do not deserve what happened to me; it came from you. You should have the same back." "The same," the act of reply, is always what the other deserves; what is rightfully his and what, in a way, the person who takes revenge rids himself of. When vengeance occurs in the heart of the family, the usual effect of exchange is reversed; in place of the confirmation of affinity, there is the assertion of enmity. The implication of vengeance between members of a family is that there is something flawed about descent. One acts as a brother, but one makes one's brother an enemy. One remains the brother or the uncle nonetheless with the result that a sometimes fatal flaw is implanted within the heart of the family.

Vengeance destroys the family because it changes what is given between family members from something that belongs to them in common into something foreign. It is precisely this possession of the foreign, of an act done to Marwan which he did not deserve, one which rightly should be given back to his uncle, that begets suspicion. It is in place of taking revenge against his uncle that Marwan seeks recognition. Marwan does not know why he is accused of betraying the organization. He never learns that it is because of his uncle. There is something about himself, namely his relation to his uncle, which he remains unaware of and which requires that he be recognized by Tan Malaka in order to be found innocent. Marwan, not knowing about his uncle, thus not knowing something about who he, Marwan himself, is, becomes suspected. He believes himself to be a nationalist, but he is thought not to be so precisely by the only ones capable of affirming his nationalism, namely, his fellow organization members. But he never inquires about why he was accused or who accused him.

Nor is the novel at all interested in finding the nature of that foreignness. Only three lines are devoted to the uncle:

> What was special was that the courageous youth was thought to be incapable of committing the treachery of which he had been accused. In this situation, Hajati secretly felt relieved because it was no longer necessary to expose the secret of Marwan's uncle, the merchant Sjahrir.

The merchant Sjahrir is never brought to light. It is not necessary. What is necessary is to prove that Marwan is innocent. Marwan is innocent in the eyes of Tan Malaka. He has proved himself incapable of being a traitor. Incapable, that is, of being like his uncle. And yet, he remains his uncle's nephew. In the logic of maternally related descent, Marwan is the descendant of his mother's brother, not his father. Marwan, in other words, continues to share his familial identity with his uncle without that identity ever being modified. But he is equally a pure and innocent nationalist. He is bound by his origins, but they do not weigh on him. This is the service that Tan Malaka performs.

It is suspicion that begets disguise and it is disguise that begets recognition. By the logic of vengeance, the uncle should be punished. But this does not happen. Thanks to Tan Malaka, Marwan is delivered into the image he has assumed. He is transformed in the way that cotton, in the movies, is made into silk. It remains cotton, but it is taken for silk. This deception is not a lie; it creates an impression on which the story is based. When the silk of the cinema is revealed to be merely cotton, it merely enhances the effect of the story. The same logic holds for the family. Marwan is born into a family, but to see that his relation to his uncle can be both maintained and put aside is precisely what makes him a genuine nationalist, one who belongs to the family and to the nation.

The Impulse toward Hierarchy

The fetish of modernity is too powerful. It stimulates undesirable forms of recognition, delivering one into identities one does not want. Tan Malaka straightens things out. We are not far from the logic of *Flower of Atjeh* with a major exception. Definitive power of recognition is now dissociated from the Dutch and made explicitly Indonesian. It is all due to Tan Malaka. He is a special image, an effect, we have said, of communication, an example of the infallible success of the transformations assumed to occur through the capacity to speak all languages but to still be "Indonesian" in language and in political faith. It is precisely this capacity to disappear into the image, to continue to transform oneself, and yet remain identical to oneself that is so wishfully portrayed in our novel. Only if one can be like Tan Malaka can one control recognition of oneself.

Meanwhile, in the Tan Malaka novels, the Dutch are shut out of the scene by Tan Malaka himself. They cannot find him; but Tan Malaka is the ultimate goal of all messages, which means that the Dutch are not. As a detective, in, for instance, *Detective Rindu*, he never traces clues to arrive at the guilty. The Sumatran detective novel reverses Sherlock Holmes. The detective merely appears and then hears everything. For instance, Detective Rindu is summoned to find some missing jewels. He goes by bus because he wants to hear what people are saying:

> . . . it was his practice when he looked for something secret to listen to the talk of the crowd [*orang banjak*]. The public (*publiek*) knew a lot and talked a lot about the things that happened in their area. (54)

One would think that we would be told what Detective Rindu heard and what he made of it, how he put it together with other clues to find the criminal. In fact, none of this is the case. The passage does not indicate that the detective interprets what he hears and goes out of his way to gather evidence. Instead, by simply finding his way to the site of the crime, the detective comes to know whatever is being said. How he solves the crime is not important enough to relate. For instance, we never see Tan Malaka ponder the question of who exactly betrayed the movement. That he solves it because the truth comes to him is more important.

Everything depends on reaching the Supreme Guide, and this is not difficult. The story is replete with his appearances and his false appearances. Marwan announces on the radio that Tan Malaka is in Moscow and he is believed. The leader of the movement's branch in Medan announces, at the beginning of the story, that Tan Malaka will arrive in Medan. Tan Malaka poses as a Bengali and fools everyone looking for him. Whoever you think is Tan Malaka is not him; if you think you know where he is, you are likely to be mistaken. His capacity for disguise is such that people look for him in the wrong places and do not see him where he is. He is always potentially present anywhere. But it is in public places, such as restaurants, that he is pictured. At one point, Marwan, wanting to find Tan Malaka, follows a Chinese thinking he is the Supreme Guide. Marwan follows the Chinese to a café where he writes one half of the movement's password, "Luctor," on a calling card hoping the Chinese/Tan Malaka will furnish the other half. Marwan then notices that a Bengali sitting next to him has in fact written the other half, "Veritas," on a piece of paper. Marwan has been completely fooled, but he has found Tan Malaka. It is not effort, calculation, or interpretation that lead to him. It is simply believing in disguise and passwords. Tan Malaka is always available to intercept messages sent to the wrong person. He is the great secret overhearer. He reverses the position of the Gouverneur Generaal in the early days of nationalist meetings who was considered the proper source of everything said. Tan Malaka is the proper address, the place messages should arrive, even those not explicitly addressed him. Receiving them, Tan Malaka accepts the sender as innocent; recognized by Tan Malaka, one is like him and one is with him.

The contrast is with recognition by the Dutch, à la Soewardi. In his formula, "If I were . . ." leads to "But I'm not. . . ." The difference between the recognizing authority and the one who imagines taking his place is restored. One imagines oneself a Dutchman. The imaginative capacity is initially found in oneself. This is not the case with Tan Malaka. It is Tan Malaka who is the master of disguise and of languages. To become like him means to take on his abilities. It means that the very capacity to change form, to become the other, when the other is Tan Malaka, precludes further change. After that, one is merely in disguise, always identical to oneself because disguise is the expression of the capacity to change form and this capacity defines identity. In Soewardi, when one imagines one is a Dutchman, one never takes on the identity "Dutch"; one merely shows that one knows what is going on in the mind of the Dutch. One inhabits

"Dutch" as a foreigner precisely because one keeps the capacity to place oneself in the position of the other for the original of oneself. However, one becomes "Tan Malaka" in a way not entirely different from the way Muhammad Bakir inhabited his text. To imagine the other is to become him. And, when he is the very control of the capacity to move between figures, one never worries about reverting to what one was.

It is just here that we can locate the impulse to hierarchy that occurs within the development of nationalism. Tan Malaka is the great over-hearer, the interceptor of all messages, the guarantor that one has the power to beget recognition and that one is recognized only for what is proper, against all false recognition. He differs from figures of recognition in other novels we have read by the purity of his nationalism. It is a nationalism based not on ideology but on communication. On the one hand, the urge for recognition stimulated by bringing the foreign inside the domestic; on the other, the need to find a domesticating figure, one where precisely one's doubleness, one's foreignness to oneself is relieved. On the one hand, the power of the fetish to transform oneself at will; the imagined capacity to take on the power of the middle. On the other hand, the need to limit this capacity. Tan Malaka is fiction but fiction with reference to the world. He represents the wish for hierarchy, a wish with two components: the domestication or making-at-home of the power of communication and a share in that power of communication itself. Hierarchy is the transformation of these wishes into social form. "Tan Malaka," the stabilization of identity, the mastery of language, is to the uncle/father what the female schoolteacher was to Sitti Saniah's mother. He is a purification, or rectification, of the linguistic faults of the father, who keeps familial structures intact by making it possible to cease to be worried about origins, which, then, remain intact.

What, then, happens to the Dutch? In the first place, Tan Malaka is also, we have said, the final address of important messages. As the idealized Indonesian father, the master of languages, he defines a hierarchy that displaces that which began with the Gouverneur Generaal as the source of messages. Is this possible? Can one say, "I no longer hear what I heard?" without also thinking one might hear? It becomes all the more important to believe in the limitations that Tan Malaka marks. Able to pass for anyone at all, one once again risks arriving in the place of the Dutch. Able to change form, one can always move away. This implies that the Dutch might see, which, after all, is the point of disguise in the first place. And if they can see, what then? Seen in the eyes of the Dutch, one might also see them. Seeing them seeing "me," I would fall back into the syntax of Soewardi: "If I were . . . But I'm not . . . I am only." It is by the redefinition of betrayal as a result of desire that the Dutch come again to define the locus of pleasure and thus become available to be put out of mind. We will see more of this when we come to consider the revolution.

HIERARCHY, VENGEANCE, AND LITERATURE: THE CROWD

The political character of these novels is marked by the transformation they show in the notion of the public. D. E. Manuturi's *Loves of a Football Player*[10] is the story of Hoesni from Sibolga who is an expert football player but who cannot reconcile his love for his sweetheart, being a sportsman and giving in to the adulation of "the public." "The public" here is designated not only by the Dutch-derived *publiek* but by the Indonesian *orang banjak*, a phrase that means also, "others" and "many." When he is praised, he tells his friend Moeanaf:

> No, Moeanaf! Don't be like the others [like the crowd, *orang banjak*] and flatter me. Whatever I might seem like in playing up till now, it is nothing other than my duty as a sportman [*sic*, in English]. (7)

Yes, his friend tells him, that is what is wanted of you, to be "a sportman, honest" and not "a god [*dewa*]. That is why you are being brought to Medan" (8). Medan is the Sumatran metropolis where important matches are to be held. Hoesni, however, does not want to go to Medan. It is not that he is afraid of being beaten, he says. It is because Hafsah, his sweetheart, lives in Medan and has warned him he must chose between football and her. Here is a situation similar to that in *Tan Malaka di Medan* when Marwan, at the opening of the story, was placed between loyalty to his political organization and his sweetheart. Hoesni goes to Medan, but he stubs his toe and does not play.

> Gossip spread between the players giving a thousand and one reasons for Hoesni's nonappearance. Each one had his suspicion and there were those who said that the youth [*pemuda*] was a coward, a betrayer [*pengchianat*], a fifth columnist. There were those too who accused him of languishing in the arms of a worldly angel.(29)

The words "betrayer" and "fifth columnist" show how the registers of sports and politics are mixed. But we shall see that team loyalty and political loyalty are nonetheless different, team loyalty being an ambiguous virtue, good if it means that one plays as one should, out of a selfless commitment, but bad if it means that, supporting the team, one gives in to their definition of who one is.

Hafsah, the girlfriend, has been brought to the game by her father. She does not like football because, according to her:

"playing football really isn't a game but a way to fight and injure. . . . Aren't there a lot of players who are kicked and hit and injured even if not intentionally?" (21)

She is, in fact, disgusted by the game and would not go if her father had not taken her. Initially, she is indifferent to who wins, but once at the stadium she begins to take sides:

> She was disgusted watching the match. . . . Of course she did not want to take sides because she hated them both. But this time Hafsah had to take sides. She had to side with her sweetheart, Hoesni. (38)

She does not approve of Hoesni's playing, but she is forced to cheer him anyway:

> There were no two ways about it; she had to! Because of her love, she did not like to hear the scorn people expressed for the club which spread to the region the losing team came from. (38)

At this moment, though in opposition to what she hears the crowd say, she becomes part of it. Her "love" (*cinta*) for him makes her part of the larger scene from which she had held herself aloof. This should be the reconciliation of love and mass action as it was in earlier political novels where the sweetheart follows her boyfriend into mass political meetings and where their love for each other is combined with their political activities. In this story, however, the opposite happens.

Hoesni is upset to see his team losing. "Apparently carried away" he reenters the game, not giving a thought to the danger to himself (39). Hafsah involuntarily begins to cheer for him. She hears the girl next to her call him "Mr. Lame-foot," and she wants to tear the girl's hair.

> She felt like she wanted to scratch and pull the hair of the girl who was so quick to insult; if only she were alone with her. But her heart froze when she heard the public [*publiek*] scream and shout for the ball which had passed over to the side of Sibolga which meant increasing danger.
>
> Hafsah was worried to death that the losing margin would widen. Consciously or not, that made her shout as loud as she could, yelling "Come on, Hoesni, come on Hoesni."

Precisely what she disliked about the game—its violence—has now infected her. The difference between spectators and the scene they watch begins to collapse as the emotions and actions she earlier attributed to the players, she now herself holds toward other spectators. At the same time, she is now united in sentiment with Hoesni, agreeing with him, at least emotionally, about football. This, however, seems to be the beginning of

Hoesni's downfall. Hoesni's sweetheart is not an object of passion but a guarantee of domesticity. If he is loyal to her, he will remain the person he always has been, selfless in his playing, a "sportman." But after she herself becomes a member of the crowd, she seems to lack the ability to restrain him. Hoesni becomes a professional and moves to Medan where he gets a job during a time when others cannot because he agrees to play for the company team. This means he has betrayed himself:

> He was aware that what he did was not right and was unjust. By joining the club from his place of work, he automatically became a professional (*beroepspeler*). The word "professional" [*beroeps*] was one he detested. (41)

With this, he makes many new friends in Medan; after all, he is a "champion" (*kampioen*). Everyone likes him; he is praised everywhere, and because of that he becomes arrogant. When he accepts the crowd's estimate of himself, however, he begins to fail. An Indo woman, Liesje, pretends to love him in order to get him to leave his job and play for the team of her "brother." The man she calls her brother, however, is really her lover. Hoesni, out of love for Liesje, takes a cut in salary. But he loses his self-respect and plays badly.

> Leisje in no way at all loved him. It was all a trick [*tipu muslihat*] of the girl's. (66)

He is fired for his poor playing and because of Liesje's lover's jealousy of him. He cannot get work because "the people (*pendoedoek*) of Medan know his playing ability has declined."

In this story, first the woman, then the man, take on the characteristics of the crowd. Doing so, the woman becomes full of passion and violent feelings, indistinguishable in that respect from others in the crowd. He, for his part, decides to play for money. He had sworn not to be misled by the crowd's flattery, but he comes to believe it. At that point, he is lost, led astray, tricked, (*ditipu*). Seduced first by the *publiek*, he is seduced by a calculating woman. Neither Hoesni nor Hafsah are who they once were after the match in Medan.

The problem is the crowd, the *orang banjak*, which was also the term at the time for "mass" and which eventually replaced the Dutch term *publiek*. Out of the crowd comes a definition of "us" that is at the same time a severing of origins and the taking on of another identity. The football crowd here is similar to the audience of the political meetings in the 1930s and to the readership of these popular novels.

The football crowd is a tissue of opinions, but one is led astray by listening to them. The best thing that can be done is to silence them, judging by the unfortunate fates of the novel's characters when they cannot resist the crowd. The public meant here the 'native' public; it was from them that nationalists drew their following, a following consisting of people who, when they became nationalists, took on a new identity. This itself, we have seen again and again, was an effect of language. But the language of the crowd provokes; it produces not nationalists but men and women whose reactions it governs and whom it leads into passion. Hafsah and Hoesni are not bundles of signs which they disseminate, needing a leader to intercept them and thus to show that they are, after all, perfectly correct in appearing as they do. Instead, they are instead tricked, swindled (*ditipu*). They are interceptors of signs, and they take them at face value. Hafsah merely repeats what she hears in the stadium, unsuccessfully trying to turn it against its originators. Hoesni is seduced, believing not simply the woman who seduces him but the crowd who tells him he is a hero.

The crowd in this novel plays a role somewhere between the anonymous gossipers threatened by the author/blackmailer of *Secrets of Bandoeng* and the nationalist organization of *Tan Malaka in Medan*. That is, it is both a source and a register of opinions as in the first novel, but it is no longer the locus of right judgment. On the other hand, it is not the mass out of which emerges figures such as Marwan who are confirmed in their allegiances and their identities. The opinions of the crowd are dangerous. Rather than needing expression, they need transformation and suppression. Were this a story of success, it might have shown how Hoesni resisted its flattery and instead became an example to others, a celebrity on the order of Tan Malaka. Here there is no Marwan and no Tan Malaka. By their absences one sees the need for them.

Instead, there is Hafsah's inability to resist replying to the crowd and thus her immersion in it. She cannot help replying and this is her weakness. Hoesni also should have disregarded what his fans said about him, but he could not. The result is a picture of violent response, a sort of vengeance in one case and of seduction in the other. Vengeance and seduction are equally the effects of the inability to withhold a response to the body of the public, as it were.

One might have expected the opposite. One might have thought that this novel, which mixes sports with politics, and was written by a member of a group that espoused nationalist ideals, would have seen "the people" as a source of sentiments that needed expression. Instead, what is shown is the failed beginnings of nationalist hierarchy, a hierarchy that starts not in the expansion of traditional structures but in the new forms introduced with "modernity." What is rejected is not sports, whose newness consisted not merely in the game introduced but in the organization of spectators on a massive scale and in the claim to represent those spectators. What is pictured in the novel, in fact, is failed representation. Spectators, loyal to their teams and, as it is said, to their regions, should be represented by those who are virtuous. The very virtue of champions should indicate the value and even the identity of spectators. The failure of virtue, however, is not the disappointment of the spectators. Hafsah and Hoesni become like the fans. One might think that they therefore represent them. It is precisely this that is feared and denied. The leader should not say what his followers say, feel, and think. He should suppress their sentiments by refusing to engage them. As a result, there would be an end to vengeance and perhaps to seduction. The multitude of sentiments of the crowd would be reduced to a single expression. The crowd of *Loves of a Football Player* incites reply; it is a stimulus to speak. It is the beginning of a thousand stories, and that is the problem. The crowd should be the mere material of hierarchy, allowing themselves to be left behind in favor of noble, if not sublime sentiments.

At the beginning of the century, in the era of the initial mass nationalist movements (*pergerakan*) and of Soewardi, the crowd formed itself when it overheard what was not meant for it and when it listened in an identity different from its everyday identity. The rallies were effective so long as they connected their audiences with the Dutch at the top of a hierarchy in which, via overhearing, they were to be included. The members of the crowd were pictured as silent aside from the signs of assent they gave. In these novels published in Medan, the object overheard is no longer the Dutch, it is the crowd itself. One might have thought that this would be welcome. It is not because it is now a locus of self-estrangement. Hafsah is disturbed by what is said about her sweetheart. Some of those who disturb her are supporters of the opposing team, others are from Hoesni's team. She is driven not merely into opposition to those with whom she disagrees, but to become a member of the crowd herself, thus someone quite the opposite of who she was before she entered the stadium. Hoesni is flattered by his supporters who come from his own region; he becomes the person he initially resolved never to become.

There were two ways of resisting this estrangement. One was through finding a new home in the structure of modernity created by the nationalist leader. A home, that is, in what we have called the nationalist hierarchy. The other is by opposing the sources of estrangement which, even when they are new, are still local. There is a third path, and that is by making a place for the foreign. This would be the path toward literature. "Literature" is the name reserved for the possibilities of language that are denied in our story. Who knows what replies Hafsah and Hoesni might have made to the crowd if they had been allowed to do so. If, that is, reply itself were no longer pictured as mere self-estrangement. What stories, what words, might have been generated then? Suppose Hafsah had begun to muse about the crowd's comments on Hoesni's character for instance, or had begun to think about club feet. Other stories, not ones culminating in technological repression, would have been the result. One sees the unrealized possibility of unplacable responses—foreign in the sense that they would be strange both to the speaker and to the auditors, of no use in supporting allegiances and identities, but still possibly of interest. Such responses open a society to heterogeneity.

We can put this in broader perspective. If one looks back at the Indies literatures from the end of the nineteenth century, one can name the important figures around which they turn. There are, for instance, the stories written in Dutch by reformers which concern those who are corrupt because they are venal. I think here, for instance, of Peralaer who in *Babu Dalima* wrote about Dutch administrators who, for money, allowed evil Chinese to oppress Javanese peasants. One thinks of the *njai* stories, not only by Daum but, of a lesser literary caliber, by many others, who wrote of their maliciousness. There are the stories of the crafty Arab who preys on innocent Javanese. Then there are the stories by Indos which warn against "Muslims," meaning 'natives.' In many of these stories, there is something stronger than a merely reformist impulse. There is a certain fear and sometimes hatred which, by contrast, one does not feel in either the Sino-Malay or Indonesian stories. There, by contrast, the villainous figures are not from other groups but from one's own "nationality." The first sort of literature calls for a stronger and less corrupt colonial authority to control the situation. This is hardly an option for, for instance, early Sino-Malay literature where the author, frequently enough, was himself the blackmailer or, even when he was short of that, needed the freedom of the market for his operations.

When the enemy becomes internal, one might expect an intensification of vengeance. But such is not the case. In the Sino-Malay literature, one begins with blackmail, which means a settling of accounts. But when the woman becomes the central figure for the market, instead of vengeance there is domestication. She is tamed rather than beaten. When the family itself contains the enemy, the result is the detective who does not detect, the movement away from reprisal. This is possible because the enemy is from the first symbolic. The starting point is no more the enmity between fathers and sons or uncles and nephews than it is the enmity between men and women. It is rather a question of first being part of the modern, a gentleman, a nationalist, and then, as we have said, finding a way to account for being estranged. Whatever strains existed in society, the move to focus on those in the interior of one's own society rather than in other groups is a function of finding oneself unaccountably somewhere else. That "elsewhere" cannot be located culturally or geographically but only in terms of opinion, communication, and language. The lack of vengeance is possible because another system is imagined, one which does what vengeance does: relieves, or attempts to relieve, one of being the repository of something foreign. Instead of repayment, there is finding the right address, one where one ends up being at home and where "home" is now an effect of communication, language, opinion.

When Tan Malaka receives all messages and they confirm who one is, the world and language are made one. This remains, of course, an imaginative possibility. This possibility is one that could always be breached, but in the face of the strength of the wish for nationalist hierarchy, it seldom has been. That is, the wish for nationalist hierarchy is the wish that language and the world coincide; that there be no leftover words, no signals that might incriminate one. This is exactly the point where vengeance is avoided in favor of the certainty of address of all messages. Vengeance is based on the assumption that the act made on me is undeserved, foreign to me, and that I must give it back; I must respond. But vengeance, by its lack of conclusion, keeps the foreign in circulation. The certainty that what is foreign to me is benign, that it forms the basis of my nationalist identity and is really, therefore, not foreign at all, makes vengeance unwanted. And, it makes it unnecessary to respond. There are no leftover signals, no leftover words. Or so it is assumed.

The crowd in *Loves of a Football Player* is a source of self-estrangement located within society. One becomes like it and unlike oneself and one does so precisely by responding to it. Becoming alien to oneself and replying, especially speaking, are one movement. Like Hafsah, one can reply in order to vindicate and to take revenge. Vengeance, in this perspective, is a reply that is made to a source of linguistic incitement that is also a sociological entity. From this perspective, literature itself, which is always the making of a reply, is easily equated with the taking of vengeance. The strongest writer of Indonesian is banned today in his country. It is because his books are thought to incite violence and disruption. This blind and deaf lumping together of vengeance and literature is the triumph of the fetish of modernity and the establishment of hierarchy. But that Pramoedya Ananta Toer, the writer to whom I refer, still works shows that this sad victory was not absolute.

PART III

Revolution

CHAPTER EIGHT

Collaboration and Cautious Rebellion

COLLABORATION

To celebrate the thirtieth anniversary of the proclamation of independence, the Indonesian state sponsored a contest. Anyone could submit writing about the revolution. The contest was announced on television, in newspapers, and in schools, and it produced numerous responses. The essays judged best were published in five volumes. The submissions were stored in Jakarta, where they are available to scholars. The essays vary considerably in form. The majority report the events of the revolution in official language, one in which the first person, for instance, might never appear. Others, however, report the experiences of the authors. I have chosen a few of the latter to discuss.

One winner was Professor Doctor Garnadi Prawirosudirjo, M.Sc., the Rektor of the Education Faculty (IKIP) in Bandung. His essay was entitled, "The Story of the Struggle for Freedom in the Period 1945–1950 as I Experienced It."[1] Professor Doctor Garnadi writes about Bogor where he was a teacher in the Veterinary School. He headed a group, a "delegation" (*delegasi*) he calls it, of youth from Bogor to the First Youth Congress in Jogjakarta in November 1945. When he returned home, he found the city in the hands of the British who had been sent to arrange the surrender of the Japanese and who, Indonesians learned, were there to restore Dutch to power. Professor Doctor Garnadi was even then an ardent nationalist. He describes the history of Bogor during the revolution and his own role. At one point, he and some friends form a "cell," a secret organization that succeeds "several times in sending medicine needed by Dr. Sudirman to the hinterland and at the same time giving them information about the situation in the city" (27). Belonging to the cell is dangerous; one might be discovered. At the point where this danger cannot be controlled, they disband their organization; he is convinced that they are known, he says.

> Once our courier, without our knowledge, brought ammunition out of the city. The Republican Regent at that time was Bapak Ipik Gandamama. We did not know how dangerous it was for us with such friends. One day a graduate came to our headquarters; he had just arrived from the Netherlands. He offered two of us scholarships [*Malino beurs*] saying, "Use this opportunity; don't continue this dangerous work." We did not know what to say. (28)

They did not know what to say not because an outsider knew of their activities but because they were confused about the correctness of what he said. Professor Doctor Garnadi continues:

> What the graduate whom we just met said was indeed true. Indonesia indeed needed many experts, many graduates. But was this not a betrayal of the national struggle? The children of high officials were satisfied with a commonwealth; the children of families who did not want to fly the red and white flag, several [high school] graduates who did not want to fight and other youngsters went to the Netherlands on Malino scholarships. And students and college students from other cities in Java and outside Java made use of the opportunity. Many of them returned to the fatherland as graduates and amongst them now there are those who hold high and respected positions. We cannot judge them. Apparently things like this are inherent [in English] in the revolution.
>
> The cell we built we declared out of existence that very day because someone from outside knew of it. If not, it could have endangered us. We looked for other activities. We formed a senior high school so the graduates of junior high school had somewhere to go. (28)

An outsider knows of the cell's existence; it is too dangerous. It is even more dangerous than they bargained for, so they disband. It is not just, however, that someone, and someone connected with the Dutch at that, knows of their secret existence. It is also that, even knowing what he knows, he offers them the attractive opportunity of studying in Holland. They are not in danger of being found out; they have been found out already. The result is not deprivation but the opposite. They are offered something attractive but, it is clear, in Professor Doctor Garnadi's opinion, to accept may well have been to betray the national cause. There is ambiguity because the country needs expertise and because those who gained it in Holland during the revolution returned with honor and with important positions. He clearly thinks this is wrong, but he is aware of the country's needs and he puts his own judgment aside.

It is evident that the offer was not without merit and was even tempting. That he refused is because he thought to accept was to betray. We cannot say that he almost betrayed his country. But it does seem that he finds it easy to end up on the side of the Dutch, all the more so since it was found acceptable by the nationalist government. The danger the Rektor ran was not simply being discovered to be a Republican activist. It is that, being discovered, he might, if he were not careful, find himself on the Dutch side.

He and his friends decide to disband their cell and start a high school. When they do that, their allegiance is clear. They are helping the *rakyat* (the people). They are in a smaller way doing what the Dutch would have done for them; they are educating those who otherwise would not have the opportunity for education. This, it is clear from the continuation of the piece, was the major contribution of the Professor Doctor, who continued throughout his life to serve his nation by educating its youth and by improving his own skills.

The passage I have quoted comes after another in which the Professor Doctor describes how, earlier, he had aided some revolutionaries with long hair in the style of the nationalist youth of the time. They asked him for medicine and bandages. Professor Doctor Garnadi and his wife give them all they could "with the hope that they would quickly leave our house. But instead in a demonstrative manner they simply sat around on the front porch of the house and only then left" (23). The problem was that there was a Gurkha soldier who patrolled the front of the house and they were in danger. Indeed, once the British, looking for revolutionary soldiers and their effects, raid the house, carrying off most of their valuables:

> Not long afterwards one of our students came to the garage to take the *putu* cake from under the firewood piled up there. *Putu* was code for hand grenade. We did not know he hid dangerous things in our house. "The Red Cross Post is the safest place to stash such things," he said. If the British soldiers had come across it, we might not have been safe. The *ekstremis* [the Dutch term] youth who hid the *putu* was Busono, now a veterinarian and assistant rektor of Gaja Mada University in Jogjakarta. (25)

The uncontrolled danger, the danger of discovery, is that he will be taken for "them"; "them" being those whose side he supports but who run risks he would not take. It is a question of identification. He is on their side, but he does not want it known that he is; he is innocent of what they do and should be thought of that way by his enemy.

Most Indonesians during the revolution naturally enough continued in their usual occupations. That they nonetheless considered themselves to have fully participated in the revolution is because they thought of themselves as being in danger. The story of the youths displaying themselves on the porch or hiding grenades in the garage, putting the teller in danger, thus have this message: "I was in danger because I could have been taken for them; I did not want to run this risk. I did so and it is proof of my nationalism that I ran risks even without knowing what I was allowing into my life."

To be taken for an *ektremis*, we have seen, was feared to have complicated effects. One could be punished, even killed, by the Dutch. But one might also be subtly wooed to their side. Perhaps without being aware of it, one could find that one changed sides. These two moments—being discovered by the Dutch to be a Republican and fearing that one might end up on the side of the Dutch—share a characteristic. They each exemplify, in our context, the easy sliding of identities across boundaries that we have thought of as an effect of the fetish of appearance.

In his description of those who accept Dutch scholarships and return with degrees, Professor Doctor Garnadi does not call them traitors or even collaborators, though the terms were in use. Taking a Dutch scholarship, as we have said, could be thought of as an act of patriotism; one could return to help Indonesia, which lacked experts. The difficulty for him is that one would never decide to change sides, but despite this one could find oneself a collaborator or even a traitor. One would not make a decision to change one's politics and one would thus lose the protection that a decision could give one. One's political identity was out of one's control. For this reason, Professor Doctor Garnadi feels himself to have been in danger. He was "almost" on the other side. The "almost" applies equally to his experiences with those who took part in what was called the "physical revolution," the actual fighting. He almost was taken for one of them. His experience in the revolution is, thus, one of "nearly." He was frequently "almost" in danger although nothing much ever actually happened.

As we have said, the resolution taken by Professor Doctor Ganardi is education; there he is distinguished from "ektremists" by being their teacher and he is at the same time safe from becoming Dutch, having found an institution that demonstrates his Republican credentials. Or, he would be safe if only he could control his students; if only he could prevent them from planting hand grenades in his garage and from becoming identified with them despite his efforts not to be. One might think that one of the effects he desired of education, the establishment of safety for the teacher and perhaps the pupils, too, failed.

A woman submitted her entry in the form of a letter to her children in Braunschweig who had just returned from Paris.[2] She had always wanted to go to Paris, but when she was in Germany she had no opportunity. Now she writes to her children in response to their question about their father's role in the revolution. Their father had been in medical school before the war, but he dropped out for lack of money and entered the civil service. He became a local administrator, or *camat*, in 1943. He spent his time, she says, preparing the masses for independence and learning to know various figures who were later to become important and whom she lists. During the revolution, he continued as administrator, supporting the revolution but working for both sides. In the view of his wife, he never wavered in either his Republican sentiments or Republican activities. The scenario his wife sets out is, in my experience, that of many people of his class.

At one point the woman is seven months pregnant; her husband decides to take her out of the city to relatives where he feels she will be safer and better taken care of. They are afraid of discovery by the allied forces, but they travel undetected through the allied lines. They arrive at Leu-wigoong, their destination, relieved. But:

> . . . no sooner had we gotten off the train when we were taken in charge by local male and female youths and told to follow them. Mother [she here adopts the fashion of some Indonesians who refer to themselves in the third person] was taken by a girl to one room and your father by a boy to another. In these rooms they didn't inspect our papers; instead they invited us to do . . . a striptease [in English]! It seems the Dutch attempt to set our people against each other had reached Leuwigoong, because it was rumored that Dutch spies had a *kroon* stamped inside their eyelid or on their genitals and so on. No healthy mind would pay the least attention. But, because of the *emosi* or because of the think-ing of simple people who easily believe things, they swallowed it. The problem was that we were arriving from a NICA city [a city administered by the Dutch]!

She is indignant; they have been humiliated, and yet there was a certain reasonableness; they had come from a Dutch-controlled city. They are sus-pected by their own side, yet she is not afraid, unlike the Professor Doctor. She is clear about who is who; "they" are simple and gullible; she knows better. It remains only to educate "them."

This is, indeed, the attitude this woman holds in other circumstances. At one point, certain places in West Java were taken over by local people. A youth tells her husband once that

> since we are free, the people are sovereign. So in Leles a merchant appointed himself *wedana* [a local official], while in Kadungora, he appointed his brother-in-law, a religious teacher, [*adjengan*] *camat*. When Father told this to Mother, he said, "This is the result of misunderstanding 'the sovereignty of the people'; it's a bad sign." Not long afterwards we heard that those who were "sovereign" in the Leles and Kadungora governments were arrested by the Armed Forces Police and Special Forces and taken to Garut. (8)

Father is appointed *camat* and is a great success. At one point, a school-teacher tells him:

> Mr. Camat, you know how to win the hearts of the people. Here is the weakness of the people. Once the *camat* has done something for them, the people are forever loyal [*taat*]. . . . Father answered, "Isn't that the result of working to-gether? In any case, Mr. Teacher, to further the well-being of the people is the first instruction for the head of a region." (9)

When the Dutch invade the region, the *camat* flees:

> Father instantly gave the necessary instructions to all the functionaries of the Kecamatan to retreat. . . . [He sent the local Chinese to another city to save them

from the *rakyat.*] This was thought necessary when one remembers the experiences of the time of the "sovereignty of the people" [when Chinese were attacked by local people]. And they [meaning Chinese] were of course grateful for this step, to the point even of being willing to surrender whatever they left behind for capital for our struggle. And Eddy [addressing her son], this last bit was given you by one of them. Even today he still has a close tie to our family. (12)

The functionaries continue to hold regular meetings in other locales. However, their tie to the regional center being broken, they receive no salary. Local textile merchants therefore send them monthly payments. The Dutch never cease searching for the *camat*, "every person they met, they asked, 'Where is the Assistant-Wedana' [i.e., *camat*]. Not a single person would tell them" (13). They move from house to house, finding themselves one day in the house of a Chinese close to the highway. The Dutch stage a raid and find the *camat* on the back porch, dressed in a *sarong*. He is taken with others and recognized by a fellow *camat*. The Dutch officer does not say much to him aside from asking him to meet the local Regent who is in the pay of the Dutch. The *camat* agrees if he can first go home and change clothes. He is put in charge of a lieutenant who is "surprised to see Father come out neatly and completely dressed in his only wool suit"(14). The regent suggests he work for the Dutch. He asks for a week to consider it, goes back and summons the various Republican forces, telling them he has been asked to continue in office. "'Now it is up to you whether I continue or put myself on the sidelines.'" They are unanimous that he should continue. "'But, are you gentlemen aware that with your decision I will be a *camat* in the pay of the Dutch! Do you gentlemen want the responsibility for that?'" They reply: "'We take the responsibility.'"

This begins a double life for him. He arranges passes for the Republican forces and at the same time impresses the Dutch with his administrative capacities.

> Maybe no one would believe it who did not see it with their own eyes. What Mother means is: the making of a situation where enemies and allies worked together without knowing it. Dutch army soldiers played badminton with [Republican] fighters who at night usually attacked Dutch army posts! It was really something! Even Mother grinned, watching them play. (16)

Father eventually is promoted and moves to Bandung, center of the Dutch puppet state, Negara Pasundan, and continues the struggle until 1950, that is, just after independence, when he feels he can do more as a teacher.

Here there are two events: in the first, he is a Republican official and the Dutch discover him. In the other, the Dutch do not discover he is a Republican by sentiment and he is an official of the Dutch-sponsored government. In the first case, he hides out, he sleeps in a different house every two or three nights, and the Dutch nevertheless find him. He tries to remain incognito, dressed as an ordinary villager, but he is recognized by a colleague and brought to Lieutenant Colonel van Dommelen. There, one would expect severe punishment. Instead, he is offered a post on their side. One expects him to refuse, true to his Republican principles. He, however, realizes that he could still be of service to his cause. It is as Professor Doctor Garnadi has said: it is easy to end up on the other side and not know it is mistaken; and maybe it is not. In fact, Dutch recognition boosts his career. He is a successful *camat*, he aides the Republicans and he is promoted to *wedana*, the next rank up, and, at the end of his career, he refuses the post of regent.

Although he hid from the Dutch, there was no danger for him in being recognized by them. One wonders why he bothered to hide. One does not doubt that he felt in danger, but the danger turned out to be imaginary. It is another example of the "almost"; a danger "almost" materialized. This sense of narrow escape is preserved rather than being exposed as false in the narrative. And it forms the core of the narrative once he begins to work for the Dutch. The Dutch only think they know who he is; they believe he is on their side, but all the time he remains a Republican. The danger comes if the Dutch should ever learn of this; that is, if the Dutch discover him and he is promoted. The danger after that is that the Dutch will discover him (again). Whatever the real danger for many whom Dutch forces came across and imprisoned or executed, it is clear that in this narrative, the danger of discovery by the Dutch is mythologized. Precisely that they do not see, that they cannot see, enables him to continue on the Republican side in a sort of disguise.

There is always thought to be a danger of revelation, however, and it comes most strongly from one's own side. We have seen how, when suspected of being collaborators, the suspicion was dismissed as an effect of the ignorance of the multitude. At the same time, the danger of the multitude continues. At one point, for instance:

> One day in Sumedang, a comrade of Father's in the struggle from the time in Bandung, Sumedang Chief of Police, R. Sadjiman, reported to Father that a copy of a letter from the TNI [Indonesian National Army] was found by the Dutch. So he said Father should be careful. (16)

What is interesting about this episode is that nothing follows from it. The next sentence reports that the *camat* was promoted by the Secretary General of the Ministry of the Interior of Pasundan, a man with whom, his wife points out, he had had close connections previously. In this post he resumes his ties with the Indonesian forces. That is, in the first place, he is not careful. He remains in the struggle despite danger. And he remains in the pay of the Dutch.

Danger here is the copy of a letter. One does not pause to ask why a secret letter should have a carbon copy any more than one asks how it is that, released by the Dutch in the care of a Dutch soldier, the *camat* calls a meeting of Republican soldiers. I do not doubt the facts so much as I wonder about the world of such occurrences. Not only does one have secret connections with nationalist forces, but the possibility of revelation comes indirectly. The fear is not that one will be discovered with incriminating evidence in hand but that those with whom one consorts have an archive in which one's name appears and which is now in Dutch hands. The danger is revelation of one's name as it circulates in places one cannot control.

This is also the danger posed by the "people" (*rakyat*). The writer of this letter draws two conclusions. Here is the first:

> Clearly the most powerful weapon of struggle is unity. If we think that there were about 31,000 inhabitants of Kadungora [where her husband was *camat*] and if we remember that among so many people there could have been someone who wanted to be an enemy and report Father's hiding place to the Dutch or that after the Dutch occupied Kadungora, someone could have told the Dutch who liked to play badminton that the Camat and the TNI were simply tricking [*tipu*] them! But it never happened. Why? God the Merciful protected us.

It is a miracle. Thirty-one thousand people could have revealed his hiding place to the Dutch (thus hastening his promotion) but did not. And thirty-one thousand people knew how, later, he was tricking the Dutch, and not one reported him.

The *rakyat*, the masses here, are the danger. Unlike the raw youths who impolitely searched them, these people knew and could have told. If the Dutch pose the danger of finding out, the people pose the danger of telling them. It is among "the people" that one's name is passed on. The same people who, in their ignorance, misunderstand the nature of sovereignty, not seeing that it means the continuation of government by those properly endowed for the task, and who lack the cultivation to withhold their desire to look for incriminating signs in embarrassing places. Sometimes "the people" suspect one, not knowing who one is. At other times, "the people" know exactly who one is, and this is also a danger. It is a danger because it is in the nature of "the people" to talk, to pass on information, to demand. One establishes a place among them by occasionally satisfying them, which means stopping them from complaining. The people here are what they are in *Loves of a Football Player*; they are the source of talk and sentiment who need a leader to be sure that only the proper talk and sentiment is expressed. It is similar to Professor Doctor Garnadi who fears not his students' enmity but that his name will be associated with their autonomous activities.

Mother has a second conclusion:

> Humanity is still pure. Think of the wages which the *rakyat* paid directly! The appreciation of the Dutch toward Father's influence on the people of Kadungora; they had full confidence in Father.

"The people" pay wages and it indicates their purity. It indicates, that is, their respect. They pay; they do not talk. Again, one sees the role of money in controlling identity. Without their wages, the functionaries would have had difficulty in continuing their work. They would have ceased to be functionaries. It is, finally, the payment of wages that ensures a difference between *rakyat*, or "people," and "functionary." But "the people" pay as a sign of their respect. Precisely, one is led to believe, for the same reason they do not report the *camat* to the Dutch. Those who do not appreciate him, who wish to be his enemy, had an opportunity. But they did not take it. Here, one sees the solidarity of the *rakyat*. They appreciate, they pay wages to mark that appreciation or they do not appreciate and they talk, spreading the word of who one really is.

Money, in this account, does not function as payment. We are not told what, precisely, the *camat* did for the people that gained him their respect. Nor did the people pay taxes in the usual sense; they did not pay for regular services, such being impossible in the situation. Their payment is, rather, pictured here as the sign of a valuable tie that links the *camat* to them and them to the *camat*. It is a gift, a token of their esteem. Here money as gift, circulating only in defined circumstances, is opposed to talk, which circulates without limit. The second is a locus of the "almost," of what could have happened but did not.

In this woman's explanation to her children, she emphasizes the communication that she insists continues with revolutionary forces after the *camat* begins to work for the Dutch. It is not that he does anything specific for the revolutionaries. It is, rather, that he remains in touch with them. That is, for instance, the significance of the letter whose contents we are never given. In this sort of thinking, which is not different from that of Professor Doctor Garnadi or many others, what one does is not so important as who one, in one's own mind, associates with. What matters is who one's significant interlocutor is, even if, most of the time, there is merely an interior dialogue: oneself and "the revolutionaries." To think that people like this were hypocritical would be to misunderstand the revolution, which drew its force from the "almost"; from feeling that one was in touch with something dangerous—"the revolution"—and that, therefore, most of the time one was in hiding or in disguise against the Dutch and even, we will see, against revolutionaries themselves. What was important was the danger of the revolution, which comes precisely from feeling oneself close to it, or, rather, at a distance, but in communication with it.

In this thinking, the Dutch were not so much the colonizing force or the punishers of those who worked for the revolution. Their position was to be someone on whose side one could be; they mark a possibly unconscious change of identity. It is an old anxiety, one we have already seen in the writing of Mas Marco from the 1920s. The fear was that one might become the other; that the translation of identities across languages and cultures could work so perfectly that the original could be forgotten. What prompts this translation of identities is, of course, recognition. The fetish is at work again, but one cannot control it.

Against the possibility of changing sides is the danger of the revolution. The "revolution" was a means of replacing one horizon of expectation with another. I do not mean that one should see "revolution" here teleologically; it is not merely that the revolution might have failed, it is that "the revolution" itself is not basic. It is another form of fascination as we have already discussed it, a feeling that, even if one knows that neither colonial nor revolutionary institutions exist, still, there exists authority with whom one is in communication. This communication for the most part was wholly imaginary. To think of this communication as both dangerous and hopeful and to think one has it in common with others was to be in the midst of the revolution and to be revolutionary even when one worked for the other side. One sees a great desire to want to be included, even when inclusion was merely imaginary.

Whether one was a collaborator or an activist, the revolution was usually at some distance. The issue was where the lines of communication led; to the Dutch or to the Republic. This issue, we have seen, could not be decided simply by who paid one. Nevertheless, pay was an issue, as we will see in another report. But it was an issue in which money, rather than being a gift, furnishes alternative systems of communication.

Suspicion Again

It was not only those who, like the *camat*, were in the pay of the Dutch feared the revolutionaries. Someone named Gani is an example.[3] He begins his essay with a sketch of the section of Jakarta called Kebayoran under the rule of the Japanese and the Dutch. There is no hint of collaboration in his case. However, he says, there were many from Kebayoran who sided with the Dutch.

> They started to ridicule the youth who were fighting for our side; they started to insult our young Republic and to praise the Dutch who, according to them, were certain to win. There were even those who joined the NICA [Dutch colonial] forces, particularly those without education. It came to the point where amongst our fighters, "Kebayoran soldier" often was a taunt because, for instance, for a

"tommygun" they would say *migen*. It is because of them that people from Kebayoran were later lumped together by those from elsewhere and were all considered to be enemies who, if one met them, and especially if one were from Banten, one would kill them without pity. That's the reason.

His activities during the revolution consist, as he tells it, of trying to avoid being found out to be from Kebayoran. Kebayoran is marked as a source of Dutch sympathizers. It is unjust, since by no means everyone from there sides with the Dutch. He concedes, however, that there were many uneducated people who fought for the colonial forces. To say, "Kabayoran soldier" comes to mean "a soldier from the other side." As a result, people think everyone from the district is procolonial. In his mind, the problem starts with a label that is a distortion. It seems this label would not have come into existence if it were not for the linguistic incompetence of the Kaboyoran soldiers who join the Dutch troops. They cannot pronounce the name of their own weapon since it is in English and they lack education. Certain people are ignorant, they change sides, they do not know what they are doing, they cannot even use the linguistic terms of the side they have chosen. Had they been educated, perhaps they would not have changed sides. Had they been linguistically able, they might, for instance, have melted into the other side. But they remain targets of ridicule because they bring the mark of their origins with them. As a result, everyone from Kebayoran, including the writer, becomes suspect.

The difficulty exists not between people from Kebayoran themselves but between Kebayoran inhabitants and those from outside.

> There was difficulty for the fighters from outside Kebayoran to distinguish friends from foes. Sometimes they fell into traps because those they thought were friends turned out to be NICA spies.
>
> So it happened, all the more so because of NICA instigation and propaganda which successfully divided people against each other, not to mention the weak will and the susceptibility to being tricked of the people of Kebayoran themselves. (11)

Some, even many people from Kebayoran, are traitors; but they are taken for friends, thus endangering revolutionaries. But whatever the initial cause that makes people from Kebayoran suspect, it is exaggerated by Dutch tactics which divide people against each other and which mislead them. In any case, many from Kebayoran are easily misled, offering no resistance. To this point, he describes the suspicion of those from Kebayoran as having a real basis. But this changes with the next phrase:

> . . . add too the easy communication between areas, either by road or by reports. So for people from outside the area, every person from Kebayoran was a traitor and a NICA dog who had already betrayed freedom fighters. (11)

Everyone is suspected once the situation in Kebayoran is communicated outside the district. One notes that it is not lack of communications that is the problem but precisely that too much is communicated too easily. There is distortion in the process of transmission: "For people outside the area, every person from Kebayoran was a traitor." Events are reported, but they are distorted by "easy communication," facilitated by the use of the label, "Kebayoran soldier." Too much is being said and it travels too far.

The problem is the revolutionary situation. We continue from where he left off:

> Indeed, such behavior is wrong because not a few people from Kebayoran joined the struggle, but the condition of revolution and war left no chance for people to think more deeply. The result was that a number of Kebayoran people were victims, killed straight off with no investigation by fighters from other districts, even though perhaps these people [those killed] were not guilty. (11)

The problem is the speed of the revolution. It left "no chance for people to think more deeply." The urgency of the revolution here is not practical. It is not simply that the revolutionaries could not afford to investigate at all. It is rather that not to do so was itself a part of the revolution. It was the implementation of revolutionary law, as the saying was at the time, that left no place for the intervention of ordinary thinking. The fighters themselves embody the revolution in this piece and in others not least because they carried out revolutionary justice.

The point of danger for him comes not simply with speed but with the formation of a "they," the fighters, who hear reports from Kebayoran. Danger for him is given a form once there is a "they" composed of people who hear about Kebayoran and who do not look beyond the term "Kebayoran soldier" or rumors for the truth. The distortion of the news is one thing; a collectivity who hears and acts on it is another. With just rumor and no "they" equatable with "revolutionary youths," his life at the time would have been different.

He hears a rumor that Kebayoran was going to be burned to the ground. The night before he thinks it will happen, he flees with his pregnant wife and their eight small children. They walk to another area of Jakarta where his wife gives birth. It is difficult to get a midwife because if he is stopped by NICA forces wearing a nationalist badge, they will make him swallow the badge. If he is stopped by revolutionary forces without the badge, and they learn he is from Kebayoran, he will be killed. He explains that he was not born in Kebayoran and his wife is from Banten, but they have lived in Kebayoran for decades and

> for that reason there is always the possibility from someone who does not know me that I will be thought to be from Kebayoran, which meant, at that time, a spy or a NICA dog. (13)

People from Kebayoran know him and, despite the division within the district and the Dutch attempt to set people against each other, he is safe from his fellow inhabitants. The danger is that he will be recognized by someone who does not know him. That is, someone from outside the area who only knows that he is from Kebayoran and will never pause to learn more about him. What he wants is recognition; what he fears is being misrecognized. But the misrecognition he fears is also the truth about himself. He is from Kebayoran. He fears anonymous surveillance because it means recognition of himself which is at once factual and alien to him. It is not the events of the revolution but the very condition of the revolution itself—the circulation of rumor, the functioning of revolutionary justice, and the accident of being from a certain place—that make him see that to others, and to a certain degree to himself, he has become someone other than who he was.

At one point, he is told by a youth that other youths know he is, and I use his quotation marks, "'a person from Kebayoran.'" He flees with his family hoping to go anywhere but "as far as possible from Kebayoran." Fortunately, there are those along the way who help him. He gets to the train station where he knows the station master, who buys tickets for himself and his family. There are British and NICA patrols along the way, but he does not note that he fears them. It is his own side he is worried about. He continues:

> Then at Cakung and Kranji the Laskar Rakyat inspected. What we heard from them were these words: "Look out for enemy spies, people from Kebayoran and former members of the police." Lucky for our whole family that the chief of the Laskar Rakyat who were doing the inspections was a former pupil called Rasyidi from Tambun. At his suggestion and the suggestion of his friends, our family was asked to stay with his father, Pak Madi, who was the agricultural inspector in Tambun. Only then did I feel safe. (15)

This is nearly the conclusion of his essay. He joins the office of the regent. The whole office flees before the Dutch and is eventually captured and detained, the worst of this being that he is paid only a quarter of his salary because he refuses to work for the Dutch.

Gani fears being recognized for what he both is and is not. He knows he is innocent, but he feels himself suspected. Suspicion is worse than guilt in this situation. Were he a reactionary, he could take appropriate measures; he could stand against those who accuse him. But he is not guilty and he is not, for the most part, even suspected. It is rather that he is afraid he will be suspected; people will find out who he is—"a person from Kebayoran," though even then not a native of the area. He is afraid that he will not be able to prove that not everyone from Kebayoran is a traitor; he believes that those who think that are wrong. Suspicion is worse than guilt in this situation because there is no recourse against it. Suspicion reigns with no means of checking it. Were it a question of guilt or innocence, he might be able to prove he had always supported the revolution, that he had never done anything for the Dutch, and so forth. But he fears suspicion because he knows that he is, in a way, worthy of it without being guilty. It is the sign that he has, during the revolution, taken on a new guise.

What is perhaps most extraordinary is that he scarcely complains of being suspected. He blames those who did in fact change sides, but he does not accuse the revolutionaries as, for instance, the *camat*'s wife did. He has no defense against being suspected except flight, the experience of many others. He worries because he knows the situation of the revolution. That is, he knows that news travels fast, that it originates in his home environment, that it is distorted as it spreads, and that people do not pause to think about what they hear. When he says this, it is not to be understood as a criticism. It was frequently said at the time as an indication of the imperatives of the revolution, a positive indication of the extraordinary character of the time. There is, for him, an enormous "they," composed of everyone who might hear (and this does not include the colonial forces) in a situation where news travels rapidly. And it is composed precisely of those with whom he stands politically. He imagines them finding him; that is, he imagines "them" seeing "him" and not being able to distinguish himself from what he fears they think he is. "I" (*saya*), here is defined by an other whom he imagines. He is unable to free himself from a fear of thinking he is necessarily what others know him to be; in short, he feels suspected. His only recourse is flight and finding someone, someplace away from Kebayoran, who recognizes him in his everyday identity.

This is a story in which nothing significant happens. He feels endangered; there are some signs that he is correct. He flees and he is safe before what happened to others who, like him, were innocent, happens to him. This is, indeed, a story of the revolution. But what makes it unnerving is that after the revolution it is told with pride. It is submitted as an entry in a contest celebrating the thirtieth anniversary of the revolution. It is not put forward as an aspect of life during the revolution that is worth knowing about even though it is not heroic. Rather, it is told as though it were heroic. Its heroism consists in having survived the revolution while his wife gave birth to a son who is now a soldier and in now having thirty-five grandchildren. The point of resistance to the Dutch, the point where he refuses to work for them despite being their prisoner, is mentioned but not emphasized.

It seems to me that he could not have told this as a story of heroism had he been guilty or had he felt guilty. Guilt would have meant a certain individuation; an identity apart from the revolution. It is almost a paradox. He sees himself as one of those who is thought guilty of being on the other

side. Had he actually sided with the Dutch, he could have defended himself. As a real traitor, he would have fought the revolution, taken issue with
it, and perhaps recanted later. But he is an imaginary traitor, one who
merely fears being identified as a traitor. He acted in terms of revolutionary
suspicion and thus he lived out what revolutionaries not thought but heard
about him and about the place he inhabited. He suffered the revolution; it
is his pride.

He puts the problem in terms of youth:

> I saw how quickly youth at that time became adult [*dewasa*] and aware of their
> responsibility. I saw children, teenagers, carrying weapons with faces that
> showed their determination and made them seem older. (14)

It is children he fears, children who, with weapons, kill on the basis of
rumors. If children quickly became adults, it means they have power. The
determination he sees on their faces is ambiguous. It is children who made
the revolution, but children who act on rumor are not responsible in the
usual sense of the term. It is not that children take on the authority of
adults as adults would do. Children with weapons acting on rumor have a
new type of authority. These children were responsible to the revolution;
that is, they acted on what they heard, on what circulated. If what they
heard did not fit the norms of truth as they exist in nonrevolutionary moments, it does not make them irresponsible. It is precisely the difference in
types of responsibility that is at the source of his pride. The circulation of
rumor with him as its target continues in his mind. His pride comes when
that circulation of language that is essential to his story is recognized by
conventional notions of verity. At that point, he is no longer the victim of
unjust rumor, which might have meant his death. Rather, that moment
when rumor ruled and children with guns saw that it did so is now to his
credit. It is to his credit because it shows how he, too, though he did little
substantial to aide the revolution, lived his life in its terms and in that way
achieved freedom (*merdeka*). Thought to be on the side of the Dutch, he
allowed that suspicion to permeate his life and still never wavered in his
allegiance. If he did not protest, it was because via that suspicion that he
was in touch with the revolution. He was in touch, once again, at a distance, hearing what circulated elsewhere. His contest entry transforms that
circulation of untruths and truths into a fixed account, a contribution to
the history of that time, hence a source of pride to him.

RED MONEY, CAUTIOUS REBELLION

This is an account written by a schoolteacher, Dayim Sostawirya, though we
only learn his occupation well into the piece.[4] He gives nothing else of his
background, writing as though he were merely reporting facts. He starts
with the geographical location: "A certain place in Majalengka regency."

He names the administrative center and the chief industry, a sugar factory, and then announces that the proclamation of independence became known there on 19 August 1945, and that it was received "with great pride." He recounts in chronological fashion the kidnapping of the regent, a Dutch collaborator, by revolutionary youth; the burning of Chinese houses; the kidnapping of an Indian merchant; and the founding of a nationalist organization. It is another story of suspicion, but seen from both sides. "They" suspect others, the "they" here being revolutionary youth with whom he sides; but at the same time, he is afraid he will be suspected of collaboration. He fears being accused of collaboration because, as a schoolteacher, he will be paid in Dutch money rather than the money of the Republic. The problem was widely discussed at the time. The exchange rate between the two currencies was closely watched, and it was a matter of pride that, for a short period, Republican money was worth more than Indies currency, which here he refers to by its color—"Red Money." In other accounts, the question of changing sides is put simply as a matter of better pay, and sometimes it was put that way with a tone of understanding.[5]

Dayim Sostawirya describes the situation in 1947 after the Dutch have returned to the area. They make assurances that inhabitants will not be bothered as they go about their daily business and that government officials who have not fled will be guaranteed protection. "And in addition they will get wages more than adequate to their needs and more than the wages of officials of the Republic of Indonesia. Traders and businessmen whose only aim is to earn a profit will be able to live luxuriously" (2). But, he says, "Officials and traders, all of them, were obliged to report any fighters who disturb peace and order" (2). And, he adds, "There were even some who were given the particular duty to be spies and guides. They had to give the names and addresses of people who did not want to give in to (*tunduk*) the Dutch so that they could be detained. He pictures this as a result of that situation:

> A condition of mutual suspicion between us and ourselves arose. Those who did not want to become refugees were suspected by those in the countryside. Those who fled were suspected by those in the city. We all had to be cautious and on the alert.

One had to be always "cautious and on the alert." Of course, he means that one had to be very careful not of the Dutch but of "us." One had to be careful, in the first place, because "us" here includes some who are in the pay of the Dutch. But it is a two-way street. Everyone is suspected of being in the pay of the Dutch if they remain behind or if they flee. So everyone has to be on the alert not only against Dutch informers but also against others who think that because one did not flee, or even if one did flee, that one is a Dutch agent. Does he exaggerate? Is there any way to know? Certainly there were people charged with working for the Dutch who were kidnapped and sometimes killed. He gives examples. But the danger is not that one actually worked for the Dutch, but that one gave some sign, no matter how small and even involuntary, that one did.

> City people too had to be careful. An expression or a move that gave rise to suspicion, or words that made light of the Government of the Republic of Indonesia [capitalized in original] of course meant that a balance would be struck and one could expect one's turn in being kidnapped and having a sentence of the sort that pertained at that time. (3)

There is a certain amount of celebration in this statement when he says that whoever is an enemy gets what they deserve. But it is clear that people felt suspected and did not always know why. "An expression or a move that might give rise to suspicion" includes a great deal. Many of those who were attacked might well have expected it either because they worked for the Dutch or on grounds of ethnic identity. "The houses of Chinese in Ciborelang [sic] were burnt to the ground, part of the scorched earth policy, by our fighters" (3). But his claim goes beyond this to include those whose expressions incite suspicion. Whichever the case, he reports that the Dutch maintain a certain order and in turn confine themselves to searching for disruptive youths. "The market in Ciborelang functioned again as before. The Dutch bothered no one." The merchants made money, he points out.

At this point, he introduces the topic that is the title of his section, "Red Money":

> The money used was the paper money of Dutch/NICA. It was usually called *Red Money* [italicized and capitalized in original] because of its color. Its value was higher than ORI [Oeang Republic Indonesia, Indonesian money]. For that reason merchants and businessmen as well as government employees were quite privileged because Red Money would circulate more easily. (3)

The circulation of money is itself for him a sign of connection to the Dutch. Those who use Red Money are, in his view, favored by the Dutch. By contrast, "the people [*masjarakyat*] still used ORI for the most part." They do so because, in the countryside, they

> were afraid to take Red Money. Because there were threats from fighters who from time to time came to Dutch held areas. Fighters came to find out the situation and evaluate the feelings [*jiwa*] of society, whether they loved the Republic of Indonesia and valued the fighters. (4)

He notes this surveillance particularly at harvest time when the market is crowded:

> When it was crowded, it was a chance for fighters in disguise to come to investigate conditions of the life of the people in the hinterland under Dutch authority.

Reports were received from people inside who were designated as contacts. So it was known just who was considered an enemy, who helped the Dutch and damaged the struggle towards independence. (4)

He continues with a story of a merchant who was kidnapped and killed, going into some detail about how the Dutch were unable to protect the man even in the marketplace itself.

Saudara Barak, brought first to Leuwiliang, proved to be saving up RED MONEY [capitalized in the original]. As a result of the investigation, it was decided to send him to Mt. Kuning, the headquarters of our fighters, to receive the sentence appropriate to the decision in effect at that time. (4)

As a result of the kidnapping, the local official, called a *wedana*, called a meeting. Present at that meeting were not only those invited but others "as investigators from the countryside disguised as merchants or ordinary people" (5). He attended the meeting, and he puts in quotation marks the speech of the *wedana*, who told them he hoped for the restoration of order and so forth. The *wedana* remarks that there are teachers whom he hopes will continue in their positions; they must think of the future, of their families and, he says, "'You will receive your wages in Red Money, whose value is higher than that of ORI' "(6). When the *wedana* finishes, the author is given a chance to speak. He is in favor, in principle, of reopening the schools, he says he told the meeting:

"But keeping in mind the present situation and thinking of the safety of government employees, for the moment we are not prepared to take our wages in Red Money. Instead, we will rely on our connections with students' parents." (7)

He comments that his remarks were well received and that "taking Red Money for certain meant being called NICA by the fighters in the countryside"(7).

The *wedana* disagrees. As a result, "it was now clear that he himself [he uses the respectful form, *beliau*, for the man throughout] had proven himself to be a tool of the enemy." A report is sent to the "fighters," who charge the *wedana* with three things. First, he did not flee with other government employees to the countryside and therefore showed that he was not sympathetic to the Republic. Next, that he "clearly was a tool of the enemy (NICA). He urged the use of Red Money and forced government employees to receive their wages in it." And finally that he no longer believed in the energy and force (*tenaga dan kekuatan*) of the fighters for the Republic. As a result, he was abducted from his house along with one of his children.

At the meeting there was also an Indian merchant who displayed Red Money and who commented that its value was higher than that of the

Republican currency, ORI. And, comments the author, "it is true that ORI was no longer valid after the Dutch took back power" (9). He says further that the man was frightened after Chinese houses were burned, and he took refuge with the Dutch, not having confidence in the republic. "Fortunately for [him], he could take shelter, and was not kidnapped. The only thing that happened was that the door of his house was damaged because it was shot at several times." (10)

In the third section, entitled "A Cautious Rebellion (SP 88)," the writer recounts the life of a certain organization. It is after the kidnappings. He is apparently in a different locality in the same region, in a small city. As part of what they called their Police Action, the Dutch invade this city. Many flee; Sostawirya, however, feels no need to do so. He is safe from the Dutch. Unlike others, he is not in the revolutionary forces or the police. He is a teacher and, without connection to any armed organization, he feels he "would not be suspected by the Dutch." And, he feels, it is an opportunity to "connect with the fighters and guerrillas in the countryside." That is, staying in the Dutch-held city provides him with a chance to help the revolution. But, he adds, "Of course within limits which had to be adjusted to the situation which from time to time could be tense and dangerous." So he is perfectly safe from the Dutch, unlikely to be suspected by them; therefore, he is prepared to help the armed fighters, but at the same time, he could only do certain things. He adds that "those who did not leave the city were in danger, because the fighters in the countryside paid attention to them." He is asked to be a messenger between the forces in the countryside and their members in the city. He does so until he fears he might be discovered. The Renville Agreement is announced, which allows him to take up his post as teacher without fear from either side. Now reestablished in a position under Dutch control, he and some friends found an organization, "a black organization" (to the Dutch), namely, "The Organization for Cautious Rebellion" (Satuan Pemberontakan Hati-hati), which they give a code name: SP 88. They are selective in their membership: "lest the Dutch find out. . . . it was necessary to pick those who could keep a secret and act without raising suspicion." The aim of this organization is "none other than to cultivate love for the Government and Country of the Republic of Indonesia as well as aid the activities of those fighters in the hinterland." Of course, their meetings are held "in deepest secrecy." For instance, one member holds a ritual feast for a newly born grandchild. But only members of the organization are invited and they consider the feast a meeting of the group. Even though, he says, it is very dangerous for the membership, no one refuses to become an officer of the organization. "It is one indication that our fighters knew no slackness as a result of the Renville Agreement, and lacked nothing in spirit simply because of the Dutch presence." In other words, the organization which, so far as he recounts, did very little except meet, had members eager to participate.

There was a potential activity that never materialized. The author received a letter asking for a list of Dutch emplacements. Dutch forces raided the organization and found the letter. All of the members were interrogated; ten were jailed for twenty days, five for three months, and he and the head of the organization were brought before the judge and sentenced for a time which he does not specify.[6] He was released after eight months, when agreement about the transfer of sovereignty had been arranged.

Revolutionaries kidnap the *wedana* and judge him guilty of collaboration. He is an example of those who were insufficiently careful of the indications they gave of themselves. It is not that he was found to be a collaborator simply because he was in the civil service of the Negara Pasundan. That alone seems insufficient to find him guilty. He is, rather, judged guilty of a certain denial:

> Bapak Wedana [bapak Behar] was insufficiently on the alert and lacked judgment.
>
> In an extremely difficult situation he showed and gave proof of his stance which was one of submission to the Dutch and of being used by them.
>
> He did not have a feeling of caution and of being on the alert. What was the opinion of the people at the meeting mentioned? For instance, who exactly was present? Did he know them all? (9)

The official gave signs that he helped the Dutch; one example is that he spoke without taking into account who might hear him speak. He was not thoroughly acquainted with those at the meeting he addressed, for instance. They might have been spies, as they were. The problem is that the *wedana* ignored the reports he might have listened to about the forces in the countryside. The account continues:

> Apparently he [*beliau*] was not really shaken by the reports of the guerrillas in the countryside because he always had powerful bodyguards and Dutch weapons.

The *wedana* is incautious; he does not listen to reports; he denies them, in effect, when they reach his ears because he believes himself invulnerable to revolutionary forces. But he is mistaken. Even with Dutch weapons, one is not invulnerable. He should have been afraid. And he should have been suspicious. Suspicion here, even the suspicion of "us by ourselves" is not condemned in this account; it is celebrated. The fact that the *wedana* was a member of the collaborationist state is not itself important. What matters is that he did not heed the guerrillas; he was not on the lookout for them. In this, the writer supports the views of other members of the Negara Pasundan who defend themselves by saying that even though they were paid by the Dutch, they were always mindful of the revolutionaries and always in touch with them.

Dayim Sostawirya's demand that everyone think themselves suspected indicates that some might escape the revolution. The difficulty is that one has trouble showing that one feels suspected. The answer is the SP 88, the organization which existed in large part, one feels, in order to have a code name. The organization's purpose was to solidify and to strengthen the devotion of its members to the Republic. They had no intention of displaying their nationalist allegiance to the Dutch by, for instance, an act of defiance or resistance.[7] The organization was their way to make a claim; namely, not to be allied to the Dutch and to be allied to the Republic. He does not feel that he made any less of a contribution to the achievement of Indonesian independence than those who fought, and in this he is like most of those whose accounts we have looked at. His assumption is not precisely one of identity in so far as this refers to a social place. It is rather a question of orientation. If he is a member of a nationalist organization and he keeps it secret from the Dutch, he is no longer oriented toward them. It is almost better than fighting which, after all, requires some contact with them. The Dutch do not know about him, do not see him. He feels himself to be in disguise, hidden from them and in communication with someone else, someplace else. It is this orientation that makes his everyday dress, whose form in no way changes, a disguise. But to be in disguise, he has to have a secret. The organization is itself the secret.

It is why he can call this section of his account, "Cautious Rebellion: SP 88." A "careful rebellion" seems nearly an oxymoron. But for him it makes sense; perhaps even the only sense. Being "careful," being in hiding when one is still in the open, not revealing oneself, as one would have to do in some way or another if one fought, one can feel that one is really keeping a secret. The secret is a form of expression. It shows to himself and to the others in the organization that one is in touch with something distant. One is in touch with the Republic. Keeping quiet, one feels in communication with something far away.

Money, Dutch or Republican, indicated with whom one communicates. To work for the Dutch is not, for him, necessarily a sign of collaboration. He himself teaches school in the occupied territories. But since he receives no salary from the Dutch, he does not consider himself a collaborator. Even the *wedana*, an important official, is not ipso facto a collaborator. He is proven to be one when he urges others to accept Red Money. Moreover, those who in no way work for the Dutch but simply use their money in business, are collaborators for that reason. They may have made no contribution at all to the side of the Dutch. But, if they used Dutch money, they are in danger of death. That is, it does not matter necessarily who one works for; that is merely a sign of what one looks like. One might wear the uniform of the Indies civil service; it is not, in this account, an infallible sign of allegiance. But if one has Dutch money in one's possession, one is a traitor. It is a matter of being connected at a distance; of being in touch with the Dutch by accepting their (monetary) communications. It does not matter how one got the money or how one spent it; mere everyday intercourse means little. It is a question of an ultimate connection. Ultimately, the money came from the Dutch. Ultimately, one is in communication with them if one has their money in one's pocket.

Distance is more important than proximity. Orientation is more important than activity. The signs one receives and one heeds come from one side rather than another. And it is a question before that of wanting to say that the signs in which one communicates, one's language, what one hears, what one uses for exchange, come from a single source, either the Republic or the Dutch. One sees here an urge for a new center and thus a new hierarchy. One feels that the money in one's pocket enters one into a vast circuit extending throughout Java, the other islands of the archipelago, and all the way to Holland as well extending into secret recesses of Java where the revolution is found. First one feels part of these circuits, as Soedjanmo, for instance, felt the currents of modernity before he recognized them for what they were. Then one distinguishes where they lead.

There are two currencies of different colors. Dayim Sostawirya knows their relative values. He thus knows that they are interchangeable. He, and everyone he knows at the time, is identifiable by which currency they have in their possession. If one were to change ORI for Red Money, one would cease being Indonesian and would be, if not a Dutch citizen, a member of their political and cultural sphere. No exchange can take place between them without a change of identity of the holder of the money. One moves from one universe to the other without changing places physically.

One can become a foreigner simply by changing money. And like the Indian merchant who simply wanted whatever currency had the better value, without intending any change of allegiance and quite possibly without knowing that to use a certain form of money would be taken as a sign of allegiance. One might go to the market and get change that included Red Money. Later, one might buy something else and pay with Red Money. This could count as "an expression or a move that gave rise to suspicion." The reality was no doubt much less exigent than that. But the words of Dayim Sostawirya imply such possibilities. One will be discovered by the revolutionaries if one has Dutch currency. One might use it innocently, but one will be taken for what one "is" nonetheless. One finds oneself defined by signs that issue from oneself without one's knowledge. It is against such a possibility that Dayim Sostawirya founds SP 88 and begins his cautious rebellion.

It is in this sense, too, that we can understand the term "fighters in the countryside" who remain anonymous not only to the Dutch but to him in his account. Twenty-five years after the revolution, he still keeps their identities to himself. During the revolution he finds himself in the middle, between the Dutch who might discover his true sympathies and the fighters who act against anyone who gives even an inadvertent sign of colonial allegiance. These fighters are larger than life, in his account and in others. They are attributed an omniscience and a power to act that makes them more to be feared than Dutch forces who are largely blind and who, in his account, inflict only moderate penalties. The might of the Dutch in this and other accounts remains abstract. They have modern weapons, great firepower, but these are invoked mainly to speak of how powerful the Republican side is armed merely with sharpened bamboo sticks. The menace of the Dutch is, as in other accounts, the temptation they offer to change sides. Their physical power seems not to threaten. The "fighters in the countryside" by contrast are feared out of proportion to their actual force. One does not know if they are present or not. And if they observe one, one might easily give a sign that does not represent political intentions at all. Fighters in many of these stories give a certain frisson to the inaction of Republican sympathizers. One keeps a secret from the Dutch, but this secret is tame next to the imagined possibility of not being able to keep anything, even the unintentional, from "fighters in the countryside." Communications end up with them, as messages end up with Tan Malaka, even when one does not know it is happening. This means that sympathizers such as Sostawirya felt charged with significance that radiated from them despite their intentions.

Dayim Sostawirya is charged with signs which, he is sure, will end up in the right place even if they carry an incriminating message. The results, he insists, could well be dire. On the other hand, discovery by the Dutch seldom brings severe consequence. Often, we have seen, it brings something one wants. Red Money in one's pocket already puts one in the world of the Dutch. Red Money is, like ORI money, a particular currency. But like other developed forms of currency, it can indicate the possibility of having whatever one wants. One difficulty of Red Money for nationalists, we recall, is that it could almost always buy more. This differential makes it a more potent catalyst for imagination than ORI. It continues to open up possibilities whose realization, as in the time of Student Hidjau, are feared not because of their content—sex and education—but because they bring one someplace else and in doing so make one someone else.

It is the exchangability of signs, Red for ORI, and *saya* ("I") for *ik* ("I") that is feared. This exchangability is possible because at the apex of the hierarchy, or to change the metaphor, at its center, there is overlapping.

The revolutionaries hear everything. But the circulation of Red Money alongside ORI indicates that signs lead equally well to the Dutch. The replaced center still exists and still exercises attraction. It is not a question of political preference or even of nostalgia. It is rather to say that even if "they no longer hear" and their signs are no longer ours, still one must attend to them. In these accounts, the Dutch had a power of attraction. It rested on feeling that one existed in the midst of various currents of signs and one could find oneself using one rather than the other without knowing it. This was undesired because it made one someone else. It was attractive because it offered possibilities one did not know were open to one. Someone else hears me, somewhere else, in another world, offering me unimagined benefits. In these accounts, the Dutch are feared at a distance. It is the power one has to broadcast signals of oneself that arrive at a distant point. But when the Dutch hear, it is not "me" that they hear; it is another that occupies the same space. "I" would not recognize myself were "I" to listen to them. Those who suspect me are therefore my allies. They recognize the estranging possibility in me. My fear of them prevents me from becoming a foreigner; it puts me on guard against myself. This is the sad conservative logic of great masses of Indonesian revolutionaries. It is at the heart of a revolution which, though anticolonial, was directed at a foreignness inherent in the colonized.

The displacement of the colonial apex occured culturally long before it happened politically. The difference between the political and the cultural should have been felt as fear. The return of the Dutch after World War II should have made them into enemies whom one avoided because of the harm they cause. But this is only partly true. The Dutch were often feared, we have seen in our examples, because they could reward. One thinks one can understand why. It is that their cultural displacement left a space behind. We see it as one source of the circulation of money and one point of exchange, thus as the possibility of being discovered, rewarded, and becoming foreign to oneself as opposed to another where one is suspected.

It seems logical enough that this should have been the case until one considers earlier Indonesian history. Colonial authority insinuated itself into the archipelago as one among other competing powers. It was normal for there to be rivalries, wars, and shifting alliances. The subjugation of one power by another, however, left little that I can recognize similar to the division we have seen. Why was the relation to the Dutch different? This, of course, can be answered in many registers. But when one remembers that colonial authorities borrowed Javanese royal insignia and that they invented modes of relationship in local idioms rather than imposing their own, the continued call from the space left by their displacement is strange. Other displaced kingdoms lived in memory and in mythology. They existed as continuous with present populations. Those who feared seduction by the Dutch, however, thought of them not only as foreign but as having the power to make Indonesians into foreigners. The division between colonial and Indonesian is a symptom of the reformulation of "foreign" that made the Dutch foreigners in a way they were not initially. Their displacement and the gap they left is not sufficient to explain their power of seduction. One must trace the path of developments within the lingua franca beginning with Muhammad Bakir and his contemporaries. One must see Dutch absence as an effect of a possible presense, one still reachable because between "I" and the world there are innumerable traces that can be followed. "I" in the lingua franca can end up anywhere at all.

CHAPTER NINE

Revolution

WITHOUT THE FETISH OF MODERNITY: "FREEDOM OR DEATH"

In chapter 8, we looked at thirtieth anniversary contest entries from the educated class. We get other views when we turn to those of the less educated. A farmer with three years of school heard of the contest on the radio and knew it had been announced in the papers. He sent in an essay, the first part of which is a historical survey that must be a repetition of what he remembers from school and from the political indoctrination that takes place in villages.[1] It is clear and unambiguous, with paragraphs often of only one or two sentences. For instance:

> The suffering from Dutch colonialism had not yet disappeared. Japan came. (1)

When, however, he makes his complaint against the Dutch precise he says:

> In the Dutch era, Indonesians with money who were close to the Dutch or, in other words, their collaborators [*kaki tangan*)], were allowed to study or to go to school. With the aim that trained Indonesians would work for and collaborate with the Dutch. (1)

He hopes "those days are over and with them the *ijon* system [whereby crops were sold before harvest, thus at a lower price] or landlords or *tengkulak* [merchants who buy crops] and so on." He views colonialism as the unjust distribution of privilege and ownership. It is question of rights to his own production and it is a question of opportunity for a better place for himself, the route to which would be education. In his view, those Indonesians lucky enough to be educated were so only in order to become the accomplices of the Dutch. We could formulate his views this way: "they take what is mine" and "those who advance in accomplishments end up on the side of the Dutch." Education is here a complex question; it is desirable, but having it, under the Dutch at least, meant complicity.

This writer has a view of Indonesian history that he learned in the ways nationalism made available to him. He applies what he learned to his life. He lives within mottos: "My motto is 'Better to die today then to live in misery' [Lebih baik mati hari ini dari pada hidup sengsara] and 'Once free forever free' [Sekali merdeka tetap merdeka]." He uses these slogans, familiar to every Indonesian of the time, to explain his actions. He describes himself uttering them in ordinary speech. In the next sentence, he describes the guerrilla group he fought with. These are not slogans, then, in the sense that one simply repeats formulas in order not to think; they bear too great an emotional weight for that. Nor are they proverbs in the sense that they contain inherited wisdom that one can apply to the world. The word he uses for motto is *semboyan*, whose meaning includes also "indication" or "sign of":

> Indication, sign. "When you hear three pistol shots, that means the attack has begun" or secret sign: "That night the passwords used by our troops were 'hawk' and 'night.' "

The citation is taken from the standard dictionary of Indonesian.[2] We could take these mottos then in the Indonesian sense of "password"—words which allow him to exit from one place and enter another, with the acquiescence of those who are equally familiar with their content.

Born in 1932, K was a teenager at the time he joined the Barisan Pelopor, his revolutionary organization, in Jakarta. When the Dutch capture one of the leaders of his group, the group starts to disintegrate, though the reason is not made clear:

> Once unexpectedly the Dutch succeeded in kidnaping one of our leaders, Bapak Wongso.
>
> I can't tell you how tortured my leader was. We felt the loss of a leader; he was a wise leader.
>
> Our strength started to disappear, one by one. Ever since my leader was captured we lacked direction.

Later the same people with the same leadership form a new group, the Barisan Banteng Republic Indonesia. Nothing is different but the name. The group leaves Jakarta for Banten, where they again meet Dutch forces.

> About 500 members were completely outfitted with weapons gotten from raids. Some had machetes, sharpened bamboo spears, grenades and so on. I was not left behind in having modern equipment; I was given two grenades. The commandant was Eming. I was only a soldier [*pembela*].

This leads him to tell the central episode of his piece. He wonders how they could get more weapons, especially modern ones.

> Finally I decided to pose as a goatherd around Mt. Kasur. This was genuinely difficult and called for a high degree of awareness since death was always on the lookout. . . .
>
> At that time for weapons I had grenades stuck into grass where the goats ate. Seen from outside there was only grass to feed the goats.
>
> As soon as the Dutch saw me, they called me over. They asked me, who are you?
>
> I answered, my name is K. . . .

Then the Dutch asked me if I were a member of the Barisan Benteng. I said no
at that time. And if I knew where those people from the Barisan Benteng were
hiding.

Acting like someone who doesn't understand the problem, I said no, *tuan*.

Then he pointed to the basket filled with dried grass, my goats' food. Looking
at his face, I trembled.

"What's that, and that?" he said, arms at his hips.

"Goat food, *tuan*," I answered.

The Dutch there all laughed and laughed hearing my story.

I was relieved that the goat food filled with grenades to kill them wasn't discovered.

I hurried off to my commandant in Mt. Kasur and told him everything that
happened.

I came back bringing food they had asked for. I brought unripe bananas, still
green. They laughed seeing what I was doing.

I said the bananas had to be baked before they were eatable; the Dutch hurriedly looked for dry leaves to cook the unripe bananas.

In this relaxed atmosphere, unsuspected by the Dutch, I looked for an opportunity.

There were two grills, one with six people around it, the other with eight.
Saying that I was going to look for grass I left the Dutch busy putting away the
unripe bananas.

They were relaxed and didn't know I had placed a grenade near their post. The
trap I had set went off and the Dutch from both groups were smashed to pieces.

The second attack I was going to make with the second grenade did not come
off because some among the Dutch were still alive and were able to stifle the
second grenade.

I was not able to get any weapons because very quickly they got reinforce-
ments. In my heart I was thankful that absolutely nothing happened to me.

With the death of several Dutch soldiers the will to fight of my comrades was
that much stronger. (11–12; extract follows K's punctuation)

He is frightened, of course, because he might be found out. He protects
himself in two ways. Disguised as a goatherd, he allays suspicion. The only
thing he has that interests the Dutch soldiers is the stack of grass in which
the grenades are stashed. There are few things worth so little as a stack of
grass. It is valuable only to goatherds and a few others; it holds no interest
for hungry soldiers. His disguise says, "poverty." The other part of his
disguise is ignorance: "Acting like someone who doesn't understand the
problem, I said no, *tuan*." He is only a goatherd. It is natural that he
knows nothing. He lacks education; he lacks knowledge. He has told us
the effects of colonialism; impoverishment by taking away the products of
labor and ignorance as the result of the refusal of education to most. He

poses, one can say, as the perfect colonial subject. That is, the perfect Indies subject as he understands what colonialists believe the colonial subject to be. If he tricks them, it is because he offers them what he thinks they think he should look like.

This means that he imagines what he looks like in their eyes. He accentuates his account by telling us how they mocked him: "'What's that, and that?' he said, arms at his hips. 'Goat food, *tuan*,' I answered. The Dutch there all laughed and laughed hearing my story." They laugh because he tells them what they can see for themselves. It is goat food they see. The simplicity of his answer, that he merely names what is in front of their eyes, that he tells the truth, if not the whole truth, without embellishment is comical to them. They think he is ignorant, and therefore simple. They lose interest in him; his disguise works, though, of course, he is continuously afraid of being discovered. We say, "his disguise works" because we believe that he has told his story accurately. That is, we believe that his assessment of their view of him is true to the facts. His version seems accurate because it invokes implicitly the images of colonialism we know from the history of the Indies.

But if he was effective and if his story is convincing it is because he surpassed the stereotypes of colonialism precisely by understanding how he looked to them. The story shows how he exits from colonialism by understanding what he is in their eyes. Seeing from their standpoint, he is able to manipulate those images and trick the Dutch. He does what Soewardi does in part; he moves between himself and himself imagining he were a Dutchman looking at himself. The Dutch never see him. That is, they never understand who he really is; just as in Soewardi's piece, the Dutch are blind. The blindness of the Dutch is necessary to his success. How else could he withstand their superior armaments, their modernity? But as we have already seen, their blindness is induced. He tricks them by his disguise.

One can ask, What gives him the courage to make his attempt? He tells us that he has certain mottos: "Better to die today then to live in misery" and "Once free forever free." One has to believe that he believes them. But one can also think of these mottos as being not merely statements of principle but, as they are in Indonesian, signals and passwords. They are passed between those who share the same beliefs. They distinguish him from, for instance, those whom the Dutch educated and who then passed to their side. Those who can utter these phrases form the nation to which he belongs. The mottos give him the courage to deceive Dutch soldiers; to imagine what he looks like to them and to conceal himself behind that image. As maxims, they enable him to imagine the blindness of the Dutch, to imagine what they see of him and what is not apparent to their eyes. In his mind, he can thus pass back and forth between "himself" and the

Dutch. The return is as important as the first step; it is, in fact, where the motto functions as a "password," letting him back through his own lines despite his disguise. The words are passed to "himself," repeated to himself, preventing him from being merely a goatherd who helps Dutch troops find food and who ends up, like those he despises, on their side. These passwords ensure that he imagines how he would see himself were he on the Dutch side without the consequence that befalls the educated. Were the Dutch to give him money for the green bananas and a job in procuring more for them later, he would refuse. Repeating his slogan, he remembers who he was at the outset.

K, the teenage revolutionary, knowing how the Dutch see him and knowing what they do not see of him, in effect repeats Soewardi's formula, "If I were a Dutchman. . . ." He is distinguished from others in the accounts we look at in completing the phrase. He lacks Professor Doctor Garnadi's fear that he might become a Dutchman, or at least end up on the Dutch side. There are two features of K that contribute to this. First, his fear centers itself on the Dutch. They, and not fellow revolutionaries, are the threat to him. This is a great aid in avoiding identification with them. K is never stuck on their side, perhaps because of his passwords: "Once free, always free" and "Better to die than to live in misery." As Ben Anderson has pointed out, during the revolution, slogans were turned into mantra, magical chants.[3] Their power for K was magical, granting him invulnerability, not to Dutch guns but to Dutch seduction. We can think of this password as a stabilizer of the first person by which "I" can see that the Dutch think "I" is a poor goatherd and, dealing with them, getting something from them, does not mean remaining what "I" sees they think "I" is. Indeed, the meaning of his mottos is precisely that: "Once free, forever free" [Sekali merdeka tetap merdeka]; that is, no longer a part of them. K is the first person we have seen who is not dazed by being in disguise.

"Better to die today then to live in misery" (Lebih baik mati hari ini dari pada hidup sengsara), his other motto, might be taken as a statement of total risk; living in misery is living the life of the colonized, associating oneself with the colonizer. Better the total negation of himself than that. This total risk is not, however, the Hegelian movement of mastery. He does not display his risk taking to the Dutch force and they do not surrender rather than take a similar risk themselves. Instead, he continues in disguise, hiding the chance he is taking. If his slogans confer magical invulnerability to identification, however, it may be because he powerfully imagines his own death, not in the mode of pathos, "I am not here," but, precisely, as part of the revolution. The words do not originate with him. Some even are from the Jacobins. They are anonymous in the sense that he does not know who first wrote them. But no one asks the name of the author; everyone knows that they are the words of the revolution itself. The invulnerability they confer comes from their source as much as from their meaning. As slogans, they are to be repeated rather than to be understood. Taking them for his motto, K, uttering them of his own will, absorbs revolutionary invulnerability. Precisely because K knows he did not say these words first and may never have pondered their implication, they are powerful. He is not the articulating subject who generates the words. He is absent from them, as though it would be possible to say, "I am dead." The words of the slogan come from somewhere else, "the revolution," and they master him. "Better to die today . . ." is not the same as "I am dead," which perhaps inevitably makes one imagine oneself as absent to oneself and therefore still alive. "Better to die today . . ." is a judgment comparing the realms of life and death. But the maker of the judgment is not the speaker of the slogan. "The revolution" makes the assertion and imposes the judgment on K. In the context in which K used it, the "misery" of the phrase formed his disguise, his view of the way he looked to them. His life depended on their acceptance of him as miserable. Refusing to accept the validity of the disguise for himself meant risking death. At that point, he illustrates the danger to the Dutch comprised in Soewardi's warning. Dutch do not see that their subjects can see their masters' thoughts and do not comprehend the limitations of their view of Indonesians.

K accepted the judgment of the revolution, that death was preferable to the misery of the goatherd. In not being the goatherd, in being the revolutionary, he stood not in the place of the Dutch but in the place of death. "Death" in this slogan has a particular meaning. The revolution somehow was able to know life and death at the same time and to prolong the moment of death, making it seem a possibility of history, the history of the revolution, and not of escape from social time. It was by adhesion to death that K escaped the difficulties of the others we have seen. He does not fear becoming a Dutchman, becoming like a Dutchman, or remaining a colonial subject. He is one of the few to be able to complete Soewardi's phrase, to be able to say, "but I'm not a Dutchman" and at the same time not to say, "I am only a colored man from the tropics."

The "I" that completes Soewardi's phrase in this time of revolution is an abstract "I," an artifact of language rather than of speech. When K repeats his slogans, they are, as we have said, not "his." The "I" of the speaker "K" is identical to the "I" of the revolution that first spoke the slogans. "K" the revolutionary is both the first and the third persons. It is as the person that is not there that he kills the Dutch troops. It is the logic of his revolutionary thinking, unlike, for instance, that of Professor Doctor Garnadi. It is the active side of his identification with death; he comes to embody it.

"Death," as in "better to die than to live in misery," is realized in the deaths of the Dutch soldiers. But "death" is no more in K's experience than it is in anyone else's alive to presumably tell about it. "Death" was a word in a slogan that took on a significance at a certain moment. The capacity of communicating "death," and the other words of the slogan, the ability to make it seem as though death were in the present, brought forward from its hiding place outside of life, is the activation of language, the hyperexcitation of the lingua franca as the possibility of traversing realms. K says what he heard when he passes on the slogan. It is not an assimilated part of his thinking; it does not fit with the rest of his understandings; it is not a conclusion he draws from his analysis of colonialism, for instance. "Death" here must be understood as interior to the slogan. "Death" is the alternative to misery and it is summoned in his dress when that dress is understood as disguise. He was miserable; before the revolution he looked, no doubt, much as he looked when he appeared "in disguise" as a goatherd to the Dutch soldiers. Beneath the disguise, hidden under the look of misery, is death. It is the message he carries in the form of his own person. "I" can embody death, however, only by being the third person, the one not there, but nonetheless somehow brought forward by a piece of language.

The slogan, "better to die . . ." is a variant of another slogan widely repeated during the revolution, "Freedom or death," which could well be translated, "la liberté ou la mort" or perhaps, "Give Me Liberty or Give Me Death." It seems quite likely that it is as much an importation as the word "revolution" (*revolusi*) itself. But its meaning, if we follow what we have been saying, is quite different from the revolutions of the eighteenth century. "Liberty" or "freedom" (*merdeka*) here is, of course, separation from the Dutch. The maxim suggests risk and that is so. It is not the absolute risk of Hegel, however. For Hegel, the slave becomes such when he refuses to risk death, unlike the person who becomes master. Death, in Hegel's sense, is the negation of the self, its removal from everything contingent; its removal from history. If everyone realized the risk of death, history would stop because, Hegel said, there would be no interest in the other. Absolute liberty, complete indifference to the other, he said when speaking of the French revolution, is itself death.

But in the sense that K thought of death, death is part of history. Merely to be able to say "It is better . . ." is already to have a connection with the revolution. To die for the revolution, even without passing through a process of memorialization, is to have one's death be a part of history. It is to retrace the path between the enunciator of the slogan and its origin, implicitly attributed not to France but to "Indonesia," to the nation rather than the universal. It is the activation of the lingua franca, the ability to cross cultural boundaries, but with the assurance that one will return to the nation. It is the insistence that the lingua franca, even in its most powerful manifestations, is a national language. To die for the revolution, in this formulation, requires no further memorialization of whomever died because the very act is traceable, via a specific path of communication, to the revolution.

K, speaking of his slogans, speaks as though they speak to him, as though he repeats them in any context, or perhaps in no context in particular, that is, speaking to himself. It as though these slogans, working through him, are motors of historical change. They appear at the beginning of his account in this framework:

> The Dutch intensified their wild attacks killing a great many fighters. From the sea as well as from the sky and the land. Innocent people who did nothing did not escape their merciless, ceaseless bullets and bombardments.
>
> Killing anyone they suspected, Indonesian youths who did not want to ally themselves [with the Dutch] were tortured and imprisoned.
>
> Bapak Damanhuri, the leader of the Barisan Pelopor, kept fighting even though secretly while trying to penetrate their fortifications.
>
> My slogans were still the same as before: "Better to die today than to live in misery" and "Once free always free."
>
> The Barisan Pelopor who became scouts and commandos fought the enemy with sharpened bamboo sticks and confused the Dutch.
>
> Finally the Dutch realized. . . .

But of course K does not die at the moment that he repeats his slogan. Its magic does not extend that far. "Death" remains, even for him, in a realm of the "almost," a word whose sense language can only almost convey. He is possessed because the almost is closer to him than to others. Via the slogan, "death"/the revolution, has entered him. It is in this possessed state that he kills. The result is that the "Dutch realize. . . ." They realize only after they are confused. What confuses them is not simply the violence and fury of their opponents, but that "The Barisan Pelopor . . . fought the enemy with sharpened bamboo sticks." They are confused because, K is convinced, they never would have imagined such determination produced out of such misery. K, once again, sees himself seen in the eyes of the Dutch. He knows how he is supposed to look in their eyes. When he wears the appearance of the impoverished peasant and yet acts in the way his slogan prompts him to act, they can only be confused and finally "realize" the truth. The truth is that misery and death are not different; the costume of the peasant is the garb of violent death. The Dutch die, and, in dying they somehow recognize who has killed them. "Death" has been brought into discourse. The revolution for K speaks the truth of appearance. Its effectiveness rests on making the Dutch see what had long been in front of their eyes; that someone, "Indonesians," know what they think, are present, and are an ultimate menace even when Dutch do not attend to them.

With K, the fetish of modernity has been set aside. He is not the out-come of the path of nationalism we have traced. That way belongs to the far greater number of people who are represented in essays of chapter 8. K brings us back to Soewardi. His importance for the Indonesia of today is his contribution to the revolution. But the ousting of the Dutch was de-cided largely through diplomatic efforts and foreign pressure. K was part of the movement that the leadership of the nation was quick to want to bring under control. Had K's stream nonetheless been dominant within Indone-sia after the revolution, the Dutch would have remained a presence. Their "realization" would have formed a critical part of the understanding of the revolution. Disengagement from them would have meant an acknowledg-ment of the outside world as today it is acknowledged, for somewhat dif-ferent reasons again, in Algeria, for instance. But Indonesia today shows the effects of the creation of a new hierarchy in which the Dutch were replaced not by a process of exchange and acknowledgment but by the substitution of one hierarchy for another.

K shows that the fetish of modernism was not the only way to indepen-dence. In contemporary Indonesia, K, who won no prize at all for his con-tribution to the contest, has been reduced to slogans of another type, figuring as a type on the posters that celebrate independence by showing fighters with sharpened bamboo sticks. None of the posters I have seen show the enemy. K nonetheless represents another possibility inherent in the lingua franca as it became a national language.

It would be a mistake, however, to see K entirely apart from the fetish of modernity or the fetish of appearance. That fetish, we have shown, was formed when a certain linguistic power became evident when it seemed to summon authority against it. The full appropriation of the force of lan-guage perhaps could only take place after such recognition awakened awareness of linguistic power.

The force of language is greater than any particle of sense it contains. To take on its full force is to supersede complete recognition. We see this in our next figure.

No Entry

"Madness"

There are two revolutionary modes. One, the one we have just seen and the least common by far, is to chose "death" when affected by the pass-word, "freedom or death." The other is to accommodate oneself to being suspected. Because the power of language in the sense we have spoken about it was so important in the revolution, to find oneself gripped by either of these possibilities meant that exiting from them into daily life

with ordinary sorts of communications was difficult. Perhaps this is particularly true for those who found themselves on the side of death. We will
call the author of the following account MNT. He begins by giving the
location of the building in Solo, Central Java, which, in 1947, housed
various youth organizations. He was a member of the Tentera Peladjar, the
Army of Students, Staf Bataljon 100, Solo Branch. He gives little else of his
background, as though whatever matters about himself begins with this
organization. To give the location of his group is to find him. He describes
the tension in Solo, but he is unclear about the causes. For him, an important word is *musuh* (enemy), which he uses not only for colonial forces but
for those he fought during the Madiun affair, the battle between communist and noncommunist forces, both of them revolutionary. He describes
the departure of his group in search of the *musuh*, leaving it unclear who
exactly is meant. They encounter several villages where there is resistance
to them. They lose a comrade to a bullet.

> The death of a comrade did not become an obstacle and in no way weakened the
> will to fight of the Tentera Peladjar. In fact this event made each member more
> determined. The organization became smoother. Every member became braver
> and more determined, even to the point of being increasingly mad (*gila*). It was
> that way too with the Commandant and the members of other companies. One
> by one battles were won and one by one villages held by the enemy were taken
> over. The use of ammunition multiplied. Enemies were no longer taken prisoner;
> they died; they had to die. The corpses of the enemy were allowed to stay where
> they were sprawled out; the attacks continued. Always forward, always attack, kill
> and only kill. (4)

The kitchen where he worked was left unattended as all went to fight the
enemy,

> shooting them no matter if the enemy ran off in complete disarray or with their
> hands up. We all had become mad; mad with killing the enemy. (4)

He calls killing the enemy under all possible conditions "madness." It is an
obsession, not simply to win but to kill, set off by the death of one their
own members. After that, they accept no surrender and they pay no respect
to the corpses of their enemies. It is a question of "must." The enemy "all
die" and they "must die," by which he means that something compels him
and his comrades to kill even when they have already won, as when they
murder surrendering would-be prisoners. We might think that they want
vengeance. But vengeance is a form of repayment and depends for its continuation on further acts requiring revenge. By contrast, their killing after
the death of their comrade is independent of the reply of the "enemy,"
which largely goes unmentioned. The killing of his comrade is forgotten as
the killing of "the enemy" continues. Whoever is an "enemy" must be

killed no matter what the circumstance in which they are found and no matter how many there are.

MNT makes only a minimal identification of those he puts to death. They are "the enemy" regardless of whether they are Dutch, working for the Dutch, or, as we will see, Indonesians suspected of being communists. Sociological identity is lost under the word "enemy." Perhaps for this reason he never uses the word "hate" (*be⟩tji*) or any other word to describe his feelings toward his opponents. Whoever "the enemy" is, they or it has too little identity to arouse hatred. We will see that this "madness" is closer to a compulsion, in that he feels he has no choice but to kill, and to an obsession, in that he reports himself as unable to think about nearly anything other than killing. He considers himself and his comrades "mad" not because they kill nearly indiscriminately but because they think about nothing else but killing. This account differs from K's precisely in erasing any awareness of the other except at the moment of death.

When MNT reviews his actions, he never speaks of regret. The killings give him a place in the new nation. The sentence after the one just quoted says this:

> In the evening we stayed in a village empty because its inhabitants had fled. I leaned against a tree in the yard of a house and stared at the flickering hearth fire. . . . I reflected on the events I had gone through that day. The face of the enemy, grimacing, I had shot with a carbine from only a few meters distance. The body of someone else which drooped, drenched in blood after its soul took flight. My memory wandered to an earlier time when I was with the Student Army in Magelang in 1947. At that time the Magelang troops served on the Kopeng front near Ambarawa. The enemy we killed were the enemy of the nation [*musuh bangsa*], that is, the colonial Dutch forces.

Here, he visualizes the persons he has killed. They are his own *bangsa*, he says, his own nationality or race and it is these, not the English or the Dutch or the Japanese whom he has also fought, on whom he dwells. He pictures their bodies at the moment of death: the grimace, the body losing its inner support. It is the last moments of animation that interest him. These mental illustrations bring him satisfaction. It is through the killings that he earns a place in the nation, but the killings themselves are more than instrumental for him; he interests himself in the physical reactions of his victims. He seems to slow their motions down in order to observe them more carefully in retrospect. As we will see, these last moments come to be typical for him. He shows us an instant in which there is animation but its source is uncertain. When the body fell or the face grimaced, was the person still alive or was he already dead? Animation is usually a sign of life, but here motion seems governed by death.

This is not a story of conflict because it is almost entirely concerned with his actions and, with the exception mentioned, very little with the enemy's. It is not comparable even to a story of the hunt, where the ruses of the animal are guessed at by the hunter. There are two moments that interest MNT. One is the instant when he and his comrades shoot. The other is the moment of reaction of the dying. Other than that, he reports moments of reflection when thoughts about killing lead him to recount how he first began to shoot. The passage above continues:

> My thoughts went on to the beginning of the revolution in 1945. At that time I was still in SMP 1 [junior high school]. My heart was moved when I saw the military activities of the students of the Ikadaigakko [the medical school] who had established their residence hall next to Prapatan junior high school and made it the headquarters of their struggle for freedom. As a youth already ripe with military training during the Japanese occupation, I joined them and became a member of the Angkatan Pemuda Indonesia (API) from the area of Petojo. Every evening we would attack. The first targets were Japanese army installations. Then we fought, opposing the British and the Dutch. It was then that I began to shoot with fire arms, no longer with *mokuju* [wooden rifles; Japanese] used during *kyoreng* [military exercises; Japanese] with Japanese soldiers as instructors. In 1945 I began to shoot the enemy. In 1946, I became a member of the BKR-TKR-TRI regiment at Cikampek, Battalion III, Company 4, led by Lieutenant Maulana Sirdar. In 1947 I shot the enemy on the Semarang front and now, here, I shot the enemy, even though the enemy was my own nationality [*bangsa*].

His serenity in recalling moments of death comes from the possibility he takes to give himself credit. He has "earned his share," as he puts it later; he knows it because it was not he only who killed but the mass of those "mad" to kill who were provoked by opponents of the revolution. He did what they did; he is one of them, is his logic. This brings him back to the moment he first became a fighter. It is when he was a student in junior high school and admired the Indonesian medical students who had formed an association. As he had Japanese military training, he joins them. In other words, he sees them as ideal versions of himself. And it leads to a certain increment in his power. He no longer uses the wooden training rifle he had under the Japanese; he has gotten real arms. "In 1945 I began to shoot the enemy," he says. The turning point for him is not when he begins to fight; in a way he has already done that when he raided the Japanese for arms. The critical moment for him is shooting. He shoots the enemy in 1947 in Semarang; and he continues up to the moment he pictures himself as he "shot the enemy, even though the enemy was of my nationality [*bangsa*]."

There is a certain progression: from seeing others whom he would be like, to joining them, to increasing his power of destruction, to shooting "the enemy," who are, nonetheless, of his nationality. He shot in the name of the Student Army, as a member of a certain organization. His shootings, his killings are expressions of the power of that group and of his own power at the same time; his power is nearly impossible to distinguish from that of his group. After the death of his comrade, that power increases, although it is not certain that it is because of the death of the comrade. In any case, not just the members of his company become *gila*, or mad. It is also "the commander and the staff members of other companies." "Every member became braver and more determined, even to the point of being increasingly mad [*gila*]."

They do what he does; he does what they do. At the apex of his power, he is not different from them. It is part of being *gila* or "mad" as well as being *nekad*. I have translated *nekad* as "determined." It has a more specific meaning, however; it means "not taking heed of anyone or anything but what one is doing"; here, of not thinking of anything but killing. The difference between *nekad* and *gila* or "mad" as he uses it is not that madness is a more intense form of *nekad*; there is no more intense form available. Everyone is *nekad* at the same time and for that reason one might say that they are merged into a single body performing a single activity. This is their "madness" and the connection between violence and the membership in the organization. Everyone kills at the same time and no one furnishes a counterexample that might restrain the violence.

Nekad means that in one's determination, one pays no heed to others. It is used, for instance, in this sense today when someone drives recklessly, intent only on getting somewhere and thus forcing others out of his way and often enough crashing into them. Here is an example from MNT:

> No more enemy were taken prisoner, they all died, they had to die. The corpses of the enemy were left sprawled out, the destruction continued. Forward, destroy, kill and kill only.

He at that time was a cook, but he left his duties to join the battle, as did his fellow kitchen workers:

> The kitchen was left behind because all its workers joined in shooting the enemy, no matter that the enemy was running away in complete disarray and with hands in the air. We were all mad; mad to shoot the enemy. (4)

Here *nekad* in the sense of "determination" is shared. If there is madness (*gila*), it is produced by having only one reflection of oneself and having that reflection repeated on every side. In the end, "madness" reverses the sense of *nekad* as being heedless of others in so far as these others are his comrades. But this sharing produces not a society but an antisociety, not merely in the sense of "attack and destruction" (*gempur*) but in that seeing oneself in the other, one sees not the regard of the other, his sense of oneself with the social control that implies, but only someone else equally "determined" to kill, equally oblivious of anyone in front of him and only another form of oneself. One has the impression that were it not the case, were some, for instance, hesitant or opposed to the killings, it would not have registered on him. The requirement for a society, that there be reciprocal communication between differentiated persons, has vanished in his account.

At the end of the Madiun affair, he says this:

> The operation to exterminate the rebellion of the PKI Musa [Indonesian Communist Party/Musa] ended. For me personally it was an addition to the experience of the battles of 1948. And there was something else additional for me: a share in freedom. In my heart a feeling of pride arose that I had a part in erecting the freedom of the Republic of Indonesia which I love. My heart was proud; but only within my heart. (7)

He did his share as others have done theirs. He has earned a place, but he keeps this pride to himself. He does not demand recognition of it, at least until later, when he submits his contest entry. In any case, he does more, perhaps making sure of his share. His commander announces that he has a new duty for him and for one of his comrades, Y. It is something he must do, the officer tells him,

> "with resolution [*tabah*], in a disciplined way and without involving feelings or thoughts of your own. This duty is to execute the death penalty on the orders of superiors." (13)[4]

His companion asks him what he thinks about this. He replies, "'Duty is duty'" (Tugas adalah tugas) (13). They proceed to a cemetery:

> The two of us were carrying L.E. rifles slung over our shoulders. At the cemetery comrades from other companies awaited us. The inhabitants we met on the road came along behind us. There were four freshly dug grave holes ready. The spectators stood far in back. Without ceremony and without announcement, two people we did not know were led up to the holes and stood on their edge, facing them. Comrade Y and I stood about 2 meters behind them. The rifles were cocked and aimed, with the left foot slightly forward. I was silent and to myself uttered, "In the name of the struggle for freedom of the Republic of Indonesia, in the name of President Sukarno and Vice-President Hatta, in the name of the commander who gave the order. Innalilllahi wainnailahi rojiun." And as a signal to Sdr. Y, I slowly counted: "One, Two, Three." The explosions from our rifles were nearly simultaneous. The 7.7 caliber bullets hit the napes of the neck and the victims fell head first into the holes. The incident was repeated at the next two holes. The utterances also.

Sometime later this special duty was carried out again and again and again. Sometimes there were 10 victims in a single day. Time went on and the number of grave holes increased with it. This time, the special duty had to be done in the city and the victims had to be gotten from their houses in the city. The entire membership of Company D went to get them. After successfully getting them, the victims were brought to the highway and shot dead there. A piece of paper with thick letters was placed on each corpse; it read: Enemy of the People!

Days changed into weeks and weeks into months. The guerrilla struggle continued without pause and the special duty went on the same way. (14–15)

He utters to himself, "in the name of. . . ." He does not say it to his victims, nor to his comrade, nor to the public, although there are spectators present. One can ask why he does not say it aloud, since the event requires a ceremony. He and his comrade have been given a duty by their officer. He acts in the name of the Republic. It would be appropriate for him to pronounce these words to those present. The words are ceremonial, but they have not been codified and given to him to say. They merely come to him at that moment. If he were to say them, he would then be the spokesman of the nation, an intermediary who conveys someone else's words to others. He would stand between a constituted authority, the revolutionary state, and the people in the cemetery. But the words do not come to him from a constituted authority, even though one exists, in the form, for instance, of his commander. These words simply appear in his mind. They do not lack authority for that, but their authority is self-evident and connected with their seemingly unmediated appearance. The phrases have evaded a structure, and yet they are the expression of the revolution.

He could still speak them aloud. And he begins to when he counts. The phrases that he repeats are not sentences. He does not say, "in the name of the struggle . . . I am obliged to kill you." Nor even "One, two three, fire." The act rather than the word "fire" completes the sentence. It is the rifle that finishes the phrase. "Rifles were cocked and aimed, left feet a little to the front." Indonesian possesses no plural form and so it is not possible to say whether "rifle" and "foot" are singular or plural. All the more so since the subject of this sentence is not named. Because of this lack, there is a second ambiguity. It is common sense to assume that the foot or feet spoken of belong to him or to him and Y and not to the rifles. And yet the sentence, in Indonesian as in English, is constructed as though there is a single subject; as though, that is, the rifle(s) had feet. They do not, so far as I know, but nonetheless the subjects of the sentence are run together in such a fashion, contrary to the usual care he takes with his prose, as to suggest that, somehow, he and his rifle are a single entity. He is here an extension of his weapon as much as it is an extension of him. It is not "him" who shoots, it is the rifle in its expanded form comprising his body and his language, both silent and audible.

MNT in this extended form merely transmits the words of the revolution. He makes the rifle the instrument of the nation, something like a loudspeaker that amplifies as much as continues his words. His victims are brought under the power of the revolution. If the rifle shots are the continuation of revolutionary words, they are not of course to be understood by those he eliminates. They are the literal continuation of his words, meaning only the power of communication without the need for sense or interpretation. Those linked by the communicative power of the revolution need only understand the most rudimentary sense ("as a signal to Sdr. Y. I slowly counted: "One, Two, Three") and none at all if one is a victim. Death here is drawn into the language of the revolution. The rifle shots, their sounds, the bullets, their effects, are linguistic. They are language, signals and their transmission, without ever being speech in a precise way.

Suspicion and Killing

> An expression or a move that gave rise to suspicion, or words that made light of the Government of the Republic of Indonesia [capitalized in original] of course meant that a balance would be struck and one could expect one's turn in being kidnapped and having a sentence of the sort that pertained at that time.

The quotation is from Dayim Sostawirya, the organizer of SP 88; we have already seen it in chapter 8. It describes the victims of the revolution from the point of view of someone afraid he might become one himself. It shows us the point of the terror. All signs that one might give of oneself are susceptible to being intercepted. They might be unintended or careless, as we have seen in the same account. But "one can expect one's turn." At that point, one can expect to be eliminated. It is the origin of feeling oneself suspect. This man was on the side of the revolution, but he felt that, were he not careful, he might be suspected. He founded SP 88 to establish his credentials. He refused Red Money because he felt it might incriminate him. He was careful to do nothing to make himself suspect, and yet he felt he, like all others, might be suspected. It is because he could not be sure, despite all his caution, what signals he was emitting. Revolutionaries, he claims, might well intercept even minor signals. There is no question of misinterpretation; the revolutionaries are right. Thus, when they detect signs of collaboration, they have discovered unintended messages, signs of being on the other side, foreign, that the sender did not know he made.

This anticolonial revolution was devoted to the elimination of the foreign, which it found at least as easily in "Indonesians" as in Dutch. The corpses are labeled and displayed: "A piece of paper with thick letters was placed on each corpse; it read: Enemy of the People!" The power of the revolution here is not merely its ability to kill. It reduces its victims to signs of itself. The corpses are not marked as the bodies of particular individuals; they are identified merely as "Enemy of the People." Moreover, these corpses are not monuments such as gravestones, which might mark the place where the corpse was buried. The bodies themselves are on display and as such they form part of a sign along with the "thick letters" placed over them. These people suspected of having Dutch sympathies, discovered by revolutionaries, now are themselves part of the language of the revolution. They no longer emit any signal other than the one given them. All signals arrive at the revolution and, one way or another, all signals belong to the revolution.

A power of recognition, able to detect even unintended signals, takes away that power from the colonial police. The corpses mark the point where one center of communication replaces another. But one can ask, is the "madness" of the revolution the simple counterpart of the fetish of modernity? Is it, at last, the manifestation of the fear that anyone, including "the people" (*publiek*; *orang banjak*; *rakyat*) are repositories of foreignness? Would such a notion produce "madness"? Or is it that this foreignness is itself produced by the appropriation of linguistic force?

The "madness" of MNT reminds one of amok, a classical form of behavior found in Malay (and other) cultures. The person who runs amok often begins with a grievance. It may be slight; perhaps something perceived as an insult. But when he runs amok, the person kills indiscriminately. Whoever comes in his way is a likely victim. The usual outcome was the death of the person who ran amok himself. Often death was thought to be the only restraint possible. Amok then was an invitation to death for the "amokker" himself.

There are differences between the "madness" of MNT and amok. The person who ran amok usually killed with a dagger rather than a rifle. This seems so often to have been the case that one thinks that there, too, killing was thought of in terms of the special quality of a certain weapon. Amok involved individuals rather than groups. But there is a similarity here as well. MNT describes himself and his comrades as one body.[5] Amok began as vengeance; as does the "madness" of MNT. But it continues with blindness about the identities of victims. If there was mere injury rather than death, it seems an accident.

I do not point to amok in order to say that the violence of the revolution was, at least in the case we deal with here, an instance of a cultural pattern. "Amok" itself as a behavior is at best on the margins of culture. How, for instance, does one learn to be amok? It is not merely that the behavior involves an altered form of consciousness. It is rather that amok, beginning with grievance, marks a moment when no exchange, even vengeance, seems possible. It is this that amok has in common with the revolutionary violence of MNT. The moment of grievance seems forgotten once the killing begins. MNT mentions the killing of his comrade as the start of "madness" and then does not refer to it again. Vengeance, by contrast, is a form of commemoration. It enshrines the grievance in the death of the adversary. Vengeance from that point of view is a form of mourning, in contrast with amok or MNT's "madness."

Common to both amok and Indonesian revolutionary violence is an invitation to death. The person who runs amok is killed. MNT sees death, and his descriptions allow us to believe that the final motions of those he killed are not theirs. They are the motions of "death" itself. That is, there is a response. The response surpasses all social categories, those that pertain in life. The fall of the body and the grimace are not expressions of intention, they are movements made when the victim is possessed by death. These motions are available therefore to be signs of death, which is how MNT takes them. It is what he looks for when he distinguishes, in his practical way, between the act of shooting and the effects. He speaks of these effects not through particular cases but as typical instances. They form for him the satisfaction he seeks. He may have silenced the enemy, but he is not content with their silence. He wants evidence of a response that comes from the other side of their silence. This evidence is the signs of death. For him, death speaks.

Beyond all exchange, there is still response. When the foreign has been eradicated, there is still something foreign left. The "madness" of the revolution is the disgorgement of the foreign no matter what nationality holds it. But even in disgorging it, it finds it again; killing continues. Beyond exchange, there is still response. When all signals have been exhausted, nonetheless there is something to be sensed. And sensing it, there is further revolutionary violence; further response because it comes from elsewhere, from an unreachable source. The sign on the corpses, "Enemy of the People," only marks the place from which further opposition will arise.

At that point, collaborators are no longer those who yielded to Dutch seduction; they are the dead whom the revolution cannot wholly appropriate for themselves. Very little of the Dutch remains in the mentality of contemporary Indonesia. The attitude toward the foreign as the site of immorality remains, though it is no longer "Dutch" but "American" and "European." That is, revolutionary violence did not eradicate the split in authorities marked by seduction and suspicion. But even if it had done so, it showed that beyond exchange there was still a response to be elicited that could not be contained even when "enemy" meant "seduction" or could be limited to foreign nationals. The battle between communists and noncommunists was one between Indonesians; it surpassed the possibility of marking in advance someone as "enemy." Thus, the foreign could always emerge again and it could do so from within fellow Indonesians. The search for "the enemy," those who respond to something from beyond the frontier of communication, was resurrected in the massacres of those called "communists" in 1965 when hundreds of thousands were slain.

No Entry, No Literature: "I" = "He"

MNT continues his account past the revolution:

> On the 10th of August, 1949, there was a cessation of shooting on the orders of the President of the R. I. [Republic of Indonesia]. Though we did not agree, we obeyed. (18)

There is a cease fire, but, in his case, not a cessation of fighting:

> We were free to wander around the city in the daytime. Every time we passed Dutch soldiers, the tension mounted and hearts pounded. Shooting was forbidden but hitting each other was not forbidden. Every time a member of Company D went to the city, there was fight with Dutch soldiers, especially those with light-brown skins. (18)

The abrupt end of a certain habit causes him difficulty:

> For myself, the cease fire was a mental shock [*schok batin*]. For friends too. The booms and the explosions that until now had ornamented life in the countryside for months and months, now were no longer. Cocking rifles, aiming them and shooting with a noise that deafened the ears had become something habitual and satisfying [*terasa puas hati*], but we could no longer enjoy it. Looking at spurting blood and victims tumbling into holes, as was experienced tens and hundreds of times, would no longer be repeated. Thinking became confused and the body felt weak. Smiles and laughter were no longer in evidence. Happy faces and welcoming natures were destroyed. Friends began to be far away. Speech was only for necessities. This is the way it seems to me now. (18)

His company is given a last assignment after the transfer of sovereignty. They take over the powers of the police in Solo from the Dutch military police. They patrol the streets in jeeps wearing white helmets.

> I myself got this duty. The form of the struggle had changed, it doesn't matter. In my heart I felt pride that I had passed through the period of guerrilla warfare successfully. My Share in Freedom had increased. Apparently now I am easily insulted and suddenly get angry. There have been several incidents between me and friends, just because of small things. Windows were smashed by fists. And I don't know what else has occurred.
>
> I no longer remember what happened after that. What duty it was I had to carry out. I don't know; I don't understand any more.

What's clear is that, after 1949 passed and 1950 arrived, I became the patient of Dokter Soejoenoes in Surabaya, a specialist in disorders of the nerves. A few years later, in 1952, Dr. Soejoenoes handed me over to Dr. Sumantri Hardjoprakoso on Nias Bandung Street, also a specialist in nerves and souls. . . . .
Assalmu'alaikum war, wab.

The ellipses in this quotation are his own. The account ends that abruptly, with a break between war and peace or between revolution and victory that he cannot manage and that occurs, as it were, in the middle of a paragraph. He is a careful writer of his sort. That a single paragraph contains two disparate subjects indicates that, at that point, he no longer controls his thoughts or his prose. His memoir gives nothing at all of his life before the war that does not directly pertain to his revolutionary experiences. After his memory of his war experience, he has nothing to say of his life except that he cannot remember what has happened to him, that he continued to be violent and that he was and possibly still is (one cannot tell the tense from the Indonesian) in the hands of doctors. "Looking at spurting blood and victims tumbling into holes, as was experienced tens and hundreds of times, would no longer be repeated. Thinking became confused and the body felt weak." One set of experiences cannot encompass another; revolution, which meant for him killing with his rifle, has no place in life after 1949.

It is just after the sentence that proclaims his pride in increasing his share in independence that he describes his mental state. The stake that he won, the pride which he kept to himself, is not transferable into everyday life. But why not? Is it, for instance, a question of trauma; of an experience that somehow exceeds the capacity to represent it? Here, there is no sign of trauma if that means that memory is somehow more powerful than the language that stabilizes memory as it expresses it and makes past experience available for recall at will rather than involuntarily. His prose is effective throughout. Nor does he complain, for instance, of not being able to forget what he experienced nor of remembering it involuntarily. On the contrary, he clearly cherishes his memories. What he regrets is that what he experienced "hundreds of times," killing, he can no longer repeat. Trauma would involve pain and incomprehension. But he is nostalgic for a source of satisfaction he no longer has access to and which he comprehends well.

When peace is established, he sometimes wears the white helmets of the military police and rides in their jeeps. It is, he says, a different sort of duty, but it does not matter, because he retains his pride. But it is evidently not sufficient. He continues to fight. But he fights, as it were, out of uniform. Now his duty is to keep the peace and yet he makes war. Further, this time when he fights there is no enemy, nor, for that matter, are there even strangers. He fights with his friends and it gives him no satisfaction. He continues, as best as he can, to do what he did during the revolution, but now he does not find it pleasurable.

Why it is that he loses his memory of events after the war? And one can ask why it is that all that he tells us of postrevolutionary life is being in the hands of doctors. Why is this fact alone pertinent? We can look again at his language. When he describes his last violent acts, he omits the first person. "Windows were smashed by fists" makes it seem as though his fists acted independently. It is true that he used the same grammatical form to describe his shooting of "enemies of the people," but then he immediately put himself back into the picture, telling us what he said to himself.

In the last paragraph of his account, he tells us about himself as others, the doctors, see him:

> Apparently now I am easily insulted and suddenly get angry. . . . windows were smashed by fists.

When he says, "apparently" about himself, he accepts someone else's version of himself. He is sure that other things have occurred, but he no longer has a memory of them; but others have. Someone else has his memory. He, the person who speaks from the time of the revolution, is not identical with the person who speaks after the revolution. The person who writes the memoir lives during a previous period, the one about which he writes, and not later. Later, after the revolution, he knows mainly what others tell him: "I don't know what else has occurred. I no longer remember what happened after that." The person who lives after the revolution is a blank to the writer. "I don't understand anymore." The "I" here who knows he does not understand is lucid. It is a lucidity he borrows from the time of the revolution, but only to say that after the revolution, "I" does not comprehend. He uses "I" as a third, not a first person. It is the "I" of a previous time, an "I" that did exist and that now complains of its nonexistence.

Now, for the first time in the memoir, he sees that others see him, but the result is that he cannot see himself. He does not agree or disagree with what they say about him. He simply accepts it to the point of suppressing his own view of himself. He has nothing to offer against their account. He does not dispute what they say, but he cannot absorb it into a social persona. One has here the mechanism of our fetish—someone else knows me better than I do—but without its proper operation. Rather than seeing that he has made himself appear to others and that has given him a place in the social world, he remains identified with moments of his past to the extent that one cannot say they are over, mere memories for him.

MNT has a "stake in freedom" for which he demands recognition when he enters the contest. And he gets it to the extent, for example, that the state recognizes his disability incurred as a fighter and takes care of him. He is not indifferent to the opinions of others, but he cannot engender the recognition he wants. It is not, for instance, that he is violent and his violence has no place in peacetime. It is not mere killing he wants or simple violence. It is violence and death as part of language. He wants death to show itself, to speak, and to speak as part of his performance.

He has something to say—the story of his experiences. But these stories do not satisfy him. He wants to use language as it was used during the revolution, when speaking, shooting, killing, and seeing death respond were a single trajectory. For him, revolutionary language was language without deferral. One did not have to wait for a reply. Revolutionary language spoke beyond the person immediately addressed. If one agrees that death can speak, it was effective; the instant the signal reached its goal, the response appeared. The signals he sent comprised words and bullets, the difference between them being distinguishable mainly by their position on the trajectory extending between him and his victims. Bullets were words and words were bullets, when language was the sheer effectiveness of transmission.

Here again, but from a different perspective, we see the absence of literature. Literature uses language to gain recognition, but it insists on deferral. The characteristic of the literary is the ability to awaken a response centuries after a sentence has been composed and without knowledge of the identity of the reader. The opposite is true with MNT, though his goal is close to the goal of literature, which also assumes an ultimate response. It is not "death" within language that distinguishes MNT's response from literature. It is MNT himself, taking him, that is, as the author and the narrator of his piece. For MNT, within the assumptions he uses, there is no alternative to immediacy of response once one has surpassed social exchange, in the form, perhaps, of vengeance. Even if he could imagine his rifle firing into the future, reaching its target, it is the deferral of response that makes him ill. It is not killing which, we repeat, was his satisfaction, nor is it the anonymity of the enemy, which it shares with the literary target which sickens him.

MNT cannot bring the first person of the past into the present. That he cannot do so indicates the foreignness of his language to himself after the revolution. Again, it is not "death" and not violence that make his language foreign. It is the inability to speak the language of the revolution after the revolution. A language without deferral was possible, he believed. But this language has disappeared and he cannot accept it. And yet he continues to try and speak it. Even though he speaks, he is not the first person in the usual sense. He is at most a medium, or an unsuccessful translator, through whom dead language passes without resonance. Inhabited by a dead language, he personifies it; MNT is a ghost of the lingua franca.

MNT cannot give up himself. He cannot separate himself from antiquated language. It is because he has no place to go. He is locked inside his text as author, narrator, and actor all at once. For him, nothing stands in the place of death, capable of substituting for it as a source of responsiveness.[6] He is trapped inside a language that now reaches no destination and that comes from elsewhere than where he exists.

It is not merely MNT's failure. It is the failure also of the hierarchy that re-formed after the revolution. That hierarchy obscures certain revolutionary activity when, for instance, it speaks only of the youth who fought and not of their opposition. It leaves out one side of the struggle, not only politically but linguistically and culturally. It credits him, and others like him, for their participation in the revolution. But it hides revolutionary "madness." It refuses to take account of a moment when response was generated from a point outside of hierarchy. That response was generated from a revolutionary language whose discourse was formed with "the enemy" (*musuh*), death, as interlocutor. There is no official interest at all in showing that there is still today an outside of hierarchy to which one can respond.

"Liberty or death" addresses no one and everyone. Nonetheless, one still needs to ask who is addressed. It was a performative, bringing about what it said in the act of saying it; stating two alternatives that excluded all other possibilities. With K and MNT we see how revolutionary words are inextricably linked within actions, bringing death into the scene of responsiveness. "Death" becomes part of the address. "Liberty" then meant Indonesia without Dutch domination. It was as free of further reference as "death." That "liberty" came to be equated with the Indonesian state and the national hierarchy went largely unquestioned. But from the perspective of the language of the revolution, this is mere historical accident. One cannot rule out the revival of this primordial language.

Pramoedya Ananta Toer's "Flunky + Maid," or Conservative Indonesian, Revolutionary Indonesian, and the Lack of Indonesian Literature

IN THE ACCOUNTS of the revolution we have read, one sees the division between pleasure associated with Dutch surveillance and guilt associated with surveillance by Indonesians. But if there is an equivalent of "Tan Malaka," it is not exact. The "fighters in the countryside" who hear inadvertent expressions of sympathy for the Dutch do not establish nationalist loyalty; they avenge betrayal. Their difference from Tan Malaka matters greatly. It is the difference between the establishment of hierarchy and revolution. Where the apex of hierarchy should have been there was, during the revolution, so far as it concerned "the fighters in the countryside," no recognition leading to integration into the nationalist cause; there was, rather, violence.

In the examples given in chapter 9, this violence is the product of curious linguistic practices: the password of K, that allows him to pass from a peasant in disguise, the colonial subject, to revolutionary; or the formula of MNT: "in the name of . . ." that forms a part of his executions. We can find here similarities with the time before the fetish of recognition was formed. K's disguise was linguistic. He was a peasant and he told himself that he looked and acted like one. In his own mind, he passed between two social identities although to anyone else's eyes, he never changed form. It was a matter of saying "I" to himself, knowing that each time "I" could be attached to a different identity. We saw this separation between language and social reality in the Muhammad Bakir of our introduction. "I" for K was a magical formula. This relation to language distinguishes him from the Tan Malaka of our novels, whose mastery of disguise and of languages was not magical but the wishful product of certain imaginations.

"Tan Malaka," moreover, was not violent. On the contrary, as often as not he solved crimes and turned the criminals over to the police. The revolutionary violence that is feared and celebrated in these accounts is not merely aided by linguistic formulas. It is, rather, the lack of difference between language and social reality that produced it. K's disguise did not produce roles in the sense of fantasies. They bring not "K" but "I" face to face with people for whom those who look like "K" arouse no difficulties at all but who denied the power inherent in the ability to pronounce "I" in the way that K did. K had a fetish of a different type. It was not the fetish of modernity, which at first at least unexpectedly produced recognition. It was a fetish in no way aimed at compelling recognition. Indeed, it was one in which the possibility of recognition was averted. This was not merely the recognition of the enemy, but nationalist recognition of the sort we have traced. It is his failure to accept this sort of recognition that left MNT mentally disabled when he could have been recognized as a hero.

What is left to such fetishism is violence. During the revolution, it produced certain marks on the bodies of its victims: "enemy of the people," for instance. It was, in fact, in the ability to produce such marks and to have them believed that the revolution consisted as it is portrayed by the people who wanted it but who feared it. They may have wished for "Tan Malaka," but they had to wait until the transfer of sovereignty for that; that is, for the reconstitution of an Indonesian hierarchy. By that time, the violent production of signs had no place. But if the revolution occurred at all, it is because revolutionary fetishism was always a possibility; one that the fetish of modernity concealed. But their source, the unexpected ability of words to stimulate response, is the same. The very success in compelling recognition and (imaginary) hierarchies in the 1920s and 1930s stifled the revolutionary fetish and so left it available to reemerge when the battle for independence began.

The Indonesian revolution was several things. It was a struggle for independence led by essentially conservative people who had a view of Indonesia as a modern nation. Their view of social order was not greatly different from the order envisioned by Dutch liberals. It was also a revolution led by "the fighters in the countryside," governed, for lack of a more accurate verb, more by slogans than by programs. These two elements came into conflict, with youths always urging more drastic and sometimes social revolutionary measures. The history of the first group is the history of nationalism but in its conservatism it makes the revolution something to be brought under control. The history of the revolutionary impulse is much more problematic. It is contained in the possibilities suppressed by the evolution of nationalistic recognition.[1]

If one wants to see the conservation of the revolutionary possibility and the emergence of literature, one can turn to the writing of Pramoedya Ananta Toer. From time to time, I have spoken of the defeat of the institution of literature in Indonesia. This phrase is so ambiguous as to be nearly contradictory. Here I furnish a translation of a story. Were there other writers with the strength of this author, Pramoedya Ananta Toer, I would not have made my claim that literature has not, or has not yet, established itself in Indonesia. Further commentary follows the story.[2]

FLUNKY + MAID

From the time of Jan Pietersz. Coen, the blood of slaves flowed down through this family. These weren't half-hearted slaves; they were faithful to their fingertips. Maybe not even from the time of Coen. There is a real possibility it was ever since Pieter Both, or the time when Houtman wandered through the archipelago. No one knows for sure. What's clear is that this family was known well before Coen became the statue the Japanese swept away from the front of the Finance Building.

The family is first known because it was noted in the big book with Latin characters—native sergeant . . . . x no . . . . At that time the rank of sergeant was something. With such a rank, a man could multiply. And that family generated forty children. Who knows from how many wombs. No one knows. Things like that aren't allowed into the big book.

Second generation—also a slave, a plain sergeant!

From then on, with each generation, the rank of these slaves descended as well. Lower and lower. Finally, in 1949, it got to the point of Sobi and Inah—their final degree of slavery. A year earlier, they were still slaves of the state. The two of them did not know: danger hung over their heads. Their degree of slavery would descend one more level—slaves of the Federal-District of Batavia! Sobi as a flunky, Inah as a maid.

If God were still as full of pity as before, willing to extend these slaves for another generation, the thirtieth generation certainly would no longer be human; it would be—worms crawling inside the earth. And this would be only logical.

The face of this family as it descended also has a story.

From the time of the sergeant, the faces of everyone in the family were awful. They never changed. After so many dozens of generations, Empok Kotek was born. Thanks to tuberculosis, she had a shining beauty. And she was called beautiful.

Empok Kotek was faithful to her tradition—she was a thorough slave. Faithful to her fingertips. So one time, even though she was a maid, her *tuan* said, "Tomorrow the missus has to go to Kopeng for a rest for a month. And *njai* will stay in the house with *tuan*. Ja?"

She did not understand why he said "*njai*" just then. She only understood when the *tuan* came back after having escorted his wife. And later—a moment that was less than good—she let something fall. And that thing could cry. People called it her child. She almost did not understand; it was so easy and so pleasurable for humans to come into being. She was astonished! But the child was already there. And it had clear chocolate-colored eyes. She did not waste time with regrets—as a slave she had real discipline.

Rodinah was born into the world. Even with chocolate eyes she was a maid, too, finally. And in Rodinah's hands, the golden age of descent opened its gates. Rodinah was the same as Victoria for the British empire. Her skin was less chocolate in color. She had a pointed nose. Her eyes were wide with lashes that curved upwards. Her lips were thin, top and bottom. Her body was like a guitar which was not yet secondhand, not yet used goods.

Astonishingly, this revolution in looks had no effect on the history of her tradition—blood and bones, she was still a slave. If by chance she had had any sort of ambition, Rodinah certainly would have steered the course of later generations. But no such ambitions arose. And no one regretted that. What's the point of life if not for enjoyment and taking pleasure in what is the right of the flesh? Ambition only upsets mankind. For that reason, she stayed a maid.

Rodinah, like ordinary humans, eventually grew up. One thing happened which she could not forget. Once someone proposed to her. The man was a foreman for *ERPOL*, an old man who people buried four years later. Of course, she refused. This had become her right. So she held on to the tradition which withstood its tests. So, too, her body whose prettiness shone as it grew.

A historic moment arrived. Suddenly. Like a meteor falling from a star. No one could calculate the time when it fell. Her *tuan* called Rodinah "Dolly." She was indeed like a Japanese doll. The name "Rodinah" was erased from history. She became "Dolly"—and a real doll through and through.

Dolly did not know the politics of *divide et impera*. But as white-skinned maid she knew that Ambonese with dark skins had to be seen as white. She had her own strategy and it worked: divide and surrender herself. She really put this strategy to work. What's more, she still disciplined herself to follow the tradition—faithful to her fingertips. Always tieing herself to slavery. But she divided, too! With this strategy, she plucked the most glittering fruit. No differently than Victoria got Africa. This was her victory: her first child was born with silvery curly hair. From the power of her strategy, greater than she was capable of understanding, came Si Sobi, son of Tuan Hendrik. Or the son of the neighbor of Tuan Hendri, Tuan Klaasen. Or the son of Tuan Giljam from France. Or the son of Tuan Koorda. Or the son of Tuan Harten. She did not know. She never bothered her head with it. What was evident was that she had a 50 percent share in the making of Sobi. And she was never aware that God had something to do with the creation of children.

Dolly was certainly faithful to her strategy. By being so, she successfully got them to act honestly and acknowledge Sobi as their child. There was a thick curtain drawn between one and the other father.

None of them knew the role of the other in the making of Sobi. From these six fathers, Dolly was able to build a masonry house inside of which were: two radios and a gramophone. Night and day these three objects sounded off one after the other! Along with the din, her heart reverberated: "This is Dolly's masonry house! Who can compete?"

But her secret remained locked up in the corner of her heart. It was this: The strategy of divide and surrender herself.

She also had the intention to start a life like a free person—a private person. She tried. She married five times the way people usually marry. That is, with the legitimacy conferred by the mosque. But never for long. The longest was two months. Her sharp thinking always brought catastrophe to legal marriage. She was able to guess the sharpness of these husbands: They did not want to hand over to her their good earnings. Just the contrary, in fact: They wanted to deceive her, wanted to use her. Finally, she let her intentions sail away with this stern wind.

Her slave's spirit did not allow her to live quietly at home. So she became a maid again—in a different area. She put her strategy to work again. And it worked—Inah was born into the world. And, as before, she took a 50 percent share in the making of this new creature. She couldn't be precise as to the father. There were more than nine. It was only the money she got that she could count.

Time went quickly on. Quite suddenly, white people were no longer agreeable in her eyes. And, quite suddenly, she could smell their odor at the distance of a yard. Before she never paid attention to their smell, even from as close as a tenth of an inch. And the smell; what staleness! Because now it was Japan which was delicious to her tastes. How happy she would be if she could have a child with slanted eyes. And why not? The sixteen dads of her second child nowadays didn't have ten cents to buy themselves a cigarette.

This world keeps turning. If mankind is not careful, all of a sudden it is going to be shocked, its body is no longer going to respond to its mental commands. Without warning, it feels old and useless to the world, which no longer pays any attention to it. So it was too with Dolly. No one knew what sickness attacked a person as pretty as that. Not even the two radios and the gramophone understood. And one unhappy day people buried her. Just before her moment of death, she had her eyes wide open and she was surprised that death was so close, so fast and so easy. But she died leaving her creations, 50 percent of Sobi and 50 percent of Inah.

Like their ancestors, these two got the instincts of real slaves, nothing half way, faithful to their fingertips. As flunky and maid of the highest quality, these two felt tortured if they had no orders. And their lives were happy when they got orders.

The two of them were on the right—not revolutionary, not, that is, flunky and maid who liked to steal forks-knives-spoons and get out quick. Not at all! The two of them regarded themselves as faithful to their duties.

Who knows, maybe there would be eternal slavery for another three generations. So they set up boundaries in the districts of their lives. Just like Renville[3] set up the status quo for the life of the Republic.

After Dolly died, Sobi became a flunky in the office of the Dai Sanka—the office of the Japanese navy spies. His latest ambition was to wear a cap with a yellow star, a white uniform with a samurai-sword with a gold handle with a patent leather sheath. These ambitions were never realized. The Japanese never gave him the chance. And he was happy when he could yell *keireit* when the Dai Sanka colonel got out of his car. Like others at the time, he hated colonialism; that is, Dutch colonialism. What colonialism was he didn't know. But, damn it all, he too hated it. Whatever came out of the mouth of Japan was the voice of truth. And everyone had to believe it. Fortunately, he could believe it. If not, his rank of flunky would disappear like the lives of the forced laborers.

Inah, too, worked there as laundress. But at that time she was just twelve. So her chest was still flat and no one was attracted to her. She had no chance to play a role.

The path of history is never straight. Japan was defeated. The English came. Indonesians went amok. And these two, the brother and sister, had to lay low. Eventually, they were brave enough to come out again. Sobi gave himself the courage to chase the Japanese and take their clothes. But this situation did not last long either. It was the turn of the English to run amok. White men were sovereign again in Jakarta. And the two of them, brother and sister, suddenly were disgusted with Japan. The two of them felt tricked as did others, even though the two of them did not know just how the trickery was practiced. And people with white skins were again high in their esteem.

The sound of shots ceased to be heard. What upset things every day was: distribution! People were fed up crying out and clenching their fists. Even those who earlier were called pioneers. Even those who had sat in the councils of government. Why not Sobi and Inah? This was why Sobi became a flunky again—a flunky for a white person who during the days of the Japanese was valueless, worth less than fingernails. And he now was able to pride himself in front of other flunkies who had Indonesian bosses. He learned to hold himself aloof from flunkies who worked for Chinese and Indonesians. He learned to sing, "yua olwees in mai haat" in a soft, indecent voice. This slavery gave him the greatest happiness of his life. Especially when he was able to suggest something for the better order of his boss's house—it was the high point of happiness for a flunky.

Flunkies, indeed, come in several classes. There are flunkies who understand politics. There are those who understand commerce. And there are even flunkies who understand diplomacy. There are those who can shoot. But Sobi was the lowest degree. He was quite happy never hearing about politics. This was because he vaguely felt that politics meant all sorts of sins. His *tuan* often said as much. And everything the *tuan* said was law [*wet*]—no different than the law made by the government. The voice of *tuan* was the voice of the Lord [Tuhan].

Inah now was an adolescent. She was no longer a maid for Japanese. Nowadays, she had become a maid in the battalion's barracks. But after no more than week, she left without asking. Not because she wanted to leave her tradition behind her—not at all. It's just that she got nervous taking orders from people who were not genuine *tuan*s—who didn't have white skin.

Her eyes were clear blue. And about this she was content. There were no Indonesians who had eyes like she had. For that reason, Indonesians had no right to give orders to anyone of her type [*karena itu orang Indonesia tak berhak memerintah matanja*]. And she had a pointed nose, too. She was really pretty. And for her, prettiness was women's capital. She did not know arithmetic. But she could evaluate her prettiness. And this capital she was going to use to take charge of her future. She had a plan. Because it was not only Russia who had a five-year plan. Inah had one, too. Dolly's strategy—her mother's—had ripened in her heart.

Once she became a maid. But her *tuan*, even though he had white skin, was as poor as she was herself. So she left. Her *tuan* made her lots of promises which raised her hopes. But she was also clever. She wasn't going to exchange her prettiness for promises.

So the day arrived—
There was a room with woven straw walls. From this room there occasionally could be heard a soft, insinuating singing, "yua olwees in mai haat." It was rather dark there. A wooden bedstead filled half the space. The two young ones were sitting on it.

"Are you happy working here?" Inah asked sadly.

'Yua olwees in mai haat' stopped. Then the answer was audible.

"Very happy. I'm at home here. I mean, Miss Mari is grown up and studying at high school. I mean, in the afternoons, lots of white kids come. Its noisy. Very noisy all the time."

And the face of this handsome man glowed—Sobi!

"There's lots of work," Sobi went on. "But when the white kids are back, I can expect it to be exciting."

"You are happy to be a flunky here," Inah interrupted jealously.

"Even more when *tuan* and the missus go to the movies. Miss Mari always calls me. I have to massage her—and there's no more talk about what I have to massage—I'm proud."

"For a flunky that's really lucky. But me, I'm sad." And Inah's beautiful blue eyes were overcast. Her pretty face was upset. "I still haven't got the right *tuan*." She looked down. In a slow voice, as though praying, she went on. "I really want to have a child with eyes bluer than mine."

"That's not right," Sobi reprimanded her. "If you try to chose you won't get anything. You know the Jakarta goats [*kambing betawi*]? The big fat ones? Not the sheep! The Jakarta goats who can even eat leather sandals. Then they're even more proud. Just think! It was only a week ago I started work. I saw that Miss Mari was already grown up. But in the house there is a small child with slanted eyes. I don't know whose it is. It's always kept locked up in a room. Three days after that *tuan* and the missus went to the movies. Miss Mari called me to her room. You see what I mean? She told me to give her a massage. My God . . . . . everywhere! Then she said, 'Can you get rid of that kid?' 'Sure, miss,' I said and was allowed to do more than massage.' "

Then he sang with his soft insinuating voice.

Inah pondered sadly. She pressed her lips together and looked vaguely out through the window.

"I learned to sing from Si Husin. It's great, Miss Mari really likes my singing. When I sing she has to get close and compliment me, 'How nice your voice is,' she says. I can sing 'yua olwees in mai haat.' And Miss Mari is mad about my voice," said Sobi in a strong voice. Then he smiled, full of hopes. "Pretty soon I'll have to study Dutch. Si Husin is really good at Dutch."

Inah kept looking sadly out the window. "But me," she said later, "me—Ah, the *tuan*s today aren't like they were when I was small."

"Stop already, don't be choosy. Just follow my advice," Sobi went on. He looked at his sister who was riddled with anxiety.

"Yesterday I went to three houses in Menteng. At the first one, I met the *tuan*. Brown eyes. And did he smell!" She sighed. "The other two—I was met by the missus. They both said nearly the same thing."

"What did they say?" Sobi said attentively.

"They said, 'I don't need a young pretty maid with blue eyes.' What do you think of that?"

"Idiot," Sobi said angrily. "The first one was already very good. What do you think you are doing trying to chose? What's the matter with choco-late-colored eyes? And don't pay any attention to the smell. I mean, don't you know you stink of piss yourself? Who are you kidding? You're too sloppy. Of course those two misses didn't want you. Much too much style. Wait a while. Wear old clothes at first. Once you're in, right, then it's easy. Once the missus is out of the house, then you dress up. Who wouldn't fall for you? It's too bad you're my own sister." And he spat on the floor.

"But listen, the *tuan*s these days are all poor. They just look rich. They aren't really marvelous like the old days." Inah groaned out these words.

"Who knows?" Sobi said regretfully.

"Listen, if I had a baby, even if its eyes were bluer than mine, without some green stuff coming in, who would take care of things? I myself would be in real trouble. You? You've already got your miss; you aren't going to pay attention to me. You're really lucky. Even more so if you get a baby with blue eyes."

Sobi pondered quietly. Then, slowly, he said, "I'ld have to think of my sister. If I could marry Miss Mari, I could become Dutch. Then I'ld ask the gouverneur-generaal for a car. Me and Miss Mari would go to Tjilintjing and go naked on the beach."

"But your skin is pocked from scabs and pimples. Wouldn't you be ashamed?" his sister asked.

Sobi laughed and laughed.

"If someone becomes Dutch," Sobi said, full of self-assurance, the old marks of scabs and pimples have to go away by themselves. When were there ever Dutch with pimples? It's only Indonesians who have scabies. Us people."

And Inah understood. She asked further: "But the Dutch are making war now. Aren't you afraid to die?"

Sobi laughed some more. He said, "You really are stupid. When did the Dutch ever fight themselves? It's mainly Indonesians who are the soldiers. They're paid to die for the Dutch, see? When I become Dutch, I'll just sit at a desk and order around the coolies."

"How could you ever become someone important," sighed Inah confused.

And Sobi himself smiled happily at the beauty and grandeur of his fantasy. But Inah was even sadder. Even more jealous. She got off the bed. She took the broken mirror stuck in the woven wall. She sat down again next to her brother. She looked carefully at her face. She smiled happily. Suddenly she frowned. Then smiled again. And Sobi sang again in his soft and insinuating voice. Then he went near the window.

Inah said to herself: "I really am pretty. If you compare me with. . . ." She was quiet. She looked at her brother.

"This is the way it goes," Sobi interrupted without looking at her. "In a little while we'll be out of this rat's nest. I'll have my own building. When you get hold of a *tuan*," he looked at his sister, "just be careful not to be disappointed. At first just give in. Then later ask for gold things. They're easy to put away. And clothes—they're easy—they'll come by themselves." He paced again. Sat down next to his sister.

Inah asked, her hopes raised, "You've already found a *tuan?*"

"Tuan Piktor is coming here. Careful how you talk, ya?"

Inah quickly looked in the mirror. Smilingly. Then she inspected her teeth. Looked at her brother and asked, "What time is it?"

"Six. Four more hours."

"What are his eyes like?" she asked half with fear, half with hope.

"Oh, I guess they're yellow. I don't like yellow eyes. Yellow eyes and a smell," said Inah happily. Her two hands wrapped themselves around her chest—tightly. And both her feet stiffened as though she had a cramp. Out of nowhere she asked, "Aren't you going to work?"

"Its only two o'clock. Another half hour."

"The bath isn't filled."

Sobi paid no attention.

"I'm not going home. You'll have to take care of it."

"This room has to be cleaned and straightened up."

He sang some more. Then he went out.

She looked at herself in the mirror again. Whispered, "How blue my eyes are. Just like Miss Jetti's eyes. Sobi's miss's can't be as blue as mine. But why aren't I Dutch? What a shame. But my body is just as good as a Dutch woman's, right? Look, I've got a pointed nose. My skin isn't so white. But it's not pockmarked. If it's too white, it's easy to get black-heads."

She put the broken mirror back into the wall and stood up next to the window. "I want to be a *njai*. I want to have a child with blue eyes. Who knows, maybe my child will become Dutch, right? It's for sure I would live well. I would have a maid—ah, she'd take away my *tuan*. Just a flunky. And I would ride in a car. I'ld go to Tjilintjing. But I'ld be ashamed to go naked."

"Oh, I can't speak Dutch. I can't read or write. What would I say when the *tuan* asked me to read that thick newspaper? Sobi can sing." She didn't know what to think next and went back to the bedstead.

Her brother reentered. Inah pushed over next to him on the bedstead and bothered him with, "What should I do? I can't sing like you can?"

"But you can sing *jali-jali*. You just call it out."

"But Dutch people don't like it, no?" Inah sighed.

"Is that right? I'ld forgotten. But it's real easy," Sobi said trying to make her feel better. "Women don't have to do anything. If you're pretty the way you are, it all comes easy. Tuan Piktor is classy. It won't need anything from you. He has a car. He doesn't have a wife. He's rich—they say he works in some business office. Just a while ago he said to me, 'Can you find me a *njai*?' And right away I came back with 'I have a sister. . . .'"

"Really? Really?" Inah asked, happy again.

Inah was struck silent, astonished as she pictured her ambition.

"I don't have to sing like Sobi," she thought. "Tuan Piktor has to have a radio. Maybe he has six radios. How nice it would be to line them up in a row next to each other. Then, lots of people would come to the front of the house to look. And I would stand on the porch. For sure they would whisper, 'Wow, Inah really has become Dutch now.' And they would all be envious. For sure, they would have to envy me. It's their own fault; why do they have dark skins and noses you don't know where the holes are? My skin isn't too dark—it's light and my nose has class." She smiled, satisfied.

"So we'll be equals, just as high up, just as low. You'll have a car, I'll have a car, too. . . ."

"But I don't want to go naked in Tjilintjing. I'ld be ashamed."

"Stupid," Sobi insulted his sister. "When we are Dutch we can't have shame. We have to have the courage to be naked. We have to be able to get drunk. We have to be able to be curt with people, to tell them 'god damn it all.' And we have to always say, 'The Japanese were really beasts, really terrible.' My *tuan* does all that. All of this I've studied and memorized. It seems easy enough to be Dutch. If someone is clever enough like me to pay attention and mimic, in a week he can be Dutch." Sobi quietly watched his sister, who was charmed by his explanation.

"But a Dutch woman isn't the same as a Dutch man, no?" Inah asked seriously.

"Of course not. Dutch women are like this—" Sobi explained. Suddenly he was quiet and regretful. "Ah," he whispered, "you can't ride a bicycle yet." But his pleasure returned nonetheless. "But Tuan Piktor has a car. Dutch women aren't supposed to say 'Goddamn it all.' It's enough to twist the dial on the radio. You can already do that. And you can sew. And your face . . . . . it's something."

And Inah smiled happily. She heard a bell from the office. The sign of closing time. Sobi leaped up. On the threshold he stopped. Looked at his sister. Ordered her, "Be careful when you speak to the *tuan*. . . ."

"Yah."

Inah, too, leaped up and went to the window. She took out the broken mirror and went back to studying her face. "You are really pretty," she whispered. Then she put her cheek next to the mirror. Looked at herself again. She said, "In a little while you will be Dutch. Aren't I an old Batavian [*orang Betawi*]?[4] I'm not Indonesian. Mother said so. She even said during the Japanese days that Sobi and I were at least as noble as the Japanese. Ah, how nice it is to be Dutch."

Suddenly her face crinkled up. She sighed, "I don't know why the Dutch now are all so poor." And suddenly the crinkles disappeared. Her voice rose as she said, "Sobi knows better than I do. There are no poor Dutch. If there are poor Dutch, it's because they mix too much with Indonesians." And she was happy again.

She put the glass back into the wall. She stood up and looked at the room. Still four more hours. Later, I'll clean up.

"Is this Sini's place?"

Inah jumped up toward the door. Her face paled. Victor[y] was in front of her. Trembling, the girl answered, "Yah, *tuan*."

And the came in and sat on the bedstead. Inah was confused. Her first thought was to sit on the floor and bow her head.

"You're his sister?" asked the white-skinned *tuan*. He took out his handkerchief and wiped the sweat from his forehead.

"Yah, *tuan*." And Inah trembled even more.

"Don't sit on the floor. Sit here next to me." And Inah did not have the courage to move. The *tuan* came closer. Gently, he picked her up and placed her on the bedstead. And Inah did not resist. . . .

And later. . . .

In fact, there are secrets between men and women that are not secrets. It can happen that women's arrogance and pride can take flight. And she consciously surrenders herself to a certain man: And this happens in every world and century, to all nationalities and moving creatures. How simple life is. As simple as this: people are hungry, they eat, they are satisfied, and they defecate. Between hunger and defecation is where the life of mankind is located. Other life comes after this. It goes on without stopping until the decay of the world. And not one head feels it is tedious. If he feels it is tedious, he kills himself.

Bukitduri Prison, 1948

The family of these slaves were slaves by blood ever since the coming of certain Europeans. Not before. Their slavishness is coterminous with the presence of the Dutch. Their genealogy begins only with their slavery. They are only known, only recognized, from the moment that their primal father is registered in the "big book" with Latin script. Where his own name might have appeared in the text, there are only ellipses. It is not his name that is important, but his rank, *inlandsch sergeant* (native sergeant), which binds a 'native' to a Dutch rank. Tracing descent ordinarily means tracing the path of a series of legitimacies, the marriages that are the points on family trees where new branches, new families emerge, and where individuals are identified by relations of kinship. But here, individuals take on identity only in relation to something Dutch, an institution, and not even always someone Dutch. There is, nonetheless, "descent." In Indonesian, as in English, the root of the word means "decline." "Decline" refers to the history of repeated illegitimacies that bind this "family" (the term is as much biological as cultural here) again and again to the Dutch. But not always in the same way. "Descent," in a second sense, means tracing the changing modes of relation to Dutch. What begins as the work of soldiers declines into a relation of servants. But the descendents are not exactly servants either because descent (decline) makes increasingly apparent the slavish quality that started, as far as one can know, when Houtman sailed the archipelago (at the end of the sixteenth century, before the flowering of colonialism). They are not exactly servants in another way. While Sobi and Inah are servants and are paid, Inah's desire is to be a *njai*, while Sobi's is to be the male equivalent. What is more, it is not exactly the *njai* as we have seen it in *The Story of Njai Dasima* or as we might have read it in certain Dutch accounts of the time. The *njai* in Francis's story worked. She did not get a salary, but rather her needs were fulfilled. In exchange, she kept track of the accounts, ran the household, and had and raised their child. It was domestic exchange that resulted, in Francis's picture, in the construction of a family. In Pramoedya's story, the *njai* is the lowest point of slavery. There is no exchange of services for money; there is only submission. One wants to say, submission in return for something. For the luxury Sobi and Inah dream about; for blue eyes. But these, of course, are their dreams and are not part of a bargain, even an implicit one, with the *tuan* who arrives in the final paragraphs. Nor are blue-eyed children or automobiles as Sobi and Inah speak of them exactly possessions. In place of earnings, Sobi and Inah dream of signs of their slavery. In place of exchange, they dream of getting something from a certain source, one called "Dutch." Submission willingly entered into in the hope of getting something later might be mere extortion. But one who extorts usually then leaves his victim. Here, there is no question of getting and leaving. Sobi and Inah dream of a permanent and defining relation in which what they acquire speaks of their status as possessed. Even when Dolly thought of turning her gain into marriage, she could not successfully do so; she could only start over again as servant and *njai*.

Even slavery, however, is not wholly adequate to designate what Inah, Sobi, Dolly, and their ancestors hoped for. A slave is the legal property of another. But *njai* was never a legal status. It existed in the Indies as a permitted form so long as it was outside the attention of Dutch society in Holland. We have already spoken of how the word designated something between a commercial and a domestic relation, and thus was not wholly reducible to prostitution, domestic service, or legal domesticity. The prospective *njai*— whose story Pramoedya set during the revolution in the Jakarta of 1948, when Jakarta was in the hands of the Dutch and Pramoedya was their prisoner—was not protected by local public opinion. But Pramoedya does not condemn the *njai* as a collaborator, the way, for instance, some women in France were condemned after World War II for their relations with Germans. Rather, he illuminates the bond that held Indonesians to Dutch. We have seen that bond even in the stories of nationalists and in the accounts of those who, during the revolution, admit to the temptation of collaboration. The slavery of which Pramoedya speaks is a state of submission to a dominating influence. But the exposure of this state does include a detailed picture of the Dutch, who appear in very few of the marvelous series of tales Pramoedya wrote during the revolution. It appears rather in the picture of the quality of the slave.

Sobi and Inah hope to win a place as slaves; their weapon is their attractiveness. But their attractiveness is, in their view, measured by the qualities they have which are of European origin. Because her mother had only a 50 percent share in her, Inah has blue eyes and a pointed nose and light skin. It is of course exactly this that she thinks will win her a *tuan*. And Sobi's dreams rest on being able to sing "yua olwees in mai haat." Sobi, of course, does not know Dutch, much less English. The words are all the more magical in his view for this reason. It is not merely that his knowledge sets him apart from most other Indonesians; it is that precisely as words whose sense he does not know, they have a magical quality. Whenever he sings them, Miss Mari (the name is not an accident: *mari* is a word of invitation in Indonesian) wants a massage. Inah, when she evaluates her looks in the mirror, tells herself that she is pretty, and, looking more closely, says "In a little while you will be Dutch." Precisely her Dutch-like looks, which were passed down, descended from Dutch men, will attract a *tuan* to her and she will be Dutch.

We see the construction of a fetish, a magical weapon. Foreign words and foreign appearance work the same way. They are endowed with the capacity to evoke recognition of the singer or the Dutch look-alike. And the effect of recognition is the transformation of identity. They will be Dutch. But not everything foreign is magical, not even everything Dutch. The foreignness Inah and Sobi possess that is magical they possess only in an incomplete and even in an illegal fashion. Legitimate descent would mean that Inah would already be Dutch and that her facial features would be irrelevant in determining her nationality. Illegitimate descent means that her features still belong in her own view to the nationality she wants to attract and to which she wants to belong. The source of her longing and thus of her belief in magic resides in this situation: she has something that is nonetheless not fully hers. She wants what she already has in the sense that her looks tell her she is already Dutch and yet she is not. Sobi too, with his song whose words he cannot fully comprehend, has something from the world to which he wants to belong. His singing of the words should show that they are his; they come from within him. And yet, as he says, he wants to learn the languages.

In the Japanese period, Dolly believes a baby with Japanese eyes would be beautiful. She changes her mind when the Dutch return. It is, of course, political power that determines what looks are desirable. But actual political force is insufficient to generate the fetish. It depends not on political power, as such, but on investing Dutch or Japanese attributes with a signification in excess of what they would mean to Dutch or Japanese. It retains the foreign as foreign and yet with the promise of possession of it. It starts, in fact, with the name in the Dutch register; a name that is only a Dutch title and is written unaccompanied by a Dutch or an Indonesian name. It starts with slavishness because slavishness means the acceptance of Dutch recognition; it takes what the Dutch say about oneself as definitive. It is not, however, that Dutch, here, say, "You are Indonesian and Indonesians are inferior, fit only to be slaves." Rather, their recognition consists in applying a Dutch term, "inlandsch sergeant"; the first in the register of ancestors takes that in place of his name. Those who follow equally desire the Dutch to endow them with a title.

From the time of the sergeant, the fetish is reconformed. The astonishing effect of illness is beauty. Kotek (the name means "to cackle" and "a plumed tail") is surprised to find herself addressed as *njai*. She only discovers what the word *njai* means, and her attractiveness to Europeans, later. We see the moment someone believes that someone else knows something more about herself, about her looks, than she does herself and believes as well that this is a revelation of identity. She is as she is called; we could say, as she is renamed. It is a further moment of decline, the result of illness. "From the time of the first sergeant, the faces of everyone in the family were awful." Pramoedya adds in the next sentence, "They never changed." Change comes with tuberculosis. It is a corruption of the body that results in this family becoming attractive to Dutch. But the result is that, from the next generation downward, in their flesh they become part Dutch. And with that there is a change of name: "Rodinah" becomes "Dolly" as the Dutchman sees something in her he can name in his own language. (The text has "Poppi" for "Dolly.") And with this, comes another change.

The fetish as we have seen it depends on someone recognizing within "me" something I did not know I had and making me think it might be possible to have a new identity. Accidentally—the accident might be tuberculosis or following fashion—I achieved a certain appearance. Then, I take it as a property of myself with which to attract recognition and legal affirmation. With Dolly we see calculation; not only the Russians have a five-year plan. Dolly and her children know what their assets are and therefore know how to make use of them. Accident drops out of the picture as they are aware of what they will be recognized for. They know that they are potential foreigners from the point of view of Indonesians. The foreign is theirs and is their asset. But they need to make use of it to fully possess it. This calculability and acceptance of the foreign as incompletely theirs and needing the Dutch to complete their possession of it is different from anything we have seen so far. It contrasts, for instance, with the feeling that one is suspected or that accident has revealed one's qualities. Accident is ruled out and, with it, the material of the fetish, the possibilities that might be recognized, are drastically limited. It puts the fetish on the side of the Dutch and against the revolution, whereas we have marked the path taken from the fetish to nationalism.

We can see the difference from the time of Tirtho, when he spoke of dress and the pass laws. Tirtho describes the recognition offered by the police and that by the man accidentally met on the street. The policeman insists the *hadji* be who he "is" and not who he looks like. But everyone would be better off if only there was a wider practice of dressing. If the Javanese woman wore Turkish clothes, there would be no harmful misunderstanding. This gesture, by the time of the revolution, is inconsequential. What matters in Pramoedya's story is that the foreign leads to colonial power. The possibility of any sort of dressing up leading to a satisfactory recognition in Tirtho is bound up with the era of translation. When anything from anywhere was translated, the power of the fetish was not firmly locatable. Recognition by "anyone" on the street, by the anonymous person, made evident the range of signs that dress could embody. The moment of recognition was not tied to an exclusive power. Widespread, indiscriminate translation and a possibility of sources of recognition other than colonial power went together. We have traced the evolution of this idea and the way it became bound to Dutch authority within Tirtho's own writings. By the time of the revolution, the fetish, at least in Pramoedya's story, depended on the illegitimate possession of foreign attributes which were then magical. And it depended on these foreign attributes binding one to a singular power from which they originated. It is the strength of Pramoedya's thinking that what he says about colonialism could as well be applied to Indonesian society after the revolution, after the time he wrote this piece.

Between Tirtho and Pramoedya there has occurred a certain nationalization, one that makes the terms of encounter with the foreign merely dyadic. By the time of the revolution, "foreign" meant "Dutch." It may seem as if this consolidation of identities applies to both sides. "Indonesians" now are who they are and need only free themselves from a rule which, in terms of their identity, is extraneous. Pramoedya's story concerns Indos, those of mixed descent. It would be possible to think of them as a special case, one left over after nationalism had arrived at its full development. To think this way would be to make Pramoedya himself a nationalist in the sense, at least, that the word is used today in Jakarta, an interpretation which I will shortly argue against. I would rather suppose that being legitimately recognized as a nationalist by nationalist authority is put into question in the story. We could read it from the point of view of the strange bifurcation of types of recognition that pertained during the revolution; on the one hand, Dutch seduction and on the other revolutionary menace.

Why should nationalists fear the threat of revolutionary fighters and brace themselves against the temptations offered by the Dutch? I have claimed that this is an effect of the very success in generating recognizing figures out of the initial fetish of appearance. It seems as if the contradiction of the time of Tirtho (that one found oneself with the power to pass for another and, if one did so, one was arrested) was resolved. But the contradiction was not resolved; it merely took another form. The authority of schoolteachers, of "Tan Malaka," and later types, left, we have seen, a residue. One was suspected for what one was not. One was suspected of other sentiments and other deeds than nationalists would find proper. Or, one bore the traces of an origin in conflict with nationalism. It indicates the retention of something within oneself which is, to use the term a bit loosely, illegally in one's possession. The opposition of Dutch/pleasure versus nationalist/suspicion and the menace of the latter during the revolution tries to reclaim a heterogeneous element, one that spoils identity.

This trace of the foreign or the illegal or the improper is essential to the feeling of being surveyed by proper authority, and it turns this authority into menace. The revolution, from this point of view, is the eruption that occurs after nationalism seems to have defined the identity of "Indonesians." Revolutionaries are feared because they recognize not national identity but everything not included in that identity. Dutch recognition in Pramoedya's story, as in the accounts of people who thought they might be suspected of collaboration, consists in finding the foreign and giving it expression. It leads to pleasure, pleasure being the release of an urge; in the case of nationalists who feared exposure as Dutch sympathizers, a hidden urge. In our story, Indos make explicit the possession of a foreign element; but this is one that the peoples of the Indies as a whole, in their intercourse with the Dutch, could have contracted. It follows from the attachment to women as this attachment becomes implicated in relations to the Dutch, as in this story or in Mas Marco's *Student Hidjau* and even in *Flower of Atjeh*. But only in our story, written during the revolution, did the implications of a division established earlier materialize.

When, with the struggle for independence, Indonesian comes to replace Dutch authority, the latter are left as a source of pleasure and revolutionaries as a threat. It is at this point that there is a break between the nationalists who led the ideological fight for independence and who remained conservative in their thinking about the structure of Indonesian society and the "fighters in the countryside" (or the city) who were clearly revolutionary. This break between nationalism and revolution depends at least as much on the phantasms of menace inadvertently generated in the course of nationalist development and held by the people we have described in chapter 8 as on the formation of revolutionaries themselves. Without the fear of revolutionaries, Indonesian nationalism may not have reached its goal of independence and the formation of a nation.

Let us return to "Flunky + Maid." It may seem as if Pramoedya's exposure of the fetish is also a wish to expel the foreign. All the more so since the story was written while, during the revolution, Pramoedya was a prisoner of the Dutch. But one should go further. The political difficulty comes with the attempt to claim the foreign for oneself by winning the recognition of those from whom it came. It is the retention of the foreign as one's own, which, finally, is the denial of its foreignness, against which the narrator sets his own interpretation of the story. The final paragraph resets the context in a surprising way. It is not a story of slaves, as one had thought all along. It is a story of "the secrets between men and women which are not secrets." That is, it is a story of men and women everywhere. It only appears to be a story peculiar to Dutch colonialism. As a story of men and women, it is well known. But this does not stop it from happening over and over again, each time as though it were a unique event. "How simple life is. As simple as this: people are hungry, they eat, they are satisfied, and they defecate." Does not the process that generates the satisfaction of eating conceal, make a secret, of what follows? That is, even the most thorough assimilation of something that originates from outside ourselves, something which becomes our flesh and bones, leaves a residue. It is this process of unavoidably incomplete assimilation that Pramoedya compares to the fate of Inah.

In the end, there is a love story. "Women's arrogance and pride can take flight." It is not at all the calculations of Sobi and Dolly that we see at work. But it is not without reference to them. They count on assimilating themselves to the foreign. But in the end, the foreign remains as such. No one, "not one head," ever "feels it has had enough." It is the head that feels this, the place of imagination, and not the stomach or the groin. It is a question of interest: "if s/he is bored, s/he kills her/himself" (the gender is not given in the Indonesian). This interest on which life depends is the willingness never to stop taking in the foreign.

It is not question, then, of doing away with the foreign. The structure of the fetish seems to remain in place by the end of the story. But the role given to it becomes immensely larger. The foreign flows through Pramoedya's story if we think of his language and particularly of the jokes. Dolly knows that dark is white, that names and things are different. She knows this from what happened to her:

Her *tuan* called Rodinah "Dolly." She was indeed like a Japanese doll. The name "Rodinah" was erased from history. She became "Dolly"—and a real doll through and through.

Because Ambonese are allies of the Dutch, they are called white. It is not simply that Rodinah/Dolly knows this; she knows also that they "had to be seen" (*harus dilihat*) as white. She can't believe her eyes; she has, "as a white-skinned maid," to see as she must see. If they can be seen as white, she also can be seen as white. It turns out to be in her interest as she comes to conceive it. The absurdity of language detached from objects generates humor here. It is a type of joke that occurs first in the opening paragraph, the time of the first slave being "before Coen became the statue the Japanese swept away from the front of the Finance Building." Jan Pieterszoon Coen was a Gouverneur-Generaal, the founder of Batavia on the site called until then Jayakarta, and is credited with establishing Dutch authority in the Indies. In whose understanding the name "Coen" is a statue and no longer a significant historical figure is at this point unclear. But it is said in the voice of the narrator; without his memory there would be no joke.

Rodinah/Dolly's strategy follows from the narrator's joke. Names differ from things; things come to look like their names. Her *tuan* calls her "Dolly" and "she is indeed like a Japanese doll." But having been named "Dolly," "she became 'Dolly'—and a real doll through and through." She takes on the attributes of her name after, first, the *tuan* had discovered these attributes in her, to her surprise. Dolly is no longer Rodinah but a doll as Coen is a statue. "Dolly's" strategy as well depends on a joke. The payoff for "Dolly" is the admission of numerous *tuan* that they might have the other 50 percent share in Dolly's productions. They pay in lieu of having their names properly attached to those who could be their children. Profiting from this illegitimacy, this gap between name not given and a thing, keeps not only Dolly but Inah and Sobi slaves. It is the invention of the fetish at the same time. "My attraction for them is my looks; and my looks are the result of illegitimate descent." Those looks, the result of sickness and contamination, left a residue which, changing my appearance, evoked words: *njai*, "Dolly."

"Rodinah" is "erased from history"; there is no lasting memory of anyone of that name, except, of course, in the mind of the narrator. This erasure suggests something more general about the relations of Indonesians to Dutch. What is at stake is the possibility of genealogy. Names are not inscribed in history. There is continuous illegitimate descent and obscuration of the bearers of Indonesian names. The narrator undoes this forgetting. His jokes restore origins whose loss is inherent in the working of the fetish of appearance.[5]

Pramoedya locates this fetish within a certain linguistic situation, one where one believes what one hears and not what one sees, as when Rodinah realizes that dark Ambonese must be seen as white. It is not that she, Rodinah, is presented as incapable of seeing the difference. The question is what she does with what she hears. The narrator, once again, establishes all facets. Ambonese are not white in color. But Ambonese are white in status. That is the joke, and it once again depends on the possibility of seeing both aspects without reduction of one to the other. The result is the freeing of language from its use to produce identity. Identity is, of course, upset when a person has more than one: "Rodinah"/"Dolly" are incompatible.

There is, in any case, another story of hearing contained in the same narrative. It is the story of the person who makes the jokes. The unidentified narrator, who never says "I," nevertheless has to be posited as the origin of sentences such as "Dolly did not know the politics of *divide et impera*." Dolly did not know the Latin phrase, but someone else who speaks from within the text, the narrator, does know. This narrator comes most clearly into view when he contrasts what he knows with what his characters know. And this happens most often when jokes are told.

But it is not always the case. The word *dan*, meaning "and," appears fifty-eight times at the head of sentences in a text that has only eleven short pages. What is more, it is often used not to introduce a new subject, but merely to add one more detail, often one which has only a tenuous connection with the subject of the previous sentence:

> No one knew what sickness attacked a person as pretty as that. Not even the two radios and the gramophone understood. And one unhappy day people buried her. Just before her moment of death. . . .

The first sentence states a fact that already contains an irony. The second sentence is only a statement of irony. As such, they make clear the narrator's stance toward Dolly and her wish for radios and a gramophone. The following sentence, beginning with "and," is again factual. The "and" here separates two tonalities. The irony clearly belongs to the narrator, but the sentence that conveys the sadness of Dolly's death either conveys his sadness as well or merely reports that people were made sad against his slight irritation at the pretention or delusion of those who do not comprehend that death also attacks pretty women and that those who want radios and gramophones greatly overestimate these objects. The last sentence comes as an interruption. Without "and" indicating something additional, the interruption would be less noticeable.

Here is another case where tonalities are separated by the initial "and":

> This was because he vaguely felt that politics meant all sorts of sins. His *tuan* often said as much. And everything the *tuan* said was law [*wet*]—no different than the law made by the government.

Here "and" introduces a sentence that intensifies and clarifies the sense of the previous sentence. In this case, "and" underscores a difference be-

tween an editorial commentary in the last sentence and a descriptive statement that could be merely the reporting of what the character feels.

"And" can indicate insistence, especially in the voice of a character:

"I can sing 'yua olwees in mai haat.' And Miss Mari is mad about my voice," said
Sobi strongly.

One piece of information is added to another. Without "and" the two
bits—that he can sing and that Miss Mari is mad about his voice—would
be discrete. With "and," one sees that they stem from a single intention:
Sobi cannot stop boasting. "And" here indicates his insistence. But perhaps "and" always indicates an insistence; always, that is, says that something further is to be heard and will be heard.

Even when "and" has the function of dividing one voice from a second,
often enough both of them the narrator's as he speaks in different tonalities, it also indicates a third source, more fundamental than either of the
first two, and which is distinct from the voice of the narrator. The insistence of "and" in contrast to the irony of the narrator indicates that there
is something else to be heard, there is something more that resides in the
very origin of the story. The narrator tells a story; he is interrupted by more
things to say, not necessarily ironic things, and this forms the text. The
narrator is interrupted by an insistent word, "and": There is something to
hear. One will hear it presently when it can be assimilated to the voice that
presumably tells the story.

The story is one of descent. It is a story of genealogy as the erasure of at
least some of the names of persons inscribed in it. There is the sergeant
who is left only with a mark in Latin letters and without a name. There is
Rodinah, a name erased from history. But their story is told nonetheless.
What has been effaced comes back. And it comes back at best only ambiguously in the voice of the narrator. It comes back, rather, as something
added, something that cannot be held back, and that upsets voice insofar
as voice is thought of as unitary.

The "and" here is not entirely a function of Indonesian, the modernized
national language. It resembles the word *maka* in traditional Malay texts.
There, every sentence often begins with *maka*. If it is translated, it is rendered usually as "thus" or "so." As in "thus the story goes" perhaps as well
as "and so this follows." *Maka* indicates that the story is retold and that the
events are related within the framework of the prosodic form; their logic is
the logic of succession and not of verisimilitude. *Dan* (and) is similar but
different. It indicates that there is in each instance something more to say.
It lacks a tradition of usage that would indicate the antiquity of the story.
Instead, this story, the story of an author, may be new; something heard
for the first time. And yet it escapes the voice of the narrator to a certain
degree by insisting and adding. The initial "and" is neither an idiosyncracy

of the narrator's style nor the revival of a tradition. It is between these two. It indicates that there is something that wants to make itself heard, and that is therefore not fully equatable with an identifiable voice.

The difference between *maka* and *dan* is that *dan*, with its uncertain provenance, remains a foreign element that is also a part of the language. Its status is evident in the title; precisely at the point one expects it to appear, it does not. Instead of "Djongos dan Babu" (Flunky and Maid), there is "Djongos + Babu" (Flunky + Maid). The "+" sign transcends particular languages. It indicates the appearance of something additional without the addition stemming from something within the phrase or from within the specific language. When one puts "+" into a particular language, saying "plus" or "and" or *dan*, one betrays its universal, repetitive quality. It exists outside of voice. Within the text, the word *dan* itself continues this function. This voiceless presence indicates only an appearance on its way or the possibilities that occur from outside of particular languages.

The languages closest to this mark in this case are the original Malay and the lingua franca from which it was derived, the predecessors of Indonesian. The language in which stories of *njai* were first told returns, a ghost of Indonesian before it became the national language.

Where does such a narrative materialize if not in the jokes it tells. These are jokes of translation. From *divide et impera* to "divide and surrender," from Rodinah to Dolly, even the Dutch name "Coen" for the statue of the person of the same name; all of these work not exactly through translation but across languages. It is, in fact, the failure of translation that is important. No true equivalents present themselves. Precisely because Indonesian does not absorb the words it takes in, there are jokes. "Dolly" is left with a name foreign to her just as the first *njai* of the line does not know that the word will apply to her. Indeed, one might say that Indonesian itself is a foreign speech if one thinks of the word for slave, *hamba*. *Hamba* is the first person singular of traditional Melayu. Here *hamba* takes its value from the foreign other. Likewise, "yua olwees in mai haat," the most potent words available to Sobi, who knows no foreign languages, remain foreign to him.

It is precisely out of this hearing of the foreign, especially if we expand the word to mean "what arrives to me from outside of myself," as in "foreign to me," that one sees the insistence of the text against its characters and, for that matter, its narrator. It is through the jokes of the text, through the acceptance of the nonequivalence of words between languages, that genealogy is restored. We know that Rodinah = Dolly; that *divide et impera* = "divide and surrender" and that these equations never balance. Exactly in this lack of balance, this irreducibility of one side to the other, forgotten genealogy, genealogy in which relationship was never legally and thus "permanently" marked, reappears. With the reappearance of genealogy, the acceptance of the foreign as foreign, the fetish disintegrates. It cannot work except by accepting that "Rodinah" "really is" "Dolly" and that therefore it is possible to become Dutch because one already looks so. The transformation of words into marks of social identities becomes impossible when words themselves refer to origins that are both factual and yet incommensurate with events after the initial naming.

When, at the end, Inah "surrenders," she follows the mistranslation from the Latin which describes Dutch colonial policy. And she repeats a universal story, one that insists on being told despite the unawareness of those who enact it. The final paragraph, with its abrupt switch of reference from the fetish to the universal story of love, shows us that Inah never got what she expected. She found herself in another story altogether. It is a question of mistranslation, "surrender" = "*impera*," from one generation to the next. The same story, the same words, result in different understandings and different consequences.

By the end of the story, words have untied themselves from identities. Signs are no longer bound into an "I" who believes herself to contain them. The property of a universal story, they repeat themselves with various effects. Genealogy returns not as an inheritance one can make use of but as history which, upsetting the very possibility of recognition and thus of the achievement of social place, opens the future to unforeseen possibilities. Without the fetish, revolution. And, and even possibly "or," literature.

The story opens with an Indonesian man who becomes a colonial army sergeant; it closes with another man, an Indo who is a servant. In between, it is the story of women not only because women furnish the genealogical linkages but because the fetish is located in them. The appearance of Sobi at the end of the story generalizes it; it makes it the story of anyone of either sex born in the Indies. But it is the attractiveness of women that is central and this attractiveness is, of course, disvalued by showing it as an effect of the Dutch. The power of seduction itself is corroded by the ironic humor. Feminine mystery is dissolved. But what replaces it is precisely the attractive power of words, the *dan* or "and" that indicates a thirst to hear more. *Dan*, locating attraction in language itself, favors no particular human voice. It retains the possiblity of the fetish, its power to command attention, but precludes recognition. By implication, neither national nor colonial authority can be sure to claim this power for its own.

There is only one story, the story says. But this one story, divide and surrender, is the story of anyone who tells a story. It is the story of one who surrenders to what she hears and who divides as Dolly did, by seducing those anonymous multitudes who hear what she repeats. Against this possibility stands the fetish of modernity that produces only one story, one that always happens, that "really happened" at a certain time in a certain place. The possibility of telling a story that never happened, of preserving the possibilities of language and languages, even and more especially when one does not know what these possibilities are, is what is denied by the fetish. It is the possibility both of revolution and of literature.

Revolutionary language, which is defeated by recognition, is similar to the workings of literature. Both depend on words whispered to oneself. And both depend on the foreignness of words, on their lack of fit with their surroundings. Literature keeps the possibility of its effectiveness open by leaving its addressee uncertain, postponing its arrival.

The fetish of modernity claims that substitution always works: "I" am what "I" am recognized to be; where "I" began (in language) is of no importance. This story of illegal genealogy says that even when origins are forgotten, they make themselves heard. Old, discarded signs return and the equation Rodinah = Dolly, the very making of which causes "Rodinah" to vanish, is reversed: Dolly = Rodinah and "Rodinah" reappears. "And," it adds, it is not that genealogy is the sole determinator of identity. Rather, identity is uncertain because it works against insistences whose provenances are always unclear, always foreign. In Indonesia, Pramoedya has not prevailed. He wrote his story from a Dutch prison. He wrote others from an Indonesian jail in the time of President Sukarno. And he wrote still more from an Indonesian camp where he, with sixty thousand others, victims of President Suharto's New Order, spent fourteen years without trial. His writings are banned in his own country at the moment I write this. If this is considered an acceptable situation in Indonesia, as it seems to be not by all but by most, it is because the culture of writing never fully established itself there. And yet, the need to silence this writer indicates how powerful the very possibility of fiction, which causes words to circulate outside the configurations of hierarchical authority, is; and how valuable the fetish of modernity is today to the Indonesian national hierarchy when it again returns all signs to the summit of that hierarchy.

Notes

Notes to Introduction

Epigraph: A. Evans, "An Eccho to the Voice of Heaven" (1653), quoted in Christopher Hill, *The World Turned Upside Down* (London: Penguin Books, 1975; 1st ed., 1972), 93.

1. John Pemberton explains what "authenticity" means in contemporary Indonesian in his book *On the Subject of "Java"* (Ithaca: Cornell University Press, 1994). See pages 152–161 for his description of the park under discussion and page 159 for the quotation.

2. Mrs. Suharto has said that the idea for the park came to her when she visited Disneyland. " 'I was inspired to build a Project of that sort in Indonesia, only more complete [*lengkap*] and more perfect [*sic*], adapted to fit the situation and developments in Indonesia, both "materially" [*materiil*] and "spiritually" [*spirituil*].' " The quotation is from an official brochure and is quoted in Pemberton, *On the Subject of Java*, 152. See N.a., *Pendjelasan Tentang Projek Miniatur Indonesia "Indonesia Indah"* (Djakarta: Badan Pelaksana Pembangunan dan Persiapan Pengusahaan Projek Miniatur Indonesia "Indonesia Indah," 1971) for the original. Another story that circulated in Jakarta at the time suggested that the First Lady was moved to outdo a similar project of Imelda Marcos after a visit to the Philippines.

3. The most prominent statement of this revolutionary genealogy is that of the writer Pramoedya Ananta Toer. Just before being jailed in the period of the change of regime from President Sukarno to President Suharto, Pramoedya ran a series of articles in the newspaper *Bintang Timur* on the "prehistory" of Indonesian language and literature. In these articles, he points out the cultural rootlessness of the lingua franca, a subject I deal with below. See chap. 1, n. 3 for a complete list of his articles on the subject.

4. The revolution seen through the westernized elite was first described by George McT. Kahin. See particularly his *Nationalism and Revolution in Indonesia* (Ithaca: Cornell University Press, 1952). The role of youth and the failure of the social revolution has been told by B. R. O'G. Anderson, *Java in a Time of Revolution: Occupation and Resistance* (Ithaca: Cornell University Press, 1972). As I write this, the Indonesian revolution is not much more than fifty years old, perhaps not old enough to have classical explanations in the way one would use that word of Tocqueville on the French Revolution. Still, these two books bear reading and rereading even by people not particularly interested in Indonesia. They are, then, likely classics.

5. I owe this observation, since confirmed by myself, to the late historian Tsuchiya Kenji. I am certain that had his life not been cut short, he would have made it the center of another of his extraordinarily insightful pieces on Indonesian culture.

6. H. M. J. Maier, "From Heteroglossia to Polyglossia: The Creation of Malay

and Dutch in the Indies," *Indonesia* 56 (1993): 37–65. Maier cites census figures. However, these figures can be misleading in the context of our work. We are speaking of the development of a language and a culture. The bulk of those classed as illiterate (which excludes literacy in Arabic and Chinese) lived their lives in the languages of the region. Those who transformed the lingua franca into a national language also spoke regional tongues. But they were obviously comfortable in the use of the lingua franca on an extended scale. If one considers the percentage of people such as these who were literate, no doubt the rate would be much higher, though I know of no figures to substantiate my claim. Moreover, the stories I analyze were often known as much or more through the theater, where literacy was of course not required. Not only were they sometimes broadly known but they expressed anxieties raised by intercultural communication. It is just there that one can see a strong stimulus to write.

7. Another question of method imposes itself here: the selection of texts to be studied. There is no canon of Melayu literature. I could well have selected other texts than the ones used. I can only assure the reader that these texts are only a small part of the number I have analyzed and that my analysis of other texts leads to quite similar conclusions. I must add that there are a few Dutch texts used. Here the question is different. I do not claim that these texts are representative of Indies Dutch literature of the epoch. It has not been my intention to pick representative Dutch texts but rather those that answer the Melayu texts we read. In general, these texts fit the tendency well described by H. M. J. Maier to separate Dutch from the languages of the Indies, even when they might seem to advocate the opposite. See the important article of H. M. J. Maier, "From Heteroglossia to Polyglossia."

8. I await the publication the lectures of Jacques Derrida on this topic, given in spring 1995 at the École des hautes études en sciences social.

9. Georg Wilhelm Friedrich Hegel's notion of the fetish can be found in *The Philosophy of History*, trans. J. Sibree (New York: Dover, 1956), 94–95. The racist bias of this section, and indeed, nearly the whole of this book, needs to be squarely faced. There is a contradiction in his analysis of Africa. On the one hand, Africans, he says, are immersed in nature, part of it, but on the other, they attempt to control it through their fetishes and rituals. Hegel's racism is enmeshed in this contradiction. He reserves productive relations to an unknown force (nature or God) to Europeans. If only Africans understood the inappropriable quality of nature, the dialectic could begin. One could universally uncover a failure in all attempts to generate productivity or signification and thus interrogate a heterogeneous element within culture itself. The notions of the fetish since Hegel, and in particular Marx's in the first volume of *Capital*, which draw on Hegel, have done this. The question of how the orientation of the fetish changes is one of the questions raised in this book. On this question, see especially Jacques Derrida, *Glas*, trans. John P. Leavey Jr. and Richard Rand (Lincoln: University of Nebraska Press, 1968), 211 ff.

NOTES TO CHAPTER ONE

1. "Malay" is sometimes used as a translation of "Melayu." I use the term "Melayu" for the language used as a lingua franca in the Dutch East Indies; I use the term "Malay" for the local, that is, first language of various peoples in the archipelago and on the Malay Peninsula.

2. There is a question of when a language is a language. Linguists commonly say that when dialects become mutually incomprehensible, they are then distinct languages. Is "Indonesian" really a different language than "Melayu"? It may be dubious from a linguist's point of view. Someone who knows Indonesian can make sense of classical Malay. But if this person were to confront the Melayu spoken in cities in the nineteenth century, he might have some difficulty and he would have more if he were introduced into a court in the Riau Archipelago. If, on the other hand, Indonesians in 1927 declared that there was one language and the language was "Indonesian," has a new language been created or acknowledged?

To make a case for the development toward a new language, we must start not with the moment of the declaration of the national language but with the break between the lingua franca from which it developed and the local language. It is then a question of how far linguistic change has proceeded. Of course, one can speak of a separation of communities over time, but this misses the point. Before the creation of the lingua franca and its conversion into a creole, there were not two communities speaking the same language which then diverged in their development. Rather, the creation of the lingua franca led to the formation of a group of speakers who constituted a "community" only if one uses "community" to refer to the group who do not necessarily share anything more than the ability to speak the language. Thus, the development of the lingua franca into a separate language is not in the first place an effect of the shared experiences of its speakers. It is initiated, rather, by the fear produced when it is abruptly realized that it is a route of contamination. It was Melayu itself that produced this effect, as one can see, for instance, from the Dutch attempts to purify their language of the corruption it underwent in the Indies. See H. M. J. Maier, "From Heteroglossia to Polyglossia," 37–65; and his "Forms of Censorship in the Dutch Indies: The Marginalization of Chinese-Malay Literature," *Indonesia*, special issue, n.n. [50] (1991): 67–81.

3. The history of Melayu as a lingua franca has yet to be written. Pramoedya Ananta Toer began to do so in the columns of the newspaper *Bintang Timur*, mainly in the Sunday edition, in 1963, but he was prevented from finishing the series when, with the change of regimes, he was sent to prison. What he accomplished then, however, and just after his release, seventeen years later, before his publications and those of his publishing house were banned again, constitutes a critical study of the beginnings of the national language and literature in its relation to the lingua franca. I list here the articles I have been able to find that are relevant to this study and from which I have benefited.

"Sekali Lagi Tentang Hikajat Njai Dasima" (Edisi Minggu), 27 December 1964.

"Sastra Novel Assimilatif," 24 November 1963.

"Sastra Puisi Assimilatif," 24 November 1963.

"Basa Indonesia Sebagai Basa Revolusi Indonesia" (also under the titles "Basa Indonesia"; Basa Revolusi Indonesia"; "Basa Revolusi Indonesia: Kritik Abdullah Munsji"), 22 September 1963; 29 September 1963; 6 October 1963; 13 October 1963; 20 October 1963; 26 January 1964; 9 February 1964; 23 February 1964; 1 March 1964; 15 March 1964; 5 April 1964.

"Bahasa pra-Indonesia dan fungsi historik dalam sastra assimilatif" (also under the title "Basa Pra Indonesia Dalam Sastra Assimilatif" and its variations), 24 November 1963; 1 December 1963; 8 December 1963; 15 December 1963; 22 December 1963; 29 December 1963.

"Setengah Abad Setelah Abdullah Munshi," 25 August 1963.

"Socio Kultural," 16 August 1963.

4. John Hoffman, "A Foreign Investment: Indies Malay to 1901," *Indonesia* 27 (1979): 65–92.

5. The attempts to classify different kinds of Malay are complicated. Kees Groeneboer cites the linguist Swellengrebel who distinguised four kinds of Malay: that spoken by those living around the Strait of Malaka for whom it was their original language; the more widely spread written language; local variations used as lingua franca; and "Pasar-Malay," or the elemental language named after its use in markets. The other distinction is between High and Low. Groeneboer calls High Malay the written form, including the Malay taught in schools, though it is not clear whether this includes the Malay used in traditional literature. He reserves the term "Low Malay" for the last two categories. The first is then neither High nor Low; it is simply a mother tongue. Its lack of classification supports Pramoedya's contention (see below) that the lingua franca was cut off from its origins, as could also be the case for written Malay and of course Pasar-Malay. Kees Groeneboer, *Weg tot het Westen: Het Nederlands voor Indie, 1600–1950*, Verhandelingen van het Koninklijk Instituut voor Taal-, Land-, en Volkenkunde, no. 158 (Leiden: KITLV Uitgeverij, 1993), 23, n. 12.

6. Jean Gelman Taylor, *The Social World of Batavia: European and Eurasian in Dutch Asia* (Madison: University of Wisconsin Press, 1983), 139 ff. The history of attempts to teach Dutch in the Indies can be found in Groeneboer, *Weg tot het Westen*. Groeneboer estimates that by the year 1900 perhaps 3,300 'natives' could speak Dutch in Java and Madura. The total population of these islands was 28,000,000. About 5,000 'natives' in the Indies as a whole could speak Dutch (210). A figure for the total population of the Indies is not available before 1907, when it was about 38,000,000. In any case, the need for Melayu was great because the use of Dutch was so limited. "At the beginning of the 19th century, Dutch in the Indies archipelago had nearly disappeared" (215). It was used on board ship and in offices, but not at home. The situation improved throughout the century. But by 1900 there were only 42,000 people with an active or passive grasp of Dutch in the Indies (216).

7. I use the term 'native' in single quotation marks to label the group that fell under Dutch law as indigenous peoples as opposed to 'Europeans' and 'foreign Orientals.' The term is invidious in English, but it is necessary to keep it to retain its reference in the colonial system. The single quotation marks signal its historical and legal meaning. The quotation marks are particularly important when one learns that a 'European,' for instance, could be someone 'equated with Europeans' by law; thus not only Indos acknowledged by their fathers but also often Japanese or certain Javanese or other 'natives,' particularly those few with European education. What is more, A. van Marle showed that most 'Europeans' of the Indies in fact were of mixed blood. A. van Marle, "De Groep der Europeanen in Nederlands-Indie:

Iets over ontstaan en groei" (The European group in the Netherlands Indies: Remarks on origins and growth), *Indonesië* 5 (2): 77–121; (3): 313–341; and (5): 481–507 (1955).

8. J. C. Furnivall, *Netherlands India* (Cambridge: Cambridge University Press, 1944), 446.

9. H. M. J. Maier, "Some Genealogical Remarks on the Emergence of Modern Malay Literature," *Journal of the Japan-Netherlands Institute* 2 (1990): 159–177.

10. See Maier, "From Heteroglossia to Polyglossia," and the articles on the topic by Pramoedya cited in n. 3 above. When the national language was discussed by the writer Sutan Takdir Alisjahbana, a member of the influential group called Pudjangga Baru, he assumed that the major languages of Indonesia would not be eliminated by the national language and, further, that this would not cause difficulties. Rather the opposite, they would be sources of enrichment. Originally published in *Pudjangga Baru* 1 (1933); republished in his essays entitled *Dari Perdjuangan dan Pertumbuhan Bahasa Indonesia*, (Djakarta: Pustaka Rakjat, 1957). For an English summary of Takdir's views, see A. Teeuw, *Modern Indonesian Literature* (The Hague: Martinus Nijhoff, 1967), 31–33.

11. Many of these were probably done from Dutch versions regardless of the original language.

12. Teuku Iskandar notes that the readers of traditional Malay texts borrowed from lending libraries included Chinese. He puts "reading public" in quotes "because the manuscripts were not read silently, but aloud to a group of listeners." "Some Manuscripts Formerly Belonging to Jakarta Lending Libraries," in *Papers on Indonesian Languages and Literatures*, ed. Nigel Phillips and Khaidir Anwar, Cahier d'Archipel, no. 13 (London: Indonesian Etymological Project; Paris: Association Archipel, École des hautes études en sciences social, 1981), 145–152.

13. In his study of a lending library in Palembang, E. U. Kratz notes that "long after the printing press had been introduced into Malaya and Indonesia it was still common practice to write and copy texts by hand." He attributes this in part to the fact that not everything one wanted to read had been printed and to the small number of literate people. "Running a Lending Library in Palembang in 1886 A.D.," *Indonesia Circle* 14 (November 1977): 3–12. The lending library rented out books, according to Teuku Iskandar, not to be read silently but to be read aloud to groups. Teuku Iskandar, "Some Manuscripts Formerly Belonging to Jakarta Lending Libraries."

14. For an excellent history of the early development of Indies newspapers, see Ahmat Adam, *The Vernacular Press and the Emergence of Modern Indonesian Consciousness* (Ithaca: Southeast Asia Program, Cornell University, 1995). For the lending library and other pertinent literature on early Melayu texts and translations see the following accounts:

Henri Chambert-Loir, "Sair Java-Bank di rampok," in *Le Moment "Sino-Malais" de la Litterature Indonesienne*, ed. Claudine Salmon, Cahier d'Archipel, no. 19 (London: Indonesian Etymological Project; Paris: Association Archipel, École des hautes études en sciences social, 1992), 43 –70.

Henri Chambert-Loir, "Malay Literature in the 19th Century: The Fadli Connection," in *Variation, Transformation, and Meaning: Studies on Indone-*

sian Literatures in Honour of A. Teeuw, ed. J. J. Ras and S. O. Robson (Leiden: KITLV Press, 1991), 87–114.

Henri Chambert-Loir, "Muhammad Bakir: A Batavian Scribe and Author in the Nineteenth Century," *Review of Indonesian and Malayan Affairs* 18 (1984): 44–71.

Teuku Iskandar, "Some Manuscripts Formerly Belonging to Jakarta Lending Libraries."

E. U. Kratz, "Running a Lending Library in Palembang in 1886 A.D."

Dede Oetomo, "'Serat Ang Dok': A Confucian Treatise in Javanese," *Archipel* 34 (1987): 181–197.

15. Translation modified; all quotations are from Chambert-Loir, "Malay Literature in the 19th Century." For the Acehnese, see James Siegel, *Shadow and Sound:The Historical Thought of a Sumatran People* (Chicago: University of Chicago Press, 1979).

16. *Review of Indonesian and Malayan Affairs* (Sydney) 18 (summer 1984): 44–72.

17. Nio Joe Lan, "Perkembangan dan Berachirnja Bahasa Melaju-Tionghoa," *Buku Kita*, no. 1, (July 1955): 301–304, and no. 8 (August 1955): 347–351.

18. The book referred to is *Hay Soey*. Nio Joe Lan does not furnish the bibliographical reference. It may be the title listed in Claudine Salmon's bibilography as *Boekoe Tjerita dahoeloe kala di Negri Tiongkok mentjeritakan Haij Soeij, alias Kong Hong djaman keizer Ban Lek Koen jang beralamat Siauw Ang Pauw*, trans. Goan Bie Ho (Batavia: Goan Hong, 1915; 5 vols., 356 pp.). Or, less likely, he may have had in mind *Tjerita Hay Soeij Taij Hong Pauw Tjoan Toan, ketika djaman keradjaan Taij Beng Tiauw Hongte Khe Tjeng Koen*, trans. Jo Tjim Goan; published in *Boekoe Boelanan* (1895–1896). It was either continued or republished in *Boekoe Roepa-roepa Tjrita Salinan dari Bahasa Tjina dan Sebaginja di Keloearkan Minggoean* (1900) under the title "Salinan dari tjerita Haij Soeij Toa Ang Pauw." Or perhaps *Tjerita dahoeloe kala di negri Tjina tersalin dari boekoe Thay Ang Pauw, ditjeritakan Haij Soeij baroe dilahirken, tempo keradjaan Khe Tjeng Koen* (Batavia: N.p., 1896). Claudine Salmon, *Literature in Malay by the Chinese of Indonesia: A Provisional Annotated Bibliography* (Paris: Éditions de la Maison des Sciences de l'Homme, 1981), 479 and 404.

19. Émile Benveniste, "The Nature of Pronouns" and "Relations of Persons in the Verb," in *Problems in General Linguistics* (Coral Gables: University of Miami Press, 1971), 217–222, and 195–204. Anyone familiar with these startling and, indeed, path-breaking articles will know how indebted I am to them.

20. E. U. Kratz, "Running a Lending Library in Palembang in 1886 A.D."

21. Tsuchiya Kenji, *Democracy and the Rise of the Taman Siswa Movement in Indonesia* (Honolulu: University of Hawaii Press, 1987). Soewardi's piece was published not only in *De Express* but as a separate pamphlet. The pamphlet has two title pages, one in a mixture of Dutch and Melayu, the title given in Dutch. The second title page lists the title in Melayu at the top followed by the name of the committee that published the pamphlet. Below that, the title and the name of the committee are given in Dutch. The first title page says that five thousand copies

were published and were free. "Als ik eens Nederlander was . . ." Vlugschrift No. 1 dikeloearkan oleh Comité Boemipoetra goena merajakan pesta seratoes tahoennja keradjaan Nederland. (Bandoeng, n.d.) The English translation appears in the excellent master's thesis of Savitri Prastit Scherer, "Harmony and Dissonance: Early Nationalist Thought in Java" (master's thesis, Cornell University, 1970). The translation comprises Appendix I, 298–304.

22. The English translation is "sarcasm," which is true if it translates the Malay *sindiran* but doubtful if it is from the Dutch *ironie*. One cannot know precisely which is appropriate. "Sarcasm" indicates a secure persona who, sure in his identity, ridicules. But irony can indicate an inversion of sense; words mean the opposite of what they say; through this inversion, ironic words can be less than securely attached to the identity of the speaker.

23. Hoffman, "A Foreign Investment."

24. I have simplified the situation. In fact, the linguistic situation in Algeria seems to have been and remains one in which most people seem to speak the language of someone else, "Algerian," "Arab," "Berber," and "French." But it is precisely this melange of languages that allowed for Algerian ideas of independence to be developed in French and often times not by Algerians. The point remains that when Algerians spoke French and voiced political ideas, French listened and political struggles that also involved identity ensued. In the Indies, Soewardi, speaking Dutch, could not get the attention of the Dutch.

25. See the articles of Pramoedya cited in n. 3 above. These articles amount to a picture of the transformations that occurred at the beginning of the century. After his release from prison seventeen years later, Pramoedya edited and published a collection of literature from this period with an important introduction. This book was banned. Pramoedya also wrote a biography of an editor and publicist of the time, Tirtho Ashisoeryo, to whom we shall refer later, pointing out the beginnings of nationalism his work. He wrote before and, clandestinely, in prison, a four-volume novel that was based on the life of this man. Had he and other scholars of his generation been able to continue their work, we would certainly have a different view of the history of nationalism, one that would entertain many more possibilities than those presently part of the recognized story of Indonesian nationalism. See *Tempo Doeloe* (Jakarta: Hasta Mitra, 1982); *Sang Pemula* (Jakarta: Hasta Mitra, 1985); and the novels *Bumi Manusia* (Jakarta: Hasta Mitra, 1980); *Jejak Langkah* (Jakarta: Hasta Mitra: 1985); *Anak Semua Bangsa* (Jakarta: Hasta Mitra, 1980); and *Rumah Kaca* (Jakarta: Hasta Mitra, 1988).

26. Takashi Shiraishi, *An Age in Motion* (Ithaca: Cornell University Press, 1990), 59.

27. Ibid., 60.

28. Protest at the time just before the rallies usually took the form of peasants assembling before the residence of authorities and waiting for the justice of their demands to be met. There were also more violent actions, such as sugar cane burning or strikes. See Shiraishi, *An Age in Motion*, 17 f., 162–169, and 209.

29. Ibid., 72.

30. Had Tjokroaminoto or others spoken Dutch at the rallies, it would not have been understood. Neither, doubtless, was Melayu understood by many. But in addition, Dutch would have been, at that point, precisely not a language that

passed between Dutch and natives; one which they, non-Dutch, excluded. See, for example, the difficulties Indo children had learning the language of their fathers. They were, Jean Taylor points out, sent to Holland to learn the language, being unable to do so in the Indies. Melayu, by contrast, at least at that moment, was heard to convey something. Taylor, *The Social World of Batavia*, 139 ff.

NOTES TO CHAPTER TWO

1. James Rush, *Opium to Java: Revenue Farming and Chinese Enterprise in Colonial Indonesia, 1860–1910* (Ithaca: Cornell University Press, 1990).

2. See, for instance, M. T. H. Perelaer, *Babu Dalima*, in *Verzamelde Romantische Werken*, vols. 8 and 9 (Amsterdam: Elsevier, n.d. [1898]). This may have been published originally in 1896. English translation by Rev. E. J. Venning (London: Vizetelly and Co., 1888). *Babu Dalima* appeared in translation in the Melayu language newspaper *Bintang Betawi*; it was translated by Gouw Peng Liang. Perelaer served four years as a noncommissioned officer in the Dutch army. He is the author of several books. See Rob Nieuwenhuys for biographical details, *Oost-Indische Spiegel: Wat Nederlandse schrijvers en dichters over Indonesië hebben geschreven, vanaf de eerste jaren der compagnie tot op heden* (Amsterdam: Querido, 1972), 197–201. Another example is "Sri Sakinem: A Story Which Actually Happened in the Mountains of the Island of Java." "Sri Sakinem" appeared *Bintang Betawi* between 9 September and 24 December 1904. It is doubtless a translation, but I have not been able to find the original.

3. Taylor, *The Social World of Batavia*, 145–158.

4. The story is told in three parts under the titles, "Met de Moeder zijner Kinderen" (With the mother of his children), "Naar Europa" (To Europa), and "Bij Grootmama" (At Grandmother's). Thérèse Hoven, *Onder de Palmen en Waringins*, 2d ed. (Amsterdam: L. J. Veen, n.d. [1899]), 28–54. For biographical material, see Wolfgang van der Meij, "Thérèse Hoven," in *Onze Letterkundigen* no. 9 (1904): 1–9. Hoven wrote not only stories and novels, but also plays and children's books and was also a journalist who wrote a women's column for the *Java-Bode*. She wrote also for an Indies women's weekly, *De Echo*, for the Sumatra-Post and contributed also to *De Amsterdammer*. Her novels appeared in such Netherlands publications as *Elsevier*, *Eigen Haard*, *Tijdspiegel*, and several others. Van der Meij lists forty-eight books of hers published between 1889 and 1904. Hoven is one of the authors Jean Taylor considers among the women writers of the times who were sympathetic to the plight of njai. Taylor, *The Social World of Batavia*, 145 ff.

5. Also in *Onder Palmen en Waringens*, 119 127. I might also mention the work of Melati van Java (Nicolina N. C. Sloot) for other examples.

6. The account is found in his *Een Kètjoegeschiedenis*, vol. 1 of *Vorstenlandsche Toestanden* (Dordrecht: J. P. Revers, 1887). Groneman was a writer and doctor who was eventually the physician of the sultan of Jogjakarta. He married a Javanese woman and, because of her and his close ties to the Jogjanese court, adapted himself to Javanese ways. See Nieuwenhuys, *Oost-Indische Spiegel*, 201–205. An abbreviated English translation of this book does not contain the material on Groneman.

7. J. A. Uilkens (1837–1893) was an Indies journalist who, according to Rob Nieuwenhuys, *Oost-Indische Spiegel*, never returned to Europe because he consid-

ered himself "Indische" (208). He was fluent enough in Melayu to translate one of his own books into that language. The pieces which concern us were published in Uilkens, *De Dochter van den Toovernaar met nog Twee Nederlandsch-Indische Novellen* (Leiden: Gualth. Kolff, 1877), 1–146, a collection of three short novels. The one cited has a Malay title: "Soekatjita Doekatjita," (199–338).

8. Compare this last quotation with the Dutch saying, *doe maar gewoon, dan do je gek genoeg* or "just act normal; that's already mad enough." I am indebted to Henk Maier for this saying.

9. J. A. Uilkens, "De Dochter van den Toovernaar," in *De Dochter van den Toovernaar met nog Twee Nederlandsch-Indische Novellen*, 1–146.

10. Karl Marx, "The Power of Money in Bourgeois Society" in *Economic and Philosophical Manuscripts of 1844*, ed. Dirk J. Struik; trans. Martin Milligan (New York: International Publishers, 1964), 167.

11. P. A. Daum, who wrote under the pseudonym "Maurits," was an editor of and contributor to Dutch language newspapers in Batavia. He was an admirer of Zola. *Nummer Elf* first appeared as a serial in the *Bataviaasch Nieuwsblad* in 1889 and as a book in 1893. It appeared in Melayu translation in *Bintang Betawi* in 1903 under the title *Lena Bruce* without mention of either the name of the translator or the author and with the additional subtitle "An Event That Actually Occurred in Java." Other translations of Daum such as Herman van Brakel and Abu Bakar also appeared in the Melayu press in the first decade of the century. The passages I have furnished are from *Bintang Betawi*.

For biographical details on Daum, see the definitive biography of G. Termorshuizen, *P. A. Daum: Journalist en Romancier van Tempo Doeloe* (Leiden: N.p., 1988). For consideration of his works, see also Rob Nieuwenhuys, *Mirror of the Indies: A History of Dutch Colonial Literature*, trans. Frans van Rosevelt (N.p.: University of Massachusetts Press, 1982); this is a translation of *Oost-Indische Spiegel*, 111–122.

12. "Yps" is not a usual name in Dutch, Melayu, or Javanese. Backwards, it spells "spy." It was the custom of Dutch fathers to give their children their name spelled backwards. Given that Ada/Yps in one scene in particular is given the ability to read the guilty thoughts of her *tuan*, the name may not be fortuitous. I thank H. Maier for the information and the observation.

NOTES TO CHAPTER THREE

1. J. A. van Doorn, *De Laatste Eeuw van Indië: Ontwikkeling en Ondergang van een Koloniaal Project* (Amsterdam: Uitgeverij Bert Bakker, 1994), 55–61.

2. See the commentary of Pramoedya Ananta Toer in the introduction to his collection of literature from the end of the century called *Tempo Doeloe* (Jakarta: Hasta Mitra, 1982), 29–32. Pramoedya republished the story we are dealing with here in this book.

3. See, for example, the story *Raden Adjeng Aidali* by F. Wiggers, which was serialized in the newspaper *Taman Sari* between 12 October 1910 and 21 July 1911. *Taman Sari* published the story in Melayu, although it may well have been originally written in Dutch. Wiggers was a prominent newspaper editor. For biographical data see Pramoedya Ananta Toer, *Tempo Doeloe*, 17–20.

4. Page numbers refer to the edition entitled *Tjerita Njai Dasima: Soewatoe Korban Dari Pada Pemboedjoek. Tjerita Bagoes Sekali jang Belon Berapa Lama Soedah Djadi di Betawi. Akan menjadi peladjaran baei sekalian prempoean jang soeka menoeroet boedjoekan laki-laki. Soewatoe Nasehat Kepada Anak-Anak Moeda* (Batavia: G. Francis, 1896). An English translation exists, but it is so unreliable that I have retranslated all the passages quoted myself.

5. A. Th. Manusama. *Njai Dasima: Het slachtoffer van bedroeg en misleiding een historisch zedenroman van Batavia* (Weltevreden: N. V. Drukkerij Favoriet, 1926).

6. The lack of place of Njai Dasima, tied as it is in the story to the danger of invasion by 'natives,' illustrates the contention of Ann Stoler that sexism was central in the foundation of racist distinctions that were at the heart of Indies colonial society. "Carnal Knowledge and Imperial Power: Gender, Race, and Morality in Colonial Asia," in *Gender at the Crossroad of Knowledge: Feminist Anthropology in the Post Modern Era*, ed. Micaela di Leonardo (Berkeley: University of California Press, 1991).

7. No previous version of Njai Dasima has been found. However, there is no general agreement among scholars as to whether it is likely that Francis originated the story. H. M. J. Maier, for instance, the professor of Malay literature at Leiden, has told me that he believes there is no strong case to be made for Francis as the first teller of the story.

8. Tsuchiya Kenji, "Popular Literature and Colonial Society in Late-Nineteenth-Century Java: Cerita Nyai Dasima," *Southeast Asian Studies* 28, no. 4 (1991): 17–30. Originally published in Japanese in *Bungaku* 57 (July 1989): 48–63.

9. The question of retelling the story as a story and its fictionality versus its truth are slightly different questions. Whether "The Story of Njai Dasima" was based on an historical incident or not, it seems, at least after the publication of Francis's text, to be believed to have happened. Whether it was true has never seemed to bother anyone except non-Indonesian commentators. That it was believed to be true can be seen by the fact that the ghost of Njai Dasima appeared in Batavia. This would not be the first time that a fictional character appeared as a ghost, if indeed Njai Dasima was entirely fictional. "Draculla," the Indonesian version of Dracula, appeared in many places in Indonesia after having been disseminated via a comedy troupe. See James T. Siegel, *Solo in the New Order* (Princeton: Princeton University Press, 1986), 92; 321, n. 3.

10. Jacques Derrida, "Parergon," in his *The Truth in Painting*, trans. Geoff Bennington and Ian MacLeod (Chicago: University of Chicago Press, 1987), 15–149.

11. I am told that Muhammad Bakir's texts had subtitles, but I have been unable to find out what they say. In any case, even if they were similar to those of Francis, as I imagine they were, the separation of the "author" from his text, and thus the establishment of the notion of "author" would not be much furthered given what happens inside the text.

12. On the notion of the center, see Soemarsaid Moertono, *State and Statecraft in Old Java* (Ithaca: Modern Indonesia Project, Cornell University, 1968); and

B. R. O'G. Anderson, "The Idea of Power in Java," in *Culture and Politics in Indonesia*, ed. Claire Holt, B. R. O'G. Anderson, and James Siegel (Ithaca: Cornell University Press, 1972), 1–69. Reprinted in Anderson, *Language and Power: Exploring Political Cultures in Indonesia* (Ithaca: Cornell University Press, 1990), 17–77.

13. Hellwig also points out that everything happens through the intermediary of women. It is through Ma' Boedjoeng that Samioen acts. One might slightly revise this to say that Samioen is merely the figure in the name of whom she acts her and very little in the picture himself. This is what happens when male authority is blind; women act. But even then in the name of men. It sheds some light on the criminality of the period. Tineke Hellwig, "Nyai Dasima, een vrouw uit de literatuur," in *A Man of Indonesian Letters: Essays in Honour of A. Teeuw*, ed. C. M. S. Hellwig and S. O. Robson (Dordrecht: Foris Publications, 1986), 48–66.

14. According to Salim Said, the director of the film was Lie Tek Swie. *Profil Dunia Film Indonesia* (Jakarta: Grafitipers, 1982), x.

15. KTH, "Film Njaie Dasima, Productie dari Tan's Film Company," *Panorama* 3 (12 November 1929).

16. Salim Said, *Profil Dunia Film Indonesia*, 20. Indeed, Tan's Film Company made more films than any other company in the Indies between 1926 and 1930. See "Le Cinema Indonesien," *Archipel* 5 (1973): 59–102. Salim Said also reports that in 1931 the film was made again with sound; it was directed by Bachtiar Effendi (138).

17. Hellwig, "Nyai Dasima, een vrouw uit de literatuur," 51.

18. One can speculate that the words before the photograph are much like the photographic negative. They are the indication of a nonappearance. With the photograph, the words, after the fact, take on substance. In any case, on the logic of the supplement, see Jacques Derrida, *Of Grammatology*, trans. Gayatri Spivak (Baltimore: Johns Hopkins University Press, 1976), 141–157 and 269–316.

19. I do not use the word "class" here in a precise sense. I refer to the mass of unskilled laborers, poorly educated, whose political life especially today under the New Order is at best intermittent and who might be referred to as "lumpen."

20. For commentary on the version made in 1971 called *Samiun and Dasima*, see Karl Heider, *Indonesian Cinema: National Culture on Screen* (Honolulu: University of Hawaii Press, 1991), 60, 64, and 69. The figures Salim Said gathered from the tax authorities, indicating numbers of ticket purchases, show that the film was not one of the most popular films of the year. It had 45,170 viewers, more than seven other films made that year but less than the other twelve. The most popular film of the year attracted 141,040 viewers. Salim Said, *Profil Dunia Film Indonesia*, 84.

21. Salim Said includes a photograph of the poster in *Profil Dunia Film Indonesia*, x. It reads as follows:

Tan's Film Coy.
It's first film just ready, the well known *Story of Njai Dasima*
All roles played by Indonesians themselves

Beneath this on the left there was a photo presumably of the actress who played Njai Dasima. To the right, in a mixture of large and small characters, is the paragraph we included in the text.

Beneath this appeared another picture, presumably of Samioen and another man drinking tea, to the left of which is a list of theaters in Batavia and elsewhere where the film was shown.

22. Pramoedya reports the story was filmed three times, in 1929, 1940, and 1970. Pramoedya Ananta Toer, *Tempo Doeloe*, 32.

23. See Kenji Tsuchiya, "Popular Literature and Colonial Society in Late-Nineteenth-Century Java: Cerita Nyai Dasima," 17–30.

24. R. S. Soerohadipoerno, *Boekoe Tipoean* (Batavia[?]: Elektronische Drukkerij "Fortuna," 1938).

25. A certain leftist rhetoric certainly was formed in Indonesia. However, it was often wedded to local forms of interpretation, yielding the strange result in the case of Tan Malaka, for instance, of an interpretation of history in which the antithesis came before the thesis. See the revealing piece of Rudolph Mrázek, "Tan Malaka: A Political Personality's Structure of Experience," *Indonesia* 14 (October 1972): 1–48. One can find interesting examples of leftist speechs in such novels as Mas Marco Kartodikromo, *Rasa Merdeka: Hikajat Soedjanmo* (Semarang: Drukkerij VSTP, 1924), which are more conventional. However, the Dutchman is still not exposed in such a way that a conflict for possession based on the illegtimacy of the other becomes apparent. Instead, in the case of Mas Marco's novel, *Student Hidjau* (Semarang: N. V. Boekhandel en Drukkerij Masman and Stroink, 1919), for instance, the danger posed by the Dutch is seduction and the possibility of oneself actually becoming Dutch. We will see this later when we treat these novels.

26. For a biography of Tirtho and a selection of his writings, see Pramoedya Ananta Toer, *Sang Pemula*. Tirtho is also the basis for a central character in his four-volume fiction.

27. The actual proverb, I am told by Henk Maier, is *Kleren maken de man* (Clothes make the man), as it is in English.

28. Pramoedya, *Sang Pemula*. The title of Pramoedya's study of Tirtho indeed means, "The Honored First."

29. *Medan Prijaji*, 3: 560–563; reprinted in Pramoedya Ananta Toer, *Sang Pemula*, 220–221. Cf. Onghokham, "The Inscrutable and the Paranoid: An Investigation into the Sources of the Brotodiningrat Affair," in *Southeast Asian Transitions: Approaches through Social History*, ed. Ruth McVey (New Haven: Yale University Press, 1978), 112–157. For the series on photography, see the articles by Tirtho entitled, "Ilmoe Menggambar Sorot," *Soenda Berita* 2, nos. 3, 4, 5, 11, 14, and 17; and 3, nos. 22 and 23 (1904, 1905).

30. "Dari Hal Advertentie," *Soenda Berita*, 29 May 1904, II: 13.

31. Republished in Pramoedya Ananta Toer, *Tempo Doeloe*, 155–220.

32. In fact, Tirtho does not name the languages used. It is certain, for the reason given earlier, that being a second language, Melayu was not strongly invested in.

33. I would like to say something about the fetish as a concept. When it is described by anthropologists, or by Hegel, the fetish is a misconception and the person who knows this is the anthropologist or Hegel. The third is not a member of the society that includes the fetishist and so the shame that I see as a necessary component in the construction of fetishism is never described.

The fetish in the traditional Indonesian societies I know bears a sacred character that means that for some of the time it is hidden or secret. No one knows for sure whether a certain Javanese dagger is really potent. There are no skeptics, however, to say that belief in magical daggers is erroneous. Its sacred character hides its imaginative quality. Here sacredness means, "in the eyes of someone else who remains indefinite, the dagger has power."

By contrast, Freud says of fetishists in Vienna that they are hard to find. They themselves know that their practices lack sense and for that reason they keep them to themselves. Any man on the street might be a shoe fetishist, for instance, and one would never know it. When, however, he buys thirty pairs of shoes, and especially if they are all men's shoes, he is a commodity fetishist and could scarcely be more public. His fetishism may well be known to himself as, for instance, a weakness for which he must pay at the end of the month. No shame is attached to it. This, however, is not because its imaginative character has not been exposed but because the very power of the fetish overwhelms the sense of shame.

34. If, in the early years of the century, there was a fetish of appearance constructed, as I claim there was, it is because of a set of circumstances that includes a belief throughout the European as well as the 'native' part of colonial society of a gap between appearance and identity. If Tirtho Adhisoeryo's reaction was not the same as Daum's or Uilkens's, it is perhaps because he felt more keenly then they did the pressure of the lingua franca. That is, he felt the interpenetration of cultures through Melayu. But one need only view the marvelous photographs gathered by Nieuwenhuys to see Europeans dressed not merely as Javanese but Japanese, Turks, Arabs and even dice (as in "a pair of dice") to see that this was a sensation Europeans shared. They, however, made another place for their fantasies.

NOTES TO CHAPTER FOUR

1. Mas Marco Kartodikromo, *Student Hidjau*. Mas Marco published other fiction, as well as much journalism and political commentary. See Takashi Shiraishi, *An Age in Motion*, 81–91, for a discussion of his role as a nationalist and for further bibliography. Henri Chambert-Loir, "Mas Marco Kartodikromo (c. 1890–1932) ou l'Éducation Politique," in *Littératures Contemporaines de l'Asie du Sud-Est*, ed. P. B. Lafont and Denys Lombard (Paris: à l'Asiatèque, 1974), 203–214.

2. Mas Marco Kartodikromo, *Mata Gelap: Tjerita jang Soenggoeh Kedjadian di Tanah Djawa*, vols. 2 and 3 (Bandung: Insulinde, 1914).

3. Henri Chambert-Loir has established that Soemantri was the pseudonym of Mas Marco. See "Mas Marco Kartodikromo (c. 1890–1932) ou l'Éducation Politique." See *Rasa Merdeka: Hikajat Soedjanmo*, 203–214, for the example.

4. Thus, after the debate, Soedjanmo discusses it with the speaker and his wife. The woman feels sorry for Abdulgani because he could not reply, but it is pointed out that he had no case to make. By contrast, they make no comment on the speech of the peasant, described below.

5. The fetish, and in particular the nationalist fetish, puts language at the service of hierarchy and hinders the development of literature. The latter would make a place for the unrecognizable qualities of language that might require long, one can

even say, if one is Walter Benjamin, indefinite deferral before they are understood. See Walter Benjamin, "The Task of the Translator," in *Illuminations*, ed. Hannah Arendt; trans. Harry Zohn (New York: Schocken Books, 1969), 69–83. The fetish collapses the space and the time between appearance and recognition. It is its demand for immediacy, recognition by the living, that makes literature difficult. The victory of the fetish in Indonesia today is shown by the fact that Mas Marco's works are nearly unheard of there. It is not by accident that Indonesia's strongest writer, Pramoedya Ananta Toer, is an exception. The victory of literature is that outside Indonesia in particular these works are still read, and read by those Mas Marco could never have imagined.

NOTES TO CHAPTER FIVE

1. Ahmat Adam, *The Vernacular Press and the Emergence of Modern Indonesian Consciousness* (Ithaca: Southeast Asia Program, Cornell University, 1995), 48.

2. On the opium monopoly, see James Rush, *Opium to Java*.

3. Lea E. Williams, *Overseas Chinese Nationalism: The Genesis of the Pan-Chinese Movement in Indonesia, 1900–1916* (Glencoe: Free Press, 1960). I am indebted to Williams as well as to Leo Suryadinata, *Peranakan Chinese Politics in Java, 1917–1942* (Singapore: Institute of Southeast Asian Studies, 1976); Leo Suryadinata, *Peranakan's Search for National Identity: Biographical Studies of Seven Indonesian Chinese* (Singapore: Institute of Southeast Asian Studies, 1976); and to G. William Skinner, "The Chinese Minority," in *Indonesia*, ed. Ruth McVey (New Haven: Human Relations Area Files, 1963).

4. In effect, there was a process of assimilation that might possibly have left Chinese as one more group in the Indies if there had not been strong anti-Sinitic feelings on the part of Europeans and 'natives.' What is necessary and what has not yet been attempted is a comparison of interethnic rivalry between 'native' groups and between 'Chinese' and others. There is a marked difference in that anti-Chinese sentiment has been preserved and developed whereas the rivalry between other ethnicities is localized and usually subordinated to Indonesian identity. It is partly a question of the conservation of memory. Here, again, the role of language is important. See my *Solo in the New Order*, 232–254.

5. Batavia: Tan Thian Soe, 1921.

6. There are narratives where rational calculation is the central assumption. For example, Tan Boen Kim, *Peroesoehan di Kudus* (Batavia: Lie Tek Long, 1922).

7. Tan Boen Kim, *Nona Fientje de Feniks, atawa djadi korban dari Tjemboeroean. Satoe Tjerita jang Betoel Terdjadi di Betawi*, 2d ed. (Batavia: N.p., 1917).

8. Anne Stoler, "Carnal Knowledge and Imperial Power," 51–101.

9. Compare with Hannah Arendt on antisemitism. *Origins of Totalitarianism* (New York: Harcourt Brace, 1948), 4 ff.

10. Liem Liang Hoo, *Roemah Tangga jang 'koe Imipiken* (Buitenzorg: Buitenzorgsche Drukkerij, n.d.) According to Claudine Salmon's catalog, this novel was published about 1930. At this point, I want to indicate my indebtedness to this catalog, which is not only indispensable to anyone interested in Indies Chinese writing but, one can say, established these writers on the historical scene of Indonesian writing. Claudine Salmon, *Literature in Malay by the Chinese of Indonesia*.

11. The evolution of the modern woman was not unilinear. Another novel, called *Nona Olanda sebagai Istri Tionghoa* (Miss Dutch as Chinese wife), begins in the theater. A young Chinese man, called John, causes a stir in the theater. He has dressed up with special care because he knows that he will otherwise be faulted by Europeans:

> So that Chinese will not be called *koprot* and *sembarangan*, that night I wore black pants and a black jacket. If I were Dutch I could be a bit careless because it is understood they understand politeness. But because I am Chinese I had to show that Chinese were not a people who were unaware of long standing and noble politeness and moreover could take on western manners when we mixed with the [Westerners]. (9)

At this point, he dresses as a Dutchman but he remains Chinese. He has to be more meticulous about his dress than a Dutchman would be. To realize he is Chinese is not to revert to Chinese ways. It is to take on Western ways in a way superior to Westerners. We see the point I have already described where identification with the image is a claim to identity; where it no longer seems possible to think that a gap between appearance and identity can mean anything other than taking a firmer grip on appearance.

The statement "But I'm not, I am a Chinese" appears here nonetheless. But it is a complicated question. John's way of being Chinese brings him into conflict with his family. At the theater, he meets a Dutch woman, Diana. They fall in love and marry against the wishes of both her family and his. Diana takes on Chinese ways and insists that their son bear a Chinese name. John's mother sees that she was wrong in her disapproval of his wife once Diana has proved how faithful she is to Chinese customs. Diana dies in the end and John is left with a beautiful memory.

The fantasy of a European woman adapting Chinese customs, becoming super-latively Chinese, which is to say, capable of convincing Chinese not that she "is" Chinese but that she can appear to be just as John becomes superlatively Chinese by dressing more meticulously as a European than most Europeans is at the heart of the story. But when Diana puts on Chinese clothes, it is not to assert her freedom and the possibility of being whatever image seems to announce her to be. Diana refuses the freedom she had once enjoyed dressed as a European. In this story, it is the approval of the traditional Chinese mother that counts. John proves that he is both Chinese and modern when his marriage to a European wins his mother's favor. But he is Chinese in the fullest sense, able to compete with Europeans, when he can do as they do, including look as they look. He can have whatever he wants. His mother recognizes that his wife obeys the constraints of Chinese ways. John's mother, seeing Diana refuse European freedoms, knows that John in freeing him-self to want what the modern world offers is also restraining himself. He gets in the end only what he should have. It is thanks to his wife. Published as the initial number of *Penghidoepan* (15 January 1925).

12. Tan Boen Kim, *Nona Fientje de Feniks.*

13. Chabanneau, *Rasia Bandoeng, atawa satoe pertjintaan jang melanggar peradatan "Bangsa Tiong Hoa." Satoe Tjerita jang benar terdjadi di kota Bndoeng dan berachir pada tahon 1917*, 2 vols. (Batavia: Drukkerij Kho Tjeng Bie and Co., 1918) In his unpublished paper entitled "Emancipation of the Indonesian Chinese

Woman," Charles A. Coppel discusses the implications of this novel for the history of Indonesian Chinese women (1993). At this point, I would like to signal the articles of Yik-Wei Faye Chan, "Chinese Emancipation as Reflected in two Peranakan Journals (c. 1927–1942)," *Archipel* 49 (1995): 45–62; Claudine Salmon, "Chinese Women Writers in Indonesia and Their Views on Female Emancipation," *Archipel* 28 (1984): 149–172; and Myra Siddharta, "The Making of the Indonesian Chinese Woman," in *Indonesian Women in Focus: Past and Present Notions*, ed. E. Locher-Scholten and A. Niehof (Dordrecht: Foris Publications, 1987), which, along with Coppel's article cited above, provides an overview of the status of Indies Chinese women and much helpful bibliography. These discussions of the status of Indies Chinese women focus by and large on ideological dimensions and in particular on the debate over whether these women should follow traditional or modern ways. My own contribution to their analyses is to say that the modernist path itself was as much conservative as liberalizing: The freeing of women to dress in Western-style clothes and to marry as they might chose was accompanied by another form of subjugation.

14. Claudine Salmon, "La notion de 'sino-malaise'; est-elle pertinente d'un point de vue linguistique?" *Archipel* 20 (1980): 177–186; and her annotated catalog, *Literature in Malay by the Chinese of Indonesia*.

15. See the articles written by Kwee Tek Hoay in *Moestika Romans* in the 1930s with titles such as "*Merosotnja Pembatjaan Melajoe Tionghoa*" (The decline in quality of Chinese-Malay reading material) [50 (February 1934): 597–599]; "*Tooneelgezelschap Dardanella poenja Bahasa Melajoe*" (Dardanella theater society speaks Malay) [54 (June 1934): 773–775]; and "*Memperbaeki Bahasa Melayoe*" (Improving the Malayu language) [53 (May 1934)].

16. "Merosotnja Pembatjaan Melajoe Tionghoa," 587–598.

17. One could take the spelling of Kwee Tek Hwee/Kwee Tek Hoay as an example. The first spelling is one sometimes used currently and one KTH used himself at times. But in the articles I have referred to, he spells his name Kwee Tek Hoay. When the reflection of one's name in print has no stability, there are various possible consequences, one of which is to feel that one may not be in control of who or what one is taken for.

18. Neil Hertz, "Freud and the Sandman," in *End of the Line* (New York: Columbia University Press, 1985), 97–121.

NOTES TO CHAPTER SIX

1. The history of Balai Pustaka, including its relations with colonial policy and its literary effects, have recently been explored in H. M. J. Maier, "Forms of Censorship in the Dutch Indies"; Hilmar Farid Setiadi, "Kolonialisme dan Budaya: Balai Poestaka di Hindia Belanda," *Prisma* 10 (October 1991): 23–41; and Doris Jedamski, "Balai Pustaka: A Colonial Wolf in Sheep's Clothing," *Archipel* 44 (1992): 23–46. See also A. Teeuw, "The Impact of Balai Poestaka on Modern Indonesian Literature," *Bulletin of the School of Oriental and African Studies* 35 (1972): 111–127; and Pramoedya Ananta Toer, "Balai Pustaka harum namanja didunia internasional-dahulu," *Star Weekly* 580 (9 February 1957): 10–11; and K. A. H. Hidding, "The Bureau for Popular Literature," *Bulletin of the Colonial*

Institute of Amsterdam 1–2 (May 1938): 185–194. For a positive statement of the achievements of Balai Pustaka, see G. W. J. (Gerardus Willebrordus Joannes) Drewes, *The Bureau of Popular Literature of Netherlands India: What It Is and What It Does* (Weltevreden [?]: Kantoor voor de Volkslectuur, 1930 [?]).

2. Quoted in H. M. J. Maier, "Forms of Censorship in the Dutch Indies."

3. H. M. Zainu'ddin, *Djeumpa Atjeh* (Weltevreden: Balai Pustaka, 1928). This work was republished in 1931 by Balai Pustaka. I have used the edition reprinted in 1958 (Medan: Pustaka Iskandar Muda). (After 1928, H. M. Zainu'ddin was written H. M. Zainuddin.)

4. "Atjeh" is the spelling used under the Dutch. Under the Republic, "tj" was replaced by "c" to give the present spelling, "Aceh."

5. For a description of Acehnese marriage customs, see Christiaan Snouck Hurgronje, *The Achehnese*, trans. A. W. S. O'Sullivan (Leiden: E. J. Brill, 1906), I: 295–371, 401–408; Chandra Jayawardena, "Acehnese Marriage Customs," *Indonesia* 23 (April 1977): 157–175; and James Siegel, *The Rope of God* (Berkeley and Los Angeles: University of California Press, 1969): 137–199.

Els. Postel-Coster has considered the picture of women in marriage relations in Minangkabau novels, in particular the relations of power within the family and the increased influence gained by women when they become mothers. See her *Het omheinde kweekbed: Machtsverhoudingen in de Minangakabause Familieroman* (Delft: Eburon, 1985). The situation she pictures is not entirely different from that in Aceh where our novel is set. Her work raises the question of how this particular social situation motivated so much writing.

I also want to call attention to the study of Tineke Hellwig, *In the Shadow of Change: Images of Women in Indonesian Literature* (Berkeley: Centers for South and Southeast Asian Studies, 1994). As the title indicates, Hellwig traces the picture given of women in a number of novels from before World War II to the 1970s. In general, she emphasizes the way in which women in these novels identify with men or for the most part need to follow rules that benefit men to the detriment of women. The immense questions of gender, it seems to me, are inflected differently at different moments. It is Hellwig's strong point to take this into account and to show that a problem of gender persists in different forms despite steps that seem to lead in another direction. It is not, in other words, that "modernity" ends the victimization of daughters, as the novel under discussion seems to suggest. One might wonder about the literary nature of writing devoted to domestication not only of women but, as we shall see, of language, under the sign of modernity. The history of Indonesian "literature," it seems to me, is just that.

6. There was, at the time the story took place, a modernist Islamic movement that introduced Western-style education and opportunity for women of the sort we see also in this novel. Against them was another sort of Islam that stressed traditional practices and was closely allied with, but by no means identical to *adat*. See James Siegel, *The Rope of God*, parts 1 and 2.

7. See A. J. Piekaar, *Atjeh en de Oorlog met Japan* (The Hague: W. van Hoeve, 1949). Piekaar notes that nationalist organizations were of little importance in Aceh in the period of our novel (13).

8. Zainu'ddin, *Djeumpa Atjeh*, 38. Nja' Ahmat is also a member of the Juliana Club. He mixes easily, we are told, with the youth of all nationalities. He is also a

member of the Steering Committee of the Vereeniging Atjeh. Although he does not use the term, he writes about the "Atjeh probleem," a term which in the 1920s and 1930s included discussion of the means to bring Aceh out of its presumed backwardness and fanaticism. See A. J. Piekaar, *Atjeh en de Oorlog met Japan*, 14.

9. They do so, taking the advice of T. B. Raman's intermediary to double its value in compensation for the "shame" they have caused. Nja' Amat refuses the gift, saying that he gave it not to them but to Sitti Saniah, thus revising its signifi-cance. It takes the effort of a judge to get him to renounce his claims on her and still not take back his gift. Nja' Amat has insisted that the gift was a gift, and therefore without the possibility of being valued in money. Sitti Saniah's side, however, has done just that, estimating the cost of the items Nja' Amat sent. One sees an empha-sis on sentiment that is foreign to traditional marriage arrangements.

10. "Normality" at the time was something promoted by the Dutch after the political disruptions of 1927. "Normality" meant the peaceful way of life the oppo-site of which could be found first in the Communist rebellions, then in the anti-societies found in the prison cum place of internal exile for political detainees in New Guinea called Boven Digul. See Takashi Shiraishi, "The Phantom World of Digoel" forthcoming in *Indonesia*, and Rudolf Mrázek, *Sjahrir: Politics and Exile in Indonesia* (Ithaca: Southeast Asia Program, Cornell University, 1994).

11. Roland Barthes, *Camera Lucida*, trans. Richard Howard (New York: Far-rar, Straus & Giroux, 1981), 96.

12. The definition is taken from R. J. Wilkinson, *A Malay-English Dictionary* (Romanized) (London: Macmillan, 1959). The word has derivitives: *mencinta*: to love or regret; and *cinta berahi*: love's longings. The last in contemporary language means sexual desire.

13. One might reconsider the effects of Dutch efforts to reform Malay. One sees that they were congruent with much nationalist effort, not merely because the language might then be a better vehicle for the modern but because the attempt to standardize and to eliminate ambiguity is congruent with the notions of transmis-sion and technology we have just considered. It would be a mistake, in other words, to see the success of Dutch efforts without considering not only nationalist but also Sino-Malay interests.

NOTES TO CHAPTER SEVEN

1. Similar novels appeared also in West Sumatra, the place of origin of many of the authors, as well as in Java. There were fewer in Java, perhaps because of the sustained popularity of works in Javanese, as Teeuw remarks in *Modern Indonesian Literature*, 75. Teeuw suggests that the format of these novels was likely to have been influenced by previous Indies-Chinese novels of the type we have already discussed. This seems to me very likely indeed.

Tamar Djaja reports that the term, "ten penny novel," or *roman picisan*, was first used by the leftist writer Parada Harap. Tamar Djaja blames the demise of these novels on the success of Sino-Malay publications. Contrary to Teeuw, he praises the Indonesian used by comparison to the language of the Sino-Malay authors. He regrets the state of Indonesian at the time of his writing (1955), which fails to attract readers because, he claims, they do not understand it. Tamar Djaja, "Roman

Pitjisan," *Buku Kita* 1, no. 5 (May 1955): 208–211. R. Roolvink also discusses these novels in "De Indonesiase 'Dubbletjesroman' " (The Indonesian ten penny novel), in *Bingkisan Budi: Een Bundel Opstellen aan Dr. Ph. S. van Ronkel anngeboden* (Leiden: A. W. Sijthoff, 1950).

2. For instance, this notice appears inside the front cover of Emnast (Moechtar Nasoetion), *Tan Malaka di Medan* (Medan: Doenia Pengalaman, vol. 3, no. 9, 1940):

Notice

Comrade M. Saleh Oemar (Editor in Chief of our journal *Poernama*) has had to relax in jail as of last 25 February for a period of three months. As a result *Poernama* has recently stopped publication. As of this April *Poernama* will be published again with new dreams, a new format and a new look; thicker in size and with articles more in demand by the public [*publik*] today.

3. See Noriaki Oshikawa, "*Patjar Merah Indonesia* and Tan Malakka: A Popular Novel and a Revolutionary Legend," in *Reading Southeast Asia*, ed. Takashi Shiraishi (Ithaca: Southeast Asia Program, Cornell University, 1990), 9–40. Originally published in Japanese in the *Journal of Sophia Asian Studies* 4 (1986): 121–155.

4. Matu Mona, *Detective Rindu (Tjintjin belian dari Golcanda)* (Medan: Doenia Pengalaman, 15 December 1939). *Detective Rindu* was published as part of a series entitled *"Doenia Pengalaman: Madjallah roman-detective popoeler"*. Each issue was a complete novel. The editors varied, but they included A. M. Pamoentjak and Matu Mona as well as the author of the next novel we will consider, Moechtar Nasoetion. I wish to thank Takashi Shiraishi for lending me his copy of this book, now difficult to find. For his excellent commentary on this and the other Medan novels, we will be considering, see Noriaki Oshikawa, "*Patjar Merah Indonesia* and Tan Malakka." Oshikawa deserves credit not only for showing how Tan Malaka was the factual model for characters of certain authors but for bringing these novels to the attention to historians and anthropologists.

5. Rudolph Mrázek, "Tan Malaka: A Political Personality's Structure of Experience."

6. Moechtar Nasoetion (Emnast), *Tan Malaka di Medan.*

7. *Spionage Dienst (Patjar Merah Indonesia)* (Medan: Centrale Courant en Boekhandel, n.d.), 108.

8. Matu Mona, *Detective Rindu.*

9. Edgar Morin, *Les stars* (Paris: Editions du Seuil, 1972).

10. Medan: Roman Indonesia, March 1941.

NOTES TO CHAPTER EIGHT

1. Drs. Maskur Sumodiharjo, ed., *Letusan di Balik Buku* (Jakarta: Aries Lima on behalf of Dewan Harian Nasional Angkatan 45, Pusat Dokumentasi Sejarah Perjuangan 45, 1976), 18–48.

2. R. S. Hardjapameko, "Manifestasi Ketahanan Nasional Dalam Bentuk Kecil: Sebuah Kecematan di Jawa Barat mempertahankan daerah Republik Indonesia selama 5 bulan (Isi sepucuk surat)." Agenda item 850, Category B.

3. Gani, "Kebayoran Lama—Tahun 1945." Agenda item 848.

4. Dayim Sostawirya, "Kisah Nyata Perjuangan." Agenda item 440, Category B.

5. After the Dutch invaded Jogja, for instance, a woman whose husband was an official who did not change sides said this:

> After Negara Pasundan was formed, the Dutch developed another strategy. They coaxed former officials of that Republic to move to West Java [the locus of Negara Pasundan]. They . . . were guaranteed a good salary. . . . Many Republican officials left; understand, they had been faithful to the Republic and had got nothing in return; they did not have enough to eat or to wear. And from time to time they feared they would be shot by the Dutch. (Suwarsih Djojopoespito, "Yang Tak Dapat Kulapakan." Agenda item 317/XVI, Category B).

She puts the question of collaboration as simply a matter of better conditions: enough pay, enough food, and less fear. Indeed, collaboration was discussed often enough as a problem of money. But it is clear from the accounts of those who did join the Negara Pasundan that they did not necessarily think of themselves as having changed political allegiance. Of course, we see their opinions after the fact. But one can give them the benefit of the doubt. They wanted Indonesian independence of some sort and at least sometimes they thought they were continuing their efforts toward it by maintaining ties with revolutionaries and by aiding them when they could. It is precisely because it was thought possible to do so that it was considered easy to change sides. It was not merely that one got more, materially, if one did so. It was also that it was apparently simple enough to think one had not abandoned one's revolutionary sentiments.

6. He told his interrogators that he knew nothing of the letter. He supposed that the letter had been delivered in his absence and his wife had forgotten to tell him about it. He claims that they believed him. Like the secret signals, it makes one remember *Tan Malaka di Medan*.

7. For an excellent description of similar activities during the Japanese occupation by the first prime minister of the republic during the Japanese occupation, see Rudolph Mrázek, *Sjahrir*, 209–268.

Notes to Chapter Nine

1. For reasons that will be evident, I have withheld the true names of the authors of this and the following accounts. The accounts are in the contest archives and are unpublished.

2. W. J. S. Poerwadarminta, *Kamus Umum Bahasa Indonesia* (Djakarata: Balai Pustaka, 1966), 4th impression. Cited under the term *sembojan*.

3. B. R. O'G. Anderson, "The Languages of Indonesian Politics," *Indonesia* 1 (April 1966): 89–116.

4. "Saya menunjuk Saudara berdua untuk melaksanakan tugas khusus yang harus dijalankan dengan tabah, berdisiplin dan tanpa menikutsertakan perasaan dan pikiran sendiri. Tugas itu ialah melakukan pelakasanaan hukuman mati atas perintah atasan."

5. It is also true that in south India there were companies of troops trained to

run amok. Amok was thus an instrument of war. See John C. Spores, *Running Amok: An Historical Inquiry* (Athens, Ohio: Ohio University Center for International Studies, 1988), 11–30.

6. The closest possibility is the sign he placed on the bodies of his victims, "enemy of the people." This, a warning for whoever might wander by whatever place the bodies were displayed, locates action in the social world. It establishes an enemy from within the body of people that until the moment of killing formed part of the Indonesian people. It thus attempts to create a basic social difference. But for him it is a futile or at least never completed task. His ceaseless killing indicates that there are always more unmarked enemies; always more of whom one must be suspicious. It is perhaps because this attempt to find an enemy from among those who are like oneself fails to be definitive that MNT looks to "death" itself for a response.

NOTES TO EPILOGUE

1. It is, indeed, the history of the youth, the *pemuda*, that raises difficulties. In the introduction to his seminal history of the role of youth in the revolution in Java, B. R. O'G. Anderson describes the places in Javanese society where males lived a life outside of conventional social bonds, for instance as students in religious schools or as traveling performers. *Java in a Time of Revolution: Revolution and Resistance*, 1–15. It is true that youths appeared out of such places to fight. But, as Anderson says, these were traditional structures, while the notion of "youth" is part of modernity. It is important not to confuse it with adolescence. The latter depends on the conflicted orientation to parents and to the wider society, particularly the market. *Pemuda* are not necessarily in conflict with their elders. Theirs is a type that proceeds first from the name, *pemuda*. Sociological histories of this type offer only partial explanations.

2. Pramoedya Ananta Toer, "Djongos + Babu," *Tjerita dari Djakarta* (Djakarta: Penerbit Grafika, 1957), 7–18; my translation. Copyright 1957 by Pramoedya Ananta Toer. Used by arrangement with William Morrow and Company, Inc.

3. An agreement between Dutch and Indonesian forces made in 1948 by which Indonesian troops withdrew from certain territories in return for the holding of plebiscites. The Dutch did not hold to the agreement.

4. "Batavia" was the name of Jakarta during colonial times.

5. The Balai Pustaka novels speak of the corruption of parents and the recognition furnished by those who embody a certain modernism. The corruption of parents makes evident that genealogy defines by force. The name I bear that my parents gave me does not refer to my entire identity. "I," somehow, am more than that, as attested to by the unexpected recognition by others. Here the name defines too broadly. There is no one to confer another name in recognition of what one looks like, a nationalist. This is the failure of the fetish. The fetish depends on the weakness of genealogy, the weakness of names exhausting identity; if not "I" would always be only the person named at birth. Pramoedya shows both the working of the fetish and what its working obscures.

About the Author

James T. Siegel is Professor of Anthropology and Asian Studies at Cornell University. He is the author of *The Rope of God, Shadow and Sound,* and *Solo in the New Order* (Princeton), which won the Ohira Memorial Prize for outstanding book about the Pacific Rim.